WORKS ISSUED BY
THE HAKLUYT SOCIETY

————————

THE ARCTIC WHALING JOURNALS
OF WILLIAM SCORESBY THE YOUNGER
VOLUME I
THE VOYAGES OF 1811, 1812 AND 1813

THIRD SERIES
NO. 12

Plate 1. Youthful engraved portrait of William Scoresby, Junior. Undated, but he is described beneath as F.R.S.E., which dates the portrait to after 25 January 1819, when he was 29. Photograph courtesy of the Whitby Museum.

THE
ARCTIC WHALING JOURNALS
OF
WILLIAM SCORESBY THE YOUNGER

VOLUME I
THE VOYAGES OF 1811, 1812 AND 1813

Edited by

C. IAN JACKSON

THE HAKLUYT SOCIETY
LONDON
2003

Published by The Hakluyt Society
c/o Map Library
The British Library, 96 Euston Road,
London NW1 2DB

SERIES EDITORS
W. F. RYAN
MICHAEL BRENNAN

© The Hakluyt Society 2003

ISBN 0 904180 82 4
ISSN 0072 9396

British Library Cataloguing-in-Publication Data
A catalogue record for this book is
available from the British Library

Typeset by Waveney Typesetters, Wymondham, Norfolk
Printed in Great Britain at
the University Press, Cambridge

CONTENTS

ILLUSTRATIONS AND MAPS

Illustrations

All illustrations from the Whitby Museum are reproduced by courtesy of the Whitby Museum and the Whitby Literary and Philosophical Society

Maps

Preface and Acknowledgements

This is the first of a probable three volumes that will contain the edited journals of the annual voyages to the Greenland Sea by William Scoresby the Younger, from the time that he took command of the *Resolution* in 1811 until the publication of his magnum opus, *An Account of the Arctic Regions*, in 1820.

The manuscript transcripts of these journals form part of the large collection of Scoresby Papers in the Whitby Museum (the relevant numbers for this volume are WHITM:SCO1252, and WHITM:SCO1253). Scoresby was one of the founders of the Whitby Literary and Philosophical Society in 1823, and it is especially gratifying that this first volume of the series will appear as the Society carries out a major physical expansion of its wonderful Museum. At a time when they were preoccupied with planning and raising funds for this expansion, the officers, committee, staff and volunteers of the Society have encouraged and assisted my work in every way possible. In particular, by making copies of the transcripts available for me to work on in Connecticut, the Honorary Chairman of the Society and Curator of the Scoresby Collection, Fred Payne, and the Honorary Keepers, Graham and Roger Pickles, have brought the completion of this volume forward by several years. The Society's Documentation Officer, Denise Gildroy, and its Archives Cataloguer, Edwin King, have saved me from several, though no doubt not all, errors related to the Scoresby Papers. For library resources, I have seldom had to look further afield than those of the 'Lit & Phil' and Yale University, where I continue to benefit immeasurably from my honorary appointment as an Associate Fellow of Timothy Dwight College. For topographic detail on Spitsbergen, I have relied on the 1:500,000 scale *Tactical Pilotage Chart TPC B-1A*. The maps included in this volume and some other illustrations have been redrawn by Ms Marilyn Croot of Calgary.

My own research interests are in the Arctic and science, rather than ships and whales. I am therefore grateful for the help on whaling provided by a former colleague in the geography department at McGill University, W. Gillies Ross, especially for permission to reproduce his illustration of the flensing process, and the advice on Royal Navy ships of the period by Michael Phillips. Mr Phillip's website on 'Ships of the Old Navy' is a mine of information, and I am glad that Scoresby's journals are helping to extend its coverage. Rosalin Barker, a member of the 'Lit & Phil's' committee, has a comprehensive knowledge of Whitby ships over the centuries, and the publication of this material is eagerly anticipated. I hope that most of the remaining nautical errors or solecisms were caught by Captain M. K. Barritt, RN, who kindly agreed to review the final manuscript as a whole. Several other people have provided information or advice on specific points, and their help is gratefully acknowledged at the relevant places in the volume. My final debt of thanks is to the

Hakluyt Society's series editor, Professor Will Ryan who is, most appropriately, yet another member of the Whitby Literary & Philosophical Society.

The format of this volume generally conforms with both Hakluyt Society practice and the layout of the transcript journals. For convenience, however, the marginal entries of date, wind directions, and latitude and longitude have been brought together at the head of each day's entry, except where the text of the journal continues uninterrupted from one day to the next. In the 1811 and 1812 journals, which adopted the nautical day beginning and ending at noon, the latitude and longitude were normally inserted in the transcripts at the end of each nautical day. In 1813, when the civil day was used, the coordinates appear in the margin close to the text that concerns the noontime period. In all three years, therefore, this means that the latitude and longitude are those determined or estimated at noon on the civil day indicated.

In her preface to the Hakluyt Society edition of *Carteret's Voyage Round the World, 1766–1769*, Helen Wallis in 1965 regretfully declined any knowledge of a relationship to that expedition's leader, Samuel Wallis. I must equally sadly make a similar admission in regard to both Robert Scoresby-Jackson, William Scoresby's nephew and biographer, and Gordon Jackson, whose 1978 study of *The British Whaling Trade* has been so helpful. The reader may find the profusion of Jacksons confusing, but I am glad to be able to join my namesakes in making Scoresby's achievements more widely known.

Hamden, Connecticut and Sneaton, Whitby   IAN JACKSON
August 2003

Table of Quantities and Conversions
(approximations in most cases)

Length
1 inch = 2.5 cm   1 foot = 30 cm   1 yard (3 feet) = 91 cm
1 fathom (6 feet) = 1.8 m   1 mile = 1.6 km

Weight
1 pound (lb) = 0.45 kg   1 quarter (28 lb) = 12.7 kg
1 hundredweight (cwt, 112 lb) = 50.8 kg   1 ton (20 cwt, 2240 lb) = 1016 kg
1 chaldron (Whitby measure) = 4927 lb or 2235 kg

Temperature
A difference of 10°C is equivalent to a difference of 18°F and the Celsius and Fahrenheit scales converge at −40°, so:

0°F = −18°C	10°F = −12°C	20°F = −7°C	32°F = 0°C
40°F = 4°C	50°F = 10°C	60°F = 16°C	

Atmospheric pressure
One inch of mercury is equivalent to 33.864 millibars or hectopascals. Therefore:

Inches of mercury	Millibars	Inches of mercury	Millibars
28	948	29.5	999
28.5	965	30.0	1016
29	982	30.5	1033

Cask capacities
In Scoresby's day, volumes and other dimensions were generally imprecise. The cask capacities listed below are therefore very approximate, and it is the hierarchy of cask sizes (e.g. as listed in the 'Manifest' at the end of the 1811 voyage) that is more important than the measure of capacity, especially because the casks contained blubber and not liquids.

Leaguer	=	159 imperial gallons		Butt	=	126 gallons, wine-measure
Puncheon	=	72 gallons		Barrel	=	31½ gallons

Miscellaneous
1. According to Scoresby (see note to journal entry for 26 May 1813), 'Four tons of blubber by measure, generally afford three tons of oil.' and 'The ton or tun of oil is 252 gallons wine measure.' A butt cask could hold half the latter amount of oil.
2. Value of the pound sterling. Based on the tables in Twigger, *Inflation: the Value of the Pound 1750-1998*, £1 in 1811 had the purchasing power of £42.92 in 1998. For £1 in 1812, the equivalent in 1998 was £37.96 and for £1 in 1813 (the year when wartime inflation peaked) the figure was £37.01.

Glossary

The entries in this glossary generally follow the spellings used in the 1811–13 journals, even if these are not the normal spellings indicated in the definitions. As will be seen, the majority of definitions quote or are based on Smyth's *Sailor's Word Book*, with others derived from Scoresby's *An Account of the Arctic Regions* and other sources.

Aboard. In the context of a journal entry such as 25 April 1811, '*To fall aboard of*, is for one vessel to run foul of another', i.e. for one ship to become entangled in the rigging of another. (Smyth)

Ancient. An alternative, and now archaic, form of 'ensign'. Normally flown from the stern to identify the ship's nationality, it was flown at the bowsprit, and there termed a jack, to signal that a whale had been harpooned, and at the top of the mizen mast to indicate that the ship was leaving the whaling grounds for home. (*Account of the Arctic Regions*, II, 523 and journal entries for 22 April and 26 June 1811)

Arctic sea-smoke. The modern meteorological term for what Scoresby called 'frost-rime' or 'frost-smoke'. Cold air is warmed as it passes over a relatively warmer sea or lake and therefore evaporates moisture from the water surface. As this air mixes with the colder air above, the moisture condenses as a 'dense frozen vapour … ascending, in high winds and turbulent seas, to the height of 80 or 100 feet' and coating rigging and other surfaces. (*Account of the Arctic Regions*, I, 434–6)

Bay-ice. 'Ice newly formed on the surface of the sea, and having the colour of water; it is then in the first stage of consolidation … also applied to ice a foot or two in thickness in bays.' (Smyth)

Bend on. 'BEND, To. To fasten one rope to another, or to an anchor.' (Smyth)

Best anchor. See *Bower anchors*.

Bit head. 'BITT-HEADS. The upright pieces of oak-timber let in and bolted to the beams of two decks at least.' (Smyth)

Blue Peter. Signal flag, used especially to indicate a ship's imminent sailing, consisting of a white square on a blue field.

Bolt. 'BOLT-ROPE. A rope sewed all round the edge of the sail, to prevent the canvas from tearing.' (Smyth)

Boring. 'In Arctic seas, the operation of forcing the ship through loose ice under a heavy press of sail; at least attempting the chance of advantage of cracks or openings in the pack.' (Smyth)

Bottlenose. The bottlenose dolphin, *Tursiops truncatus*.

Bouge. 'BOUGE OR BOWGE AND CHINE, OR BILGE AND CHINE. The end of one cask stowed against the bilge of another.' (Smyth) The bilge of a cask is its largest circumference, where the bung-hole is located; the chine is the flat end of the cask. 'Chine and chine' therefore describes casks stowed end to end, whereas bilge and chine (Scoresby also used the term 'bilge and head') means stowage with the long axis of each cask at right-angles to its neighbours in the row.

Bower anchors. 'Those at the bows ... They are called best and small, not from a difference in size, but as to the bow on which they are placed; starboard being the best bower, and port the small bower.' (Smyth)

Braces. 'The braces are ropes belonging to all the yards of a ship' (Smyth), and are therefore the means of adjusting the alignment of the sails.

Bran. The 'bran-boat' was a whaleboat that was launched and manned, in places where the appearance of whales seemed likely. (*Account of the Arctic Regions*, II, 237–8)

Brash. 'Small fragments of crushed ice, collected by wind or currents, near the shore; or such that the ship can easily force through.' (Smyth)

Cannonade/carronade. The carronade was a light cannon, with a short barrel and large calibre, produced in large numbers by the Carron Company of Falkirk, Scotland, between 1778 and 1852, primarily though not exclusively for use on ships.

Cant/kent. 'A cut made in a whale between the neck and the fins, to which the cant-purchase is made fast ... .' (Smyth)

Canting tackle/cant-purchase/cant-blocks. The system of pulleys between the main-mast-head and the cant cut in the whale to enable the whale to be rotated as it is flensed.

Cap. A strong block of wood, with holes, used to link mast or bowsprit extensions to the main structure.

Careening. 'The operation of heaving the ship down on one side, by arranging the ballast, or the application of a strong purchase to her masts, which require to be expressly supported for the occasion to prevent their springing; by these means one side of the bottom, elevated above the surface of the water, may be cleansed or repaired.' (Smyth)

Carlines. 'CARLINES, OR CARLINGS. Pieces of timber about five inches square, lying fore and aft, along from one beam to another.' (Smyth)

Cat head. 'The cat-head ... is used to lift the anchor from the surface of the water ... [and] serves to suspend the anchor clear of the bow, when it is necessary to let it go.' (Smyth)

Chains. 'CHAINS, properly CHAIN-WALES or CHANNELS. Broad and thick planks projecting horizontally from the ship's outside to which they are fayed and bolted, abreast of and somewhat behind the masts ... they are respectively designated fore, main, and mizen.' (Smyth)

Chaldron. A measure of the weight or volume of coal, now archaic. Inherently imprecise, its amount also varied from place to place. In Whitby it appears to have been approximately 4927 lbs (2235 kg). See note to journal entry for 21 March 1812.

Chine. See 'Bouge'.

Chock aft. '[A]s far aft as possible.' (Smyth)

Chop. 'Of the wind: To change, veer, or shift its direction suddenly.' (*OED*)

Clag. Northern English dialect word (*OED*). 'To adhere as paste' (Robinson, *A Glossary of Yorkshire Words and Phrase, Collected in Whitby and the Neighbourhood*).

Clew. The lower corner of a square sail, or lower after corner of a fore-and-aft sail. Clewing-up is hauling up the clews to the spar or mast before furling the sail.

Clinch. 'A particular method of fastening large ropes by a half hitch.' (Smyth)

Come home. 'COMING-HOME. 'Said of the anchor when it has been dropped on bad holding ground, or is dislodged from its bed by the violence of the wind and sea, and is dragged along by the vessel, or is tripped by insufficient length of cable.' (Smyth)

Corn. 'To preserve meat for a time by salting it slightly.' (Smyth)

Cross/cross-sea. 'A sea not caused by the wind then blowing. During a heavy gale which changes quickly ... each change of wind produces a direction of the sea, which lasts for some hours after the wind which caused it has changed ... .' (Smyth) Scoresby also used the term to describe drifting ice moved by a cross-sea.

Dark lights. A variant of 'deadlights', q.v. (*OED*, s.v. 'dark'), shutters used to protect cabin windows in heavy weather.

Dead-lights. 'Strong wooden shutters made exactly to fit the cabin windows externally; they are fixed on the approach of bad weather.' (Smyth)

Dolphin. In the context of Whitby harbour, 'a stout post on a quayside, or in a beach, to make hawsers fast to.' (Smyth). See note to journal entry for 18 March 1812.

Doubling. 'DOUBLE, To. To cover a ship with an extra planking, usually of 4 inches, either internally or externally ... Doubling, however, is a term applied only where the plank thus used is not less than 2 inches thick.' (Smyth) In the sense of 'doubling a cape', as in the navigation exercise noted in the Introduction (p. xxviii, n. 2), it means to sail or pass round the cape.

Fid. Several nautical meanings; in the context of equipping a whaleboat (e.g. journal entry of 17 April 1813), 'a conical pin of hard wood, of any size from 10 inches downwards, tapering to a point, used to open the strands of a rope in splicing'. (Smyth)

Finner. Scoresby described the finner in *An Account of the Arctic Regions* (II, pp. 484–5), but that description might fit more than one whale species recognized nowadays.

Fish/fishery. The terms used always in contemporary documents (including legislation) for whales and whaling, though it was well understood that whales were mammals.

Flat-aback. 'When all the sails are blown with their after-surface against the mast, so as to give stern-way.' (Smyth)

Flinch-gut. The place in the ship's hold where the blubber is temporarily stored before making-off.

Floating anchor. 'A simple machine consisting of a fourfold canvas, stretched by two cross-bars of iron ... It is made to hang perpendicularly at some distance below the surface, where it [diminishes] a ship's leeward drift in a gale.' (Smyth)

Foot. 'The lower end of a mast or sail.' (Smyth)

Foreganger. A length of untarred rope ('white line') that, by its lighter weight and flexibility, makes it easier for the harpoon to be thrown manually. '4¼ Fathoms in length, is similar to the whale lines, except the deficiency of tar whereby it is more supple & better adapted for heaving out. The one end of the foreganger is spliced closely round the small shank of the harpoon, the other is spliced to the whale lines.' (1813 journal, 17 April)

Fox. '[A] fastening formed by twisting several rope-yarns together by hand and rubbing it with hard tarred canvas.' (Smyth)

Fresh. In the context of Whitby harbour, run-off from heavy rain or melting snow, carried by the River Esk.

Frost-rime/Frost-smoke. See *Arctic sea-smoke.*

Galliot/galleot. In the context of Scoresby's voyages, 'a Dutch or Flemish vessel for cargoes, with very rounded ribs and flattish bottom, with a mizen-mast stept far aft, carrying a square-mainsail and main-topsail, a fore-stay to the main-mast (there being no fore-mast), with fore-staysail and jibs'. (Smyth)

Grapnel. 'A sort of small anchor for boats, having a ring at one end, and flour palmed claws at the other.' (Smyth)

Grog. 'A drink … consisting of one part of spirits diluted with three of water … The addition of sugar and lemon-juice now makes grog an agreeable anti-scorbutic.' (Smyth)

Guess warp. 'GUESS-WARP, OR GUEST-ROPE. A rope carried to a distant object, in order to warp a vessel towards it, or to make fast a boat.' (Smyth)

Gumming. The first stage of the preparation of whalebone for commerce. It is the removal of the *gum* that separates these bones, described by Scoresby 'white, fibrous, tender and tasteless. It cuts like cheese. It has the appearance of the interior or kernel of the cocoa-nut.' (*Account of the Arctic Regions*, II, 416, 418, 458)

Hand money. As used by Scoresby (e.g. journal entry for 12 March 1813), this appears to have been a specific cash payment to certain members of the crew at the outset of a voyage, that was not an advance on wages but more in the nature of a 'signing bonus'.

Harponeer. 'HARPOONER, HARPONEER, OR HAPINEER. The expert bowman in a whale-boat, whose duty it is to throw or fire the harpoon.' (Smyth)

Hawse. 'This is a term of great meaning. Strictly, it is that part of a vessel's bow where holes are cut for her cables to pass through … Also, said of a vessel a little in advance of the stem; as, she sails *athwart hawses* … .' (Smyth)

Head, by the. A ship that has been loaded or ballasted so as to draw more water forward than aft.

Heavy ice/heavy drift-ice. 'Dense ice, which has a great depth in the water in proportion to ts size, and is not in a state of decay … .' (Smyth)

Ice blink. An intense whiteness visible close to the horizon, caused by reflection of light by the ice-covered sea beneath.

Junk. To Smyth, 'any remnants or pieces of old cable, or condemned rope, cut into small portions' for various purposes. In his journal entry for 18 March 1812, Scoresby applied the term to an uncut old rope used for mooring in Whitby harbour.

Kedge. 'A small anchor used to keep a ship steady and clear from her bower-anchor … especially at the turn of the tide.' (Smyth)

Kent. Alternative form of 'cant' (q.v.).

Kiel. 'KEELING. Rolling on her keel.' (Smyth) See Scoresby's journal entry for 26 April 1811.

Kilson. 'KEELSON, OR KELSON. An internal keel, laid upon the middle of the floor-timbers, immediately over the keel, and serving to bind all together by means of long bolts driven from without, and clinched on the upper side of the keelson.' (Smyth)

Knee. 'Naturally grown timber, or bars of iron, bent to a right angle, or to fit the surfaces, and to secure bodies firmly together.' (Smyth, who listed several types of knee, but did not include the 'ice-knees' mentioned by Scoresby when describing the construction of the *Esk*, at the beginning of the 1813 journal.)

Lamellar. In the form of a thin plate or layer (term used by Scoresby to describe snowflake features).

Lipper. 'A sea which washed over the weather chess-tree, perhaps *leaper*. Also, the spray from small waves breaking against a ship's bows.' (Smyth)

Longer. 'Each row of casks in the hold, athwart.' (Smyth)

Loose fall. An attempt to capture a whale that is unsuccessful because the harpoon does not remain secured to the whale.

Mallemuching. 'MALLEMAROKING. The visiting and carousing of seamen in the Greenland ships.' (Smyth)

Matt. 'Mat ... A thick web of rope yarn used to protect the standing rigging from the friction of other ropes.' (*OED*)

Mill-dolling. 'Mill-dolling, consists in breaking a passage through thin ice, for a ship, by a sort of *ram*, let fall from the bowsprit; or by one or more boats attached to the jib-boom, having several men in each, who move from side to side, and keep them in continual motion. As the ship advances, the rope by which the boats are attached to the jib-boom, draws them forward, and prevents them from being run down.' (*Account of the Arctic Regions*, I, 310n)

Mouse. 'To mouse a hook, to put a turn or two of rope-yarn round the point of a tackle-hook and its neck to prevent it unhooking.' (Smyth)

Nautical day. 'This day commences at noon, twelve hours before the civil day, and ends at noon of the day following.' The journals of 1811 and 1812 are based on the nautical day, that for 1813 on the civil day from midnight to midnight.

Nittles. Presumably what Smyth terms 'nippers': 'formed of clean, unchafed yarns, drawn from condemned rope, unlaid ... . [U]sed in various ways, viz. to bind the messenger to the cable, and to form slings for wet spars, &c'.

Orlop. 'The lowest deck, formerly called "over-lop," consisting of a platform laid over the beams in ships of war. whereon the cables were usually coiled, and containing some cabins as well as the chief store-rooms.' (Smyth)

Piggin. 'A little pail having a long stave for a handle, used to bail water out of a boat.' (Smyth)

Ply. '... to work to windward, to beat'. (Smyth)

Preventer. 'Applied to ropes, &c., when used as additional securities to aid other ropes in supporting spars, &c., during a strong gale.' (Smyth)

Quicksilver. An alternative term for the element mercury.

Rabbit. 'RABBET, OR REBATE. An angular incision cut longitudinally in a piece of timber, to receive the ends of a number of planks, to be securely fastened therein.' (Smyth)

Rank. 'In close array, crowded together, thick, dense.' (*OED*, which regarded the term as obsolete, except in northern dialect.)

Rattle. 'To rattle the rigging' is to fix small lines ('ratlines') across a ship's shrouds like ladder-rungs.

Razor back. 'The fin-whale (*Balænoptera*), so called from its prominent dorsal fin.' (Smyth)

Refraction. 'TERRESTRIAL REFRACTION. The property of the atmosphere by which objects appear to be higher than they really are, and in certain cases producing the effect called *deceptio visus*, and *fata morgana*.' (Smyth)

Rough. As used by Scoresby (e.g. journal entry of 26 June 1812), the term appears to describe uncoiled whale lines, in contrast to those that were properly coiled in a tub in the whaleboat.

Sallying. 'To rock (a stationary or slow-moving ship) by running from side to side in order to assist its progress.' (*OED*)

Scant. 'A term applied to the wind when it heads a ship off.' (Smyth)

Scarf. 'SCARPH, OR SCARFING. Is the junction of wood or metal by sloping off the edges, and maintaining the same thickness throughout the joint.' (Smyth)

Shake. '*To shake a cask*. To take it to pieces, and pack up the parts, then termed "shakes".' (Smyth)

Short sea. 'A confused cross sea where the waves assume a jerking rippling action.' (Smyth)

Skids. Smyth defined these as 'Massive fenders; they consist of long compassing pices of timber, formed to answer the vertical curve of a shp's side … mostly used in whalers.' In the context of the journal entry of 23 May 1811, however, they refer to fenders on a whaleboat.

Small anchor. See *Bower anchors*.

Spanning. 'SPANNING A HARPOON: Fixing the line which connects the harpoon and its staff … on striking the whale the staff leaps out of the socket and does not interfere with the iron, which otherwise might be wrenched out.' (Smyth) The foreganger is that connecting line.

Specksioneer. 'SPECKTIONEER. The chief harpooner in a Greenland ship. He also directs the cutting operation in clearing the whale of its blubber and bones.' (Smyth)

Sprung 'SPRING. A crack running obliquely through any part of a mast or yard, which renders it unsafe to carry the usual sail thereon, and the spar is then said to be sprung.' (Smyth)

Stantions. 'STANCHIONS. Any fixed upright support. Also, those posts of wood or iron which, being placed pillar-wise, support the waist-trees and guns.' (Smyth)

Stay. '*In stays*, or *hove in stays*, is the situation of a vessel when she is staying, or in the act of going about … '*to miss stays*, is to fail in the attempt to go about.' (Smyth)

Steering sails. 'STUDDING-SAILS. Fine-weather sails set outside the square-sails; the term "scudding sails" was formerly used.' (Smyth, who also defined 'steering-sail' as 'An incorrect name for a studding-sail.')

Streak. 'STRAKE. One breadth of plank in a ship, either within or without board, wrought from the stem to the stern-post.' (Smyth)

Streams (of ice). 'STREAM-ICE. A collection of pieces of drift or bay ice, joining each other in a ridge following in the line of current.' (Smyth)

Strop. '[A] piece of rope, spliced generally into a circular wreath, and used to surround the body of a block, so that the latter may be hung to any particular situation about the masts, yards, or rigging.' (Smyth) Used in the journals to describe the rope suspended from the ship and attached to the whale's cant during flensing.

Stuff. 'A *coat of stuff*, a term used for any composition laid on to ships' spars, bottom, &c ... .' (Smyth)

Thole. A wooden (or later, metal) pin used on the gunwale of a boat as an alternative to a rowlock.

Tracking machine. Scoresby's term for a floating anchor (q.v.).

Twice laid. 'Rope made from a selection of the best yarns of old rope.' (Smyth)

Wear. To change tack by turning a vessel downwind instead of the more usual turn against the wind. '[E]specially when strong gales render [turning into the wind] dangerous, unseamanlike, or impossible, the head of the vessel is put away from the wind, and turned round 20 points of the compass instead of 12, and, without strain or danger, is brought to the wind on the opposite tack.' (Smyth, s.v. 'VEER')

Whither/wither feather. 'The harpoon ... consists of three conjoined parts, called the "socket," "shank," and "mouth;" the latter of which includes the barbs or "withers".' (*Account of the Arctic Regions*, II, 223)

Winger. 'Small casks stowed close to the side in a ship's hold, where the large casks would cause too great a rising in that part of the tier.' (Smyth)

Introduction

The memorial to William Scoresby the Younger (1789–1857) in Upton Church, Torquay includes a text from the Epistle to the Hebrews 11:4: 'He being dead, yet speaketh'.[1] The choice of text was remarkably prescient, for, on the subject of arctic whaling at least, Scoresby's voice has continued to be the dominant one. His two-volume work *An Account of the Arctic Regions* was published in 1820 and reprinted in 1969. Although much of the scientific data and evaluation in the first volume ('The Arctic') has been superseded by later research, the second volume on 'The Whale Fishery' remains the authoritative text.[2]

As a whaling captain, scientist, and then a minister of religion, Scoresby was a prolific writer. His biographer[3] listed twenty-seven published items on religious subjects and sixty-four on science, but he also wrote much that remained unpublished, most notably the journals of his annual voyages to the Greenland Sea in search of whales. From 1811 until 1823 (1819 excepted) he sailed from Whitby as master of the *Resolution* and then of the *Esk* and *Fame*, and from Liverpool in command of the *Baffin*. Even before 1811 he had assumed responsibility for maintaining the journal of the *Resolution* while chief mate under his father's command.

In 1822 Scoresby combined whaling with exploration and survey along the east coast of Greenland, and in 1823 made his final whaling voyage from Liverpool in the *Baffin*. In the same year the Whitby Literary and Philosophical Society was founded, and one of its first acts was to honour Scoresby. When he died in 1857, he bequeathed to the Society the magnets and other scientific instruments that he had made or used, 'my specimens of Arctic birds, narwal, bears, and sea-horse heads' and other biological items together with

> ... the following books, drawings, manuscripts, &c., namely, all my manuscript journals of voyages and travels, and original maps, drawings, and sketches illustrative thereof. All my other scientific manuscripts, notes of experiments, and investigations; my autobiography and notes referring thereto; my original manuscripts of published works, manuscripts of literary, narrative, and biographic subjects; my select correspondence ... [etc.][4]

The Whitby Literary and Philosophical Society is still in vigorous existence. It

[1] The memorial tablet is described in detail in Scoresby-Jackson, *Life*, pp. 398–9.
[2] Gordon Jackson ended the preface to his book *The British Whaling Trade* with the following apt remark (p. xv): 'In one matter I must crave the indulgence of the zoologist. The whale was *not* a fish, but in the past it was often so regarded and invariably so described, both in whaling parlance and in Acts of Parliament. I have followed this inaccurate terminology because of the difficulties that would have arisen in quotations and legal definitions.'
[3] Scoresby-Jackson, *Life*, pp. 401–4.
[4] Ibid., pp. 405–6.

maintains the Whitby Museum, where many of the items bequeathed by Scoresby are exhibited and where his papers are preserved, including the manuscript autobiography[1] mentioned in the will. This was used by Scoresby's nephew, Robert Edmund Scoresby-Jackson, in the preparation of his *Life* of Scoresby (1861), and also by Tom and Cordelia Stamp, the authors of a more recent biography (1975).

As can be seen from the present volume, Scoresby's arctic journals are much more than summary records of the annual voyages. In part, although only in part, the topics and the detail are a response to the requirements imposed by Parliament for payment of the bounty available to British whaling ships. This bounty, based on a ship's tonnage, dated from 1733 and both its amount and the conditions for its award had been altered several times by subsequent legislation. By the early nineteenth century the bounty was twenty shillings per ton, to a maximum of 300 tons, and among the conditions was the following:

> No bounty shall be paid to any person or persons whatever, on account of any ship employed in the said fishery, unless a log-book shall have been constantly kept on board, in which log-book the various situations and occurrences respecting such ship, during the whole course of the voyage, shall be inserted every day, and particularly the times when such ship shall have been in sight of land, distinguishing what land, and the bearings thereof, and the supposed distances therefrom, and the soundings; and also the times when, and the latitude in which, any whale, or other creature living in the sea, shall have been killed, taken, or caught by the crew of such ship; which log-book shall be delivered by the master, or other person having the command of such ship, at the time of his making a report, to the Collector of the Customs, at the port in Great Britain where such ship shall arrive on her return from the said fishery, for his inspection and examination; and the said master, or other person having the command of such ship, together with the mate thereof, shall jointly and severally verify on oath the contents of such log-book before such collector.[2]

Scoresby's journals contain far more than information of this type. They increasingly became the personal journals of an individual whose abilities matched his wide and diverse interests. They contain social anecdote, religious conviction, humour, and scientific inquiry. There is a wide variation in the length of the journals, although all of them are much longer than was required or normal: the already-substantial 25,000 words in 1811 expanded to twice as much only two years later. One doubts that the Collector of Customs found it necessary to read every word.

The journals have also remained largely unread since that time. The account of his 1822 voyage of exploration along the coast of east Greenland was published in the following year, and reprinted in 1980.[3] A facsimile of the journal of the 1806 voyage

---

[1] WHITM:SCO843. The autobiography is in several sections ('Personal Memoirs No. 1' to number 10) and there is a note at the beginning of the fifth section (where Scoresby begins a description of the journey to Scotland with his wife after their marriage), as follows: 'NB. 74 foregoing sheets [Personal memoirs No. 1 to 4 inclusive] were written during a Greenland voyage in 1821; the Continuation was begun on the 2nd of May, 1823, in latitude 71°0'N.' The autobiography breaks off at the end of 1818.

[2] 26th Geo. III. c. 41. §10. Quoted in Scoresby, *Account of The Arctic Regions*, II, p. 499.

[3] Scoresby, *Journal of a Voyage to the Northern Whale-Fishery.*

of the *Resolution*, commanded by William Scoresby, Senior, with his son as mate and journal-keeper, was published in 1981.[1] It is intended that this Hakluyt Society volume, covering the voyages in 1811, 1812 and 1813, will be the first of several devoted to the voyages commanded by William Scoresby, Junior, that preceded the publication of *An Account of the Arctic Regions* in 1820.

The Journals

Although the bounty legislation used the term 'log-books', Scoresby preferred the term 'journal'. The terms were recognized as synonymous by Smyth: 'a daily register of the ship's course and distance, the winds and weather, and a general account of whatever is of importance'.[2]

The journals vary considerably in length, but the length is unrelated to the duration of each voyage: Scoresby normally sailed from Whitby in mid-March and returned in the first half of August. In terms of the number of manuscript pages, the following list indicates a gradual increase, and places the 1811–1813 journals in context. The number of pages is, however, only an approximate guide to the actual length of each journal, as demonstrated by the 1811–1813 journals.

1811	*Resolution*	68 pages	24,726 words	WHITM:SCO1252
1812	*Resolution*	96 pages	30,889 words	
1813	*Esk*	98 pages	51,251 words	WHITM:SCO1253
1814	*Esk*	66 pages		
1815	*Esk*	74 pages		
1816	*Esk*	96 pages		WHITM:SCO1254
1817	*Esk*	64 pages		
1818	*Fame*	78 pages		WHITM:SCO1255.1
1819	(No voyage)			
1820	*Baffin*	74 pages		WHITM:SCO1255.2
1821	*Baffin*	146 pages		WHITM:SCO1256

It is important to note here that all these journals are later transcriptions from the original journals written during the voyages. Exactly when, or by whom, these transcriptions were made is not clear, but there is some evidence that they were made after the publication of *An Account of the Arctic Regions* in 1820, and that they were not transcribed by Scoresby himself, but were done at his request and, to varying extents, under his direct supervision. At the end of the transcript of the 1810 journal, the last one in which William Scoresby, Junior sailed under his father's captaincy, there is a closing memorandum in which he stated that:

---

[1] Scoresby, *The 1806 Log Book*. Although both Caedmon, the publisher (in a flyleaf note) and the keeper of the Whitby Museum, in his foreword, refer to this as a facsimile of the 'original manuscript', it seems more probable that it is a facsimile of a 'fair copy' of the original journal, prepared some time after the voyage was completed. The consistency and even character of the handwriting, and the almost complete absence of corrections, suggest this, especially when compared to the undoubted original journals of the voyages of 1811 and 1812 (WHITM:SCO651), preserved in the Scoresby Papers in Whitby.

[2] Smyth, v.i. 'Journal'.

The preceding Journal has been copied from the original by Mr Thomas Hewitt, on board the Baffin, 1821, and was afterwards examined and corrected throughout by myself.[1]

In several places in the transcripts, there are blank spaces, often in mid-sentence, with the text continuing, apparently without omission, on a new page. This perhaps indicates that some of the journals were transcribed by more than one person, working simultaneously, although the changes in handwriting are not substantial. It does not appear that the transcriber or transcribers had detailed understanding of the material in the journals, so that occasional transcription errors occur.

Many of these errors can be identified, and corrected, by comparison with what are evidently the original log-books or journals for 1811 and 1812, which are also among the Scoresby Papers.[2] These originals show many pencil markings, suggesting that Scoresby wanted to produce an edited version of the original journals, with both additions and deletions as well as corrections. The changes are not substantial, or particularly important.

A significant feature of the original journals for 1811 and 1812 is that they are each in three parts. On the outward and homeward voyages, a printed log-book was used, with space for navigational entries at two-hour intervals, and a fixed amount of space available for additional remarks. Virtually all the pencil alterations are in these pages. During the actual whaling in the Greenland Sea, however, the pages were initially completely blank, allowing Scoresby to write entries of whatever length he thought appropriate. These two page formats appear to have been sewn together at the time the journal was prepared.[3] In 1811 the printed format was abandoned after 18 April and resumed on 15 July; in 1812 the respective dates were 6 April and 27 July, with the Whitby port entries prior to 29 March also written on blank sheets.

The minor nature of the changes from originals to transcripts can be exemplified from two instances, both taken from the first few pages of the 1811 journal. On 11 March 1811, the day the *Resolution* left Whitby, the original noted that only after the vessel had passed out of the harbour entrance was it discovered that two of its crew had been left behind, and a boat had to be sent to bring them on board. Scoresby appears to have decided that this brief incident should be omitted from the transcription. Similarly, in the entry for 15 March, as the *Resolution* approached Shetland, there are minor omissions and changes in the transcript from the original:

(Original)
The other Ships came up about 7½ PM several spoke they continued their course for two hours and followed them all then all lay too[.] In the morning it was clear weather at Day break made sail to the NbE or NNEd for an hour, one ship ahead several miles the other to the Ed & still and seeing no Land I suspected we were to the Ed hauled westerly

[1] Signed and dated 'William Scoresby Junr, Greenland Sea, 2d Augt 1821'.
[2] As can be seen from the opening paragraphs of the 1813 journal, this and subsequent voyages involved not merely a new ship but also a change in ownership. One can speculate that these proprietors retained the original journals, but permitted Scoresby to transcribe them.
[3] The journal for 1811 appears to have utilized the remaining pages of an earlier log: it begins on the reverse side of a page recording the conclusion of a passage by the 'Ship Victory from the Lizard towards St Michael' (S. Miguel in the Azores) on 13–14 July 1785.

first NNW & W & NW about 9 o clock hauled close by the wind[.] At 10½ AM made the land Noss Island bearing about NWbW distance 10 miles[.] At noon had come very near it found we sh^d not fetch it even tho' the tide came in our favour.

(Transcript)
The other Ships came up about 7½ PM several spoke they continued their course for two hours then all lay too[.] In the morning it was clear weather at Day break made sail to the NbE or NNE^d for an hour and seeing no Land I suspected we were to the E^d hauled up NNW or NW and about 9 o clock close by the wind[.] At 10½ AM made the land Noss Island bearing about NWbW distance 10 miles[.] At noon had come very near it but found we should not fetch the entrance of Brassa sound to which we were bound[.]

In this instance the changes appear to have been made in the interests of clarification.

As would be expected, the transcript is easier to read than the original journal written on board. In some cases it has been possible to use the originals to correct inaccurate transcriptions, or to identify words that are doubtful or illegible in the transcript, though in many cases the problem lies in the legibility of the original. For example, in the very first sentence of the 1811 journal, the transcription reads 'I was prepared to succeed him' but the original text is clearly 'I was proposed to succeed him', and in this case the word 'proposed' was inserted above the line in the transcript, perhaps by Scoresby himself. Where corrections can be made to the transcript versions, this is indicated in the footnotes.

It is appropriate to mention at this point that the log-books of seven whaling voyages commanded by William Scoresby, Senior, were published in facsimile by The Explorers Club of New York in 1917. These log-books had been brought to the United States by Louisa Scoresby in 1876[1] and at the date of their publication were still in the possession of the family in Ellenville, NY. On none of these voyages did William Scoresby, Junior, sail with his father; they are for the years and vessels as follows:

1786	*Henrietta*	(Only beginning and end of voyage recorded)
1787	*Henrietta*	(Scoresby Senior as specksioneer [i.e. chief harpooner])
1791–1797	*Henrietta*	(Scoresby, Senior as master)
1798	*Dundee*	(Facsimile ends on 3 July, in lat.70°12′N, long. 7°48′E)
1801	*Dundee*	
1817	*Mars*	
1820	*Fame*	
1822	*Fame*	

These log-books therefore span the career of William Scoresby, Senior, from his earliest whaling voyage in 1785 under the command of Captain Crispin Bean, until his final completed voyage in 1822 (in 1823 the *Fame* was destroyed by fire at Kirkwall, Orkney, en route to the whaling grounds). The journals are brief compared with

---

[1] Louisa (b. 1831) was the daughter of Thomas Scoresby, younger brother of William Scoresby, Junior. The family had emigrated to the United States in 1834, but Louisa later returned temporarily to Whitby to care for her widowed aunt, Mary Clark, until the latter's death in 1876. See Stamp, *The Scoresby Family*, p. 12; Dellenbaugh, *Seven Log-Books ...*, p. 13.

those when his son was master, or even when his son was responsible for maintaining the journals for his father, as appears to have been the case for the *Resolution* journals from about 1806 to 1810.

The Scoresby Family[1]

William Scoresby, Senior, was born at Cropton, a small agricultural village on the southern edge of the North York Moors, on 3 May 1760. In 1783 he married Lady Mary Smith, whose first name was apparently one traditionally given to girls born on 25 March, Lady Day or the feast of the Annunciation.[2] There was no family tradition of seafaring, but William Senior began as an apprentice sailor in 1780, and made his first whaling voyage in 1785. There is general agreement that, over a period of three decades, he was an outstandingly successful whaling captain, and he is also credited with the invention of the crow's-nest.[3] During his long career, he commanded several different ships, from various British ports:

1791–1797	*Henrietta*	Whitby
1798–1802	*Dundee*	London
1803–1810	*Resolution*	Whitby
1811–1814	*John*	Greenock
1816–1817	*Mars*	Whitby
1819–1823	*Fame*	Hull

He died in Whitby in 1829, apparently of a self-inflicted gunshot wound.[4]

William Scoresby, Junior, was the third child and eldest son of William and Lady Mary. He and his elder sisters, Sarah and Mary, were born at Cropton, though the family moved soon after his birth to Whitby. Another sister, Arabella, was born in

[1] As indicated in the previous footnote, Cordelia Stamp published a valuable (though in places speculative) family tree of the Scoresby family from the thirteenth to the twentieth centuries.

[2] '… he married; the object of his choice being Lady Mary, (viz. Mary, with the prefix of Lady, taken, not ostentatiously, but in rural simplicity, from the characteristic designation of the day of her birth, which was on *Lady-day* [i.e. 25 March]) …': Scoresby, *My Father*, p. 36.

[3] There is an illustration of a 'Barrel crow's nest of the type devised by William Scoresby Senr. in 1807' in Credland, *Hull Whaling Trade*, p. 33. 'Slung from the top of the main mast on chains it was entered from the bottom by a trap door. A canvas hood could be rotated to give shelter from the wind. The occupant was provided with a telescope for observation along with a signal flag and speaking trumpet to communicate with the crew below.' A more detailed description was provided by his son in *Account of the Arctic Regions*, II, pp. 203–5. That description was playfully satirized by Melville in chapter 35 of *Moby-Dick*. Although Scoresby clearly credited his father with the invention, Melville described Scoresby Junior ('Captain Sleet') as 'the original inventor and patentee.' A replica, built according to Scoresby's description, is exhibited at Whitby Museum.

[4] 'On Tuesday [28 April 1829], a Coroner's Inquest was held on the body of Mr. William Scoresby, of Whitby, aged 69, late ship-owner, who put an end to his existence, at his house in Bagdale, Whitby, the same afternoon, by shooting himself through the heart with a pistol. He appears to have been in a state of temporary derangement for several months past. He was for many years commander of the ships Henrietta, Dundee, Resolution, Mars, and owner of the Fame, in the Greenland trade.': *Hull Advertiser*, 1 May 1829, p. 3. See also Credland, *Hull Whaling Trade*, p. 38. The circumstances of his death are seldom mentioned elsewhere, and not at all by his son in the affectionate memoir *My Father*, published in 1851, or in the page devoted to the death in Scoresby-Jackson's biography of his son (p. 258).

1792; thereafter three brothers and two daughters died in infancy between 1794 and 1802. Thomas Scoresby was born in 1804, and another brother died in infancy in 1806. Scoresby-Jackson said that in his early years William Junior 'Physically, ... was tall, weak, and delicate in constitution; mentally, he was timid, anxious, and scrupulously conscientious.'[1]

Because of Scoresby's subsequent achievements as scientist and writer, his early education is of more than usual interest. After acquiring 'the rudiments of learning'[2] at a dame school, he then attended a boys' school. In a well-known passage from the autobiography, Scoresby described the schoolmaster:

> He not only had recourse to the ordinary means of punishment, such as the cane or the ferule – both of which he was in the habit of applying with terror-awakening dexterity, and they were of unusual magnitude, – but he was also in the habit of locking the offending boys in the school, and keeping them several hours in darkness after the rest of the scholars had departed – of strapping the little culprits to a bench, and keeping them immovably fixed for a half a day together – and, at other times, of fastening a cord to their thumbs, an inquisition-like torture, and then passing it through a pulley above them, hoisted them up so as to leave only their toes on the ground. In this cruel posture, with their arms above their heads, and with their thumbs almost disjointed, he was known to detain those who seriously offended him during the absence of the school at dinner!'[3]

A more productive experience was his period at a school near Blackwall Dock in London. His father was by now commanding the London whaler *Dundee*, and William and his mother joined the ship at Whitby during the homeward voyage in 1802.

> I was put to an excellent school in the neighbourhood, superintended by Mr. Stock. This was the first instance in which my faculties were brought into exercise. Mr. Stock was a rigid disciplinarian, but a teacher of the first order ... For my own part, the advantage I gained was incalculable. In grammar I attained uncommon proficiency; in calculation much facility; in writing much improvement. On the first weekly examination of exercise copies I was almost at the bottom of my list, my number being below seventy: at the conclusion of a quarter of a year I stood number two. ... The exertion, however, on a delicate frame was severe. I had to rise at five in the morning and to pursue the routine of the seminary until the same hour in the evening ... after which I never failed to have some exercise for my employment at home; and sometimes, which was optional, attended the familiar lectures of Mr. Stock, on interesting branches of science, in the evening.[4]

Even before this date, at the age of ten William Junior had made his first voyage to the Arctic, having persuaded, fairly easily, his father to take him on the *Dundee*'s voyage in 1800. When his father returned to Whitby to command the *Resolution* in

---

[1] Scoresby-Jackson, *Life*, p. 16. There is no reason to doubt this statement, though it needs to be remembered that Thomas Scoresby-Jackson was born in 1816, and the *Life* was published in 1861, after the death of its subject.

[2] Ibid., p. 18.

[3] Ibid., pp. 18–19.

[4] Ibid., pp. 25–6.

1803, his son became a regular crew member. His formal education continued, though Scoresby later recalled it as inadequate:

> After I left Mr. Stock's admirable academy in 1802, no opportunity was afforded me of improving myself in scholastic knowledge, excepting what little was within my reach at the school in Whitby, conducted by Mr. Routh. Here, in the intervals of the fishery, I attended to geometry (plane and spherical), algebra, navigation, and other branches of mathematics; but having, in every branch, run the teachers beyond their usual practice, I found their explanations of any difficulties that occurred neither satisfactory nor intelligible. Hence, what I learned perfectly was merely the rudiments of each division of the science.[1]

If such educational inadequacies seem unremarkable in the context of the period, it also needs to be said that Scoresby's judgment may be a little harsh. There are two surviving exercise-books from this period in the Scoresby Papers in Whitby, concerned with geometry and navigation respectively, and the tasks and solutions in the latter do indicate a real concern by the school for the future needs of Scoresby and other boys preparing for a maritime career.[2] The schoolroom could never be a substitute for the actual task of navigation at sea, but it does seem to have provided a theoretical basis for what Scoresby would soon learn from practice. It seems evident from the journals in the present volume that older and more experienced captains were glad to trust in Scoresby's navigational skills, especially on the more hazardous return journeys from the Arctic, and the Whitby school surely deserves some of the credit.

As Scoresby-Jackson noted in his *Life*, 1806 was an eventful year for William Scoresby. He was promoted to chief mate of the *Resolution*, under his father's command; the voyage reached 81°30′N, a 'furthest north' that was not surpassed until 1827 (by Parry);[3] and he met Mary Lockwood, the woman whom he would later marry. Perhaps of greatest significance, however, he spent the winter of 1806–7 studying at the University of Edinburgh.

There is a long-standing and widespread belief that the educational system in Scotland was, at least until well into the nineteenth century, superior to that in England, and accessible to a much greater proportion of the population. At the level of higher education, Scotland had four universities from the late sixteenth century, whereas Oxford and Cambridge remained unchallenged in England until the 1820s. This view

---

[1] *Life*, pp. 30–31.

[2] WHITM:SCO681 and 682. Two examples taken from Scoresby's exercise book on navigation (undated, but probably 1803 or 1804). (1) 'A Ship bound to a port that bears NE by N¼E, must double a cape to the eastward with the wind at N.N.E. After having sailed 10 leagues on her larboard tack, 5¼ points from the wnd, with a point lee way, the port bore NW by W. How near the wind must she lie on her starboard tack? What dist. must she sail to reach her port? And what distance was she from the port when she set sail?' (2) 'Being at sea in latitude 35°S. on 11th of Nov. 1802, the sun's altitude being 13°20′, when his magnetic azimuth was ESE. Required the variation of the compass?'

[3] In *An Account of the Arctic Regions*, I, pp. 42–6, Scoresby reviewed earlier claims to have reached higher latitudes, including one to 89½°N! Though dismissing such extreme claims, he wrote (p. 44) 'I by no means wish to infer ... that no voyager has ever sailed beyond the latitude of 81° or 82°', though he saw no real evidence that this had been achieved.

of the Scottish system has been contested,[1] but there is no doubt that, in terms of both accessibility and intellectual vigour, Edinburgh was the ideal choice for Scoresby. Birse, though scarcely an unbiased observer, has suggested that the Scottish Enlightenment of the mid-eighteenth century was just the beginning of

> a remarkable outburst of scientific and technological activity in Scotland [that] began, slowly at first, in the second half of the seventeenth century, gathering momentum throughout the eighteenth century to reach a peak in about 1850 ... Philosophy and science led the way, much of it centred in Edinburgh University and its assembly of distinguished professors.[2]

Birse suggested that a principal reason for this vigour was the 'revolution in higher education' initiated in Edinburgh in 1708 in which, instead of a single 'regent' or tutor being responsible for the entire teaching of a student, the latter could henceforth

> pick and choose between courses given by famous professors vying with each other to attract students (and income!) by making sure that their lectures were interesting, and covered the applications as well as the principles of their subjects.[3]

The initiative to go to Edinburgh was Scoresby's own, but he was subsequently encouraged and financially supported by his father. The choice of subjects to be studied was also his own, and in that choice

> ... I was, perhaps, more than commonly fortunate; the classes I attended being chemistry (Dr. Hope, professor), natural philosophy (Professor Playfair), with occasional lectures on anatomy, and a French school.[4]

The introduction to science, and the boundaries of scientific research, undoubtedly helped to shape Scoresby's future, but of equal importance, especially in regard to the character of his journals and other writings, was the study habits he developed during this winter at Edinburgh.

> I took full notes of both classes I attended in the university, and on my return to my lodgings extended them. ... I found my notes daily extend, until at length the writing of them used to occupy me three or four hours. By this exercise each subject was more particularly fixed on my memory than it could have been by an extensive course of reading – an employment to which I felt considerable aversion – and I was necessarily led, at the same

[1] See, for example, Houston, *Scottish Literacy and the Scottish Identity*: 'The further we go into the subject of Scottish education the more its much-vaunted achievements fade away into a range of mythology.' (p. 247).
[2] Birse, *Science at the University of Edinburgh, 1583–1993*, p. 45.
[3] Ibid., p. 46.
[4] John Playfair (1748–1819) was mathematician, physicist and astronomer, but is best remembered for the establishment of uniformitarianism (see p. xxxi) as the basis of geology, based on his association with James Hutton. Discovering Scoresby's arctic experience, this 'so far excited his attention as to lead to a future correspondence'(*Life*, pp. 32, 33–4). Scoresby was only seventeen at this time, but he was not unusually young to attend the university; Birse, *Science at the University of Edinburgh*, p. 52 cited the evidence from a later Royal Commission indicating that in the 1820s 'the average age at entry to Edinburgh University was about fourteen and a half'.

time, into habits of composition; for although I often took down the words of the lecturer, yet more frequently the ideas only were preserved.[1]

Scoresby had to leave Edinburgh in mid-March 1807 'just when Professor Playfair was entering on astronomy – a subject which, to me, had uncommon attractions' to join the *Resolution* again.

If he had plans to return to Edinburgh in the autumn, these were preempted by his role as a volunteer in bringing the captured Danish fleet from Copenhagen to Portsmouth. For this duty, occupying him from 23 September to 21 December, 'I received £11. 19s. 2d., the amount of bounty, travelling money, and wages for three months' service'.[2]

It was during Scoresby's return from Gosport to Whitby that he met Sir Joseph Banks, already an acquaintance of his father. Scoresby, still a diffident teenager, understandably found it an 'extraordinary *trial*' to call upon the baronet, educated at Harrow, Eton and Oxford, who had sailed with Cook two decades before Scoresby was born, and who had been President of the Royal Society since 1778. He was warmly received, however, invited to one of Banks' weekly breakfast meetings, and afterwards began

> a correspondence which was continued pretty regularly, until within a few weeks of his lamented death; and gave rise to a personal intercourse at every opportunity, from which I derived very great mental advantages.[3]

Scoresby did not return to the University of Edinburgh after the 1808 voyage, but he did so in November 1809. He claimed in his autobiography that he felt more confident about his studies than in 1806 and

> I therefore entered upon an extensive field of inquiry, and took out tickets for natural history, two classes of mathematics, and logic; in all four daily classes. These, with anatomy and some gymnastic exercises, completed the routine of my studies ....[4]

This appears to have been at some risk to his health; it is surprising to find that, despite all his travels and exertions, and the similar activities that were to follow, he was still in early manhood noting that 'For years I had been of a consumptive habit. For years my appetite was so bad that I knew not what it was to enjoy a dinner; and for the same period I was liable to severe colds.'[5]

Apart from the formal learning that Scoresby acquired at the university, two other influences helped to shape his future scientific interests, and are reflected in his major work, *An Account of the Arctic Regions*. In the first decade of the nineteenth century, the arrangement of science into discrete disciplines was still more a matter of convenience than of rigid distinctions and specialist training. Banks in London was fighting a rearguard action to keep the Royal Society as the meeting place for all of science, so

---

[1] *Life*, p. 34.
[2] *Life*, p. 65. In terms of UK purchasing power in 1998, this sum was equivalent to approximately £585 (Twigger, *Inflation*, Table 1).
[3] This and the preceding quotations are from the *Life*, pp. 66–7. Banks died in 1820.
[4] *Life*, p. 70.
[5] Loc. cit.

that single-discipline societies (for geologists, astronomers and others) would not arise as competing venues.[1] In Edinburgh, the legacy of the eighteenth-century Enlightenment still encouraged a broad view of intellectual activity, so that, for example, Playfair's *Illustrations of the Huttonian Theory of the Earth*, his best-known work, was published while he was still the Professor of Mathematics. Scoresby's natural curiosity about all forms of arctic science was enhanced, rather than channelled or curtailed by the intellectual climate he found in Edinburgh.

Probably the greatest influence on Scoresby the scientist, however, was Robert Jameson, Professor of Natural History from 1804 until his death in 1854; it is to Jameson, 'at whose suggestion this work was undertaken, and to whose early and uniform friendship the author is deeply indebted', that *An Account of the Arctic Regions* is dedicated.

> In taking out my ticket for admission to the natural history class, Professor Jameson inquired my object in attending the University, and the profession for which I was designed. He was surprised when I announced myself as a sailor (being, I daresay, the only one in the College), and still more so when he understood my usual voyage was to the whale fishery of Spitzbergen. This led him to make many inquiries respecting the natural history of the Polar Sea, and especially of the whale. When I informed him that I had drawn up descriptions of the whale, and had kept regular meteorological journals for two or three years, he expressed such an interest in these things that I ventured to offer for his inspection the book in which my observation [*sic*] were recorded, an offer which he seemed eager to embrace.[2]

As when meeting Banks in 1807, this led to social invitations by Jameson and introductions to Edinburgh's intellectual élite, and to the publication of Scoresby's meteorological records and notes on the whale in the *Memoirs* of the Wernerian Society, in which he was quickly elected to membership.[3]

It is amusingly ironic that, in the city in which the uniformitarian view of earth history was first propounded by Hutton and made widely known by Playfair, Scoresby's mentor should be an unyielding defender of the contrary, neptunist, argument.[4] Jameson had studied in Freiburg under Abraham Gottlob Werner and had

---

[1] Hall, *All Scientists Now*, pp. 5–7.

[2] *Life*, p. 72.

[3] Scoresby's meteorological records from 1807 to 1812 were published in volumes 1 and 2 of the Society's *Memoirs*. In *Account of the Arctic Regions*, I, Appendix 1, these were reprinted with corrections and extended to 1818. Scoresby noted in this appendix (p. 48) that 'The direction of the winds will appear to be totally different throughout the two series. This arises from the winds in the Tables first published [in the *Memoirs*] being quoted according to the magnetic meridian, while those now presented to the public, have, by the application of the variation, been reduced to the true meridian.' He also stated (p. 46) that civil days, commencing at midnight, were used for all the records in the *Account* from 1810 onwards (but not 1807–9), whereas in the 1811 and 1812 journals in the present volume, the nautical day is used. Taking 1 June 1812 as an example, the wind direction in the journal is 'Serly'; in the Wernerian *Memoirs* it is 'SW to W' and in the Appendix to *Account of the Arctic Regions* it is 'SW.erly'.

[4] The basic principle of the uniformitarian view of geology is that 'the present is the key to the past', i.e. the processes responsible for geological formations and physiography are those that are observable today. A consequence of this principle is that vast amounts of time are required for such

adopted Werner's theory that granite was the original rock of the earth, and therefore the oldest, that basalt was not of volcanic origin but had been formed by crystallization from water, and several other beliefs that were gradually disproved during the first half of the nineteenth century.

This scientific debate had both religious and political overtones:

> Hutton's theory reflects the calm inquiring rational spirit of the eighteenth-century Enlightenment; ... [It] was attacked immediately as being dangerous to religion, and the force of this criticism was sharpened by the political consequences of the French Revolution. In Great Britain the French Revolution was felt to endanger the whole fabric of social order, of which the Christian religion was the essential foundation. Hutton's theory left no place for the Mosaic account of Creation and of the Flood. ... At Edinburgh, where Hutton's friends continued to support his theory after his death in 1797, Robert Jameson ... was one of the most vigorous exponents of the Wernerian theory. Consequently, the controversy between the Wernerians and the Huttonians raged with a special vigor at Edinburgh between 1800 and 1810. Hutton's friends ... tended to be liberal in their outlook, whereas the Wernerians were Tories, and these political associations tended to deepen and embitter the scientific controversy.[1]

For Jameson to name named the scientific society that he founded the 'Wernerian Society' was therefore clearly provocative, and Birse noted that in the museum that he established, Jameson 'arranged the geological exhibits to support his Wernerian tenets; and he kept hidden any specimens which he conceived to be anti-Wernerian'.[2] Given the vigour of this controversy, it seems very unlikely that Scoresby remained unaware of it, especially as he studied under Playfair during his first period at the university, and under Jameson during the second. There is, however no mention of the controversy in *An Account of the Arctic Regions*, or in the passages from his autobiography that are quoted in the *Life*. What is clear is that, despite its title, the Wernerian Society was a true scientific society, and its *Memoirs* were not propaganda for a particular viewpoint. Scoresby's scientific observations on his arctic voyages, apart from those involving the magnetic compass, involved the ocean and the atmosphere, and therefore had little or no relevance to the Huttonian-Wernerian debate. They were nevertheless of great interest to Jameson, and he encouraged Scoresby in every way possible.[3]

---

processes to operate. In Hutton's own words, 'we find no vestige of a beginning, no prospect of an end'. By contrast, the Wernerian or neptunist view represented a catastrophist approach, in which many geological features were attributed to dramatic events, such as the biblical Flood. The terms 'uniformitarian' and 'catastrophist' were not introduced until 1837 (see the comprehensive review by Wilson, cited in the next footnote).

[1] Wilson, 'Uniformitarianism and Catastrophism', p. 419.

[2] Birse, *Science at the University of Edinburgh*, p. 77.

[3] Birse (ibid., p. 75) mentioned Charles Darwin's autobiographical comment 'During my second year (1826) at Edinburgh I attended Jameson's lectures on geology and zoology, but they were incredibly dull. The whole effect they produced on me was the determination never to read a book on geology or in any way to study the science ...'. Birse, however, listed others who were inspired by Jameson and went on (p. 76) 'By all accounts he was a respected and influential, if unexciting, teacher, who put considerable emphasis on demonstrations and field trips.' It is also worth noting that one of Scoresby's earliest scientific papers, 'Account of the *Balaena mysticetus*, or great northern or Greenland whale', published in the Wernerian Society's *Memoirs* in 1810, was cited in the 1993 definitive volume on *The Bowhead Whale*.

Scoresby's second winter at Edinburgh University was even shorter than his first, but it was very rewarding. He ended his formal education with the knowledge that any observations, measurements or discoveries he might make in arctic latitudes would be valued by some of the leading scientists of the day.

> The calls of my profession obliged me to proceed to Whitby before the end of February, a considerable time prior to the conclusion of the session. I took leave of Edinburgh with regret. Not four months before this I had entered it without a single literary acquaintance in the place – I quitted it enriched by the friendship of some of the most eminent men of science in the Scottish metropolis.[1]

Whitby and the Whaling Industry in the Early Nineteenth Century

Any account of whaling up to the 1820s faces a dilemma that is not easy to resolve. On the one hand, the amount of writing on the subject is enormous. In the preface to his own study from the perspective of an economic historian, Gordon Jackson commented that 'It is doubtful if any trade, save that in human beings, has attracted so much attention as whaling.'[2] But Jackson also went on to emphasize that

> ... any work on the traditional whaling trade must be deeply indebted to William Scoresby, whaling captain turned Divine, whose monumental work, describing every aspect of the Northern Whale Fishery, will never be surpassed. The most difficult period to write about is, in fact, that which follows Scoresby's terminal date around 1820.[3]

That view has been echoed by others, and is evident in Herman Melville's *Moby-Dick or, The Whale* (1851). Melville was writing about the sperm whale in the South Seas, not the bowhead[4] whale in the Greenland Sea, but Melville recognized the value of Scoresby's first hand knowledge:

> Many are the men, small and great, old and new, landsmen and seamen who have at large or in little, written of the whale ...

> Of the names in this list of whale authors, ... but one of them was a real professional harpooner and whaleman. I mean Captain Scoresby. On the subject of the Greenland or right-whale, he is the best existing authority.[5]

The dilemma is therefore that it is difficult or impossible to find an account of the whaling industry in Scoresby's day that does not ultimately depend on Scoresby himself, and specifically on the second volume, devoted to 'The Whale-Fishery', of his monumental *An Account of the Arctic Regions*, published in 1820. There are several first-hand accounts of what it was like to participate on a whaling voyage, including at least one account by someone who served under Scoresby.[6] There is,

---

[1] *Life*, p. 75.
[2] Jackson, *British Whaling Trade*, p. xi.
[3] Ibid., p. xiii.
[4] The term bowhead is American, and modern; to Scoresby the same creature was the Greenland or Right whale. See the next section of this Introduction.
[5] Melville, *Moby-Dick*, ch. 32.
[6] Charles Steward's account of the 1814 voyage in the *Esk* is in the Whaling Museum, New Bedford, Massachusetts.

however, nothing like Scoresby's comprehensive review of whaling, covering its history, zoology, methods, and the uses to which the products were put.

Despite attempts in the early seventeenth century, the British were relative late-comers to arctic whaling on a substantial scale, and it took almost half a century for them to replace the Dutch, from whom they learned the requirements and techniques. The British Government's bounty was first introduced in 1733, but it had little or no effect until it was doubled to 40 shillings per ton in 1750. Even then, according to Gordon Jackson, the rapid growth that followed was due more to increasing demand than to the subsidy: 'The rapidly growing woollen textile industry ... consumed oil on a grand scale for the cleansing of wool prior to spinning', and whale oil was 'ideal for cheap coarse cloths'. At the same time whale oil was used for illumination both indoors and externally: 'The city of London had become the best lit city in the world when five thousand street lamps were installed in the 1740s.'[1]

In the expansion of British whaling during the 1750s, Whitby was one of the places that benefited from the fact that

> the very newness of the trade ensured that no particular port or ports enjoyed advantages derived from experience. All the ports were starting more or less from scratch ...

> Since whaling did not have to be in a place with existing trade, it could develop anywhere where there was, for whatever reason, an easy access to shipping and seamen, and a reasonable coastal trade to places that were major trading ports. Thus Dunbar or Anstruther in Scotland and Whitby in England could become whaling centres on the basis of a shipowning or fishing tradition.[2]

In Whitby's case, that tradition was founded on the coastwise transport of coal; as Girouard has noted,

> ... whaling has captured the imagination of the local people and visitors, while the less romantic coal trade has been forgotten. Coal came first at Whitby, however, and was economically more important ...

> In 1702-4 Whitby had the third largest number of ships engaged in the Newcastle [to London] coal trade, with 98 ships as compared to Yarmouth's 211 and London's 168.[3]

Another reason for this rapid expansion of British whaling during the 1750s was the Seven Years' War, which severely restricted the whaling activities of the American colonies. The colonies, enjoying free access to the British market, were effective competitors, and whaling from Britain itself might have gone into decline again but for the American War of Independence. This, incidentally, encouraged not merely Whitby whaling, but another activity that was even more remunerative than the coal trade or whaling: the use of its ships as military transports.[4]

---

[1] Jackson, *British Whaling Trade*, pp. 55–6.
[2] Ibid., pp. 59, 62.
[3] Girouard, *Town and Country*, p. 69.
[4] Girouard (ibid., p. 73) noted that Whitby benefited in this way during the Seven Years War, the American Revolution and then the wars with Revolutionary and Napoleonic France. One symbol of this is Cook's *Endeavour*. Originally a Whitby collier named the *Earl of Pembroke*, she was used after Cook's circumnavigation to supply the Falkland Islands from 1771 to 1775 and, then, with

American independence represented a major gain for British whaling:

> the peace of 1783 was the signal for an immense expansion of the British economy and a consequent rise in the demand for all manner of raw materials. So far as the oil trade was concerned, the peace terms removed at a stroke the most damaging competitors ... Imports from America, which now bore heavy duty, were running at about a tenth of pre-war levels, and ceased altogether by 1793.[1]

This gap was filled by British expansion, and in fact over-expansion. The 44 British whalers in the Greenland Sea in 1782 rose to 102 in 1784, and to 250 vessels in 1787–78. The bounty had been doubled to 40 shillings per ton at the beginning of the decade, but was cut back to 30 shillings per ton in 1786, to 25s in 1792, and then to 20s in 1795. Meanwhile the average price of oil dropped from £28 a tun in 1781 to £17 in 1787; whalebone from £345 a ton in 1782 to £200 in 1787.[2]

To the difficulties caused by these declining returns were added the French wars after 1793, which not merely cut exports but also reduced the number of available seamen, as the Royal Navy and its press-gangs expanded rapidly. In Jackson's words, 'The reduction of the bounty and the troubles of the Revolutionary war finally separated the men from the boys in whaling, the professionals from the amateurs.'[3] Whitby whalers were certainly among the professionals, though Hull became and remained the pre-eminent British whaling port.[4]

Although the Scoresbys sailed always to the Greenland Sea in search of whales, this was only one of three principal areas of whaling activity, and not necessarily the most important. One of the admirable characteristics of the *Account of the Arctic Regions* is that, although its author had no personal knowledge of either the area west of Greenland, or of southern whaling, he went out of his way to provide as much information about whaling in these areas as he could obtain.[5]

At the time that William Scoresby joined his father on the annual whaling voyages from Whitby, therefore, the trade had settled into a pattern that was much more stable than in the eighteenth century, and this stability was essentially maintained

---

another change of name to *Lord Sandwich*, to transport Hessian mercenaries to New York in 1776. By the end of that year she was in Newport, Rhode Island, where with other vessels she was scuttled in August 1778 as part of the successful British defence of the town against the French fleet (Abbass, '*Endeavour* and *Resolution* Revisited', p. 18). Scoresby noted that 'from 1761 to 1766, during the [Seven Years] war, when the transport service was more profitable, the whale trade from Whitby was suspended (*Account of the Arctic Regions*, II, p. 127).

[1] Jackson, *British Whaling Trade*, p. 70.
[2] All data in this paragraph are from Jackson, *British Whaling Trade*, pp. 70–75.
[3] Ibid., p. 76.
[4] Credland, *Hull Whaling Trade*, *passim*.
[5] Chapter V of volume II (pp. 382–96) is an 'Account of the Davis' Strait Whale-Fishery, and a Comparison with that of Greenland, with Statements of Expences and Profits of a Fishing Ship'; Appendix VIII (pp. 529–37) is 'Some Account of the Whale Fishery Conducted in the Southern Seas', based on information provided by Captain Day of London, which was the principal British port for whaling in that region. Elsewhere in the same volume, he noted (p. 127) that 'In the year 1777, only 9 ships sailed from the different ports of Britain to the whale-fishery of Davis' Straits, 6 of which were from Whitby.' By the time Scoresby took command of the *Resolution* in 1811, only a single ship sailed from Whitby to Davis Strait.

until the early 1820s. Average prices for whale oil recovered after the 1780s, reaching £38 10s in 1800. Wartime inflation reduced the benefits of this gain, and a more severe blow was dealt by changing fashions. Women, exemplified by Jane Austen's heroines, abandoned the whalebone corsets and stays that, before the late 1790s, enabled about half the income from whaling to be derived from whalebone.[1]

Within this overall pattern of stability and reasonable returns for the principal surviving British whaling ports, there was substantial variation in the fortunes of individual ships and their masters. Before turning to this aspect, however, it needs to be noted that, in a small town of only about 10,000 people, whaling had a particular significance for Whitby:

> Whitby never sent out more than twenty whalers a year, less than eight percent of its merchant fleet, but the whalers figured prominently in the life of the town because of the great profits enjoyed by all classes as the result of a successful season, and because, unlike most of the cargoes carried by Whitby ships, the whales came back to Whitby and were processed in the town.[2]

From the contemporary lists of vessels engaged in the *Greenland & Davis's Streights Whale-Fisheries*,[3] which are not completely reliable, the British whaling fleet in the years 1811–13 is summarized in the following table.

British ports engaged in the whaling trade in the Greenland Sea or Davis Strait

	1811		1812		1813	
	G'land Sea	Davis St.	G'land Sea	Davis St.	G'land Sea	Davis St.
Hull	12	31	18	31	25	30
London	13	3	12[a]	3	14[b]	5
Whitby	6	1	6	1	7	1[c]
Other English	4	5	4	5	4	7
Scottish[d]	9	14	14	15	23	23

[a] Excludes the *Effort* and *Reliance*, both of which were lost on the outward voyage.

[b] Includes the *Eweretta*, omitted from the printed list, but added by hand to the list in the Scoresby Papers.

[c] The *James* failed to reach Davis Strait in 1813, and eventually joined the Greenland Sea fleet.

[d] This table follows the convention in the contemporary printed list by including Berwick-on-Tweed as a Scottish port. In all three years the port sent one vessel to Davis Strait; in 1813 it also sent one vessel to the Greenland Sea.

[1] Jackson, *British Whaling Trade*, p. 84.

[2] Girouard, *Town and Country*, p. 73. Something of the significance of whaling in the Whitby community is illustrated by the reception on his return that Scoresby described in his journal entry for 12 August 1813. However it does not appear that this gave him or his father an exalted place in society; neither of them is mentioned in vol. II, chapter V, 'Biography and Family History', of Young's 1817 *History of Whitby*.

[3] These annual lists, in pamphlet form, are preserved in the Scoresby Papers. The list for 1812 contains the statement '[Rodgers, Printer, Whitby.]' and its seems probable that the lists for the others years came from the same local source. They appear to have been produced during the whaling season, because they contain notes such as 'The ships marked thus * are intended for Davis's Streights' and the 1812 list notes against two of the London whalers (*Effort* and *Reliance*) that the vessel was 'lost on her passage out'.

In 1811 and 1812 the Whitby ships sailing to the Greenland Sea, with their captains, were the *Aimwell* (Johnson or Johnstone[1]), *Henrietta* (Kearsley), *Lively* (Wilson), *Resolution* (Scoresby, Junior), *Volunteer* (Dawson), and the *William and Ann* (Stevens). In 1813 Scoresby took command of the *Esk* and another Kearsley replaced him as captain of the *Resolution*.[2] The *James* (Smith) normally sailed early in the year to Davis Strait. As Scoresby's journal entry for 9 May 1813 records, however, the *James* 'with many others was not able to make a passage to Davis's Streights' because of adverse weather, and therefore joined the other Whitby whalers in the Greenland Sea.

The Bowhead Whale

Writing in 1978, Gordon Jackson commented that '*Balaena mysticetus* has never been scientifically investigated and, in view of its size and scarcity, probably never will be, so that much about it remains a mystery.'[3]

He was too pessimistic. At the time he was writing, intensive research on the species was being carried out, and a major comprehensive review of the bowhead whale, *Balaena mysticetus*, was published by the Society for Marine Mammalogy in 1993. Its eighteen chapters cover the subject from the whale's fossil antecedents, through its anatomy, physiology and behaviour, commercial and subsistence whaling, to its current status as a protected species. Ironically, much of the vast amount of research that is synthesized in this volume, and the volume itself, was funded by the United States and Canadian governments and the oil industry, because of the potential impact on the species of oil drilling in the Beaufort Sea.

> Many people closely associated with the bowhead issue viewed these intensive research efforts, spanning 20 yr and costing more than $56 million, as a benchmark achievement in the methods employed and the results obtained on this difficult-to-study species.[4]

The existence of this comprehensive scientific study text is one justification for the adoption in this Introduction of the term 'bowhead whale', a late nineteenth-century name of American origin[5] that Scoresby would not have recognized and that does not appear anywhere in *Moby-Dick* (Melville always referred to the species as the Greenland or Right whale.) To Scoresby himself, it was the Common or Right Whale, but Montague listed as many as 13 common names in English and 55 others in 20 additional languages.[6]

---

[1] In these printed lists, the spelling is always 'Johnson'; in Scoresby's journals it is always 'Johnstone'.

[2] Credland, *Hull Whaling Trade*, p. 137, lists a Kearsley as master of the *Sarah and Elizabeth* from 1810 to 1813. However the contemporary annual list indicates that in 1813 the *Sarah and Elizabeth* of Hull was commanded by a Captain Foster. It therefore seems probable that this Kearsley moved from Hull to Whitby to assume command of the *Resolution* for the 1813 voyage. He may have been a son of the *Henrietta*'s captain who, according to the journal entry for 30 June 1812, had made his first voyage to the Greenland Sea in 1785 and was therefore of the same generation as William Scoresby Senior.

[3] Jackson, *British Whaling Trade*, p. 7.

[4] Montague, 'Introduction', p. 15.

[5] The earliest citation in *OED* is British, in 1887, but the term was in American usage before that, e.g. in Scammon, *Marine Mammals of the North-Western Coast of North America* (1874).

[6] Montague, 'Introduction', Table 1.1.

It would nowadays be incorrect to use the term right whale for the species that the Scoresbys sought in the Greenland Sea. The term is now used for two species distinct from bowheads, the Southern right whale, *Eubalaena australis*, and its Northern Hemisphere counterpart, the Northern right whale, *Eubalaena glacialis*. In size and other major physical characteristics, bowheads and right whales have many similarities, but there seems no doubt that Scoresby was correct in identifying the whales he sought as *Balaena mysticetus*, what is now termed the bowhead, for one very good reason:

> The morphological and behavioral similarities of bowheads and right whales (*Eubalaena glacialis*) have caused confusion both historically and recently in attempts to define the bowhead's range. The ranges of the two species closely approach or overlap in a number of areas (e.g., the Sea of Okhotsk, Labrador Sea, Gulf of St. Lawrence, Denmark Strait, and southern Barents Sea). This does not mean that bowheads and right whales occur in close proximity, however, since bowheads are associated with ice and right whales are not. By the time right whales migrate into a summer feeding area, the bowheads, which might have been there during winter and spring, usually will have migrated to higher latitudes.[1]

After reviewing the available evidence, Woodby and Botkin have estimated that the size of the population of bowhead whales prior to the beginning of commercial exploitation in the early sixteenth century was a minimum of 50,000, of which almost half (24,000) were in the 'Spitsbergen stock' of the Greenland Sea.[2] By compiling the incomplete and sometimes fragmentary data on whale catches from Dutch, German and British sources, Ross has shown that the greatest reductions in this stock – 10,000 or more whales taken each decade – took place during the early phase of 'bay whaling' in the late seventeenth century.[3] Even if the pre-whaling figure of 24,000 is a substantial under-estimate, the stock could not sustain such massive depredation. The available evidence suggests that bowheads grow more slowly, and reproduce less frequently than other baleen whales:

> Most female bowheads become sexually mature when they are 12.5–14.0 m long, probably at an age exceeding 15 years … . In contrast, females of other species of baleen whales become sexually mature at age 5–10 yr …

[1] Moore and Reeves, 'Distribution and Movement', pp. 357–8. At the risk of being pedantic, it can therefore be said that Melville was correct when he referred to the right whale in the context of the voyage described in *Moby-Dick* (e.g. chapter 16: '… the long, huge slabs of limber black bone taken from the middle and highest parts of the right-whale') but wrong when he equated this whale with the 'Greenland or right-whale' of Scoresby.

[2] Woodby and Botkin, 'Stock Sizes Prior to Commercial Whaling', p. 404.

[3] Ross, 'Commercial Whaling in the North Atlantic Sector', Table 13.1. 'Bay whaling', as its name suggests was located on the bays and inshore waters of Spitsbergen and Jan Mayen. It was distinct from the later deep-sea (pelagic) whaling of Scoresby's era by the fact that the blubber was rendered down into oil at cookeries on the shores of these islands. The Dutch base of Smeerenburg (i.e. 'Blubbertown'), on Amsterdanøya (79°44′N, 10°50′E) was the most famous of these cookeries in the seventeenth century, although modern research suggests it was a relatively small and seasonal facility, rather than the roistering community of 12,000 to 18,000 suggested by Scoresby (*Account of the Arctic Regions*, II, pp. 143–4). See Ross, pp. 525–8.

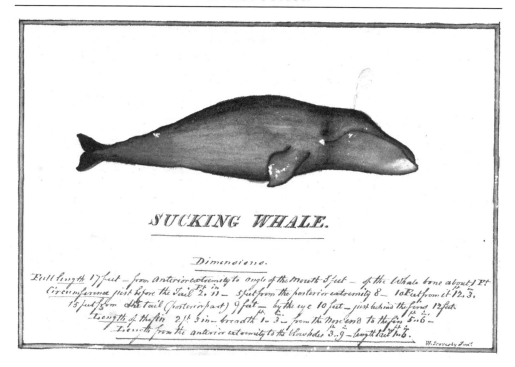

Dimensions.

Full length 17 feet — from Anterior extremity to angle of the mouth 5 feet — of the Whale bone about 1 Ft — Circumference just before the Tail 2.11 — 5 feet from the posterior extremity 8 — 10 Feet from it 12.3. 15 feet from the tail (posterior part) 9 feet — by the eye 10 feet — just behind the fins 12 feet — Length of the fin 2 ft 3 in — breadth 1.3 — from the Nose end to the fins 5.6 — Length from the anterior extremity to the Blowholes 3..9 — length tail 1.6 .

W. Scoresby Jun.

Plate 2. Sucking Whale. Drawing by Scoresby. Whitby Museum (SCO825.1). Photograph courtesy of the Whitby Museum.

The mean calving interval appears to be 3–4 yr based on limited indirect evidence, but could be longer. A 3–4 yr interval would be similar to calving intervals in northern and southern right whales, but longer than the 2–yr intervals of most other species of baleen whales.[1]

It was precisely because the bowhead was adapted to living at the ice margin that it was so attractive to commercial whalers.

The bowhead … is found only in waters seasonally covered by sea ice. It has adapted to life in waters that average less than 0°C in the Beaufort and Chukchi seas … by possessing a blubber layer that, at 43 to 50 cm thick …, exceeds that of any other animal. Further, it has the lowest surface area to body volume ratio of perhaps any mammal.[2]

Apart from this thickness of blubber, the distinctive characteristic of the bowhead is the size of its head, accounting for up to one-third of the total body length.[3] This is an evolutionary adaptation to the bowhead's feeding method, which depends on capture by filtration of vast quantities of very small organisms. The filtration device is the two rows of baleen plates (several hundred in number) from which is derived the

[1] Koski *et al.*, 'Reproduction', pp. 268–9.
[2] Montague, 'Introduction', p. 1.
[3] Haldiman and Tarpley, 'Physiology', p. 71.

second important economic product, whalebone. There is a close relationship between the body length of the whale and the length of the baleen.[1] This relationship was recognized by Scoresby and his contemporaries, who used the maximum length of baleen (which he referred to as *laminæ*) as a convenient measure of the size of each whale caught.

> The laminæ are about 300 in number, in each side of the head. The length of the longest blade, which occurs near the middle of the series, is the criterion fixed on by the fishers for designating the size of the fish. Its greatest length is about 15 feet; but an instance very rarely occurs of any being met with above 12½ or 13 feet.[2]

It is this length that is used, for example, in the margin of Scoresby's 1813 journal, when a whale was caught. Scoresby also developed a table showing the relationship between the average quantity of oil derived from a whale and the length of its longest blade of whalebone:[3]

Length of whalebone in feet	1	2	3	4	5	6	7	8	9	10	11	12
Oil yielded in tons	1½	2¼	2¾	3¼	4	5	6½	8	11	13½	17	21

By custom, the term 'size' was used in whaling and whaling journals to indicate whales in which the maximum whalebone length was six feet or greater, not least because

> Whalebone becomes more valuable as it increases in length and thickness. ... The *size-bone*, or such pieces as measure six feet or upward in length, is kept separate from the *under-size*; the latter usually being sold at half the price of the former.[4]

Bowheads and right whales 'feed principally by straining small organisms from the water while swimming slowly forward with their mouths open'.[5] That simple statement tends to minimize the effort involved. Recent studies, based on Alaskan data, suggest that 'The organisms most commonly eaten [crustacean zooplankton] ... were usually from 3 to 30 mm long' but an individual whale would need to consume about 100 metric tons of such crustaceans per year.[6]

It should be noted at this point that the economic historian Cornelius de Jong has argued that what he termed 'the great slaughter of the Greenland whale' began about 1790. In particular, he suggested that the strengthening of, and other technical

[1] Lowry, 'Foods and Feeding Ecology', Fig. 6.1.
[2] Scoresby, *Account of the Arctic Regions*, II, p. 416.
[3] Ibid., I, p. 462. In a footnote, Scoresby mentioned that this was an improved version, based on more data, of a similar table in his 1810 paper in the *Memoirs of the Wernerian Society*. It is possible, however, that the amount of oil (8 tons) indicated for an 8-foot whale is understated; in what appears to be a typographical error, Scoresby's table was printed as 8[1], i.e. with the numerator of a fraction but no horizontal bar or denominator.
[4] Ibid., II, pp. 418, 419. See also Jackson, *British Whaling Trade*, p. 81.
[5] Lowry, 'Foods and Feeding Ecology', p. 205.
[6] Ibid., pp. 217, 229. The removal by commercial whaling of thousands of bowheads must have had a major impact on trophic relationships, i.e. the food chain. Lowry suggested (p. 231) that 'it is possible that when bowhead stocks were decimated by commercial whalers, the numbers of arctic cod and ringed seals increased and took advantage of the increased availability of zooplankton'.

improvements to whaleships introduced by the British made possible a much earlier start (late April and May) to the whaling season than had been possible for the Dutch and German vessels that generally abandoned whaling around that time.

> The greatest disadvantage of the opening of the catch earlier in the year was that the nursing females, 'suckers' and immature animals had not yet hidden themselves in the drift ice in the north and were within reach of the whalers. They were slaughtered in great numbers. Other disadvantages were that in spring the whales are meager and produce little blubber and whale oil, and that the baleen plates of young animals are short, undersized and low-priced.

> Because Scoresby Senior was one of the innovators in British whaling and because he and his famous author-son participated in the wholesale slaughter, the son is silent in his publications on the predatory traits which whaling assumed after 1790.[1]

It may be, of course, that Scoresby had been silent on these matters because De Jong's assertions lack validity. There is no doubt, for example, that Scoresby and other whalers took young as well as mature whales, and the 1811 journal describes one such incident in great detail. But that incident took place on 15 June 1811, not in late April or May. In the 'open' year of 1813, the *Esk* harpooned a sucking whale on 23 April, but both the calf and its mother escaped. Only the second whale taken in the 1813 season, on 3 May, clearly fits De Jong's scenario; its newborn calf presumably did not survive its mother's death. Of the five whales taken by the *Esk* between 22 April and the end of May 1813, all were 'size', with whalebone lengths between 8 feet and 10 feet 8 inches; only two of the five were females. In 1811, the first whale was not killed until 19 May, and of the three that the *Resolution* took that month two were 'size', one male, one female, and the third was a male with 5 feet of whalebone. In 1812 (another close season) no whale was caught by the *Resolution* before June. The evidence of these three journals, during what Ross has recognized as the decade of maximum British effort in the Greenland Sea,[2] does not suggest that pursuit of calves and their mothers early in the season was as important a factor as De Jong asserted. Scoresby's journal entry for 30 June 1812 provides an alternative explanation for the increased catches after 1790; before that date British whaling captains may not have taken their task as seriously as they did in later years.

The Whaling Process

What commercial whaling involved in the early nineteenth century has been described in many places, and nowhere better than by Scoresby himself, particularly in the two hundred pages of chapter IV of the second volume of *An Account of the Arctic Regions*: 'Account of the Modern Whale-Fishery, as conducted at Spitzbergen'. The following is therefore only a brief summary, to enable those without background knowledge to understand the entries in Scoresby's journals.

The successive stages can be summarized as follows: searching; killing; flensing; and making off. The search might take days or even weeks; the kill was normally accomplished in an hour or so but could stretch into a day of hard and dangerous

---

[1] De Jong, 'Hunt of the Greenland Whale', p. 89.
[2] Ross, 'Commercial Whaling', p. 533.

activity (e.g. journal entry for 25 June 1812); flensing took several hours and had to be accomplished immediately after the whale was killed. Making off had to be undertaken several times on a season's voyage, but could normally be scheduled for times when weather and ice conditions were favourable, and the immediate prospects for capturing more whales seemed small. Occasionally it became an urgent task, because the amount and location of the blubber awaiting making off affected the ship's safety (journal entry for 14 June 1812).

1. *Search*. Because the bowhead was always found in close proximity to the arctic sea-ice, the search did not begin until the Greenland Sea whaling ships reached a latitude of about 75°N.[1] Before reaching the area, the ship's rigging was adjusted so as to make the ship navigable with the smallest number of crew, while most of the crew were away in the whaleboats,[2] and the crow's nest was mounted at the very top of the mainmast. In clear weather (a rare phenomenon in the arctic summer, as the journals indicate[3]) the distance to the horizon at 90 feet above the sea is 12.8 miles; at 50 feet 9.5 miles and at 15 feet (approximately the height of the quarter-deck) 5.2 miles. This last horizon distance would in fact have been adequate for the immediate pursuit of a whale by seamen rowing a whaleboat; the advantage of the crow's nest was that it provided a 360° panorama, unobscured by sails, masts etc., and it was as valuable in the task of navigation through the ice (frequently reduced to the attempt to avoid being trapped or 'beset') as it was in the search for whales.[4] Scoresby also noted that

> The commanding view which is obtained from a ship's mast-head, enables a person on the look-out in the crow's nest to form a much more correct idea of the movements of a whale, and of the position of boats, ice, &c. than it is possible for the most experienced person to do from a boat moving on the surface of the water. Hence it is usual for the captain of every whale-fishing ship, to adopt a few simple signals, whereby he can direct his boats when at a distance beyond the reach of his voice.[5]

[1] See, for example, the journal entry for 21 April 1811. Whaling vessels searching for sperm whales (*Physeter catodon*) or right whales (*Eubalaena* spp.), by contrast, might encounter their prey any moment after leaving their home port. 'Even though the whale population in the waters to the southeast of the island [of Nantucket] ... had been greatly diminished over the years, it was still quite possible to come across what Nantucketers called a shoal of sperm whales.': Philbrick, *In the Heart of the Sea*, p. 36.

[2] 'As it is an object of some importance, that a fishing ship should be easily navigated, under common circumstances, by a boat's crew of six or seven men, it is usual to take down royal masts, and even some of the top-gallant-masts, and sometimes to substitute a long light pole in place of a mizen-top-mast; also to adopt such sails as require the least management.': Scoresby, *Account of the Arctic Regions*, II, p. 197. See, for example, the journal entry for 3 June 1811: 'In the absence of the Boats I worked and steered the Ship by myself alone tacked once.' In *My Father*, pp. 196–7, Scoresby claimed that this was one of the innovations in arctic whaling initiated by William Scoresby Senior, both to enable the ship to be handled by a small crew while the boats were hunting whales, and to sail as close as possible to the direction from which the wind is blowing ('windward sailing').

[3] '... in general it is very rare to see a clear Day in July or even a clear hour'. (7 July 1812.)

[4] See for example the journal entry for 4 June 1811, when Scoresby used a telescopic sighting of whales from the masthead as the basis for setting the ship's direction rather than as an immediate pursuit of these whales from whaleboats.

[5] *Account of the Arctic Regions*, II, pp. 521–2. See for example the journal entry for 18 June 1812.

2. *Killing.* Scoresby observed that 'a whale seldom abides longer on the surface of the water than two minutes'[1] and that during the much longer period that it was submerged it might travel half a mile or more in any direction. It was therefore difficult for the whaleboats to approach a whale on the surface, or to know where a submerged whale would eventually reappear. 'A well constructed "Greenland boat"', Scoresby stated,

possesses the following properties. It floats lightly and safely on the water, – is capable of being rowed with great speed, and readily turned around, it is of such capacity that it carries six or seven men, seven or eight hundred weight of whale-lines, and various other materials, and yet retains the necessary properties of safety, buoyancy, and speed, either in smooth water, or where it is exposed to a considerable sea.[2]

Clearly, safety, buoyancy and speed are not easy to reconcile in a rowboat on the open ocean, and speed was the vital requirement. The task of the whaleboat was to get the harpooner within range of the whale:

the harpoon is thrown from the hand, or fired from a gun, the former of which, when skilfully practised, is efficient at the distance of eight or ten yards, and the latter at the distance of thirty yards, or upward.[3]

In practice, it was close range for the hand-held harpoon that mattered in the journals in this volume. Scoresby was well aware of the potential benefits of the harpoon gun, but, as the journal entries for 5, 7 and 9 July 1812 indicate, these benefits were not easily realized in practice. As he noted in 1820, not merely were whales sometimes lost that could have been caught with a hand-held harpoon, but the gun was also liable to misfire and injure its users, so that 'it has not been so generally adopted as might have been expected'.[4]

The harpoon had to avoid the massive head of the bowhead, because of the thickness of the skull, 'but any part of the body, between the head and the tail, will admit of the full length of the instrument, without danger of obstruction'.[5]

Immediately after being struck, the normal behaviour of the whale was to dive deep, taking with it great lengths of the whale-line (i.e. rope) stored in the whaleboat and fastened to the harpoon. To slow this descent as much as possible, several turns of the whale-line would be made around a bollard in the whaleboat, but

Such is the friction of the line, when running round the bollard, that it frequently envelopes the harpooner in smoke; and if the wood were not repeatedly wetted, would probably set fire to the boat.[6]

Scoresby noted that the whale normally stayed under water for about thirty

---

[1] Ibid., II, p. 239
[2] Ibid., II, pp. 221–2.
[3] Ibid., II, p. 242.
[4] Ibid., II, p. 228.
[5] Ibid., II, p. 242.
[6] Ibid., II, p. 245. Scoresby estimated (II, p. 247) that during the first 300 fathoms of the dive, 'the average velocity was usually after the rate of eight to ten miles *per* hour'; that is, between 12 and 15 feet per second.

minutes after being struck, and descended to a depth of '700 or 800 fathoms perpendicular', i.e. over 4000 feet. He was well aware of the immense pressure on the whale that such depths must involve, and saw this, rather than the injuries of one or more harpoons, as the principal reason for the 'remarkable exhaustion of the whale after returning to the surface'.[1]

Meanwhile, additional whaleboats converged on the scene, and additional harpoons were thrown; then the whale 'is afterwards actively plied with lances, which are thrust into its body, aiming at its vitals'. As it died, 'The sea, to a great extent around, is dyed with its blood, and the ice, boats, and men, are sometimes drenched with the same.'[2]

Killing a harpooned whale was a dangerous as well as a bloody business. In its reaction to being harpooned, in its rapid dives and resurfacing, and in its death-throes, a whale of forty to seventy tons could easily capsize the whaleboat or, as described in the journal entry for 26 June 1812, tow the whaleboat under the ice.[3]

3. *Flensing (flinching)*.[4] The dead whale was then towed back to the ship by the whaleboats, which was no easy task: 'A large whale, by means of six boats, can be towed at the rate of nearly a mile *per* hour.'[5] It was then secured to the side of the ship, which itself was often moored to a convenient edge of sea-ice. The flensing process, i.e. the removal of the blubber, was complicated by the fact that 'The enormous weight of a whale, prevents the possibility of raising it more than one-fourth or one-fifth part out of the water' unless it had been dead for several days. The process began by securing the 'kent' – 'A band of blubber, 2 or 3 feet in width, encircling the fish's body, and lying between the fins and the head' – to a block and tackle suspended from the ship's mainmast and connected to a windlass. As this kent was gradually cut away into a strip of about 30 feet in length, the whale could thereby be rotated, enabling the blubber on the rest of the body to be cut away and hoisted on board 'in pieces of half a ton to a ton each'.[6] It was there cut into smaller pieces and stored temporarily in the ship's hold in an area termed the 'flens-gut' ('flinch gut' in these journals).

During the flensing process, as the dead whale was rotated, the whalebone from the head was also removed.

---

[1] Ibid., II, p. 249. The modern authoritative text, *The Bowhead Whale*, is silent on the depth to which whales can dive.

[2] Ibid., II, p. 248.

[3] Ibid., II, p. 462: 'A stout whale of sixty feet in length, is of the enormous weight of seventy tons; the blubber weighs about thirty tons, the bones of the head, whalebone, fins and tail, eight or ten' carcass thirty or thirty-two.'

[4] These two terms (and others like them, e.g. 'flinsing') all describe the same process. Scoresby always used the term 'flinching' in the journals in the present volume, but in *An Account of the Arctic Regions* he described the process as flensing.

[5] This and the next two quotations are from Scoresby, *Account of the Arctic Regions*, II, pp. 296–7.

[6] Ibid., II, p. 299. A sperm whale that died on the shore of Nantucket on 31 December 1997 was flensed using nineteenth century tools from the local whaling museum. 'A single four-foot-square slab of eight-inch-thick blubber weighed as much as four hundred pounds.': Philbrick, *In the Heart of the Sea*, p. 233.

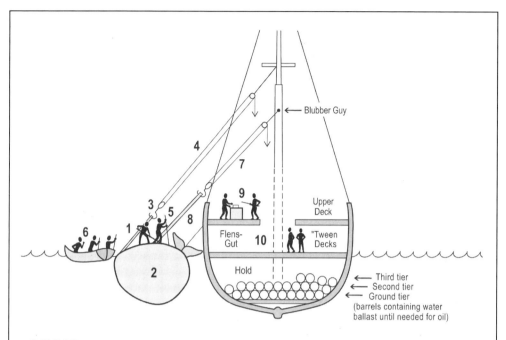

FLENSING

'A band of blubber, 2 or 3 feet in width, encircling the fish's body, and lying between the fins and the head... is called the *kent* [1]; because, by means of it, the fish [2] is turned over or *kented*. Now, to the commencement of this imaginary band of fat or kent, is fixed the lower extremity [3] of a combination of powerful blocks, called the *kent-purchase* [4]. Its upper extremity is fixed round the head of the main-mast, and its *fall* or rope is applied to the windlass...'

'After the whale is properly secured alongside of the ship... the harpooners [5] having their feet armed with "spurs," ...to prevent them from slipping, descend upon the fish. Two boats [6]... attend upon them, and serve to hold all their knives and other apparatus. Thus provided, the harpooners, directed by the specksioneer, divide the fat into oblong pieces or "slips,"... then affixing a "speck-tackle" [7] to each slip [8] progressively flay it off, as it is drawn upward. The speck-tackles, which are two or three in number, are rendered effective by capsterns, winches, or other mechanical powers.'

'The blubber, in pieces of half a ton to a ton each, is received upon the deck by the boat-steerers and line-managers [9]: the former with "strand knives," ... divide it into portable cubical, or oblong pieces, ... while the latter, furnished with "pick-haaks," ... pass it between decks, down a hole in the main hatches. It is then received by two men styled *kings*, who pack it in a receptacle provided for it in the hold, or other suitable place, called the *flens-gut* [10]...'

Plate 3. Flensing a whale. This is a redrawn version of a diagram by W. Gillies Ross in his book *Arctic Whalers, Icy Seas*. The original illustrated a description of flensing in Davis Strait in 1834 but Scoresby's own words (from *An Account of the Arctic Regions*, vol. 2, pp. 296–300) are equally applicable.

Whalebone is generally brought from Greenland in the same state as when taken from the fish, after being divided into portable *junks*, or pieces, comprising 10 or 12 laminæ in each; but occasionally it is separated into separate blades, and the gum and hair removed when at sea.[1]

4. *Making off.* The final stage of the whaling process was that of preserving the blubber from deterioration during the remainder of the voyage. Essentially this meant cutting up the large pieces of blubber 'into oblong pieces, not exceeding four inches in diameter', and filling wooden casks with these pieces by hand, through the bung-holes of the casks. As Scoresby declared, 'it is evident that the process of making-off must be tedious, disagreeable and laborious. Fifty men actively employed, can prepare and pack about three tons of blubber in an hour; though more frequently they are contented with making off little more than one-half of that quantity.'[2]

It was not simply that making off was tedious and time-consuming. The casks in which the blubber was stored were previously filled with water as ballast for the ship. Before making off could begin, these casks had to be brought up from the hold and emptied of their water ('started' was the term used in the journals).[3] Further, the blubber-filled casks needed to be stored in the hold below any tiers of casks still containing water, so that the latter were accessible when needed in subsequent making offs. All this meant that making off was not a process undertaken whale by whale, as each was caught, but was carried out only when conditions were favourable or when there was no space to store the blubber before making off. Since making off the blubber from several whales was time consuming and involved rearrangement of the ship's ballast,

> The ship must be moored to a convenient piece of ice, or placed in an open situation, and the sails so reduced as to require no further attention in the event of bad weather occurring.[4]

It will be observed that one process that did not occur on the ships of the whaling fleets of the Greenland Sea or Davis Strait was the extraction of the oil from the blubber. In the early days of bay whaling off Spitsbergen, this was done on shore, e.g. at

[1] Ibid., II, p. 417. Elsewhere (p. 415) Scoresby noted that whalebone is 'sometimes, though incorrectly' named whale-fins, and that is how, for example, the whalebone is listed in the manifests prepared towards the end of each of the voyages in the present volume. Scoresby recognized (p . 417) that 'The smaller extremity and interior edge of each blade of bone, or the edge annexed to the tongue, are covered with a long fringe of hair, consisting of a similar kind of substance as that constituting the interior of the bone.' That observation is confirmed by modern research (cf. Haldiman and Tarpley, 'Anatomy and Physiology', p. 105).

[2] Scoresby, *Account of the Arctic Regions*, II, pp. 309–11.

[3] Scoresby noted (ibid., II, p. 305) that the water from old casks 'gives out a great quantity of a strong disagreeable vapour, consisting probably of sulphuretted and phosphuretted hydrogen, with a mixture of other gaseous fluids, produced by the decomposition of the oleaginous, and other animal substances, left in the casks after former voyages. ... This gas blackens metals, even gold, restored some metallic oxides, is disagreeable in respiration, and affects the eyes of the persons employed in the hold, where it is most abundant, so as to occasion ophthalmic inflammation, and frequently temporary blindness'. The principal component of this gas was probably hydrogen sulphide H_2S, and Scoresby did not exaggerate its dangers. See the vivid journal entry for 1 July 1812.

[4] Loc. cit. See also the journal entry for 5 June 1811.

Smeerenberg. On whaling voyages to the South Seas, such as that described in *Moby-Dick*, the blubber was boiled down into oil in 'trypots' on the deck of the ship, because deterioration of the blubber was otherwise inevitable, given the length of the voyages and the tropical latitudes that had to be crossed.

The Greenland and Davis Strait whaling fleets could avoid this task, substituting the making off process for the still more time-consuming process of reducing the blubber to oil. Though universally adopted by these fleets, it was a choice made on a more delicate balance of advantages and disadvantages than is often recognized. Scoresby noted in 1820 that

> When blubber is boiled in Greenland, the oil produced from it is much brighter, paler, more limpid, and more inflammable, than that extracted in Britain. It is also totally free from any unpleasant flavour, and burns without smell.

Scoresby's father experimented with ways to achieve this higher quality of oil by processing the blubber during the voyage, but found that as much as one-third of the oil was retained in the fibre. His son concluded therefore that although the blubber tended to putrefy during the voyage, even after the casks had been sealed,

> … the putrefying process serves to relax the tenacity of the cellular substance of the blubber, and permits nearly the whole oil to ooze out, and is therefore serviceable to the manufacturer, though injurious to the quality of the oil.[1]

In short, the increased quantity of oil gained by reduction on shore, after the ship returned to port, more than compensated for the lower quality that was inevitable. Greenland Sea whale oil was competitive only at the lower end of the market, especially for street lighting and in making cheap cloth, but at least until the 1820s, this was an adequate market for Scoresby and the other whaling captains.

Whaling in Wartime
The whaling voyages of 1811–1813 took place against the background of the Napoleonic Wars. Britain and France had been at war since 1793, apart from the year-long interlude initiated by the Treaty of Amiens in 1802. But France was not the only enemy; during his return from the Greenland Sea in August 1812, Scoresby was surprised to be informed by the Royal Navy that the United States had also declared war on Britain two months earlier.

As the journals show, explicitly or implicitly, war influenced the British whaling fleet in at least four ways: (a) there was the threat of direct attack on the whaling ships by French warships or privateers, or those of France's allies, at least during the period when the whalers were travelling to or from the Greenland Sea; (b) After the USA joined the hostilities, there was a similar threat from the US navy and American privateers; (c) Though the whaling ships were in theory and law protected from the actions of Royal Navy press-gangs, this protection was less complete in practice, and in any case both the military and the merchant ships were competing for a limited number of qualified sailors; (d) wartime conditions provided some economic stimulus to whaling, e.g. in the continual demand for whale oil used in the manufacture of cheap uniforms.

[1] Ibid., p. 412.

The whaling fleet was under attack from 1793 onwards, both by naval ships as well as privateers. Conflicts reached their peak in 1806, when French naval ships pursued the whaling fleet into the arctic ice. British whalers captured or destroyed included the *Dingwall* of London, *Boyne* of Yarmouth, *Simes* of Leith, *William* of Greenock, and the *Molly*, *Blenheim* and *Holderness* of Hull.[1]

By 1811, the threat was considerably reduced but as the journals show, Scoresby continued his father's practice, made possible by letters of marque, of mounting guns and designating gun crews on both the outward and return voyages. Meanwhile the Royal Navy continued its practice of sending one or more ships into the sea area between Shetland and Norway to protect the whaling fleet, especially on its return journey.

The danger from American vessels was not substantial until 1814, although in 1813 the USS *President* captured two whaling ships, the *Eliza Swan* of Montrose and the *Lion* of Liverpool.[2] At the same time what has been described as 'the republic's private navy', i.e. American privateers,[3] was already evident in the area, the *Scourge* (New York) and the *Rattlesnake* (Philadelphia) attacking British ships carrying grain from Archangel.[4]

By 1811, the demands of the Royal Navy, through impressment, were also more moderate than they had been a decade or so earlier.[5] Whaling was regarded as a vital activity, and by Act of Parliament harpooners, line-managers and boat-steerers were protected from impressment both during a whaling voyage and in the intervals between such voyages, while ordinary seamen engaged in whaling were similarly protected from the first of February until the end of a voyage.[6]

As well as volunteering and impressment, the Royal Navy gained seamen as a result of the Quota Acts of 1795 and 1796. Emsley has described the purpose and effects of these Acts in what was then the North Riding of Yorkshire, including Whitby.[7] It was a mechanism that stood between volunteering and impressment, and

[1] Lubbock, *Arctic Whalers*, pp. 170–79.
[2] Ibid., pp. 193–4.
[3] Privateering has been defined as a 'former usage of war permitting privately owned and operated war vessels (privateers) under commission of a belligerent government to capture enemy shipping. ... Privateersmen, who kept all or a part of their booty, often gained great wealth. ... Privateersmen were free of naval discipline, and their desire for prize often led them to make no distinction between friendly and enemy shipping, to violate the rules of war, and to indulge in lawlessness after the conclusion of peace.': *Columbia Encyclopedia*, s.v. 'privateering'.
[4] Lubbock, *Arctic Whalers*, p. 193. See also Garitee, *The Republic's Private Navy*, p. 171.
[5] 'In some areas the local population took positive action against [press] gangs. At the beginning of the war against revolutionary France, two lieutenants were ordered to open a rendezvous house in Whitby. After some difficulty they found a landlord prepared to accommodate them, but before they could commence recruiting a crowd of several hundred smashed their way in and severely assaulted the lieutenants, their gang and their landlord.': Emsley, *North Riding Naval Recruits*, p. 8 (based on Hutchinson, *Impressment*, pp. 220–22, who gave the date of this incident as 23 February 1793).
[6] The specific provisions of the legislation were reprinted by Scoresby in *Account of the Arctic Regions*, II, pp. 503–4.
[7] Emsley, *North Riding Naval Recruits*, pp. 7–13. The 1796 Act provided that English coastal counties should provide 6,142 men for the navy (385 from the North Riding, of whom 19 were required from Whitby and nearby parishes), while landlocked counties and Wales had to provide 6,525 men for the army. Under a separate Act, Scotland was to provide 2,108.

was therefore more acceptable than the latter. However, as Scoresby described in his journal entry for 25 March 1813, it was a method that could not be depended on to deliver the quota in full, and impressment was used as a method of enforcement.[1]

It might be expected that the recruiting demands of the Royal Navy would affect the ability of whaling captains to find competent crews for their own ships. Credland saw this as typical for the Hull whalers:

> During the French wars when so many men had been swept up by the army and navy it was increasingly difficult to make up a crew. It became the custom therefore to leave home port with a basic sailing crew, harpooners, and specialists such as a cooper, carpenter and blacksmith. There were enough men to handle the ship and keep watch, but the rest of the complement was made up by the doughty island men of Shetland and Orkney ... The Orkney men were taken aboard at Stromness by the Davis Strait vessels and the Shetland men at Lerwick when bound for the Greenland fishery.[2]

Credland also went on to note that the practice outlived the wars, so that 'in the 1850s and 1860s, when the fleet was greatly reduced, as many as half the total crew might be recruited in the north.'[3]

The rules for qualifying for the government bounty on whaling voyages originally required ships to muster their entire crew in their home port before sailing, but these rules were relaxed under the pressure of wartime conditions about 1806, and were not restored after 1815.[4] However important it was for Hull's and other whaling ships to complete their crews in Shetland, this seems to have been of minor significance for Scoresby and for the other Whitby ships that travelled in company with him, especially on the homeward voyage.

The variation in the price of whale oil between 1800 and 1818, based on data provided by Scoresby,[5] does not suggest that whether Britain was at war or peace had much immediate influence on whaling as a commercial venture.

Price of Whale Oil (£ per ton) 1800–1818

1800	35	1810	38
1801	46	1811	31
1802	31	1812	35
1803	38	1813	50
1804	31	1814	32
1805	30	1815	38
1806	29	1816	28
1807	21	1817	46
1808	27	1818	38
1809	36		

[1] Scoresby noted that care was taken to release from the impressment those whaling men who were protected, and those from parishes in Shetland that had met their quota. This supports Emsley's remark (ibid., p. 7) that 'Not all of the regulating officers were the villains of popular fiction; they released men with exemptions ... and often they permitted seamen to "volunteer" after they had been seized by the gang, thus enabling the seamen to receive the recruiting bounty.'
[2] Credland, *Hull Whaling Trade*, p. 32.
[3] Ibid.
[4] Scoresby, *Account of the Arctic Regions*, II, pp. 494–5.
[5] Scoresby, *Account of the Arctic Regions*, II, p. 410.

In his study of whaling from the standpoint of an economic historian, Gordon Jackson contrasted 'The Boom in the Northern Fishery, 1783–c.1808' (his chapter 4) with 'Decline in the North in the Early Nineteenth Century' (chapter 6). The decline, however, really began after 1821 and Jackson agreed that 'there is every reason for accepting Scoresby's assertion that 1814, for instance, was "uncommonly prosperous", and the years immediately following the war were no worse'.[1]

In the period covered by the journals in the present volume. i.e. 1811–13, and for the years immediately before and after, the characteristic of the northern whaling trade seems to be stability, rather than either expansion or decline. Whale oil briefly reached a price of £60 a ton at the end of 1813[2] but this was a function of reduced supply rather than increasing demand. Eight ships returned from Davis Strait without a whale among them, and Scoresby used his 1813 experience to make the point that

> In certain years, it is curious to observe, that the whales commence a simultaneous retreat throughout the whole fishing limits, and all disappear within a very few days. ... In the year 1813, whales were found in considerable numbers in the open sea ... but in the greatest abundance about the end of June and the beginning of July. On the 6th of July they departed into the ice ... [and] they wholly disappeared after the 9th.[3]

Supply rather than demand equally explains the rapid fall in price the following year. The wars with France and the United States are therefore more of a background context to these whaling journals than a significant factor. In Jackson's memorable phrase, 'Climate, luck, and things known only to whales, might produce one good season in three before the present [twentieth] century',[4] and these factors were much more important than Napoleon or American privateers.

Father and Son: The Scoresbys and their Ships 1811–13

The 1811 journal opens with the statement that 'my Father having resigned the command of the Resolution, I was proposed to succeed him and appointed by the general voice of the owners.' Two questions are clearly begged by this statement: why did Captain Scoresby, Senior resign his command, and why was his son so readily appointed to succeed him?

The second question is easier to answer than the first. Although the appointment took place on the day that the younger Scoresby marked his twenty-first birthday,[5] his arctic experience was already substantial; through eight annual voyages from 1803 he had rapidly risen to become the second-in-command to his father. He had learned the task from one of the most successful of all whaling captains of the period, and the owners probably felt that, if the father was leaving Whitby, they 'might look

---

[1] Jackson, *The British Whaling Trade*, p. 118.
[2] Scoresby, *Account of the Arctic Regions*, I, p. 281. See also the details provided by Scoresby at the end of the 1813 journal, concerning the prices obtained by the Whitby fleet.
[3] Scoresby, *Account of the Arctic Regions*, II, p. 214. See also Lubbock, *Arctic Whalers*, p. 194.
[4] Jackson, *The British Whaling Trade*, p. 252.
[5] '... the earliest at which, by reason of age, I could legally hold a command': Scoresby, *My Father*, p. 125.

a lot further, but do a lot worse' than to appoint someone with the son's experience. It was, after all, initially only a one-year commitment.[1]

The more interesting question is why the elder Scoresby relinquished command of the *Resolution*, of which he had been a part-owner (an eighth share)[2] and in which he had been extremely successful. In eight voyages, he had brought back 194 whales, yielding 1617 tuns of oil.[3] One consequence of this success was that the elder Scoresby received many attractive offers from owners and ports. The one that he accepted involved the creation of a new company, based in Greenock, with Scoresby himself owning one of four equal shares in the company and the ability to purchase a suitable ship.[4]

It was an attractive proposition, fully justified by Scoresby's success in the *John* from 1811 to 1814, but it seems clear that the financial 'pull' to Greenock was not the only factor in the elder Scoresby's decision to leave the *Resolution* and Whitby. His son believed that his father's action represented 'a kindly and parental consideration for myself'.[5] Writing four decades later, however, his son also made it clear that there was another powerful factor in his father's decision: the jealousy and resentment generated by less successful whaling captains in Whitby:

> In my Father's case, where sometimes the owners, captains, and crews of near a dozen ships sailing from the same port had their most ardent enterprises, year by year, altogether eclipsed by his superior success, – and where, by reason of relative or interested association, the majority of a town's population became participators in the mortifying competition, – the measure in which the ungenerous feelings might possibly have their existence and impulses, may be well imagined to have been very extensive. That it was so in an extraordinary degree in the early progress of my Father's adventures, and during many years of his singular prosperity, every member of his family had too painful evidence.[6]

The significance of these comments, the validity of which there seems no reason to doubt, is increased if they are kept in mind when reading Scoresby's account of the dispute with his father that is described in the journal entry for 21 July 1812. The crew of the *John* had harpooned a whale, but the harpoon fell out ('drew'). The whale was then captured by the *Resolution*'s crew, whose determination to retain it was supported by whaling tradition. Whether the dilemma described by Scoresby was a real one, or was mainly created by his father's angry insistence that the whale be given up to the *John*, is probably less important than Scoresby's eventual decision to support his crew. 'As there might appear to be some partiality towards My Father or

---

[1] Although Scoresby might seem unusually young to take command, Rosalin Barker, who has compiled data from a very large number of muster-rolls of Whitby sailing ships, has found that in the period 1700–1748 more masters were to be found aged 21 to 30 than in any subsequent decennial cohort (personal communication, based on her *A Nursery for Seamen: Whitby's Merchant Sailing Fleet 1600–1820*, in preparation).

[2] Scoresby, *My Father*, pp. 116–17.

[3] Scoresby, *My Father*, pp. 185–6.

[4] According to Scoresby (ibid., p. 172), the *John* was a teak ship of 316 tons, built in Batavia (now Jakarta, Indonesia), and bought by the elder Scoresby in London.

[5] Ibid., p. 125.

[6] Ibid., p. 64.

that I was awed by his influence I could not exert that authority which I could command in any other Case.' It may have needed an incident such as that to persuade the crew, and later the people of Whitby, that Scoresby was his own man, despite his evident sense of filial duty to his father.

The *Resolution*, built in Whitby during the Peace of Amiens, had been a successful ship for Scoresby, Senior, and the voyages of 1811 and 1812 proved to be equally satisfactory for his son.[1] In 1811 he returned with what became over 210 tons of oil from thirty whales; the following year's catch was twenty-five whales and over 200 tons of oil.[2] The *Resolution* continued as a whaler long after both Scoresbys had left the sea[3] but during the winter of 1812–13 Scoresby worked with Thomas Brodrick and Thomas Fishburn, the builders and owners of the *Resolution*, in the design of a larger vessel, the *Esk*.

It was Scoresby's opinion, stated in 1820 and supported by substantial physical and economic argument, that

> A ship of intermediate size between 300 and 400 tons, is best adapted for the fishery. And, on the whole, perhaps, a roomy ship of 330 or 340 tons, possesses more advantages, with fewer disadvantages, than a vessel of similar build of any other capacity.[4]

The principal argument against a ship of more than 400 tons was that it was most unlikely that it would ever be filled in the course of a season's voyage. Further, although the government bounty paid to whaling vessels was based on the tonnage of the vessel, the bounty paid to ships built after 1786 of more than 300 tons was limited to the bounty paid on a 300-ton vessel. At the other end of the spectrum, Scoresby claimed that

> In the most favourable and prosperous cases, a ship of 330 tons burthen may receive on board about 150 tons of blubber at once; a ship of 250 tons scarcely 100. Hence, being soon crowded with blubber, the smaller vessel is not capable of deriving the same advantage from any extraordinary 'run of fish' as the larger; the fishing is necessarily suspended, until the blubber obtained is packed in casks, an operation requiring so much time, that a favourable opportunity, such as a run of fish, rarely continues until it is completed, nor often recurs in one season.[5]

The *Resolution* was a vessel of 291 tons; the *Esk* was 354 tons. As well as general considerations of the type mentioned by Scoresby in the preceding quotations, there were also constraints on the size of vessel imposed by the nature of Whitby harbour. One problem was the existence of the bridge separating the inner and outer harbours, through which the whaling ships had to pass. Originally constructed in 1766, it took

---

[1] There is an illustration of the *Resolution* under sail, painted by Thomas Butterworth, Senior, in Barrow, *Whaling Trade of North-East England*. The original is in the New Bedford Whaling Museum in Massachusetts.

[2] From the table 'State of the Whale-Fishery from 1803 to 1816, Inclusive' in Young, *History of Whitby*, II, at p. 568.

[3] According to Lubbock, *Arctic Whalers*, pp. 278, 364, 469, she was sold to Captain James Hogg of Peterhead in 1829, and may have continued arctic voyages until the middle of the century.

[4] Scoresby, *Account of the Arctic Regions*, II. p. 189. See also appendix II (1) in the same volume (pp. 506–7): 'Some Remarks on the Most Advantageous Dimensions of a Whale-Ship.'

[5] Ibid., II, p. 506.

the form of a two-leaf drawbridge, between stone abutments, with a maximum width for shipping of 32½ feet, and a strong possibility of entangling the ship's rigging as it passed through.[1] The *Resolution* was 26 feet 2 inches in the beam; the *Esk* was 27 feet 11 inches.

Scoresby's description of the beginning of the 1813 voyage, in mid-March, illustrates a second problem: the shallow depth of the harbour caused by the material brought down by the River Esk.[2] Scoresby may have been quite correct that a ship of 350 tons was the optimum size for northern whaling, but it seems clear that it was also close to the limits imposed by the contemporary conditions in Whitby harbour.

Within these limits, the *Esk* appears to have embodied all the experience of its owners and builders, Fishburn and Brodrick, and that of Scoresby himself. Credland remarked that 'Only one British whaler was ever comprehensively designed and built for the Arctic fishery and that was the *Baffin* launched at Liverpool in 1820.'[3] That seems difficult to reconcile with the very detailed comments made by Scoresby at the beginning of the 1813 journal about the construction of the *Esk*.

The Scoresby Papers in Whitby Museum contain an indication that Scoresby's partnership with Fishburn and Brodrick was not his only option at this time. WHITM:SCO688 is a 'Notarial Copy, Contract of Copartnery among Messrs. William Forsyth James Hunter William Scoresby Senr and William Scoresby Junr, dated 10 March 1813. It was signed by the first three, but not by William Scoresby Junior. The contract was a general revision of the original agreement made by the elder Scoresby with three Greenock merchants in 1810. It noted that one of the merchants, David Hyde, 'has now transferred his share and interest in the concern to the said William Forsyth and James Hunter.' The first substantive clause extended the agreement until 31 December 1820; the second provided for the purchase of land and construction of buildings for reducing the blubber to oil, and other needs such as 'seasonal lodgings' and office space. The third and fourth clauses arranged for Thomas Jackson, the elder Scoresby's son-in-law, to be included in the Greenock Whale Fishery Company, though not as a partner, so that

[1] In his 1817 *History of Whitby*, George Young commented that 'Were the passage for the ships widened, the leaves and the apparatus for suspending them would not be so frequently injured: but a much greater improvement would be effected, were the moveable part made to turn on a pivot, instead of being hoisted. There would then be nothing to entangle the rigging of the vessels ...' (II, pp. 543–4) Such a bridge, opening by a horizontal swivel to a width of 45 feet replaced the 18th century structure in 1835, and was itself replaced by the present swing bridge in the first decade of the twentieth century. See also Weatherill, *Ancient Port of Whitby*, pp. 13–15.
[2] '*Whitby* is a Tide Haven, and falls almost dry at low Water. On the East Side of the Haven is a Beacon, which at your going up you must leave on the larboard Side, and so you may run up as high as the Bridge. ... If you lie up there you must go above Bridge and lie upon the Sand called the *Bell*, which is dry at low Water.': *English Pilot*, p. 8. That was the situation in 1770. In 1817 Young claimed that the outer harbour, below the bridge, had been improved by pier extensions and constriction of the entrance. The improvements, however, still left much to be desired. 'Small banks of sand, or mud, are occasionally formed, especially above the bridge; but ... they are nothing to the banks with which this port was formerly obstructed. ... [V]essels in stormy weather must go above the bridge to escape the swell ... The channel, however, is not very broad in some parts, being confined on the west by a large bank called the *Bell isle*.': Young, *History of Whitby*, II, p. 539.
[3] Credland, *Hull Whaling Trade*, p. 119.

...as soon as the said Thomas Jackson is experienced in the fishing business to the satisfaction of the said William Scoresby his father in law he shall be entitled to the sole
command of the said ship John or some other Vessel in the employ of the Company and
be allowed the wages following ...

It is, however, the fifth clause that is of greatest interest:

... It is agreed that William Scoresby Junior of Whitby Son of the said William Scoresby
shall become a Partner in the Greenock Whale Fishery Company have a part of his
fathers one fourth share of that Concern and shall have a ship purchased by the
Company and be allowed to fit her out from any Port of Britain he may judge best to
[***] the fishery to Greenock and shall be allowed ...

The sixth clause stated that the agreement on wages in the original contract of
1810 would end in August 1815, but 'nevertheless the business is to Continue in the
Management of the said William Scoresby Senior, or in case of his resignation or
death to devolve on the said William Scoresby Junior ...'. The final substantive clause
provided for the winding-up of the Company, should this eventually prove necessary.

Signed by the elder Scoresby and his Greenock partners in March 1813, as the son
was about to take the newly-built *Esk* to sea, the contract appears to have been an
attempt by the elder Scoresby to make the Greenock company a 'family business',
with the ready agreement of the other land-based partners. Perhaps the elder
Scoresby envisaged purchasing the *Esk* from its shipbuilding owners, Fishburn and
Brodrick. Whatever the father's hopes, his son seems never to have mentioned the
proposal, then or later, and continued to sail from Whitby.

'Open' and 'Close' Seasons

In *An Account of the Arctic Regions*, Scoresby devoted many pages (I, pp. 266–84) to
the difficulty of reaching the principal whaling area in the Greenland Sea, west of
Spitsbergen in latitude 78–79°N. On the one hand, even early in the season, the ships
could take advantage of what Scoresby called (p. 266) '*The Whale-fisher's Bight*' – a
broad tongue of open water between longitudes 0° and 10°E and extending north-
wards usually as far as the latitude of southern Spitsbergen (77°N).[1] However, once
the whalers had reached the northern end of this bight, they might or might not be
confronted with a formidable barrier of ice separating them from more open water
(what Scoresby called the 'land water') in the whaling grounds further north. As
Scoresby summarized the situation in this crucial area,

When the ice at the extremity of this bay occurs so strong and compact, as to prevent the
approach to the shores of Spitzbergen, and the advance northward beyond the latitude
of 75° or 76°, it is said to be a *close season*; and, on the contrary, it is called an *open
season*, when an uninterrupted navigation extends along the western coast of Spitzbergen ... In an open season, therefore, a large channel of water lies between the land and
the ice, from 20 to 50 leagues in breadth. extending to the latitude of 79° or 80°, and
gradually approximating the coast ... .[2]

---

[1] Italics in original. This bight is shown in modern atlas maps such as *The Times Atlas*, Plate 48,
where it forms part of the line indicating the 'Maximum limit of drift ice'.

[2] Scoresby, *Account of the Arctic Regions*, I, p. 266.

The journals in the present volume illustrate this contrast in ice conditions very clearly. In what must have been a frustrating month for Scoresby on his first voyage in command, the *Resolution* reached the ice barrier in latitude 76°30′N on 22 April, but it was not until 25 May that the ship was able to pass through it, and 30 May before the *Resolution* succeeded in capturing a whale. What made things even more frustrating was the fact that three ships (*Henrietta* of Whitby and *Aurora* and 'Old' *Manchester* of Hull) had succeeded in getting through the ice in mid-May, and had been very successful in capturing whales by the time *Resolution* and the rest of the fleet joined them.[1] As Scoresby wrote later,

> The season of 1811 was uncommonly close. Though the most arduous exertions were made by the fishers for four or five weeks, few ships passed the barrier before the 26th of May. Whales occurred in great plenty, and the fishery was generally good.[2]

It was even more difficult to penetrate the ice barrier in 1812. The *Resolution* did not reach 75°N until 12 May and did not get through the ice barrier to the land water until 1 June.

> The barrier consisted of a compact body of floes and fields. In each of the preceding years, the obstruction invariably consisted of packed ice, consolidated by the intervention of bay ice into a continuous sheet; but, on this occasion, the most ponderous field-ice barred the navigation … . This barrier was one of the most formidable that had ever been encountered. All attempts to pass it before the close of the month of May were attended with imminent danger, and were generally nugatory. But after a week's continuance of mild calm weather, the fields and flows were released by the partial destruction of the bay-ice among them, and a winding navigation of about sixty miles in extent, opened into a clear sea adjoining the land. For some time after passing the barrier, but few whales were seen; the fishery was late, and only partially successful.[3]

Because of the problems encountered in 1811 and 1812, it is surprising that Scoresby was confident enough to have predicted (journal entry for 17 April 1813)

> Before leaving England …, that Greenland the present year would exhibit an open country, or in other words that there would no obstruction from Ice offer, to the Navigation to a proper Fishing Latitude. I affirmed this to Several of my Friends.

By that date, however, the *Esk* was already at 79°N latitude, and Scoresby had the leisure to write a lengthy entry in his journal (almost 1500 words) to celebrate and also to endeavour to explain his good fortune. Reaching the whaling grounds so easily, however, did not mean ready access to whales; it was 'uncommonly tempestuous', especially in May and 'In consequence of the prevalence of easterly winds, the ice was generally packed, and the fishery was bad.'[4]

Scoresby's Navigation

In his journal entry for 9 July 1811, as he started his homeward journey, Scoresby

---

[1] See the journal entries for 1 June and 17 June 1811.
[2] Scoresby, *An Account of the Arctic Regions*, I, p. 279.
[3] Ibid., I, pp. 279–80.
[4] Ibid., I, p. 281. Because whaling in Davis Strait was also poor in 1813, the price of whale oil reached £60 per ton, as already noted (p. 1).

noted that the *Resolution* was 'under all sail running to the SSW or sailed by the Wind to the S^d in company with the Enterprize and Aimwell which ships nominated us Commodore'. To these were later added the *Volunteer* and, for shorter periods, the *Perseverance* and *Lively*. Ships tended to travel in convoy after leaving the Arctic, for defensive reasons, but to make Scoresby the commodore of the convoy, during his first voyage as master, clearly seems an expression of confidence (shown by vessels from Peterhead as well as Whitby) in his superior ability as a navigator.

There were two interrelated problems in regard to navigating between the British Isles and the Greenland Sea, and these problems were much more serious on the return journeys than when sailing northward in the spring. The principal difficulty was the one that had hindered navigation for centuries, that of determining longitude. A subsidiary problem, but one to which Scoresby devoted much attention in the journals and in scientific papers, was the unreliability of the magnetic compass in northern latitudes.

In principle, the longitude problem had been solved by the development of reliable chronometers in the eighteenth century. In practice, such chronometers were extremely expensive until the middle of the nineteenth century,[1] and the whaling fleet, Scoresby included, relied on much less accurate watches. On the outward voyage, this was a relatively small problem. The watch could be set at Greenwich time by reference to local noon at Lerwick the longitude of which was known (1°9'W). Although a watch gained or lost several seconds per day, the approximate error could be determined by solar observations (e.g. journal entry 29 April 1812) and after allowing for this error the longitude could be determined with sufficient accuracy to bring a ship to the western coast of Spitsbergen.

During the months spent whaling in the Greenland Sea, the ship's geographical position was of less significance than its relationship to ice distribution and the presence or absence of whales. Scoresby recorded both latitude and longitude almost every day, but the longitudes must have been estimates, occasionally confirmed or corrected by sightings of the Spitsbergen coast.[2]

In the lengthy Appendix I of volume 1 of *An Account of the Arctic Regions*, Scoresby listed the latitudes and longitudes for the daily meteorological observations taken throughout most of the duration of all his voyages from 1807 to 1818. From these it seems that he made no astronomical determinations of longitude in high latitudes (north of 70°) before 1817, and only occasional determinations of latitude (e.g in July 1812, on the 2nd, 13th, 17th and 24th of that month, with an additional measurement on the 31st when the *Resolution*, was already south of 70°N).

---

[1] 'It was not until the middle of the 19th century that the mechanical construction of these timekeepers had attained an unexampled and high standard of efficiency, the improvement in manufacture having, at the same time, been accompanied by a reduction in the cost of production.': Cotter, *History of Nautical Astronomy*, pp. 52–3.

[2] Even when Spitsbergen could be sighted, the charts used by Scoresby contained errors. In Appendix IV of volume 1 of *An Account of the Arctic Regions*, he provided coordinates for 42 locations on Spitsbergen and 12 on Jan Mayen 'derived chiefly from original surveys' that he had undertaken since 1815. Elsewhere in the volume (p. 113) he noted that 'In several particular situations I found an error of 10 miles of latitude and 2 or 3 degrees of longitude, in our most approved charts.'

On the return journey, careful navigation was much more important than on the outward voyage.

> Vessels returning from Greenland or Archangel are so very liable to make the coast of Norway, when the navigators imagine themselves at the distance of some degrees, that the circumstance is notorious. An error of 5 or 6 degrees of longitude, in the reckoning of a Greenland ship, is by no means uncommon, notwithstanding the coast of Spitzbergen may have been seen immediately before setting out on the passage homeward. ... This error has usually been attributed to an easterly current; if such a cause, however, do operate at all, most certainly it is not the sole cause. There is little doubt but it is chiefly owing to the increase of the westerly variation of the compass, in consequence of the "local attraction" of the ship on the magnetic needle, when steering on a course to the westward of the magnetic meridian; and partly to an error in the departure of the Greenland ships, arising from the situation of the southern parts of Spitzbergen being laid down 3 or 4 degrees too far to the westward in the charts.[1]

One of the remarkable things about the preceding statement is that it was written after large numbers of British whaling ships had been making annual voyages to and from the Greenland Sea for almost seventy years. One might reasonably expect that some 'rule of thumb' would have emerged to ensure that ships on their return stayed well clear of the Norwegian coast, whereas in 1820 it still remained a 'notorious circumstance'.

A rule of thumb was probably all that many whaling captains could have used. As Scoresby put it:

> It is not unusual for a ship to bear away [homeward], without the navigators having first obtained any certain knowledge as to their situation in longitude. Not having, perhaps, seen any land for some weeks, or even months, or possibly not since their arrival on the fishing stations; having neither a chronometer on board, nor the means of taking a lunar observation; they set out ignorant of the meridian on which they sail, and sensible of their being liable to an error of 5 or 6 degrees of longitude.[2]

Scoresby, however, was both a competent and confident navigator, even during his first years of command, and his journals show that he used judiciously all the evidence available. to him. The entry for 1 May 1811 shows that he had learned to determine longitude by lunar distances, using the *Nautical Almanac* and the *Requisite Tables*.[3] On his return from the Greenland Sea that year, he preferred his own determination of the ship's position to that estimated by HMS *Niobe* 'since I suspect the Niobes Reckoning to be too far Westerly they having had no Lunar observation or

---

[1] Scoresby, *Account of the Arctic Regions*, II, pp. 375–7.
[2] Ibid., II, p. 369.
[3] *Requisite Tables* was the familiar name of the *Tables Requisite to be used with the Nautical Ephemeris for finding the Latitude and Longitude at Sea*; like the *Nautical Almanac* they originated with Nevil Maskelyne, the Astronomer Royal, in 1765. 'The method of finding longitude at sea by lunar distance was to become the standard astronomical method for finding longitude at sea and was to remain so for the whole of the 19th century.': Cotter, *History of Nautical Astronomy*, p. 205. In the Scoresby Papers there is a set of forms (WHITM:SCO650), for calculating longitude, using Mendoza Rios's method (Norie, *Formulae for Finding the Longitude*, 1816); with completed calculations for 10 and 31 July 1820 and 24 July 1821.

Correction of Timekeeper since they saw the North Cape' two weeks earlier (journal entry 15 July 1811).

Scoresby's confidence in his ability to determine his longitude by the careful observation and complex calculations required by the method of lunar distances is shown even more clearly in the journal entry for 9 August 1812, and the commentary on that situation that he included years later in *An Account of the Arctic Regions*. Based on a lunar observation, Scoresby believed himself to be in latitude 60°N, longitude 3½°W, i.e. west of Foula and southern Shetland. He took a sounding 'As a matter of curiosity',[1] and found bottom in 73 fathoms. This was totally unexpected, because 'it is generally or universally supposed that no soundings are to be met with to the Wd of Shetland out of sight of Land'.[2] As the journal indicates, Scoresby had some other evidence to support his astronomical determination – the pattern of sea swell suggesting they had recently passed east of the Faroes – but

> Had I not had the greatest confidence in my lunar observation, (especially as we had left Greenland with out [sic] obtaining any departure, and without having seen land for two months previous,) I should undoubtedly, have steered a south-westerly course, which would have run us to the westward of Scotland. My mate, and some other experienced officers on board, felt assured that we were to the eastward of Shetland.[3]

In the tables of meteorological and other records that Scoresby included in *An Account of the Arctic Regions*, an asterisk following a latitude or longitude indicated a position determined by astronomical methods. In these journals, he appears to have used a plus sign ('+') for the same purpose (e.g. the latitude on 13 March 1811). There are, however, some inconsistencies if the journals are compared to the *Account*.

Conclusion: The Emerging Arctic Scientist

Less than a decade after the first of the voyages recorded in ths present volume, William Scoresby the Younger would publish what has been described as 'one of the most remarkable books in the English language' and 'the foundation stone of Arctic science'.[4] It is natural that these 1811–13 journals, and the ones that follow them, should be valued for the evidence that they provide of how *An Account of the Arctic Regions* came to be written.

In the journals for 1811, 1812 and 1813, there is not much to suggest that the notion of book writing had entered Scoresby's head, and this is confirmed by Scoresby's correspondence, in the archives of the Whitby Literary and Philosophical Society.[5] It seems

---

[1] Scoresby, *Account of the Arctic Regions*, II, p. 372.

[2] Journal entry 9 August 1812.

[3] Scoresby, *Account of the Arctic Regions*, II, p. 372. This might appear as the wisdom of hindsight, but the journal entries for 8 and 9 August 1812 express a similar confidence.

[4] The first remark was made by Sir Sidney Harmer in 1928, and the second is from the entry for Scoresby in the *Dictionary of National Biography*; both were quoted by Sir Alister Hardy in his introduction to the 1969 reprint of *An Account of the Arctic Regions*.

[5] It should be mentioned here, however, that in 1812 Scoresby appears to have attempted, though not very seriously, another form of writing. In the Scoresby Papers at Whitby Museum (WHITM:SCO691) there is a 33–page manuscript, dated 24 April 1812, entitled 'Williame and

clear that Robert Jameson in Edinburgh – and perhaps William Playfair and Joseph Banks even earlier – had made Scoresby aware that his arctic observations and experience, whether of meteorology, zoology or any other branch of science, would be regarded as valuable, but one or more papers in the *Memoirs* of the Wernerian Society was as much as could have been expected.[1] During these years, Scoresby took weather observations on a regular basis; he experimented, with moderate success, on temperature soundings at depth in the Greenland Sea; he indicated a growing interest in geomagnetism, and especially its implications for navigation by compass; he began a lengthy interest in the structure of snowflakes. But during these three years, he was still primarily a whaling captain. If one is to look ahead, his experiences in 1811 to 1813 contributed more to volume II, 'The Whale Fishery', of the *Account of the Arctic Regions* than to the scientific survey that is provided in volume I.

The journal entry for 13 June 1811, in which Scoresby mentioned that 'the modification of the nimbus was particularly marked and much resembled the drawing given by Luke Howard Esqr.', caused confusion when transcribed (the unfamiliar term 'nimbus' was transcribed as 'numbers'), but is of some importance. Luke Howard's essay 'On the Modification of Clouds …' had been published in the *Philosophical Magazine* in 1803. In his recent survey of the significance of that essay, Hamblyn emphasized that

> The readers of the *Philosophical Magazine* were … hardworking members of the professional, practical classes who were beginning to swell the audiences of the fast-proliferating lectures, demonstrations, and museum exhibitions. …
>
> This readership, broader than that of the [Royal Society's] Philosophical Transactions was also in many respects better informed, at least on day-to-day technical matters, and it was certainly more demanding. It included artisans and industrialists, professional and working people, some of whom were wealthy and successful, most of whom were not. Learning was for them a new and uplifting opportunity … [2]

Scoresby fits that description like a glove, and Hamblyn used him as its exemplar:

Eliza, or, Norwegian Gratitude, A Tale, Founded on Facts which occurred within those last two Years, by William Scoresby Junr MWS. Greenland Seas. Published as the Act directs for all the Booksellers and Manuscript Venders from Spitzbergen's farthest Mount, down to Johny Maine and Cherry Islands.' The latter terms are presumably facetious references to Jan Mayen and Cherie or Bear Island.

[1] On 13 January 1810, 'The Secretary laid before the [Wernerian] Society a Communication from Mr WILLIAM SCORESBY of Whitby, comprising a Meteorological Journal of several Voyages to Greenland, and an account of different Crystallisations of Snow observed there. The Journals are published in 1st vol. Mem. p. 249–57.' (From the Appendix on the 'History of the Society' published at the end of volume 2 of the *Memoirs of the Wernerian Natural History Society*, at p. 641.) The same source noted (p. 642) that on 22 February 1812 'Professor JAMESON read extracts from a Meteorological Journal kept by Mr SCORESBY *junior* in Greenland, in 1811, which is inserted in vol. ii. Mem. p. 155–166.' and (p. 650) that on 16 January 1813 'The Secretary read a communication from Mr SCORESBY, containing his Greenland Journal for 1812, with some curious particulars concerning some Greenland animals, especially the Polar Bear.' This meteorological journal was also published in volume 2 of the *Memoirs*, pp. 167–73, although there is an error on p. 167 where it is stated that the paper was read on 22 February 1812, i.e. before the observations were made!

[2] Hamblyn, *Invention of Clouds*, chapter 7.

> Scoresby ... had become an early convert to Luke Howard's nomenclature [of cloud types], having come across it in a copy of the *Philosophical Magazine* in the library at Edinburgh University ...
>
> Scoresby used the full Howard cloud classification in the ship's log of the *Resolution* in his first journey as captain ... This was the first navigational use of the new nomenclature ... [1]

Howard's symbols for different cloud types were occasionally also employed by Scoresby, e.g. in the journal entries for 1 and 8 August 1813.

Scoresby's attempts to measure the variation of temperature and specific gravity with depth (i.e. the thermohaline profile) in the Greenland Sea, even before he assumed command of the *Resolution*, are the best evidence of the emerging experimental scientist in these early journals, though the journal entries themselves are inadequate. In the 1811 journal, for example, Scoresby described the measurements made on 23 April, but there is no mention of similar experiments, with an improved device, on 1 May. From his description in *An Account of the Arctic Regions* (I, pp. 184–8) and the accompanying table of results, the early experiments passed through three stages. In April 1810 Scoresby used a wooden cask fitted with valves at each end. As the cask was lowered, the valves were open and water passed through. These valves closed when the descent was stopped, so that the cask contained about 10 gallons of water from that depth. The cask

> was generally allowed to remain about half an hour at rest, so that the wood might attain the temperature of the sea in that situation, and then hauled briskly up without stopping, and the temperature of the contained water immediately ascertained.

The specific gravity would have been determined later, at atmospheric pressure, and would therefore provide a measure of salinity.

These initial trials on 19 and 23 April 1810 were encouraging but 'after a few experiments had been made, the wood of the cask became soaked with water; several of the staves rent from end to end; and the apparatus became leaky and useless'.

The measurements made on 23 April 1811, in almost the same location and on one of the same dates as in 1810, used the device provided by Sir Joseph Banks. This was again wooden, but bound in brass, and contained a recording thermometer. The journal entry for that date, however, suggests an error in Scoresby's table in *Account of the Arctic Regions* (II, p. 187). Scoresby has an asterisk at the last measurement on 23 April 1811, noting that

> Down to this experiment, the apparatus used for bringing up the water, was the fir-cask; and the mode of finding the temperature, was by a common thermometer, after it came to the surface. Hence some slight change in the temperature might possibly take place during its passage upward; but, in all the subsequent experiments, a Six's thermometer accompanied the marine-diver, and consequently marked with accuracy the extremes of temperature through which it passed.

There are two problems with this footnote. First, attaching a self-recording thermometer to the device would indeed record the extremes, but not necessarily the

[1] Ibid., chapter 10.

temperature of the water at the depth where the sample was obtained. It is clear from the journal entry for 23 April 1811 that Scoresby recognized this, and continued to measure the temperature of the water sample after it had been recovered. Secondly, it seems evident from the journal entry that the asterisk and the associated note in the table are misplaced: they should refer to the last experiment on 23 April 1810, not 23 April 1811.

The third stage in these experiments was the replacement of Banks's brassbound wooden device by one made entirely of brass, but using the valves from the previous model. It is illustrated in *An Account of the Arctic Regions*, II, Plate II, Fig. 2. Scoresby did not say when or where this was made, but it must have been in late April 1811, on the *Resolution*; otherwise the measurements made on 1 May would not have been possible, because the device provided by Banks was beyond repair. Why there is no mention of these experiments in the journal entry for that date is not clear.

Two more general comments also seem justified from these three journals. The first is that they show that Scoresby's relatively short periods at Edinburgh University had taught him something that every graduate student comes to realize: the task of turning observation and analysis into a written record is itself the most effective way of remembering things that would otherwise be likely to remain forgotten or unremarked. Scoresby had found in 1806–7 in Edinburgh that 'my notes daily extend, until at length the writing of them used to occupy me three or four hours. By this exercise each subject was more particularly fixed on my memory than it could have been by an extensive course of reading',[1] and he seems to have had no hesitation in similarly extending the daily entries in his journals to whatever length the topics required.

The second comment is that there does seem to be a significant difference between the journals for 1811 and 1812 on the one hand, and that for 1813 on the other. In 1813 there is much greater detail about matters that in the preceding years were taken for granted. In the entry for 17 April 1813, for example, the whale lines used in the whaleboats are described in great detail: number, length, weight, diameter and even the number of yarns in each strand. The other equipment of the whaleboats is also described in detail. The *Esk* was, of course, a new vessel, but the quantity of detail and explanation about the ship and its equipment, or the voyage, do not seem intended as a comparison with experience in the *Resolution*. The impression one gets is that Scoresby had realized that the journals may have a wider interest, and be read by those without a detailed understanding of whaling, so that it was necessary to explain what was involved. To that extent (but no more), the 1813 journal seems in some respects the first rough draft of chapter IV of volume II of *An Account of the Arctic Regions*: 'Account of the Modern Whale-Fishery, as conducted at Spitzbergen'.

Rightly or wrongly, this editor has not 'read ahead' to the journals of subsequent voyages, before editing these journals for 1811–1813. He believes that Scoresby as arctic scientist will become more evident in those later journals, as the prospect of the 1820 book emerges and increases in importance to its author. Meanwhile, these journals of a young man in his twenties, already with great arctic experience and clear evidence of scientific ability, seem fascinating in themselves.

[1] See p. xxix.

Journal for 1811

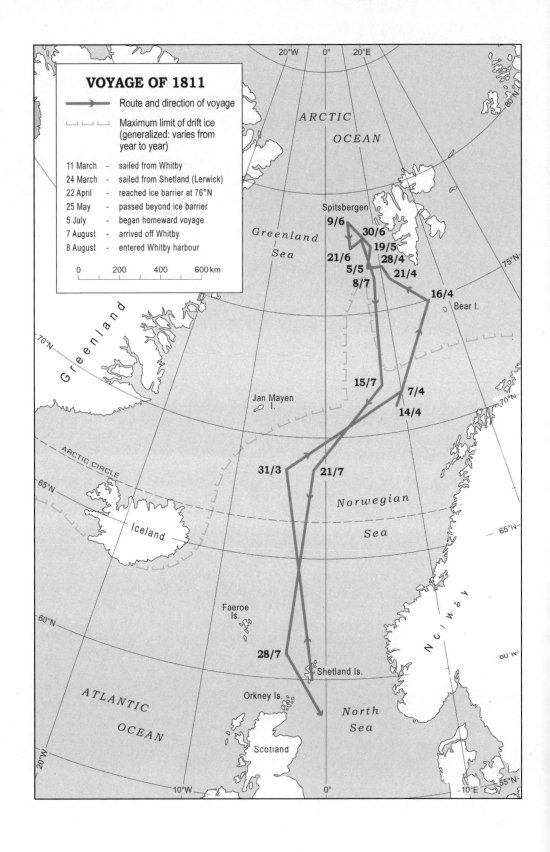

VOYAGE OF 1811

→ Route and direction of voyage

Maximum limit of drift ice
(generalized: varies from
year to year)

11 March	-	sailed from Whitby
24 March	-	sailed from Shetland (Lerwick)
22 April	-	reached ice barrier at 76°N
25 May	-	passed beyond ice barrier
5 July	-	began homeward voyage
7 August	-	arrived off Whitby
8 August	-	entered Whitby harbour

0   200   400   600 km

ARCTIC

OCEAN

Greenland
Sea

Spitsbergen
9/6   30/6
       19/5
21/6   28/4
5/5   21/4
8/7
              16/4   Bear I.

Greenland

70°N

15/7   7/4
            14/4

Jan Mayen
I.

31/3   21/7

Norwegian

Sea

ARCTIC CIRCLE

65°N

Iceland

65°N

Faeroe
Is.

28/7   Shetland Is.

Orkney Is.   North

ATLANTIC   Sea

OCEAN

Scotland

Norway

80°N

75°N

70°N

60°N

55°N

20°W   0°   20°E

10°W   0°   10°E

Journal of a Greenland or Whale Fishing Voyage (under Divine Providence) in the ship Resolution of Whitby. By Wm. Scoresby, Junr. Commander 1811.

['Introduction' *inserted in another hand*]

The Day on which I became of age October 5th 1810 my Father having resigned the command of the Resolution[1] I was proposed[2] to succeed him and appointed by the general voice of the owners[.]

I spent the Autumn and part of the Winter in excursions for pleasure and improvement to Edinburgh Loch Lomond Greenock Glasgow Hull and London and about Christmas proceeded homeward to superintend the preparation of provisions and the equipment of the Ship for the fishery[.][3]

On the 9th of March all our arrangements were completed and on the tenth we put to Sea[4] and proceeded on the fishery according to the succeeding Journal[.]

This was my tenth voyage to the Polar seas. My first voyage was performed in the Ship Dundee from London in the year 1800 being then only ten years of age. The next 8 voyages I sailed in the <u>Resolution</u> during the year [*sic*] 1803 to 1810 inclusive: my first 3 voyages in this ship I served in the Capacity of Apprentice only but in 1806 I was advanced to the office of Chief mate and in 1809 to that of Chief mate and Harponeer.[5] Previous to my being appointed harponeer I struck two whales the first in the year 1806 the second in 1808 and in the voyages 1809 and 1810 was fortunate enough to strike and capture 12 fish though in the last of the two I was off duty from an accident during the best of the fishery[.][6]

---

[1] See Introduction, p. l.

[2] The transcript has 'prepared' but 'proposed' had been written above this in another hand, probably a correction by Scoresby himself. The word in the original journal is clearly 'proposed'. Where such obvious transcription errors can be checked against the original, I have corrected the error, normally without further comment. See also Introduction, p. xxiv.

[3] More details about these travels are provided in Scoresby-Jackson, *Life*, pp. 75–7, including the following quotation (p. 77) from Scoresby's manuscript autobiography: 'During my stay in London I visited Sir Joseph Banks weekly, was constantly present at his *conversaziones* on the Sabbath evenings! and sometimes attended his public breakfasts.'

[4] In this introduction, Scoresby uses the civil day, commencing at midnight. However the daily entries in the 1811 journal (and also 1812, but not 1813) use the nautical day, commencing at noon on the preceding civil day. The *Resolution* therefore sailed from Whitby on the afternoon of 10 March, civil time, but 11 March in nautical time.

[5] This spelling is adopted consistently in the journals, though in *Account of the Arctic Regions* Scoresby used 'harpooner'. *OED* lists several spellings and indicates that 'harponeer' was an 18th-century form.

[6] 'Wednesday June 6 ... During the making off I had the misfortune to slip into the hold pitching on the edge of a tub with my side: I was so much hurt that I was obliged to retire from duty & had my boatsteerer, Isaac Wilson. appointed for my substitute harponeer.': Journal of the 1810 voyage in the *Resolution*, Scoresby Papers, Whitby Museum, WHITM:SCO1251. The *Resolution* returned

Monday 11th March 1811. The Ship not having floated on the Morning tide some things were moved forward to trim her being near one foot by the [Stern?] as regards the draught of water[.]

The weather fine and wind favourable made preparation for sailing[.] At 3 PM several of the other Greenland Ships were in motion it was not until near full tide however that we were enabled to heave the Resolution off the Ground we presently afterwards hauled through the Bridge nearly as far as the pier where we made sail and got safe out of the Harbour[.][1] At 5½ PM the Pilot left us we then made sail loaded a few of the Guns[.] In the Morning fine weather moderate or fresh breezes and hazy[.] Whitby in Latitude 54°28′30″ Long 31′30″[.][2] Steering to the NNE the rate of 6 to 8 knots[.]

Tuesday 12th March 1811. Little wind fine weather and rather cloudy dinner finished called all hands on deck divided them into Watches and placed them to their different stations in case of actions viz three men to each 4lb Gun 4 to each 18 canonade[3] and 6 lbs Guns except to the foremast Guns to these were allotted 6 Men[.] All to fight Gun and opposite others were reserved for the Helm, braces, &c. After this each gang cleaned their Guns and loaded them[.] Light airs and delightful clear weather towards noon[.] Course NE, E & NbE velocity 1 to 4 knots[.]

[From here on the journal is laid out in three columns: 'Dates' 'Winds' and 'Occurences [sic] the [date]'. In this edition this information is arranged sequentially on separate lines. Note that in 1811 and 1812 the latitudes and longitudes are those observed or estimated at the end of the nautical day, e.g. the entry for 'Wednesday March 13th' was taken at noon on that date, civil day, immediately before the commencement of the nautical day of 14 March.]

Wednesday March 13th Lat. 58°13+N Long 0°56′W[4]
WbN
Fresh breezes and fine clear weather in the Evening. In the morning light airs a

---

to Whitby on 17 July 1810. See also Scoresby-Jackson, *Life,* p. 75: 'A serious accident occurred to Mr. Scoresby about the middle of the voyage – a heavy fall into the hold of the vessel, whereby a renewal of chest symptoms was threatened. In order to allay these he spent the summer of 1810 in uninterrupted repose; and when, at length, his health was moderately re-established, he undertook a pleasure tour into Scotland.'

[1] The original journal continued: 'we then found two of the Crew were in wanting, sent the [Troy?] boat on shore which soon brought them off'. See Introduction, p. xxiv.

[2] The actual coordinates of the parish church on Whitby's East Cliff are 54°29′21″N 0°36′33″W. This entry was presumably intended to serve as the basis for subsequent dead reckoning. In subsequent log entries, 'N' was usually omitted in the latitude, but the longitude normally always specified 'E' or 'W' of the Greenwich meridian.

[3] *Sic.* Presumably the 'carronade', a light cannon suitable for use by ships, distinguished by its short barrel and large calibre, and produced in large numbers between 1778 and 1852 by the Carron Company of Falkirk, Scotland. The word is not clear in the original.

[4] This longitude is from the original; the transcript is 'Long 59°8'. Similarly, in the next entry for 14 March, the transcript version is 'Long 37°13E'.

Galliot[1] in sight standing to the SE[.] at noon Thermo*meter* 53°[.][2] Course NbE or NNE velocity 0 to 6 knots.

Thursday March 14th Lat 58°46 Long 0°53′W
calm

Calm fine weather in the afternoon succeeded by light breezes a heavy north sea the fore part which drove the vessel to the SE about 6 miles[.] At noon rather freshening[.] Five ships hove in sight bearing about WbN supposed to be the Whitby fleet course NNE and NbE made very little progress[.]

Friday March 15th
SW

The wind at first moderate but towards evening it increased to a fresh gale we steered at NbE and then N½ W and at 5 PM were as far west of the 5 ships descried yesterday 4 miles a head of them we changed our course to the NNE steered thus till after sun set then shortened sail and hove the Ship too supposing ourselves to be near Fair Island[3] we even thought we saw it through the haze. The other Ships came up about 7½ PM several spoke they continued their course for two hours then all lay too[.] In the morning it was clear weather at Day break made sail to the NbE or NNE[d] for an hour and seeing no Land I suspected we were to the E[d] hauled up NNW or NW and about 9 o clock close by the wind[.] At 10½ AM made the land Noss Island bearing about NWbW distance 10 miles[.][4] At noon had come very near it but found we should not fetch the entrance of Brassa sound to which we were bound[.][5]

Saturday March 16th
SW

Fresh breezes fine clear weather at ½ PM tacked within ½ a mile of the Point[6] of Brassa Island made a tack ¾ of an hour then doubled Brassa Island and up the Channel first NbW then NNW then NNE to NEbN[.] At 2 PM came to an anchor in Brassa Sound about the middle ground[.] Four Whitby ships were already arrived the remainder of the fleet soon followed together with the Egginton the Harmony of Hull the Fountain of Lynn &c[.] The sails being already furled sent down Top Gallt masts made the customary changes in the rigging[7] bent best sails and filled water in the after hold in the Morning[.]

Sunday March 17th
SW

Fine weather and a moderate breeze most of the crew went on shore to church[.]

---

[1] OED: 'A Dutch cargo-boat or fishing-vessel'. See also Smyth, *Sailor's Word Book*, s.v. 'Galleot'.
[2] Throughout the journals, Scoresby recorded temperatures in Fahrenheit and atmospheric pressure in inches of mercury.
[3] Fair Isle, 59°32′N 1°38′W.
[4] Isle of Noss, 60°9′N 1°1′W.
[5] Bressay Sound separates the island of that name from Lerwick and the Mainland of Shetland.
[6] Presumably Bard Head, the end of the peninsula on the southeast coast of Bressay.
[7] See Introduction, p. xlii.

Monday March 18th

The fore part fine moderate weather moderately cloudy a shower of rain in the Evening. In the morning began to fill water in the Main afterwards in the fore hold brought the Ship down to 13^{ft} 3 in aft and 12^{ft} 10 in forward[1] then stayed our pumps greased mast and top sail Sheets[.]

Tuesday March 19th 20th 21st 22nd 23rd

NW

During the most of this time the wind blew constantly strong from the NW occasionally NNW or WNW[.] A remarkable sudden change was observed[2] one morning a severe gale had sprung up from the SW[.] I heard it blow excessively hard and rang the Bell to enquire the particulars the Spieksmeer[3] came down and while he yet stood talking with me a heavy shower of Hail or rain commenced and on a sudden the vessel hauled to one side[.] I thought she was drifting with her two anchors but on running up to see the occasion we found the wind had chopped[4] round to the NNW and the Ship was in the act of swinging[.] The 19th or 20th the packet sailed and I forwarded a Letter to Miss L[5] the Cherokee Sloop of War of 12 Guns came in[.][6]

Sunday March 24th Lat 60°20 Long 0°38W

WSW or SW

The wind being favourable at about 6AM "knocked out"[7] all hands and as quickly as possible weighed the anchor hanging the Ship in the mean time by the Henrietta[8] with a warp sailed safely out of the Harbour and hove too at the mouth gave the Pilots some Beef Pease and Oatmeal a little Brandy also their fee for Pilotage and attendance then dismissed them made sail[.] At noon moss head[9] bore about SWbW distance 15 miles[.]

Monday March 25th Lat 62°51 23 Long 46"W[10]

WSW SW

Fresh gales fine weather [running?] along the land accompanied by the fleet[.] At 4

---

[1] This indicates that the available draught in Whitby harbour was insufficient to allow the *Resolution* to sail fully ballasted.

[2] In the original 'early' is inserted in pencil here.

[3] A transcription error, from 'specksioneer'. in the original journal. The term does exist in a variety of spellings, though not the one used in the transcript. 'The specksioneer or chief harpooner …': Scoresby, *Account of the Arctic Regions*, II, p. 200; Smyth, *Sailor's Word Book*, s.v. 'Specktioneer'; *OED* lists additional variants.

[4] 'Chop' in a nautical context, *OED*: 'Of the wind: To change, veer, or shift its direction suddenly'; Smyth, *Sailor's Word Book*, s.v. 'Chop-about, To'.

[5] Presumably his future wife, Mary Eliza Lockwood.

[6] HMS *Cherokee*, actually with 10 guns, built 1808.

[7] The meaning of this phrase is evident from the context, but it is not listed in *OED*, Partridge's *Dictionary of Slang*, or Smyth's *Sailor's Word Book*.

[8] One of the most famous Whitby whalers, 251 tons, built in 1764 and active in whaling until it was wrecked in 1834: Lubbock, *Arctic Whalers*, p. 299. William Scoresby Senior began his whaling career in the *Henrietta* in 1785, and commanded her from 1791 to 1797 (see Introduction, p. xxvi).

[9] A transcription error: 'Noss' in original. Noss Head, on the eastern coast of the Isle of Noss, is the highest point on the island (181 m).

[10] Another transcription error: '0° 46′W' in original.

PM passed Balta sound[.] at 5 PM the northernmost point of Zetland in Lat 60°50 North and Long 0°38W[1] bore WbN distance about 8 Leagues. In the evening when we had cleared the land we met a very heavy NW sea. This not suiting our Ships narrow bearings forward all the other ship [sic] out sailed us[.] The Sarah and Elizabeth[2] astern[.] In the morning about 9 AM called all hands secured anchors unbent the cables and sent them on deck to dry set steering sails[.][3] At noon charming fine weather course NbE or NNE velocity 2 to 7 knots[.]

Tuesday March 26th Lat 65°34N Long 2°9W
SWbS
The fore part fresh gales and fine weather coiled cables under seamens cabins divided men into boats crews lotted for the boats and crews amongst the Harponeers[.] In the evening 8 sail of ships in sight.

Observations of the time by Sun setting

Time p[4] Tables in this Lat with sun's Dec reduced 1° 41N	6	13	28
Equation of time	+		6 19
True time of sun setting	6	19	47
Time p watch 6h 21 40			
Long. 52W -3 40	6	18	0
Watch too slow	0	1	47

In the evening the wind increased took in studding sails top gallant sails and reefed the top sail[.] In the morning the wind increased to a hard gale [rate?] 7 or 7½ knots ship scudding before the wind[.]

Wednesday March 27th Lat 66°56N Long 1°28W
SWbW
The wind increased in the night and about 6 AM suddenly shifted to the NNE when a heavy gale again commenced[.] reduced sails to reefed fore sail main top sail and storm trysail[.] towards noon the wind rather subsided[.] The Thermometer fell to 25° and the Barometer at 10 AM was 29.29[.] Courses NEbN and NW[.]

Thursday March 28th Lat 66°52+N Long 1°45W
N NNE
The weather more moderate in the afternoon frost increasing set jib and mizen main stay sail &c[.] In the evening cloudy with some snow[.] Calm for 2 hours in the night suddenly a breeze sprung up from the NNE which increased to a strong gale[.] In the morning the Thermometer was at 22° and at noon at 19° courses WNW to NE[.]

---

[1] Lamda Ness, on the northeast coast of Yell, is at 60°49'06"N 0°45'52"W.

[2] A Hull whaler, 270 tons, built in Maryland in 1775: Credland, *Hull Whaling Trade*, p. 126.

[3] Smyth, *Sailor's Word Book*, s.v. 'Studding sails': 'Fine-weather sails set outside the square-sails; the term "scudding sails" was formerly used.' At p. 654, Smyth declares 'steering-sail' 'an incorrect name for a studding-sail'.

[4] Used regularly in Scoresby's journal, 'p' appears to be an abbreviation for 'per', i.e. 'by means of'.

Friday March 29ᵗʰ Lat 67°0N Long 2°27W
N
Moderate breezes in the afternoon severe frost with some snow sea high[.] In the evening the Aurora Borealis was uncommonly brilliant[.] Calm for the space of 2 hours in the night and then a light breeze sprung up which towards noon had increased to a Brisk gale[.] A good deal of snow fell courses WNW, NbW, NNE &c.

Saturday March 30ᵗʰ
ESE
Fresh breezes cloudy weather with almost constant snow[.] In the evening I fancied we were near Ice from the snow not dissolved in the water[.] To satisfy myself of this I procured a bucket of Sea water and found its temperature was 33°[.] This degree of coldness indicated our near approach to some Ice[.] I gave orders for a particular look out accordingly[.]¹ At ½ 5 PM saw a few scattered pieces of Ice and afterwards we passed through what appeared to be broken up streams[.]

All hands were turned up at 9 AM to unload dismount the carriage Guns and stow them away[.]²

Sunday March 31ˢᵗ Lat 68°30+N Long 5°02W
ENE
Light moderate or breezes fine clear but cold weather meeting with several pieces of Ice seeing no seals and the wind being light tacked and stood to the ESE or SE[.] At 6 PM a ship hove in sight a head standing towards us which proved to be the Sarah and Elizabeth of Hull. she tacked and and [sic] stood after us[.] At mid'nt we tacked and stood in towards the Ice which we made about 6½ am consisting of disseminated heavy pieces and brash streams[.] stood in NbW tacking occasionally until we came to Ice so close as to be impassable[.] A few miles west appeared to be an impervious[.] The Ice was washed and moderately heavy[.] Saw but one seal which was in the water[.] Tacked and steered close hauled by the wind towards the Sea[.] The Sarah and Elizabeth and [sic] few miles to leeward of us. The sea rather turbulent from the Ewᵈ· About noon the moon and Sun being visible took seven sets of observations on the time distance and altitudes from which and the time regulated again in the afternoon the Longitude of the Ship proved to be 5°2W[.] Watch per Greenwich 1'35 too slow[.]

Monday April 1ˢᵗ Lat +69°41 Long 3°31W
Nerly NWbW
Light airs fine clear frosty weather[.] A Fresh springing up in the Afternoon stopped our Course to the NE passed straggling small pieces of Ice. The Aurora Borealis was uncommonly brilliant in the twilight it assumed a smoky tinge[.] About 8 AM passed several streams of heavy Ice left some to the Eᵈ of us afterwards found ourselves

¹ At the end of March, in latitude 68°N, the sun would be above the horizon for rather less than 14 hours, with approximately another hour of civil twilight (sun 6° or less below horizon.)
² The whaling fleet was vulnerable to attack by privateers and enemy vessels only in ice-free areas. See Introduction, p. xlviii.

within much Ice steered out to ESE until we again got clear saw one large seal on a piece of Ice in the midst of a stream[.]

Tuesday Apl 2ⁿᵈ Lat 69°40 Long 1°11E
NWbW
The fore part fresh breezes and squally fine clear weather found ourselves somewhat entangled in the Ice steered to the ESE and SE when being clear of the Ice hauled by the wind[.] The latter part light breezes inclinable to calm[.] Cloudy weather with snow[.] cut foregangers[1] spliced in harpoons and placed 2 boats at the Qarters [sic] of the Ship course EbS to SE[.]

Wednesday Apl 3ʳᵈ
SW
The fore part moderate or fresh breezes cloudy some small showers chryst snow running under brisk sail to the ENE no Ice to see[.]

At 10 PM passing some pieces of heavy Ice hauled the Ship by the wind and reduced the sails. The latter part the wind increased to a severe gale accompanied with thick showers of snow. Through carelessness or mistake of orders the Ship was allowed to drift to leeward so far that in the morning entangled in a difficulty[.] we were amidst a number of heavy pieces of Ice the sea very high made as much sail as we could carry and steered Southwᵈ by the wind (9 AM) met a rugged patch of Ice[,] wore[2] and at 10 wore again the wind having shifted. The snow now cleared away we were yet amongst many pieces of heavy Ice[.] A Ship in sight to SW made sail by the wind to the SWᵈ[.]

Thursday Apl 4th Lat 70°53N Long 5°4E
WNW
The fore part fresh gales squally sea high more moderate towards evening. Lay too during the night and at Day light made all sail to the ENEᵈ[.]

The Day being charmingly fine hauled on deck the part of the small bower cable[3] which was put below damp[.] At noon no Ice to see[.]

Friday Apl 5ᵗʰ Lat 70°49′ Long 7°15E
NW
Fresh breezes the sky became suddenly overcast with clouds and the wind skimmed

---

[1] These preparations were described in detail by Scoresby, *Account of the Arctic Regions*, II, pp. 230–32. Briefly, the foreganger was a piece of rope about eight or nine yards in length that was spliced to the shank of the harpoon, and its other end spliced to the whale-line. It was stronger and more flexible than the tarred whale-line, and therefore less of a drag when the harpoon was thrown.
[2] Smyth, *Sailor's Word Book*, s.v. 'Veer, To': 'In tacking it is a necessary condition that the ship be brought up to the wind as close-hauled, and put round against the wind on the opposite tack. But in veering or wearing, especially when strong gales render it dangerous, unseamanlike, or impossible, the head of the vessel is put away from the wind, and turned round 20 points of the compass instead of 12, and, without strain or danger, is brought to the wind on the opposite tack.'
[3] Smyth, *Sailor's Word Book*, s.v. 'Bower-Anchors': 'They are called best and small, not from a difference of size, but as to the bow on which they are placed; starboard being the best bower, and port the small bower.'

along the water in the heavy squalls[.] Snow showers quickly followed. Coyled away the cable[.] About 4 PM fell in with Ice[.] lay too during the night[.] The Fountain of Lynn near us[.]

At 4 PM Longitude p Watch 5° 51 E[.]

Very squally throughout the night snow Showers and frost rime. At 9 AM the Therm*ometer* stood at 18°[.] At that time made sail passing the skirts of the Ice amongst disseminated pieces streams &c saw no seals[.] At noon met a strong ENE sea indicating that there is no Ice in that direction[.]

Saturday Apl 6ᵗʰ Lat 71 25 Long 10 53E
North
Fresh gales and squally showers of snow and sometimes thick frost rime[.][1] found ourselves at Sea at 1 PM after that saw no Ice so we went to the Eᵈ[.] The Fountain to leeward of us[.] In the morning [snow?] moderate weather thick frost rime made sail no ships or Ice to see[.] at 9 AM Therm*ometer* 10°[.]

Sunday Apl 7ᵗʰ Lat 71°29 Long 10°41
NNW EbS
Moderate breezes at noon which towards sun set increased to a fresh gale exceedingly squally and variable accompanied with thick showers of snow[.] At 3 PM the Therm*ometer* had risen to 17° and at 6 PM to 27° this remarkable rise of 17° in about 9 hours made me suspect a SE wind and as the Barometer lowered to 29.50 It might be expected to be a severe gale[.] I walked the deck somewhat alarmed at the appearance of the sky in the intervals of the Showers. At one time a strong light like an Ice blink[2] appeared from NNE to ESE or EbS though there was no Ice in that Quarter. In

---

[1] Scoresby, *Account of the Arctic Regions*, I, pp. 434–6: '*Frost-rime* or frost-smoke, is a meteor peculiar to those parts of the globe, where a very low temperature prevails for a considerable time. It consists of a dense frozen vapour, apparently arising out of the sea or any large sheet of water, and ascending, in high winds and turbulent seas, to the height of 80 or 100 feet … The particles of which it consists are as small as dust, and cleave to the rigging of ships, or almost any substance against which they are driven by the wind, and afford a coating of an inch or upwards in depth ….'

'Frost-rime sometimes appears at a temperature of 20° or 22° [F.]; but generally, it is not observed until the cold is reduced to 14°. It is most abundant in the lowest temperatures, with a high sea and strong winds ….'

Modern terms for the phenomenon are 'steaming water' or 'arctic sea-smoke'. It therefore differs in formation from *hoar frost*, i.e. 'a crystalline icy deposit formed in the same manner as dew when the temperature is below freezing point' (UK, Meteorological Office, *Observer's Handbook*, p. 53) through the transformation of water vapour into ice without passing through the liquid stage, and is closer to *rime*, a similar deposit from supercooled water droplets in a fog. Scoresby's description in *An Account of the Arctic Regions* is an accurate explanation of its formation, as air is warmed by the sea surface over which it passes, and therefore evaporates moisture from the surface. The warming causes the air to rise, which leads to cooling and consequent condensation of the moisture as the saturation vapour pressure is reached.

[2] Scoresby, *Account of the Arctic Regions*, II, pp. 299–300: 'On approaching a pack, field, or other compact aggregation of ice, the phenomenon of the *ice-blink* is seen whenever the horizon is tolerably free from clouds, and in some cases even under a thick sky. The *ice-blink* consists in a stratum of lucid whiteness, which appears over ice in that part of the atmosphere adjoining the horizon.' Scoresby

the midst of a thick shower (wind NNE) it cleared up to the SE^d [.] I instantly suspected the wind would prevail from that Quarter so it proved for about 10 minutes afterwards a shake of the Sails was observed and immediately they were taken flat a back.[1] The wind had veered[2] to ESE steered Nward 2 hours the wind tho increased so much that we were obliged to raise all hands to take in and reef top sails and Troy sail[3] till Day light and then wore. At 6 blowing an excessive hard gale furled all sail but M T Sail and [***] Troy sail under this sail lay too[.] The sea became immensely high the vessel was very kindly[4] and shipped very little water laying quite close to the wind[.] Thus the us [sic] of a Thermo*meter* connected with Barometer. The Cabin smoking [sic] we could not have a fire[.]

Monday Apr 8th Lat 70°56 Long 10°[30?]E
ENE
The whole of this Day very severe gales with heavy squalls frequent showers of rough unchryst snow laying too and drifting to the Southw^d[.] Had occasion to lift up the lee quarter boat and lash the rings to the head of the Davits[.] In the morning a cross sea arose from the NNE which combining with the Easterly swell formed a very danger-ous sea rising very high in knots so that it was impossible for a vessel to rise over it[.] About 10½ AM a heavy sea of this description struck the ship on the quarters. It lifted up the [weather?] [5]and unhooked one of the tackcles [sic] though moused[6] and let it drop into the Ground (***) it had filled the lee quarter boat with water lifted [a lee Gun?] over its cleats and turned it fore and aft filled the Chock boat stove in the waist boards on both sides and most of the quarter boards mercifully however the Men all got secure themselves from its violence and no serious damage was done we were obliged to put in the dark lights[7] and then wore the Ship[.]

[*At this point the date headings for four pages indicate the year 1812. They later revert to 1811 and it is clear that a later hand corrected some but not of all of these pages.*]

---

provides an explanation for its appearance, and states that it 'enables the experienced observer to judge whether the ice thus pictured be field or packed ice: if the latter, whether it be compact or open, bay or heavy ice'. The *OED*, s.v. 'ice-blink', gives Scoresby as one of the first to use this term in print.

[1] Smyth, *Sailor's Word Book*, s.v. 'Flat-aback': 'When all the sails are blown with their after-surface against the mast, so as to give stern-way.'

[2] In modern maritime meteorological terminology, 'veer' is used to denote a change of direction that, as here, is clockwise or 'follows the sun', and the verb 'back' is used for wind changes in an anticlockwise direction. Scoresby, however, used the term 'veer' for changes in either direction.

[3] A variant spelling of 'trysail', a fore and aft sail set on the lower main mast. See Smyth, *Sailor's Word Book*, s.vv. 'Trysail' and 'Storm-trysail'.

[4] Layton, *Dictionary of Nautical Words and Terms*, s.v. 'sea kindliness': 'that characteristic of a ship by which she behaves well in heavy weather, and accommodates herself to varying states of the sea'.

[5] If this reading is correct, Scoresby may have intended to write 'weather-side', i.e. the side of the ship facing the wind.

[6] Smyth, *Sailor's Word Book*, s.v. 'Mouse': '*to mouse a hook*, to put a turn or two of rope-yarn round the point of a tackle-hook and its neck to prevent its unhooking.'

[7] A variant of 'deadlights' (*OED*, s.v. 'dark'), shutters used to protect cabin windows in heavy weather.

Tuesday Apl 9ᵗʰ Lat +70°25 Long 8°15E
NNE
The fore part very hard Gales and squally with Showers of Snow or opaque hail[.] Laying too as before Sea still very high but the Nerly Sea meeting the Ship a head she was uncommonly dry never scarcely shipping a spray[.] The latter part the wind decreased but was yet squally[.] at 8 AM it was pretty moderate set the fore Top sail and Fore sail[.] At 11 AM made as much sail as we could prudently carry[.] No ships or Ice in sight.

Wednesday Apl 10ᵗʰ Lat 70°32N Long 6°58E
NNE
Fresh or Strong Gales and Squally[.] Variable with some Showers of Snow. Thermo*meter* fell from 28° to 15[.] At 8 PM saw a large hummock of Ice which at first appeared like a Ship – tacked. Towards morning the wind increased and becoming very squally reduced the Sails to close reefed Top sails. Frost rime now began to make its appearance. Courses NW EbS and NWbN[.]

Thursday Apl 11ᵗʰ
NE
Dark Cloudy Weather and fresh or Strong Gales of Wind accompanied with Frost rime[.] At 3 PM passed a piece of Ice like a Brig. At 8 PM tacked[.] At 4 AM again tacked and at 9 fell in with disseminated pieces of Ice amongst which we went. Afterwards fell in with Streams[.] At 10½ AM tacked and stood out to Sea[.] Snow showers sometimes cryst at others opaque shapeless[.] Masses of hail[.] Courses NNW SEbE NbW[.]

Friday Apl 12ᵗʰ Lat 70°52N Long 6°0E
ENE NEbE
Fresh gales squally with Showers of Snow and strong ESE Sea. The fore part stood to the SE the latter to NWbW[.] At 8½ AM fell in with loose Ice and at 9 with streams composed of mixed Ice[.] Passed a very heavy Ice Berg 100 feet in length round on the top and shaped like a [*blank space*][1] Buoy[.] At noon were come to the edge of a continuous pack seemingly composed of pieces of heavy and light Ice indiscriminately mixed. Did not see a single Seal. Tacked and stood back by the wind[.]

Saturday Apl 13ᵗʰ Lat 70°18N Long 8°57E
NEbE
Fresh breezes with strong squalls[.] Met a heavy ESE Sea on the Larboard[2] tack which caused the Ship to pitch uncommonly heavy[.] About 3 PM passed through an opening in a heavy stream the passage crossed by many heavy pieces of Ice in a state of great agitation, some of them actually were forced at the rate of a knot to Windwᵈ[.]

---

[1] In the original a short word was inserted above the line of text, but it is illegible, as it presumably was also to the transcriber.
[2] Port or left side of the ship. The similarity of 'larboard' and 'starboard' (right side) caused so many errors that the Admiralty ordered the term 'larboard' to be dropped in 1844.

About 6 PM were out at Sea. Took in the Main Sail for Squalls in the night. In the Morn[g] charming fine weather[.] Employed Harponeers splicing in foregangers, and initiated the Seamen into the art of reefing Sails in the best and neatest manner[.] Courses steered SEbE, SE[.]

Sunday Apl 14th Lat +70°52N Long 8°59E
Var EbN East
Moderate breezes fine Clear Weather. Sea high from the ENE[.]. At 2 AM in a Snow Shower of thick flakes it fell [***]. The Snow became powdered and a gale of a sudden sprang up from the SE it scarcely continued 5 minutes when again it fell calm[.] this continued 10 or 13 Minutes Snowing in the meantime when a EbN Gale commenced which gradually fell to a fresh or moderate breeze[.] In the morning delightful Clear weather saw some Bottlenoses Finners[.][1] Steered to the E[d] or NE[.]

Monday Apl 15th Lat 72°36+N Long 13°30
EbS
Fine moderate weather towards noon fresh gales uncommonly clear[.] Therm*ometer* at 3 PM 34°[.] At 6 AM until 9 AM passed through some newly formed Ice – Called by the Sailors sludge. courses steered NEbN to ENE[.]

Tuesday Apl 16th Lat 74°31N Long 16°32E
SEbS
The fore part fresh Gales and fine Clear Weather [Running?] in open water to the NE at the rate of 7 knots[.] At 10 PM reduced Sails to two treble reefed Top Sails Fore Sail and Troy Sail[.] The latter part fresh or Strong Gales and cloudy[.] At 5 AM came

---

[1] 'Bottlenoses' refers to the bottlenose dolphin: *Tursiops truncatus*. Scoresby's description of the 'finner' in *Account of the Arctic Regions*, II, pp. 484–5 may refer to the Sei whale (*Balaenoptera borealis*), but it also seems possible that whalers described more than one species as 'finners'.

As with other biological forms, the taxonomy of cetaceans (whales, dolphins and porpoises) has become much more complex than it appeared to be in Scoresby's day. In *Account of the Arctic Regions*, I, pp. 449–501 he described the following 'Animals, of the Cetaceous Kind, frequenting the Greenland Sea' and used the classification of both Linnaeus (Linné) and La Cépède:

BALÆNA MYSTICETUS: – The Common Whale, or Greenland Whale.
BALÆNOPTERA *Gibbar* (La Cepède:) – *B. physalis* of Linné, or Razor-back of the whalers.
BALÆNOPTERA *Rorqual* (La Cepède:) – *Balæna Musculus* of Linné, or Broad-nosed Whale.
BALÆNOPTERA *Jubartes*, (La Cepède:) – *Balæna Boops* of Linné, or Finner of the whale-fishers.
BALÆNOPTERA *Avuto-rostrata*, (La Cepède:) – *Balæna rostrata* of Linné, or Beaked Whale.
MONODON *Monoceros* (Linné:) – *Narwhal*, or Unicorn of the whalers.
DELPHINUS *Deductor*, (Traill). – Ca'ing or Leading Whale.
DELPHINAPTERUS *Beluga* (La Cepède:) – *Delphinus leucas* of Linné; *Beluga* of Pennant, or White Whale of the fishers.

Nowadays the aquatic mammals (order Cetacea) are divided into two main sub-orders, Odontoceti and Mysticeti. The toothed whales (Odontoceti) are divided into several families, in which are found beaked, bottlenose, sperm and beluga whales, narwhals, porpoises and dolphins. There are three families of baleen, or toothless, whales (Mysticeti); the Balænidae, which includes the bowhead; the Eschrichtidae, containing only the gray whale of the North Pacific, and the Balænopteridae or rorquals, including humpback, sei, minke, fin and blue whales, among others.

in thick with snow[.] At 5½ AM hauled by the wind to the E^d and lay too[.] soon after saw some pieces of Ice made sail to the S^d and at 10 AM tacked. Passed a very high piece of a Berg supposed it might be 50 or 60 feet Above the Sea. From this and some Ducks seen suppose we may be near Cherry Island[1] and too far to the E^d for a passage North[.] Steered by the Wind[.] At noon no Ice to see[.] Weather hazy[.]

Wednesday Apl 17th Lat 75°24N Long 15°4W
WbS
Fresh gales or fresh breezes constantly hazy. Sometimes the eye could not penetrate more than ¼ a mile thro' the fog. Having stood off to the NW for 4 hours at 4 PM bore away NNE[.] At 11½ PM hove too head to the N^d soon after saw a piece of Ice[.] At 6 saw many small pieces[.] At 8 AM clearing up somewhat – saw a pack of Ice to leeward 4 or 5 Miles from us extending as far as could be seen in a direction NWbN to SEbS or NNW to SSE some small portions of water were observable in it though chiefly it was close seemingly composed of <u>heavy</u> or <u>light</u> or <u>bay</u> Ice indiscriminately mixed. Tacked at 8 AM and made sail to the NW^d at a Distance from the pack edge; at noon fell in with several brash Streams[.]

Thursday Apl 18th Lat 75°34N Long 13°46°E
SWbW
The fore part fresh the latter strong gales constantly hazy or foggy[.] (By hazy I mean that wetting haze and which resembles very small rain and is sometimes termed <u>Scotch Mist</u>. By Fog I would imply the thick mist often occurs here in particular seasons and which wets very little.[)] Tacked at 2 PM for streams of Brash intermixed with heavy Ice[.] pursued our course again at 3 PM to the NW into open water[.] About 4¾ PM saw two Ships laying under easy sail to the N^d bore down supposing there must be some reason for it. They proved to be the Henrietta of Whitby and Bernie of Grimsby[.] Captn Kearsly[2] informed me that he had been in a bight or Bay of the Ice to the Westward three Day ago had seen many seals but only got 11.[3] He had since that been at the bottom of the which[4] we are now in and about to survey –

---

[1] Now Bjørnøya or Bear Island (74°30′N 19°E) but also known to the British earlier as Cherie Island. In *Account of the Arctic Regions*, I, pp. 79, 152, Scoresby explained the derivation of both names. If his position on this date was accurate, the *Resolution* was rather less than 50 miles west of Bear Island.

[2] *Sic*. Captain Kearsley was master of the *Henrietta*.

[3] Gordon Jackson noted (*British Whaling Trade*, p. 144) that 'seals had always been a possible make-weight on unsuccessful whaling expeditions'. Both skins and oil were important, especially in the mid-19th century; 'Almost a million skins were taken by British vessels in the years 1848–57.' In Scoresby's day, however, 'Not above one or two vessels, at a time, have been fitted out of Britain, entirely for the seal-fishery, for many years, but from the ports of the Elbe and the Weser a number of sealers are annually despatched.': *Account of the Arctic Regions*, I, p. 512. For the Greenland Sea whaling fleet, in normal circumstances sealing was a distraction from the main purpose, for two reasons: (a) forty to fifty seals were needed to yield a ton of oil; (b) the principal area for commercial sealing was around Jan Mayen in March and April, when the whaling captains were anxious to find a way through the ice barrier further north (see Scoresby's *Account*, I, pp. 508–17).

[4] A transcription error; 'the sinuosity which' in the original.

a Pack lay about 8 or 10 Miles further to leeward[.] The Sea being too high to attempt a passage into the Pack we thought it prudent to remain in our present situation until some change, therefore put the Ship under and [*sic*] easy sail and plyed across between the two bodies of Ice found a breadth of about 20 Miles [Wore?] at 2 AM and 10 AM.[.] At noon the Bernie only in sight[.]

Friday Apl 19ᵗʰ Lat 75°59N Long 12°E
SW
Strong Gales which decreased to a light breeze by noon[.] Plying too and fro by the wind[.] At 7 AM were near loose Ice and made some sail to the Northᵈ[.] At noon were amongst scattered pieces of Ice and brash streams[.] 5 Sail of Ships in Sight[.] At 10 AM saw the Land near Point Look out[1] bearing NE½E[.] Distance thirty six Miles. From this it appears that my reckoning was nearly correct even within ten English Miles[.][2]

Saturday Apl 20ᵗʰ Lat 76°21 Long 12°E
NW
Calm for a Short time in the afternoon afterwards a fresh increasing to a Strong breeze sprung up – Made a board to Windwᵈ to clear a close stream[.] The Sea considerable. Saw from the Mast head a large opening of water to the NNW or NW[.] Coming in thick we could only proceed according to the estimated bearing pursued a NW to NWbN course for two hours amongst open Ice fell in occasionally with very awkward and difficult passages where nothing but very cross openings appeared. At 4½ PM found ourselves in the opening at which we aimed. Steered NNW or NbW for other 4 hours[.] At 7 PM came across streams which we avoided as well as we could in the thick snow. At 9 PM found ourselves stopped by a barrier of heavy Ice. Shortened Sail and dodged the rest of the Day[.] At 10 PM clearing up saw the Land. In the Morning Captⁿ Volum of the Enterprize[3] took Breakfast with me. He is a good Scotch Character and a person of intelligence. I found the Ice closely packed to the Eastward NE and Nᵈ of us a little slack to the NWᵈ[.] A few Ships in Company[.] At noon the Land was particularly clear Point Look Out bearing E½S[.] Distance about 35 to 40 Miles[.]

Sunday Apl 21ˢᵗ Lat 76°30 Long 11°E
NbE
Light breezes sometimes calm. At noon called all hands (Saturday civil Day) got all the Whale Lines on deck took one boat out of the tween decks, sorted all the Lines and coyled away those of 4 Boats viz two in the tween decks, the six oared Boat on

---

[1] Then the British name for the southern tip of Spitsbergen (76°34′N, 16°40′E), close to which the land rises to 695 m: Scoresby, *Account of the Arctic Regions*, II, Plate VII.

[2] If Scoresby was indeed close to 76°N, 12°E at 10 a.m. he would have been approximately 75 nautical miles from the southern headland.

[3] The *Enterprise* of Peterhead. There are several references to Captain W. Volum and the *Enterprise* from 1804 onwards in Lubbock, *Arctic Whalers*. Lubbock also noted (Appendix G) that Captain J. Volum was master of the Peterhead whaler *Joseph Green* from 1832 onwards.

deck and the Stern Boat fitted them for the fishery. Saw several Razor Backs. The Ice is somewhat open to the N[d] but still impervious with a plying wind.[1] The Ice around us open 23 Sail of Ships in sight mostly to the S[d][.] At noon Point Look out at EbS½[.] Distance 40 Miles[.]

Monday Apl 22nd Long 10°50E
Erly
Light airs calm or a moderate breeze. The Ice opening some Distance to the North-ward made sail amongst loose pieces. I Dined on board the Burnie Captn Hornbie[2] by whom I together with Cap[tn] Johnson W Kearsley, Kearsly[3] and Robinson were well entertained[.] At 10 PM were becalmed. the water began to freeze. In the night the Ice closed upon and beset us.

The Ice hereabouts is not heavy chiefly small pieces[.] From the <u>formation of Clouds</u>[4] to the Northward of us and even the <u>breeding</u> of Showers I am strongly persuaded there is much water to the North[d][.] I have little doubt but if a Ship had been hereabouts immediately after the strong Easterly gale of the 6th to 10th Ap[l] a free passage as far as wished might have been obtained. The Western Sky shews much water in that direc-tion. From the SE to NNW or NW is a body of closely packed Ice. At 10 PM had a Boat in pursuit of a whale the first seen this year by us. In the Morning the Sarah and Eliza-beth hoisted her Jack as a signal of having struck a Whale.[5] Towards noon the Ice slacked but left not room sufficient to get under sail therefore lay moored to two pieces of Ice drifting fast however to the Southw[d][.] 4 Ships a Mile N 3 to leeward in sight[.]

Tuesday Apl 23rd Lat +76°34 Long 10°E
North
Moderate or light breezes. Charming clear weather very cold. Icy particles were seen in great abundance floating in the Atmosphere during during [sic] the Evening; they consisted of elegantly formed slender crystals[.][6] About 15 sail of Ships were yester-day 15 miles to the SSW to Day at 2 PM they bore SE 15 and at noon ENE Distance 7 or 8 Miles yet I believe they made little progress thro' the Ice but have obtained this advantage merely by the Currents[.] We drifted much to leeward the fore part altho' moored to two pieces of Ice the middle and latter parts by the formation of bay Ice were kept pretty stationary amongst the heavy Ice about us which in a great measure beset us. Little water to be seen. No prospect of moving the Ship[.] Five sail of Ships within 2 or 3 miles of us 23 altogether in sight[.]

Since nothing could be done with the Ship I thought this opportunity of trying the

[1] Scoresby implies that ice-breaking was impossible when beating into the wind from NbE.
[2] *Sic*. Correctly, Capt. Hornby of the *Birnie*.
[3] The original journal is: '... together with Capt[ns] Johnson, W. Kearsley, J [or I?] Kearsley, & Robinson ...'.
[4] In the original this phrase is not underlined, but 'breeding' in the same sentence is.
[5] See Scoresby, *Arctic Regions*, II, pp. 521–5: 'Signals Used in the Whale-Fishery.' See also the journal entry for 26 June 1811.
[6] These were probably ice prisms, 'unbranched ice crystals, in the form of needles, columns or plates, often so tiny that they seem to be suspended in the air. These crystals may fall from a cloud or from a cloudless sky.': World Meteorological Organization, *International Cloud Atlas*, p. 56.

Instrument Sir J Banks politely presented me with for ascertaining the Temperature of the Ocean at considerable depths.[1] Having suspended it with cords and adjusted the Therm*ometer* by bringing the Metallic pieces to the surface of the Quicksilver when standing at the Teperature [*sic*] of the Water at the Surface (30)[2] I allowed it to sink first 20 then 40 then 60 and lastly to the depth of 100 fathoms each time noting the range of the register Thermometer and the Temp when arrived at the top by A Common Therm*ometer* also the time of drawing up which in the last was 2′,40[.][3] The Instrument however was not water tight in the Valves & after the last Experiment two of the seams were opened the wood soaked with water and much swelled out in the middle between the two Strong Brass Hoops supporting the ends[.] The curve formed by this swelling broke both the glass plates on the sides. From these Experiments similar conclusions were drawn with those last year an increase of 6⅔° of Temp took place in a descent of 60 Fathoms the same occurred at more at 100. At 40 Fathoms the Temp was 36° and at 20 – 32°[.] Tho' the wind was very light and the drift of the Ice inconsiderable the line by which the Instrument was let down was drawn much from the Perpendicular towards the NE shewing an under current running with considerable velocity in that direction, which also agrees with my surmises of last year. I was afraid to risque the Instrument at any greater depth than 600 feet lest it should have been rent to pieces and prevent the possibility of performing more experiments on this interesting topic[.][4] At noon Point Look Out bore ESE Distant 15 Lea*gues*[.]

Wednesday Apl 24th Lat 76°45N Long 10°E
NW
The fore part light breezes the middle part calm, the latter fresh Gales[.] Altho' we were surrounded by Bay Ice and heavy Ice intermixed I thought it practicable getting to the E[d] into a small opening about two miles Distant – At 2 PM Cast off and made sail crashing the Bay Ice by means of a Boat which also carried out a Grapnel occasionally fixed to a Whale line to any piece of Ice sufficient to pull along the Ship. In 4 Hours got into this opening were soon thro' it persevered to the NE[d] or N[d] towing

[1] Sir Joseph Banks, President of the Royal Society. See Introduction, p. xxx and note 3, p. 183.
[2] Scoresby was describing the normal procedure for setting either a maximum or minimum thermometer. A ferrous marker is drawn by an external magnet held by the observer until the marker rests on top of the mercury of the thermometer. Subsequent fall (minimum thermometer) or rise (maximum thermometer) of the mercury will then push the marker to a new location, where it will remain until read and reset by the observer. '(30)' presumably means a sea-surface temperature of 30° F., a normal reading in saline water close to the ice margin. In the original the phrase is '… when standing at the Temp. of the Water at the Surface (30°) …'.
[3] Presumably 2 minutes and 40 seconds.
[4] Scoresby summarized his measurements of sea temperature at various depths between 1810 and 1817 in *Account of the Arctic Regions*, I, pp. 184–8. See Introduction, pp. lx–lxi. The table on p. 187 includes the measurements on 23 April 1811, but differs from the journal in that the temperature at 20 fathoms (120 feet) is given as 31.0°, not 32°, and at 40 fathoms 35.0°, not 36°. The table also indicates a smaller rise in temperature with depth (from 30.0° F. at the surface to 35.0° at 360 feet) than the journal statement of 6⅔°. Note also that the journal entry indicates that Scoresby did not risk using the device below 100 fathoms, whereas in *An Account of the Arctic Regions* Scoresby stated that the device was damaged at 300 fathoms.

warping &c. amongst moderately open Ice. About mid'nt having come to a pretty large opening lay in it until morning. The Neptune[1] in Company. – A constant Snow commenced about 7 AM[.] At 11 altho' thick weather bore away before the wind amongst Bay intermixed with heavy pices [sic] of Ice; at first the heavy pieces were pretty much scattered. The Neptune followed[.]

Thursday Apl 25ᵗʰ Lat 76°58 Long 10°⅓E
S to W
Fresh or strong Gales of Wind the Middle of the night light or Moderate breezes. – All the Day constant snow frequently very thick always and finely crystallized.

Continued running almost in the dark for some miles having come to close Ice lay too purposing to drift thro' it [.] About 2½ PM several Ships came near us and two passed us[.] Made sail and bored through the Ice (¼ mile) steered away to the Nᵈ amongst open Ice [.] At 3½ PM were arrived at what had the appearance of a close pack wore amongst Bay Ice and sailed out again worked a little to Windwᵈ an [sic] lay too. In the Night the opening closed run out to the SEᵈ. – At 8 AM while dressing myself I heard a bustle on deck ran up and observed a Ship (the Hope) of London[2] almost aboard of us. He attempted to come to Windward of us while we were in the act of Stays[3] or immediately following. consequently our Ship was under no command[.] Our Sprit sail Yard carried away one of his Quarter Boats Davids [sic]. the Boat was precipitated bottom upwards into the water. Two men in her escaped with a wetting. I believe the lines which were in the Boat were not lost. From what I could learn it evidently appeared the Hope alone was to blame[.]

Having got clear of this vessel made sail to the SEᵈ[.] Afterwards tho' blowing very fresh began to ply to Windward seeing a trifling opening merely to get from amongst the Ships 5 being together in a small opening endangered each other. Found the Ice being Cross and rather heavy however made good progress were followed presently by the Vigilant[4] Bernie Enterprize &c[.]

Friday Apl 26ᵗʰ Lat +77°0N Long 10⅓E
ENE
Sailed very safely until about 1 PM when having worked up into a very narrow passage opening into a small vacancy to the SEᵈ we were attacked by such a heavy

---

[1] There were whalers of this name from several ports, but the contemporary printed list shows this as a London vessel (Captain Robertson).

[2] Captain Gallaway. There was another *Hope* from Peterhead (Captain Sangster) in the 1811 whaling fleet: Lubbock, *Arctic Whalers*, p. 189; the contemporary printed list shows the master's name as 'Sangsten'.

[3] Smyth, *Sailor's Word Book*, s.v. 'Stay': '*In stays*, or *hove in stays*, is the situation of a vessel when she is staying, or in the act of going about.' The similar definition in *OED* includes a citation from Scoresby's *Voyage* (p. 91). I am grateful to Captain Barritt for observing that Scoresby was making the point that it was impossible for his ship to take action to avert collision. In the next century the international regulations for the prevention of collisions at sea codified the term 'not under command' to describe a vessel which is not under full powers of manoeuvrability so that other ships should keep clear of her.

[4] Of London.

squall that the Ship could scarcely sustain the pressure she kieled amazingly the Main Stay sail (an old sail) gave way in the <u>foot</u> were obliged to take it in[.] Not having room to take <u>in</u> Sail the Ship was overburthened by this insomuch that she became almost unmanageable. We drifted very heavily against one piece of Ice but avoided the rest of the heavy pieces[.] We were just drifting on the pack when I perceived room to tack bore downwind far aft to get room to turn in and then stayed[1] in the least room possible. Sailed into more room and then reefed the Top sails. Lay too a little then being more moderate altho' still thick with snow again made sail worked to Windw^d and passed the narrow to the SE^d steered thence by the wind or near it several miles to the SSE SE &c among rather open Ice. At 6½ PM found ourselves in a considerable opening surrounded by a Close Pack except to the NW^d from whence we had come[.] here rested for the Night[.] 27 Ships in sight half of them beset. In the Even^g wind moderate[.]

The wind continued light until 5 AM when it increased to a Strong Gale which at noon had somewhat moderated. Continued plying about in the same opening we arrived at last Evening. The Ships which were yesterday to the NW^d of us are now at the WNW or W[.] At noon the Land was in sight from SE to NNE[.]

Saturday Apl 27th
ENE
The wind decreased to a light breeze which continued until 7 AM when a strong breeze increasing to a fresh or strong Gale sprung up. The Ship being much out of trim and consequently in danger in the Evening filled 16 casks with water in the 3rd and 4th tiars [*sic*] of the Fore Hold this brought the Ship nearly upon an even keel[.] In the Morning I found the opening in which we dodged frozen over with Bay Ice of considerable thickness[.] At the edge of the Pack to Windw^d appeared a new opening being unfrozen[.] For this we aimed made much sail to force the Ship thro' the Bay Ice. Found the passage very difficult being thickly set with scattered pieces of heavy Ice[.] Several Ships gave up the point. ['**Sunday Apl 28th** Lat 77°4N' *in margin*] We persevered and about 4½ PM had reached this opening of Comfortable Magnitude and at 5 PM lay too at the weather edge. Soon after us several Ships arrived The Aimwell Vigilant James of Liverpool Enterprise Hope &c[.] The Aimwell Captn Johnston informed me was yesterday Morning <u>stove</u> in the <u>Bow</u> by running for an opening between several large pieces of Ice which closed upon this[.] The Captain was in bed. The Land in sight far distant one Ship to the NE^d of us 10 or 15 miles from us[.]

Monday Apl 29th
ENE
The wind continued strong all night the weather clear. At 10 AM a large opening having formed partly encompassed by heavy Ice to the North^d of us sailed into it where we saw two or three whales. The Hope and Vigilant each struck one both were lost. In the Afternoon the wind decreased to a light breeze – the water began to freeze

---

[1] Again in the sense of 'going about', not 'remaining'.

in several places[.] The Sun and Moon being both very clear took 9 Sets of Observations for finding the true distance from the mean of which the marginal Long*itude* was ascertained. I also took a set consisting of 3 observations of the Suns alt*itude* in which without the use of the Dec*lination* or Lat*itude* by account ascertained the Lat*itude* to 12 miles and the Declination pretty nearly consequently had given the Day of the month.[1] In the Evening the atmosphere was in a very uncommon state. The Air near the horizon though cloudless was so variable in Density that the Circumferential boundary appeared hilly replete with [ringes?] of ⅓ or ½ a degree of Alt*itude*[.][2] A ship also to the NE^d appeared to be upon her beam ends, but whether this were the Case or it was an optical deception I could not at this time determine[.] 8 Ships in Compa^y three of which ran off in the Evening to the SE 14 sail lay beset to the W^d of us[.] In the morning fine moderate weather water freezing in most places in sight. The case of the Ship last night proved to have been an optical deception for this morning she appeared in her natural position. Last night a Telescope of high magnifying power and Dollands construction was of little service owing to the bad state of the atmosphere every object at any distance appeared to have a tremulous motion. The refraction of the air was highly extraordinary proved by the Ship already mentioned. with regard to us her position is stationary being beset in close Ice[.] Now yesterday morning and this morning she appeared so far beyond the Horizon that all her hull and half her lower masts as seen by a good Telescope were intercepted by the Horizon (the Ice) so that she must be at least 4¼ Miles (the part intercepted being called 22 feet beyond the horizon and being seen from 90 feet elevation gives 9 miles to the horizon[3] and 4¼ beyond is 13¼ Miles the Distance of the Ship. Now such was the extraordinary retraction [*sic*] that this vessel though not the least altered in Distance appeared last evening far within the horizon a full Distance of 4 miles of Ice being seen beyond her and her hull appeared uncommonly high and her mast uncommonly short which gave the Idea to the Officer of the Watch who called me up saying "The Ship to the NE^d seems to be laid on her side or beam ends.["] Hence the refraction has been so great that the eye elevated 90 feet discerned the Horizon at the Distance of at least 17¼ miles which is more by 8¼ miles than is calculable from the Dip of the Horizon[.][4]

[1] These 'celestial observations' for latitude and longitude are not included in Scoresby's *Account of the Arctic Regions*, I, Appendix I.

[2] Scoresby provided a clearer description of this phenomenon in *Account of the Arctic Regions*, I, p. 390: 'The horizon on this occasion, between the east and north, though continuous, appeared curiously undulated. There appeared a difference of nearly a quarter of a degree, between the elevation of the highest and lowest portions of the circumferential boundary.'

[3] Scoresby was incorrect. At 90 feet elevation, the horizon distance is 12.8 statute miles, or 11.1 nautical miles. See Introduction, p. xlii.

[4] Scoresby again provided a clearer summary of these observations and calculations in *Account of the Arctic Regions*, I, pp. 389–90. His proposed explanation for such optical phenomena is 'That they are, probably, occasioned by the commixture, near the surface of the land or sea, of two streams of air of different temperatures, so as to occasion an irregular deposition of imperfectly condensed vapour, which, when passing the verge of the horizon, may produce the phenomenon observed.' Compare this to a more modern explanation: 'two layers of air of contrasting density – a cool and denser one under a warm one – act as a lens to bend light rays. This brings a distant, low-lying object into focus and makes it appear close at hand.': Ley, *The Poles*, p. 28.

Tuesday Apl 30th
North
Towards noon the Ice closed amazingly five Ships were crowded in a very small space; At mid'nt the Ice was nearly close being little wind. In the Morning a fresh breeze with constant snow came on from the S[d] at which time we were completely beset in bay and heavy Ice intermixed[.] To the E[d] and NE[d] and SE[d] appears nothing but a close pack of heavy Ice no chance at present of extricating ourselves. Several Ships in similar situations[.] The Aimwell which I before mentioned to have received a blow on the bow came near us and careened by means of shifting cables Guns boats; the canting tackle upon the Ice with a Kedge and the Top sails braced to the mast and hoisted up. By these means the place of the blow was got above the surface of the water – a small piece of the doubling was removed and renewed by the means of the Carpenters of the Aimwell and Resolution. Our Armourer supplied them with Bolts a complete job was made of it in a short time after which the Ship which was before leaky became tight[.]

Wednesday May 1st
SbE
In the Afternoon wind and weather continuing could not remove[.] The situation of our Ships not pleasant we are afraid we shall have sometime to remain here before we get to the N[d] what is most alarming is our drifting so fast from the Land with NE winds we have drifted off direct West. Have not now seen the Land since Sunday suppose we may be about 70 miles distant from it. estimated our distance at 60 miles at the time I got the last Lunar observation (viz last sunday Evening) and from which it would appear that the situation of [lands?] is pretty correctly stated in this Latitude. The usual ceremonies on suspending the Garland at Mid night[.][1]

Thursday May 2nd Lat 77°17 Long 8°10
SSE
The wind moderate snow showers occasionally – little alteration in our situation except that the Ship tho' beset gradually turned her head from NbE to ENE[.] A large opening formed to Windw[d] of us in which we saw some whales. The ship to the SE[d] came much nearer us and one which lay within 200 yards was removed to the distance of 3 Miles[.] 27 or 28 sail were in sight about this time. Fitted a Gaf Top sail[2] out of a Flying Jib which stood well[.] Unbent the Fore Sail and Fore Top Sail and bent other older sails[.]

Friday May 3rd
E to ENE
In the morning of Friday being clear weather and a fresh gale of wind I thought it

[1] See the more detailed descriptions of the Mayday celebrations in the 1812 and 1813 journals.
[2] Smyth, *Sailor's Word Book*, s.v. 'Gaff-topsail': 'A light triangular or quadrilateral sail, the head being extended on a small gaff which hoists on the topmast, and the foot on the lower gaff.' In *Account of the Arctic Regions*, II, pp. 197–8, Scoresby explained the value of this and other special sails in enabling the ship to be navigated through icy seas when most of the sailors were away in the whaleboats.

possible to remove the Ship into the opening above mentioned which lay not more than 200 yards from us. Therefore began to break the bay Ice near the Ship by means of a Boat which we run quite into the water; a small portion we severed by means of a small Ice Saw. The Ship lay with her head ENE we broke a passage a head carried out a Warp which we hove well tight and then forced the ['**Saturday May 4**[th]' *in margin*] Ship by Sallying.[1] Hove out with some difficulty employing all Hands for 2 or 3 hours in which time we moved the Ship through bay Floes about 120 yards nearly head <u>to wind</u> then coming to Ice which the Boats could not Break and at the same time the opening filling with Ice at which we aimed desisted and moored the Ship[.] The Aimwell came up our tract and lay close to us. Procured some Fresh Ice[.] Saw many Whales in the water to windw[d] one one [*sic*] near the Ship[.] The Chance

of Capture if even struck but small[.]

Sunday May 5th
E
The Wind continued to blow and increased to a Gale all accompanied with almost constant Snow, very little water to see[.] Many Ships in sight. Towards noon the Wind fell to nearly calm much Water appeared to the Southw[d][.] A probability of coming nearer it. I was not fond of the situation in which we now lay the Ice had frozen so thick about us that a Boat could scarcely break it. We were in the midst of a field of heavy pieces of Ice frozen together by Bay Ice. This should the Frost continue would in the space of a week or two, (were we to be so long detained) become impervious to our feeble efforts and be displaced by nothing less than a heavy Gale of Wind or great Swell[.] Therefore anxious ['Lat +77°34 **Monday May 6**[th]' *in margin*] to be in a less confined spot where the Ice would be more inclined to seperate[2] about noon set all Hands to work to break the Ice with two Boats for the space of about 150 yards where was a slacker place with more Bay Ice and tho' thinner than what we lay amongst. In some parts of the way we employed two Saws to cut the heavy pieces[.] The Aimwell being close by us took her men on board the Resolution employed also two of her Boats and lasked[3] her Bowsprit to our Stern thus we hove both Ships through together[.] we often stuck fast confined between two heavy pieces of Ice where was scarcely room for the Ship[.] here we made use of an occillatory Motion of the Ship by causing the Seamen to run from side to side to free her from the Ice which almost always succeedded [*sic*] whenever we were able to Sally the Ship was sure instantly to be in a state capable of Removal. This excellent plan was first used by my Father[.]

About 6 PM had accomplished our end in obtaining the recently frozen Bay Floes.

---

[1] *OED*: 'To rock (a stationary or slow-moving ship) by running from side to side in order to assist its progress.' See also the journal entry for the next day, 5 May 1811. In *My Father*, pp. 204–9 (and also in that journal entry), Scoresby claimed that his father was the first to adopt this method in an 'ice-bound ship for relieving her of any remediable pressure ... For the relief of this *lateral* pressure, no mechanical force, except the action of the wind on the sails ... had heretofore been considered as available, or had been applied. But my Father's device afforded a novel, as well as a powerfully available, agency'.

[2] *Sic*. This word is frequently misspelled in this form in the journals.

[3] *Sic*. 'Lashed' in the original.

Cut across one with a Boat to the SW^d in a direction for the nearest slack it however rapidly closed and over flapped in the tract of the boat[.] therefore changed our direction to about S warping along in the tract broken by means of one or more Boats made but slow progress for want of wind. Several Ships in sight employed in a similar manner to us. About mid night having come again to heavy Ice took in the Sails and let the Ship remain until morning[.] At [8?] AM again made sail the wind blowing a strong breeze and a swell apparently from the S^d having come in upon us, which in many places broke the Bay and seperated the heavy Ice[.] Warped and bore to the SE or ESE aiming at a large opening several miles distant[.] made good progress whilst the strength of the swell continued which until about 1 PM when it having much fallen ['**Tuesday May 7**^th Lat 77° 28 Long 8° 4E' *in margin*] and the Ice becoming closer the heavy pieces more approximated us made little progress. continued however to persevere breaking the Ice with a Boat sawing occasionally loosing the Ship by sallying warping &c at intervals or together. We frequently cut the Bay Ice round the larger pieces or heavy Ice at considerable distance whereby loosening that next the Ship[.] At 6 PM the wind had fallen much and at 11 PM it again increased scarcely any appearance of a swell at that time. The Aimwell near us[.] Many Ships in sight. About Mid Night had come to the edge of a Bay Floe which connected with several others extended quite out into the opening at which we aimed with very few heavy pieces of Ice intervening. With the Assistance of a Boat suspended at the Jib boom end and occasionally of a Whale line made good progress so that at 5½ AM had obtained the ['**Wednesday May 8**^th NNW' *in margin*] opening where we reefed Top Sails the wind blowing strong and plyed about until 2 PM when the heavy Ice setting together circumscribed our bounds in so small a space that we ran the Ship amongst the Bay Ice and furled the sails made fast to a piece of Ice soon afterwards.[1] The Aimwell came to us and moored to the same piece[.] Many ships in sight in a similar situation[.] The wind continued a Gale accompanied with showers of Snow the fore part of the Gale finely crystallized in the lamellar forms towards this time fell in granulated small particles – Several large lanes of Water break out commencing 4 Miles to the ESE of us and extending as far in a NNE direction or N as can be seen from the Mast head. Much heavy Ice intervenes and the wind being too far Nerly or we should attempt to get into them. Being now employed I commenced a set of observations on the freezing and thawing of water preparing materials for future Experiments and Analysis[.][2] I expelled most of the air from a 6 oz vial previously half-filled with water then corked it close first cooling it by means of Ice and Snow I exposed it to a Temp of 10° the Mouth downwards to observe the phenomen (*sic*) of its freezing it remained thus situated after being coold (*sic*) to near the freezing point for the space of 1½ hours ere it began to freeze[.] the process then went on rapidly and it was in a few hours quite consolidated[.] The Ice however had a remarkable appearance being so completely filled with air bubbles as to render it only translucent [.] I poured next into a quart Bottle about 1½ Pints of fine water got from

[1] The original is 'so afterwards'.
[2] These 1811 experiments do not appear to be the ones described by Scoresby in *Account of the Arctic Regions*, I, pp. 235–6.

Fresh Ice exposed it uncorked to the Temp of 10° in the open air. The process of freezing soon commenced first on the top next [started?] obliquely downwards in crystals, then the sides. When the sides were solid I could perceive plainly small bubbles of air rising upwards from the bottom in pretty rapid succession frequently many together[.] I left the Bottle exposed all night in the morning found the side burst out but the whole although intersected by small rents going across the bottle horizontally or diagonally as it stood on its base[.] I took out the Ice by breaking the Glass first gently heating it the cylinder had the following characters a semi trans mass or cone arose from the bottom having its base nearly equal to that of the bottle[.] at the top of the cylinder of Ice it had come nearly to a point. A lamina of about ½ an inch on the surface was also trans lucient[.] the rest perfectly transparent without a single air bubble. The semi transpart [*sic*] or translucient parts were so from the quantity of air bubbles these were very small and were partly arranged in lines shooting from the surface of the opacity diagonally upwards towards the centre[.] This curious form I think may be easily accounted for by considering the process of the freezing: The sides next the bottle first became congealed the evolved air had room to escape towards the centre if not through[.] the Ice at the surface freezing more rapidly towards the top than at the base caused the semi transparent Mass to assume the form of a Cone. Now when the centre began to freze [*sic*] the air had no where to make its escape therefore formed into bubbles lay confined in the last congeled [*sic*] part of the Water[.] It was then that the Bottle burst. I neglected mentioning that in the last Exp*erimen*t the vial was not injured altho' the cork was forced quite out and the Ice filled the neck of the vial yet not a drop of water was lost[.]

Thursday May 9th
NNW
Fresh gales small showers of snow. No alterations in our position this 24 hours. Had hoped the SW wind would be of service to us but it came on too feebly and was of short continuance[.] 30 sail of Ships were now in sight. The land seen at ENE Dist about 70 miles[.]

Friday May 10th Lat 77°10 Long 8 1/6E[1]
SW
Moderate breezes slight showers of snow. The water to the NE cloudy 4 Ships 12 miles to the S^d underway. Most of the other Ships like us beset. To Day made another observation on the freezing of water without air. The air being expelled by boiling in the vial it was removed on deck into a Temp of 12° or 14° where it continued boiling exposed to the Air for at least ½ an hour[.] It had long ceased and was a very considerable time ere the freezing commenced it then proceeded pretty rapidly and when the process was nearly complete the vial burst. The Ice had a similar to the last being semi-transp^t filled with small air bubbles throughout. Had the bottle not burst it would have been curious to have examined the air remaining above the Ice (the vial was reversed to prevent the admission of any external air) This might shew the quality of the air evolved when water freezes[.]

[1] Presumably an alternative form of '8°10′E'.

Saturday May 11th

North

Fresh Gales cloudy. Ice particles constantly floating in the air[.] Frost severe Thermo*meter* 9° did not rise to 12 for 24 hours removed the bread from the After hold into the Lockers and shaked the Casks[.][1]

Several lanes of water broke out some near us most of them closed again – Four fresh Ships appeared to the SE suppose if it were clear should be able to see at least 33 or 34 sail[.] It is very likely no Ships are to the North^d of this Ice.[2] 20 of the Ships in sight are like us closely beset amongst mixed Ice. A vast quantity of birds have been seen to Day. About 4 PM our Surgeon either induced by the love of gain of a 5^s/ bet or the fear of being called a coward stripped off the most of his clothes and committed his body to the water alongside the Aimwell swam a few yards and returned amidst the acclamations of the sailors who pronounced him mad[.]

Sunday May 12th Lat 77° Long 8°5E

NNW

Light or fresh breezes snow showers, small openings break out in many places but presently freeze[.] Whales seen in them as well as Narwhales and seals[.] Had a boat on one near the Ship but could not get fast[.]

Monday May 13th

SSE

The wind in the evening increased to a heavy Gale accompanied with thick Snow but was of short continuance. In the morning moderate again increased with Snow Showers[.] Many lanes of Water broke out to the N^d frost diminished. Thermo*meter* rose to 31° at 8 AM but about noon or 2 to 4 PM the 14° had fallen again to 18[3] the Wind then blowing a Gale[.] employed filling casks with Ice. Doubling Top Sail Sheets &c &c[.] several Ships to the S^d and W^d of us forcing to the E^d or N^d. We purposed trying to bore that way but in the interval of preparing the Ice closed. The William and Ann[4] near us Aimwell not ½ her length from us Enterprize and Hope within a Mile as well as the Bernie, Vigilant, James of Liverpool, Lyon, Volunteer and [*blank space*] to the Southw^d and Westw^{d,} 7 or 8 Miles[.] Dundee[5] Hope of London &c to the NW^d of us some Ships beset others in small openings pursuing the Whales[.] The land was seen last night at East of us Distant about 60 miles[.] This Morning had great hopes of being liberated the Wind however seeming to Shift too often to have any material

---

[1] Smyth, *Sailor's Word Book*, s.v. 'Shake, To': '*To shake a cask*. To take it to pieces and pack up the parts, then termed "shakes".'

[2] See journal entries for 1 and 17 June, and Introduction, p. lv.

[3] A transcription error. In the original it is '... about Noon or 2 to 4 Pm on the 14th had fallen again to 18° ...'.

[4] Of Whitby (Captain George Stevens). A painting of the *William and Ann* is reproduced in Lubbock, *Arctic Whalers*, at p. 176.

[5] *Dundee* (Captain Cooper) was the London whaler commanded by William Scoresby Senior from 1798 to 1802, in which his son made his first arctic voyage in 1800.

impression upon the Ice[.] Expected a swell the wind there also was too far Westerly[.][1] A swell is now our Chief hope although dangerous when heavy and amongst close Ice yet is little chance of getting to the N[d] without its aid to break up the Bay and thereby disentangle and set the heavy Ice at liberty[.][2]

Tuesday May 14th
WbN

The westerly Wind soon increased to a strong Gale accompanied with Snow Showers and followed by a severe frost[.] the Change of the Therm*ometer* in 15 hours was remarkable not less than 20°[.] At 9 AM 13th Therm*ometer* 31° 4 PM 18° and 11 PM 11° The Barometer also fell from 30.00 to 29.63 within 24 hours. The Wind blowing so hard we took out two towlines of 6 and 8 inches to the Ice to prevent us drifting foul of the Aimwell which lay within ½ her lenth [*sic*] astern. In the Evening the Ice began to seperate, the Bay from the heavy and not further from us than 100 yards towards the SW[d][.] In the morning this opening had so increased as to be of considerable size[.] supposing it might lead to the NE which we could not ascertain from the constant snow about noon prepared to sail[.]

Wednesday May 15th
NW

The Aimwell breaking the Bay Ice with a boat got out first we followed and worked to the N[n] extremity of the opening amongst patches and loose Ice; here we found nothing but fields Bay Ice containing masses of older formation disseminated throughout[.] Lay too[.] The opening increased to about 6 Miles N & S and 1½ to 2 miles E and Wwise. In the Morning it closed E and Wwise so that we had scarcely room to work the Ship[.] perceiving a large opening to the E or ESE made sail run down a narrow passage and went through another to the E[d] running from the first about 4 Miles EbN ENE where we again lay too at 7 AM[.] The Ice seems now to be inclined to open in a general way. Lanes may be seen all over to the N[d] and E[d] which increasing large sheets break off and drive to leeward thus closing on one hand as it opens on the other. This seems a good prospect for getting to the N[d] should the NW wind continue with sufficient force but am afraid but am afraid [*sic*] from the rising of the ['**Thursday May 16**[th] **NW**' *in margin*] Barometer it will soon fail us being already far less considerable than yesterday. The Aimwell and Sarah and Elizabeth in Company[.] 7 ships to the W[d] under sail others beset to the S[d][.] At 3 PM lay

[1] In *Account of the Arctic Regions*, II, p. 220, Scoresby stated that 'The most favourable opportunity for prosecuting the fishery, commonly occurs with north, north-west, or west winds. At such times, the sea near the ice is almost always smooth ....' By contrast, 'South-east or east winds, though of themselves disagreeable, on account of the thick weather with which they are in general accompanied, and exceedingly dangerous, from the high swells which they often occasion, when they are boisterous, have nevertheless their advantages.'

[2] Ibid, I, p. 246: 'The power of a swell in breaking the heaviest fields, is not a little remarkable. A *grown* swell, that is so inconsiderable as not to be observed in open water, frequently breaks up the largest fields, and converts them wholly into floes and drift-ice in the space of a few hours; while fields composed of bay-ice or light-ice, being more flexible, endure the same swell without any destructive effect.'

too again close by the NE boundary. The Enterprize which lay close by us before we got <u>under way</u> is now SW of us 10 miles or more[.] I don't see any ships to the N^d or NE^d of us[.] As I feared so it proved the Wind fell to nearly calm towards morning and the water was soon coated with Ice. Towards noon the Ice had closed around us began to tow with a boat or 2 a head towards the NE or E warping occasionally[.] The Aimwell and Sarah and Elizabeth 3 or 4 miles to the E^d of us[.] continued this exercise all Day occasionally employing ['**Friday May 17**th Lat 77° Long 9°E Incl to calm' *in margin*] all Hands and 4 Boats. 14 Sail lay to the SW of us within 4 or 5 miles[.] 3 sail were discovered 10 miles N^d of us supposed to be the Henrietta and others[.] In the night plying to Windward amongst Bay Ice with the assistance of one or two Boats a light breeze of wind having sprung up accompanied with almost constant snow. At 1 AM made fast cast off soon afterwards the Ice setting upon us. In the morning being within 400 or 500 yards yards [*sic*] of the [Wⁿ?] boundary of the opening where appeared water breaking out and being unable to ply further upon account of the Bay Ice sent a boat up with 2 whale lines leaving one end on board the Ship and making the other fast to the weather Ice then taking in the Sails prepared to heave the Ship up but lo! ['**Saturday May 18**th Lat 76°46 Long 9°E NbE' *in margin*] the line became suddenly so stretched so as to be like to break[.] we fastened the end and the Ship was turned round and pulled out to Windward of the Bay Ice without heaving in the least upon the line a Distance of 200 or 300 yards. Coming then into clear water hove the Ship up to the Ice which accomplished found the place from which we set out at a miles distance. Moored to the Ice. In the Afternoon finding the Ice setting fast to the W^d cast off and worked about in the opening which had formed since morning. To Day 40 sail of Ships were seen the greatest part of the British in Greenland. In the night wind or fresh breeze[.] The Ice closed around and beset us[.]

Sunday May 19th Lat 77°56 Long 8°50E
Nerly
In the morning warped &c out of the Ice into a small opening where we lay too until afternoon much water to the NW several Ships have sailed in that direction as far as they can be seen[.] worked up a very narrow opening which had broken out and broke with a Boat a passage through.[1] Bay Ice where we sailed by the wind to the NW then running a little to leeward obtained a large opening to the NW^d up which we plyed [.] Saw a whale or more sent two Boats away[.] Afterwards (8 PM) a Mysticetus was struck apparently in a good situation open Ice all round except to the NW where was a frozen patch of Ice 2 miles across apparently without <u>holes</u> and this at a Miles Distance[.] The Whale however instinctively ran to this place for Shelter and obtained it ere one of the boats could come nearer than ½ a ships length at which distance they were several times. She reached the patch took under it after the first Boats (which were) new lines[2] spliced on the lines of 2 boats in order that we might be

[1] Full stop clearly inserted, but out of place.
[2] The original reads: 'She reached the patch took under it. After the first Boats' which were new lines, spliced on the lines of two Boats is order that we might be assured losing no more than …'.

assured of losing no more than those of the first Boat should she persist in running forward[.]

Some of the officers ran over the Ice with lances in two parties and at length discovered her blowing in a soft place of the Ice full ¾ of a mile from the fast boat. In it they lanced her which drove her forward[.] They succeeded in killing after pursuing her to several situations[.] She then sunk under the Ice and disappeared we hoped to rise no more until along side the Ship. In this however we were too sanguine. I was informed that the whale broke the Ice nearly a foot in thickness wherein to breathe.[1] We now put the Ship into some Bay Ice which lay at the Patch Edge where we moored her with two whale lines out of the Stern thereby to keep her from the Ice would have a good effect in drawing out the whale. She had run out 7½ lines[.] took an end to the Ship and began to heave on the Capstern[.] after getting in about a line we had a very heavy strain as much as the line was calculated to bear with safety[.] the line lay very horizontal from which we supposed the whale had not sunk but lay under some rough Ice or behind some hummock under the surface. Thence to release her suspended a kedge[2] of about 2¼ cwt by a Snatch Block upon the stretched line having another fastened to the Kedge[.] Slacked away the lines of both allowing the Kedge to sink and slip along the longer line[.] The Kedge was sent to the Distance of two lines. Where it stopped bringing the line on which it run much towards a perpendicular[.] After resting about ½ an hour began to heave on the lines which we supposed fast to the fish got in to the length of 6½ lines without when the line was at its utmost and keeping at this for 100 yards at length broke. 3½ lines were lost and 3 of those saved nearly spoiled by being over strained. The Mate with 3 men went to the place where she died. Here the [sic] sounded with Boathook &c on the further edges of all the heavy pieces of Ice near within 200 yards altho[3] through numerous places of the then flat of Ice under which she went. They found her not.

It is probable by her rolling much about whenever she appeared that the line had then thrown over or round some submarine hummocks and it is a query whether the whale was fast to the line since on her dying the Harpoon had very slight hold by one whither feather or barb[.][4] Thus after having laboured until 2 AM lost or rendered almost useless 7 of our best whale lines (5 had never been used before[.] Two of these totally lost were new last year hence nearly as good as the rest perhaps equally as strong) we set the Watch and cast the Ship adrift from the Ice[.]

After this the wind shifted to the SE[d] or SSE and gradually increased in strength until noon when it blew a hard gale accompanied with showers of small [grandinous?] snow[.]

[1] 'Researchers have documented whales pushing up through ice at least 20 cm thick to breathe …, and Eskimo hunters report whales breaking up through ice up to 60 cm thick.': Philo et al., 'Morbidity and Mortality', p. 301.

[2] A small anchor. Scoresby was evidently trying to use the weight of the anchor to exert a downward pressure on one of the lines to the dead whale, in order to free it from the ice under which the whale was trapped.

[3] Sic; 'also' presumably intended.

[4] Scoresby, Account of the Arctic Regions, II, p. 223: 'The harpoon … consists of three conjoined parts, called the "socket", "shank", and "mouth;" the latter of which includes the barbs or "withers".'

Monday May 20th
SEbS
The place where we then remained was by the situation of the Ice near where the whale was struck hereabout we dodged[.] Much water appears to the NE the wind is so strong that it would be dangerous attempting to get into it since it cannot be accomplished without boring thro' a heavy stream. Reduced the sails to two close reefed Top sails and Fore Stay sail under which we easily kept our situations laying too and wearing occasionally[.] Several Ships in sight some near us[.] One of them appears to be <u>fished</u> (This is known from the custom of suspending the Spacktackle[1] Blocks when a Ship is clean which are let down on the Capture of a Whale)[.] In the Evening the wind still blowing very hard and snow thick allowed the Ship to drift NW or Wward into open water thro' which were disseminated many masses of heavy Ice streams and patches or floes[.] Towards morning plying about to keep ground under small sails[.][2]

Tuesday May 21st Lat 77°20+ Long 8°00E
EbS
About noon the wind a little more [moderate?] set main stay sail Troy sail and Fore sail under which sail with the two close reefed Top Sails and F, T, M, Stay sail began to ply to Windw[d] most of the Ships in sight under easy sail[.] At 3 PM clearing up and wind still more decreased saw an opening to the ENE or NE 8 or 10 miles distant for this we aimed all the fleet followed us about 7 PM lay too in it having seen a whale had a Boat away[.]

   The Ice to the N and E seems a close pack still as before strongly cemented together by Bay Ice which even in a hard favorable [*sic*] Gale of wind renders it impenetrable must yet resist until a more general opening or breaking of the Bay Ice by a swell[.]

   All the Ships near us yesterday arrived at or about this opening in the Evening amounting to 21 sail only three of which have each got a fish. A Whale was struck by the Vigilant but lost presently afterwards[.] About Mid night the wind had fallen to nearly calm, water freezing[.]

Wednesday May 22nd Lat 77° 22N Long 8°E
Erly
Light breezes charming fine weather the fore part of this Day[.] with the Assistance of

---

[1] *Sic*. Scoresby, *Account of the Arctic Regions*, II, p. 299, in his description of the process of flensing, notes that 'the harpooners ... divide the fat into oblong pieces or "slips" by means of "blubber-spades" ... and "blubber-knives" ...; then affixing a "speck-tackle" to each slip, progressively flay it off, as it is drawn upward ... Each of [the speck-tackles] consists of a simple combination of two single blocks, one of which is securely fixed on a strong rope, extended between the main-top and the fore-sop, called a *guy*; and the other is attached by a *strap* to the blubber of the whale.' See also ibid. Appendix III, p. 511, and Introduction p. xliv.

[2] Smyth, *Sailor's Word Book*, s.v. 'Small sails' defines these as 'Topgallant-studding-sails and the *kites*.' 'Flying-kites' are in turn defined as 'The very lofty sails ... such as sky-sails, royal studding-sails, and all above them.'

a Boat and the sails got from amongst the Bay Ice of a 12 hours formation into a fresh opening to the SE^d[.] here amongst loose Ice occasionally saw whales which in general were vigorously pursued by a dozen or more Boats. 20 Sail of Ships by us lay in a circle of 1½ or 2 miles Diameter. The Fountain of Lynn Barton[1] to leeward careening suppose she is stove[.] The Augusta of Hull found a <u>Dead fish</u> she seemed to tow very heavy it is not unlikely but it may be the Fish we killed on Saturday & Sunday last. About 29 sail are in sight 4 to the S or SW^d under sail some boring this way 2 to the SE beset and 2 to the EbS seemingly in close Ice 10 miles distant[.]

In the Evening an opening to the SE^d or E increased much in size whilst we lay in close made sail and with our utmost efforts and managements were enabled to get through a stream which lay athwart the wind without any boring: the Ship sailed a considerable distance with 4½ or 5 points of the wind. One Ship found a passage before us by boring 12 or 13 sail accomplished the end also most of them boring some made many attempts before they succeeded[.] worked up to the Eastern boundary of the opening and lay too. Ice to the East^d a little slack to the N^d and NE^d impervious to the NW or W open to the SW, S and SE pretty close approximated into extensive patches. Last night Captn Hornby of the Burnie[2] took Tea with us he said when beset within 1½ or 2 miles of us about 10th May while we lay secured and comfortable in Bay Ice the Bernie was caught between two heavy pieces best[3] in Bay Floes and so pressed that he thinks if it had not been for their activity and exirtion in launching Boats across the Bay Ice near the pieces which pressed them that the Ship must have been stove. The pressure was severe.

Thursday May 23rd
East
In the [first?] morning watch (Wednesday) attempting to weather a heavy piece of Ice the Ship came against it and slightly stove a boat[,] carried away one of the Boats Skids[4] one of the Gangway steps &c[.]

In the Evening wind rather increased accompanied with Snow showers the Ice close rapidly around us so that it was a difficult matter to keep clear of it and the Ships by us (14 in number) within a circuit of 3 miles some of them made fast to pieces of Ice at 6 PM [.] Perceiving a large opening two miles to the S^d made sail at 6 PM to bore through the immediately Ice consisting of heavy pieces and Bay packes [*sic*] accomplosed [*sic*] and by 11 PM without striking any piece of Ice with considerable force. Found much water 3 or 4 vessels lay in it amongst which were the Aimwell Sarah and

---

[1] *Sic*. Captain Barton was the master of the *Fountain*: Lubbock, *Arctic Whalers*, p. 196.

[2] According to Lubbock, *Arctic Whalers*, p. 187 and Appendix E, the *Birnie* was a Spanish prize, sailing from Grimsby. Scoresby's log entries give varied spellings of the name, as does Lubbock himself (e.g. Appendix E: '*Bernie*'). Appendix E also indicates 1811 as the ship's first whaling voyage, whereas elsewhere (pp. 165, 167) she is mentioned in the contexts of the seasons of 1804 and 1805.

[3] *Sic*. 'Beset' in original.

[4] Smyth, *Sailor's Word Book* gives the principal use of this term as 'Massive fenders; they consist of long compassing pieces of timber, formed to answer the vertical curve of the ship's side ... mostly used in whalers.' From the context, however, it seems more probable that 'skids' refers to the permanent fenders fitted to whaleboats 'to prevent chafing and fretting'.

Elizabeth[.] About 10 sail of Ships in the Northern opening followed us presently after we started. Saw but one or 2 whales the whole Day.

In the morning light winds fine clear weather. A considerable opening to the E and SE seperated by Ice of about 2 miles across[.] Two Ships 15 miles to the NE^d 4 about 13 to the W^d. Several a little to the N^d the rest of the Ships in sight in Company together amounting to 29 sail[.] Mr Johnstone[1] says the Henrietta and other 2 or 4 Ships have got to the N^d I think it probable. It appears several Ships are fishing to the S^d of us amongst slack Ice. Several in sight have got some one some two fish[.]

The Dead whale which the Augusta found on Wednesday we were informed was that which we killed 19th Inst and that the Harpoon and lines were saved therefore sent a boat on board to the Captn Beedland[2] to express my desire of having the Harpoon returned which one would have supposed he could scarcely refuse[.][3] To my astonishment however he did refuse giving some frivolous excuse and that he had a wish to try the Harpoon, being one of Flinns make[.][4] I sent back the boat desiring that it might be brought on board for the Armourer to erase the name upon it whereby to endeavour as far as possible to present [sic] mistakes and disputes in Fishing[.] if he would not trust on the Resolution that I would send the Armourer on board the Augusta to accomply it. I Dunbar carried the Message as he mounted the side the Master accosted him with "Have you [comed?] again" Yes replied Dunbar "I've [comed?] again Sir then delivered his Message to which answered that he would not have the name erased the fortune of fishing had thrown the Harpoon into his Hands & he was determined not only to keep it but to refuse indulging my request which one would have supposed was undeniable. I troubled him no more and accounted for his ridiculous behaviour attributing it to want of <u>sense</u>. I treated him

[1] This spelling is consistent in the journal, but the master of the *Aimwell* is identified as Captain Johnson in Lubbock, *Arctic Whalers*. The contemporary lists of ships engaged in the *Greenland & Davis's Streights Whale Fisheries* in 1811 and other years consistently identified the master of the *Aimwell* as 'Johnson' but these lists are not reliable, e.g. the *Augusta* of Hull was listed in 1811 as the *Angusta*.

[2] Actually William Beadling, like Scoresby on his first voyage as a whaling master: Credland, *Hull Whaling Trade*, p. 135.

[3] Despite the firm conviction expressed here that the harpoon and ropes, but not the whale, should have been returned, Scoresby made no similar assertion when describing the 'Laws of the Whale-fishery' in *Account of the Arctic Regions*, II, pp. 312–33. By then he had been made aware of the case of Gale vs. Wilkinson, which was summarized in Appendix V of that volume, pp. 518–21. In 1804, a whaleboat belonging to the *Neptune* was abandoned by its crew because a whale that they had harpooned dived and towed the boat down with it. Whale, harpoon, line and boat were subsequently retrieved by crew members of the *Experiment*, whose captain then claimed ownership of all items. In his judgment, Lord Ellenborough, the Lord Chief Justice, found that the boat should be returned to the *Neptune*'s owners, since the crew had quitted it only in order to save their lives. However, 'With regard to the harpoon and line, the fish, when it made off with them, acquired, if he might use the term, a kind of property in them, and any body who afterwards took the fish had a right to the harpoon in it.' Herman Melville appears to have derived much of chapter 89 of *Moby-Dick*, 'Fast-Fish and Loose-Fish', from this chapter and this appendix of *An Account of the Arctic Regions*.

[4] 'Robert Flinn, blacksmith and whitesmith, of North Shields advertised his harpoons in the Hull press in 1809 and by the evidence of surviving examples the workshop was active over a considerable period.': Credland. *Hull Whaling Trade*, p. 23.

with the negligence of contempt which he deserved and almost wished I had given Dunbar liberty to use his oratorial powers in mortifying the fellow since at wit his no contemptible votary. The following instance of it related by the Surgeon who heard it fully [evinces?] the above an Idea started which would not have disgraced a Poet. [A?] youth on board not remarkable for the beauty of his person or face relating his love affairs &c Dunbar wondered any women should have any liking for so ordinary a looking person as him for he observes he [*sic*] "If I hadn't known that God Almighty made every body, I'll be d – nd but I sho*u*ld have taken you for a <u>counterfeit</u>.["]

Friday May 24th
Nerly
Light breezes fine cloudy weather. A large opening appearing to the E[d] extending a considerable distance in that direction in the morning made sail worked a little to Windw[d] to gain leads into the opening and then proceeded to its NEern boundary an apparent pack where we lay too[.] We had scarcely set our sails when our example was followed by all the Ships near us 20 in number which followed as fast as they were able. Our prospect[1] hitherto of gaining the Northern water or Fishing ground have been rarely favourable. They however now brighten a little from the appearance of a strong blink of much water from NE to SE of us and so high as would prompt me to judge its distance could not be more than 15 or 20 miles[2] – a few patches of Ice are probably scattered through also it is an assurance of the above since the two Ships mentioned yesterday as being 15 miles Distant to the NE[d] of us have disappeared and indeed do not come in sight altho' we have approached the spot to within 8 or 9 miles[.] Hence it is more than probable that we were[3] able to accomplish a passage a few miles Erly we should find open or sailing Ice. Several breaks in the Ice are seen especially to the NE, E and SE seperated from us by what appears to be a pretty close pack of moderately heavy Ice[.]

Saturday May 25th
NNW
Light breezes fine cloudy weather. In the Evening two Ships the Burnie and another made sail to the ENE amongst the Ice at first they made great progress[.] made sail altho' the wind was very slight as [far?] as the Ship could sail to the E then began to bore warp &c most of the fleet similarly employed two a head the rest behind us[.] About 8 got into slacker Ice[.] 8° at 9½ AM obtained a large opening to the E[d] of the place from where we set out. Made all sail to the NE[d] ['**Sunday May 26 NNW**' *in margin*] by the wind tacking occasionally for close patches or floes of Ice[.] About 4 PM wind increasing attained slack Ice and kept our reach to the NE or E for

---

[1] *Sic*, despite plural verbs following.
[2] An unexpected remark: Scoresby is clearly talking about the blink being an indication of open water, but the blink phenomenon is associated with ice, not water. However, in *Account of the Arctic Regions*, I, p. 384, Scoresby mentioned that on one occasion his father, 'Observing by the blink, a field of ice surrounded with open water, at a great distance northward, he immediately stood towards it …'.
[3] A transcription error: the original is 'were we'.

5 or 6 hours amongst loose pieces of lightish Ice and small Patches. About 7 got sight of what appeared to be the NErn Water. The Sea at which we aimed and about 10 PM by making three boards passed through a sea stream into it[.] The James of Liverpool opened a passage we followed when we reached this water we were from two to 8 or 10 miles a head of several of the Ships which started with us. The Aimwell came up to us soon afterwards. No Ice is here to be seen between us and the land and none to the North except disseminated pieces and small patches of light Ice. Worked up along the [edge?] of the Main but loose Ice the rest of this Day[.] The wind being exceedingly variable several Ships got to Windward of us[.] Others again are several miles to leeward[.] 23 sail in sight two amongst the loose Ice to the Westward the rest in this Water[.] Saw no Whales [on?] coming out[.] The land in sight[.] At noon the Middle Hook of the Foreland bore NNE Distance about 45 miles[.][1]

Monday May 27th
NbW
Moderate breezes the fore part with fine clear weather[.] in the Evening it increased to a brisk and afterwards strong or hard gale[.] after the commencement of the brisk gale being amongst brash streams and patches of light Ice we frequently weathered and gained of all the Ships to Windward of us (carrying a press of sail) and about 10 PM and weathered the Aimwell which was 2 hours before 2 miles to Windw^d[.] About this time coming into a [swell?] took in the Jib and Mizen 3 reefs in the Top S^l and 2 in the Main. Under this sail the main staysail the Main Stay S^l Troy S^l and F T M Stay S^l we continued the rest of the Night and Morning altho at times it blew exceedingly hard. Took in the Waist Boats. Notwithstanding the Sea became high yet the Ship never missed stays[2] – we had frequently to tack working to Windward between streams of Ice and amongst scattered heavy washed pieces which were very dangerous[.] Most of the Ships about us were obliged to wear.[3] At noon had passed the Aimwell[,] Mary and Elizabeth[,] James of Liverpool[,] Augusta[,] Guilder[4] etc., some of which were 4 miles to leeward which when the Gale commenced were further to Windward. The active[5] was about 8 miles to Windward and was weathered on much several of the Ships carried the same sail on as us[.]

About 8 PM sea high wind a hard gale close reefed Top Sails and reefed Troy Sail[.] A few washed pieces of Ice and brash streams passed occasionally amongst which we endeavoured to work to Windward. I believe we kept our ground[.] At 8 P.M. Middle

[1] This suggests that the *Resolution*'s position was approximately 77°45′N 10°E.
[2] Smyth, *Sailor's Word Book*, s.v. 'Stay': '… to *miss stays*, is to fail in the attempt to go about'.
[3] A touch of youthful pride seems evident here. Scoresby was saying that, whereas the *Resolution* was able to go about in the normal way (i.e. into the wind), most of the accompanying ships were compelled by the strong winds and heavy seas to turn in the opposite direction through 20 points of the compass instead of 12.
[4] *Sic*. The *Augusta* and the *Gilder* made their first whaling voyages from Hull in 1811: Credland, *Hull Whaling Trade*, pp. 120, 123.
[5] Of Peterhead, Captain J. Suttar (Lubbock, *Arctic Whalers*, pp. 51, 189), but the contemporary lists identified the master as 'Sultar'.

Hook of Foreland[1] at NEbN Distant 27 miles[.] Two Ships in sight to Windw[d] 5 or 6 to leeward[.]

Wednesday May 29th Lat 78°22′ Long 9°30E
NbE
About Noon the Wind began to moderate[.] About 6 PM the clouds cleared away let out 2 reefs in the M S and one in the F TS[l] also set the Jib and reefed Mizen. In the Morning we were to Windward of every Ship in sight but since we having been working in a Sea and sometimes amongst streams of Ice nearer the land one of them weathered us 2 or 3 miles other 6 Sail in sight all to leeward[.] About 8 PM began to work to windward amongst streams of washed but light Ice at 12 or 13 miles Distance from the land and about 17 miles SSW of the Middle Hook of the Foreland[.] The Sarah and Elizabeth near us to leeward[.] Saw a whale last night.

The Wind however increasing again to a strong Gale early in the morning we were obliged to put the Ship under her former sail (close reefed Top sails &c) At 11 AM tacked close by some streams of Ice near the land. Middle Hook of Foreland NNE Distance 15 miles[.] Stood off found nothing but clear water during many hours sail except a few disseminated pieces of Ice.

Thursday May 30th Lat 78°26 Long 5°40E
NbE
Strong gales fine clear weather – towards night the wind somewhat abated made a little more sail. From the Bar's rising I expected an abatement of the Gale. Therefore thought it best to reach across to the Western Ice lest it should fall calmed little wind.[2] Then we might have some chance of meeting with Fish one Ship only in sight Astern. The Sea being short and turbulent we made little better than a West course. At mid night had sailed about 30[3] miles yet no Ice but straggling pieces to be seen[.] Saw many sporting animals suppose they were Bottlenoses. The Clouds in the afternoon had a remarkable motion[.] The upper region a light fleecy cloud seemed to move fast in the direction of the wind the lower regions of pieces of heavy Masses which divided from dense horizontal clouds as they arose above the Sea had a similar motion whilst a middle region of cloud plain to be seen and somewhat similar in appearance to that of the higher region being a kind of [Confiner?] and in some places Distinct Cirri (\)[4] was either stationary or had a motion to Windward the latter appeared to the case it might however from the nature of the motion of the others be a deception[.] At Mid night Observed in Lat by Suns alt below the Pole 78°24′18N[5] continued our reach off to the NW by the wind which became moderate towards morning[.] About 6 AM

---

[1] Plate III.3 in *Account of the Arctic Regions*, II, is Scoresby's sketch of the 'MIDDLE HOOK of the FORELAND or CHARLES' ISLAND, bearing E.bS. 25 Miles. Elevation 4000 to 4500 feet.' Modern maps gives the maximum elevation of this part of the island of Prins Karls Forland (78°30′N 11°E) on Svalbard's west coast as 3,560 ft.
[2] A transcription error; the original is 'lest is should fall Calm or little wind, thus we might ...'.
[3] Possibly '50'.
[4] See Introduction, p. lix, and the footnote to the journal entry for 1 August 1813.
[5] Scoresby's journal entry makes the observation sound unremarkable, but determining the latitude by the sun's altitude at midnight (i.e. when it is directly below *Polaris*) is a reversal of the

having passed some small streams of Ice and approaching what appeared to be a loose pack saw several small whales one of which we struck and killed in about 2 hours[.] Took a Quantity of casks out of the Main hold to form a Flinch Gut,[1] Got the fish alonside [sic] flinched it and then sent away 4 Boats again in pursuit[.]

Friday May 31st
North

The Vigilant near us the Bernie to Windward 8 sail to leeward in sight. In the afternoon struck and killed another whale. Flinched her like the former the ship under sail sometimes the Fore tack down so that we worked to Windward nearly as well as at other times. Breeze now freshened weather still fine and cloudy seeing a blink to the NNW which appeared to be that of a field worked up towards it. At 9 AM struck and presently killed a small whale had the boats in pursuit of many others but could entangle no more. The fish being flinched (the Ship on the way) made sail to work up to the Ice to Windward apparently a Field[.] 2 Ships made fast to it. In all 13 sail in sight several of which have got fish this Morning. The Henrietta to Windw^d.

Saturday June 1st
NNW

Fresh or moderate breezes in the Evening showers of snow, working to Windward at 4½ PM a Fish was struck and with some difficulty killed made the Ship fast to the Ice to Windward which instead of a Field proved to be an aggregation of floes[.] flinched the Fish. In the interval Captn Kearsly came on board they have 20 or 21 Fish about 90 or 100 Tons of oil. 60 Tons of which is made off. They got thro' the Ice 16th May; where [sic] within sight of us Apl 30th were not many yards distance from the Northern water which presently afterwards was covered with Bay Ice. Two Ships got through with them the Aurora and Old Manchester[2] both of which must be well fished [.] He says several Vessels lay beset to the N^d of us amongst Floes that a large Field lays to the NE^d of us &c[.] About mid night cast off made sail to the West^d where we got another fish in 4 miles sailing made fast and flinched. The wind a light breeze in the Evening accompanied with snow in the morning fine weather and clear[.] About noon wind again freshened – Cast off to search for fish being here very scarce[.] Ice to the N^d packed and frozen together to the NE or ENE open[.] 14 Ships in sight[.]

---

normal calculation based on the sun's altitude at noon that is not mentioned in the standard textbooks of nautical navigation. It is, of course, a method only available to ships in high latitudes.

[1] Smyth, *Sailor's Word Book*, s.v. 'Flinch-gut': '… the part of the hold into which [the blubber] is thrown before being barrelled up.' See also Scoresby, *Account of the Arctic Regions*, II, pp. 299–300 and Introduction, p. xliv.

[2] The 'Old' *Manchester* of 266 tons was built in New York in 1762 and the 'New' *Manchester*, 285 tons, was built at West Stockwith, on the River Trent near Gainsborough, in 1789 In 1811 both vessels were in the Greenland fleet from Hull: Credland, *Hull Whaling Trade*, p. 125, where they are identified as *Manchester I* and *II*. Credland and the contemporary list agree that the master of the 'New' *Manchester* in 1811 was Archibald Hunter, but Credland listed the master of the 'Old' *Manchester* as John Allan or Allen, whereas the contemporary list identified a Captain Bennett. The *Aurora* (368 tons, Captain Sadler), built at Selby in 1782, was making its first whaling voyage from Hull in 1811.

Sunday June 2nd

Nerly

Having now five Whales broached a cask given us by Mr Fishburn filled with fine ale[.] I delivered to each of the sailors a glass containing about a pint being at M^{rs} F's request (to be repeated should we be fortunate enough to get 5 more whales.[)] In the night fresh breezes variable weather cloudy or hazy. Being in Company with many Ships the Fish being scarce and water very blue and clear seeing a light blink as of a field to the NE made sail by the wind to the E^d amongst very open Ice small Streams and floes for the Distance of about 15[1] miles where we again came into thick water of a deep green colour favourable for fishing since in the transparent Sea the Whales see at such a distance that they become easily alarmed and set off.[2] Here we saw two or three fish and presently struck (by a heave)[3] one of them killed it with little difficulty and flinched it while we drifted to leeward with the Top Sails lowered down[.] The Aimwell and the Active in sight to leeward together with other 17 sail to the N^d and W^d soon after we had set the sails and reached a little to the NE^d two fish were struck (8½ & 9 AM.) The first we lost and the latter killed and flinched the Ship under sails[.]

Monday June 3rd Lat 78°34 Long 6°10E

NE

Moderate breezes fine cloudy weather. Plying to Windward or laying too amongst loose pieces of Ice in much water many whales seen 3 or 4 in a place together. Had three Boats in pursuit but altho' they several times came near they could not get fast. I imagine the failure amongst 10 whales was owing to the clearness of the water which was of a transparent blue colour[.] In the absence of the Boats I worked and steered the Ship by myself alone tacked once. Several Ships to the W^d or NW^d have got fish lately[.] The Aimwell[4] those which were successful in their pursuits they all lay at the edge of Floes or frozen Packs[.] There they had small whales here middle sized or larger[.] After labouring in vain until passed Mid nt made sail by the wind to the E^d for a small patch of Ice I observed at the distance of about 10 miles here I expected to meet whales even more numerous than hitherto for the whale delight [*sic*] in the vicinity of small open Patches or even close streams they find either a real or imaginary shelter[.] As I thus surmised so it proved we met with whales of all sizes in great numbers 6 or 8 might be seen blowing at the same time. Sent 6 Boats away in <u>chase</u> from one of which John Hall our Spicksoneer struck a large fish she the next moment with her tail struck so forcibly at the boat the Boatsteerer Wm Welburn was

---

[1] Possibly '13'.

[2] Scoresby believed that the bowhead's 'sense of seeing is acute' when submerged (*Account of the Arctic Regions*, I, p. 465), but what he regarded as evidence of sight is now known to be the whale's ability to communicate by sound. What he described in this journal entry may perhaps be interpreted as the whales' behaviour when feeding in plankton-rich ('deep green') waters as compared to their movement when not feeding.

[3] Scoresby may mean that the harpoon was thrown from the *Resolution* instead of from one of its boats.

[4] Transcription omission; the original is 'The Aimwell amongst those which were ...'.

thrown overboard[.][1] the stroke was repeated when the Spicksoneer and Lineman-ager shared the same fate[.] Welburn recovered the Boat the two latter were not so fortunate[.] The Boat by the lines was instantly drawn from the spot[2] and the two men left swimming[.] Another Boat rowed from alongside Ship and picked the men up in about 2 minutes[.] Hall was a good deal shocked and apparently hurt by a Blow from the Fin or Tail which carried him overboard the rest escaped with wetting and fright[.] The Linemanager supported himself on the Surface of the Water until he got assistance altho' quite unacquainted with the art of swimming[.] It is not to be expected that the whale struck the Boat intentionally or premeditated they are scarcely ever known to do it[.] the accidents they occasion in general proceed from an adventitious Blow whilst in the agony of pain or the effort of making a speedy retreat.

The above fish took out 8½[3] and with them made such a sweep that it was some-time ere a second harpoon was struck. When killed made the ship fast to a flat piece of Ice got the fish alongside and immediately afterwards the whales being numerous sent all the Boats away in pursuit they succeeded in presently sticking and killing another which we took alongside (10 AM)[.]

Tuesday June 4th
NEbE
The wind now shifted to the S[d] or SSE[d] accompanied with snow showers[.] At noon a Whale was struck another at 4 PM both of which we got[.] The Ship [moored?] to two pieces of Ice began to flinch at 6 PM the wind a moderate breeze accompanied with thick snow showers[.] at 1 AM finished flinching – Sent all hands to Bed except a Boats crew for 6 hours. The Aimwell came up to us and lay too close by us[.] She had 7 fish 2 of which were size (8ft)[4] Between 30 and 40 tons of oil[.] In the morning the Snow which had lately fallen in frequent showers ceased[.] The Wind fell to Calm[.] a fish we got during its continuance Flinched we Cast off (a breeze of wind NErly having sprung up) and began to work to the NE towards the opposite side of an open patch of Ice to that on which we lay. I having seen with a Telescope from the masthead several Fish in that direction.

Wednesday June 4[th][5] Lat 78°29 Long 5°54E
NEbN
We presently afterwards without much trouble struck and killed 2 fine whales both of which we took alongside towed them to a piece of Ice made the Ship fast and began to flinch[.] Found the Ship much by the head in draught of water consequently were unhandy nay so much so that with all our art we could not wear her with the two

[1] This incident was retold by Scoresby in *Account of the Arctic Regions*, II, pp. 358–9.
[2] I.e. the boat was towed away by the stricken whale.
[3] 8½ lines, or 6,120 feet of rope.
[4] As noted in the Introduction (p. xl), 'size' meant a whale with whalebone six feet in length or greater. This parenthesis therefore presumably indicates the actual length of whalebone in the two whales caught by the *Aimwell*.
[5] *Sic*. The error was corrected at the head of the next page of the transcript.

fish.[1] One of the whales the last we got is a handsome animal his party coloured coat of black and white being somewhat uncommon in the mixture and his fine bright black back shews him to be a gentleman whale, perhaps one of their brightest beaus. Having flinched the whale notwithstanding we had yet room to take in 20 [ton?] more cleared the Fore hold started[2] water and began to make off[.] About 10 AM Lowered the Waist Boats down to the Water's edge as a safety to prevent the Ship falling over or upsetting since it is common for her in such cases to be dangerously [tender?][.][3] 17 sail in sight. Capt Johnstone came on board and took Breakfast with us they got 3 fish within 24 hours last have now about 70 tons of oil[.]

Thursday June 6th
NW
Light to fresh breezes with snow Showers[.] Early in the Morng having filled [*Blank space*] Casks with Blubber of the two lower tiers and 3rd tier of wingers[4] in the forehold and seeing several Ships fishing around us [***] got on the [***] and made sail by the wind to the NNE met with open Ice and streams in 2 hours tacked and worked to Windward off their edge[.] Saw whales occasionally had a boat in pursuit[.] ['**Friday June 7th** at 79°10″ [*sic*] Long 8°E Easterly' *in margin*] In the afternoon 4 PM began to reach to the NE along the weather edge of what seemed to be a Field several miles Distant from us. Passed the Margaret with 20 Fish Henrietta with 26.

Wind freshened. Snow became constant towards Mid nt soon afterwards fell in with Ice loose pieces and small patches – reached in amongst it to explore it 4 or 5 miles to explore if possible the termination[.] The wind then increasing to a fresh gale and the Snow thickening I thought it most prudent to return least we should get entangled amongst the Ice in the thick. Saw no whales. The colour of the water last night before we cast off from the Ice was of a transparent Blue. On sailing 4 Miles NE it became of a thickish green and now as we tacked was of a very deep green. The Ice all around at the edges tinged of a deep yellow colour from the deposit of some substance in the water which probably gives it the deep green colour. This Colour is evidently permanent not changing in fine weather or foul. Clear or Cloudy, fair or Snowy. Calm or Stormy[.] I preserve a Bottle of it for future Analysis[.][5] Wind a

[1] Smyth, *Sailor's Word Book*, s.v. 'Head': '*By the head*, the state of a ship which, by her lading, draws more water forward than aft.' Smyth went on to say that one consequence is that the ship then tends to gripe, i.e. 'tends to come up into the wind while sailing close-hauled'. The ship is also 'uneasy', a term probably synonymous with Scoresby's 'unhandy'.
[2] To start a liquid, is to empty it, in this case, ballast water from casks in the fore-hold. See Smyth, *Sailor's Word Book*, s.v. 'Start'.
[3] Scoresby seems to be saying that in the interval between clearing the fore-hold of casks containing ballast water, and replacing them with casks containing blubber, the ship would be in a dangerous, inadequately-ballasted, condition. See Introduction, p. xlvi.
[4] Smyth, *Sailor's Word Book*, s.v.: 'Small casks stowed close to the side in a ship's hold, where the large casks would cause too great a rising in that part of the tier.'
[5] In *An Account of the Arctic Regions* (I, pp. 176–7), Scoresby implied that his principal work relating these colour changes to the presence of the organisms on which whales feed was initiated in 1817. 'I at first imagined that this appearance was derived from the nature of the bottom of the sea. But on observing that the water was very imperfectly transparent … and that the ice floating in the

strong gale accompanied with thick snow or haze[.] Plying to Windward tacking or wearing at the Ice every 4 hours[.] Streams on the larboard a kind of Pack we met on the starboard tack. The Sea high 4 or 5 sail of Ships in sight Lively of Whitby 4 Fish Experiment of London 8[.]

Saturday June 8th
SSE The fore part strong gales with constant Snow the latter occasionally clear or hazy or Snow Showers. Plying to Windward[.] Employed gumming[1] whale bone[.] At 1 AM tacked amongst brash Ice on the Weather side of a Pack run a little to leeward and then steered by the wind to the SSW^d [.] At 9 AM began to clear away the Blubber in mid ships of the main hold to make off being alarmed lest the Iron <u>stantions</u>[2] supporting the Beams and Blubber on each side of the main Hatch way and twin decks from coming into mid ships should break the stress on them being very heavy and they bending very much altho' we had supported them by pieces of wood between each <u>stantion</u> we had not been long begun ere one of them actually broke. Cleared away the main Hold started[3] the Water and coals took provisions upon deck and ['**Sunday June 9th** Lat 78°58 Long 7°E' *in margin*] about 2 PM got begun making off. Previously we had close reefed the Top Sails and took in all sail but those. the F T Mast Stay S^l and reefed Troy Sail[.] the Sea still considerable. Several Ships but no fish seen[.] Water deep green[.] wore the Ship about 2 PM[.] At 8 AM wore again and sailed larboard tacked. Two Ships in sight making off probably. Towards noon small showers of prismatic Snow or haze sailing with helm lashed partly [a?] lee to the NW^d at the rate of about 2 knots P hour. In the Evening while making ['**Monday June 10th**' *in margin*] off in the 2nd breaking out of the Main Hold fell in with Ice on the lee bow and beam it proved to be a close Pack or ragged Ice bore for it 4 sail in sight[.]

Weather fine light breezes inclinable to calm the Fore part[.] At 1PM made sail tacked ship and steered by the wind to the SW or WSW on the [n^n?] edge of the Pack which lay about ENE and WSW[.]

Tuesday June 11th
Serly
At 8 PM finished making off having filled 106 casks with Blubber which together

---

olive-green sea was often marked with an orange-yellow stain, I was convinced, that it must be occasioned by some yellow substance held in suspension by the water, capable of discolouring the ice, and of so combining with the natural blue of the sea, as to produce the peculiar tinge observed.' The 1811 journal entry clearly foreshadows these conclusions.

[1] Scoresby, *Account of the Arctic Regions*, II, , p. 416 describing whalebone: 'This substance, when taken from the whale, consists of laminae, connected by what is called the *gum* in a parallel series, and ranged along the mouth of the animal.' Later (p. 418) he mentioned that removal of the gum (i.e. gumming) is the first step in preparation of the whalebone for commercial uses. See also p. 458: 'This substance (the gum) is white, fibrous, tender and tasteless. It cuts like cheese. It has the appearance of the interior or kernel of the cocoa-nut.'

[2] *Sic.* Smyth: *Sailor's Word Book*, s.v. 'Stanchions': 'Any fixed upright support. Also, those posts of wood or iron which, being placed pillar-wise, support the waist-trees and guns.'

[3] Scoresby was again reducing the amount of water and other ballast as the weight of blubber increased.

with 48 before makes in all 154 casks 80–90 tons of oil[.] About midnight we came amongst Fish where the Pack now laid about ESE and WNW bore away before the wind 6 or 8 miles and fell in with several whales sent 3 boats in pursuit. The Aimwell flinching to leeward 19 sail in sight chiefly to the West^wd most of them fishing[.]

By noon had killed and taken along side 2 small fish another was struck but lost. A great number were seen[.] one of these we got was struck close by the Pack edge and got into it but not before two Harpoons were fast. Having flinched the Whales began to ply to the NE along the Pack edge seeing then no Fish. Lay too occasionally[.]

Wednesday June 12th
Erly
Light or moderate breezes fine cloudy weather, small showers of <u>prismatical</u> Snow[.] seeing few Fish to the E^d made sail by the wind to the NW^d several miles until the Pack turned down to the SW[.] in the [Corner?] lay too running a little to leeward no fish worked back again[.] Yesterday from Mr Johnstone heard by the Neptune of Aberdeen news of my Father in the John had 2 large fish 29th May. To Day were informed by the Effort who heard it of the Reliance[1] that he had 7 large whales the 1st Inst. Good news. Yesterday was the first acct we have have [sic] had[.] A Ship seen beset to the N^d of us 17 sail in sight Enterprize 15 Fish Henrietta 29 Egginton 10 Effort [blank space] Volunteer [blank space] Aimwell [blank space][.]

Thursday June 13th
NErly
Light airs or inclinable to calm with showers of small prismatic snow which skimmed along the surface of the water like clouds of smoke rising out of it[.] The modification of the numbers.[2] was particularly marked and much resembled the drawing given by Luke Howard Esqr. Whales being here very scarce (in a deep sinuosity or bight of the pack it being seen from ESE to SbW) made sail and run down along the edge of it in many places consisting of large floes first to the SW and then to the S^d or SSE examining every Bay point for Fish saw but 2 or 3 in 10 hours sailing at the rate of 2 or 3 knots P hour[.] In the morn^g (8 AM) lay too and about 11 AM made sail towards the Ice to the WSW for a slack place which appeared in the Seaward boundary leading amongst open Ice considerable water to the SW^d and W^d where appeared 2 Ships Fishing. Several other Ships in sight chiefly plying to Windward the Enterprize in the Ice a head of us[.]

Friday June 14th Nrly NW Made passage in a Stream into a loose patch by means of a

---

[1] The *Effort* (Captain Paterson) and the *Reliance* (Captain Cutter) were included as London whalers in the contemporary list, *Greenland and Davis's Streights Whale-Fisheries, 1811*.

[2] *Sic.* A transcription error for 'nimbus' or rain cloud. Scoresby was presumably referring to the illustration of 'nimbus' in Howard's 1804 paper 'On the Modifications of Clouds …': see Introduction, p. lix. The term 'modification' was distinctively Howard's; in his 1804 paper he explained (p. 98) that 'By modification is to be understood simply the structure or manner of aggregation, not the precise form or magnitude, which indeed varies every moment in most clouds.' In this context the term is therefore synonymous with 'type'.

Boat and sailed or towed thro' saw 4 or 5 whales immediately afterwards the water being very clear and Blue and the weather still (nearly calm) could not entangle any of them. With the Assistance of two Boats towing for about 4 hours had worked to Windward thro the Patch into a large Sea of water extending to the W^d and SW^d as far as the eye from the Mast head could discern bounded on the NW, N^d and NE by open or close patches streams and loose Ice. Calm chiefly thro' the night[.] in the Morning light airs Serly accompanied with showers of Haze or small rain sprung up made sail to the W^d saw large fish occasionally had 2 Boats in pursuit[.] About 10 AM the colour of the water changed from Blue to deep green[.] I had observed it at 9 AM to be of a clear blue we had sailed in the interval little more that [sic] 1½ or 2 miles. Many Narwhales were seen near the Ship I observed them swimming from the Mast Head with a Spy Glass; their Fins were stretched out horizontally (from the Body) and appeared motionless while an undulating motion of the rump with the flexibility of the posterior part of the Tail seemed to give the propelling force[.] occasionally a lateral motion was observed this might either be for velocity or turning. When the Unicorn[1] wished to descend like as the whale the tail was forcibly pressed downwards which elevated the <u>crown</u> or head and then immediately forced upwards caused the head to descend. The larger of these animals which I took to be the old ones were only spotted with black on a white ground the smaller ones were of a dark Blackish colour on the Back marked with still deeper spots. I observed no <u>horns</u> amongst them comparatively few of them are possessed of this Instrument. I noticed a large one of the whitish kind accompanied by a very small one of the Dark coloured skin which appeared to be its young from its following it very close on its side.

Saturday June 15th
Serly
Got a Whale (struck at 1 PM) the lines of the boat were run out all except about ½ dozen fathoms when a boat came up to bend on[2] they had scarcely time to take a <u>hitch</u>[.] Pursued several other fish but could not come at more[.] Flinched the one we killed set the Watch and began to ply to Windward seeing fish occasionally. Several Ships in sight employed in the various avocations of a Fishing voyage[.] Spoke the <u>Prince of Brazils</u>[3] with 10 or 11 Fish 180 Butts of Blubber she had seen the John on the 30th of May with three large Fish[.] The Captn (Taylor) of the Prince of Brazils in indifferent health[.]

In the night it fell calm yet not withstanding the disadvantages of fishing were great Wm Rippon very artfully manoeuvered a Fish and got fast she was easily killed. The situation of the Fish was ascertained by the eddie also by the motion of the Birds (Fulmars) which flattening their wings alighted in the Water over the place then quickly ascending again descended fluttering this is a sure sign of the Whale being not

[1] The term 'unicorn' was applied to the narwhal as far back as the seventeenth century; its similar application to the one-horned rhinoceros is even older: *OED*, s.v.

[2] Smyth, *Sailor's Word Book*, s.v. 'Bend': 'To fasten one rope to another …'.

[3] *Sic.* Correctly, *Prince of Brazil*, 237 tons, of Hull. Lubbock, *Arctic Whalers*, p. 185, noted that in 1810 its previous master, Captain Milner, 'committed suicide soon after his ship reached the ice by jumping out of the cabin window'.

far Distant beneath the Surface[1] thus by observing this, the Boat was enabled to keep near the spot by sculling &c so that she arose ½ a Ships length. Flinched had several Boats in pursuit of Fish of which we saw not a few, with one sweep of the Glass round the Horizon I counted no less than 14. Being near an open Patch of Ice a sucking Fish came up close by a Boat laid on the Watch they struck it and presently the Mother arose nearly touching them and having got entangled with the line drew it out pretty briskly for 100 Fathoms[.] 5 other Boats were now sent around the spot to endeavour to entangle the mother[.] she was presently seen running furiously and frequently stopping short and returning seemingly in great agony for the loss of her young which it appeared she could not find out[.] For many several times she acted in a similar manner seeming not to fear the Boats which constantly pursued her[.] At length one of the Harponeers hove at her and drew another struck and shared the same fate another delivered by a boatsteerer held fast and not long afterwards four Harpoons were fast[.] in about an hour after this she was killed thus becoming a prey from mutual affection her young one was all at which she aimed its safety was her peculiar care in danger she feared nought nor neglected aught to accomplish its rescue[.] The young one was purposely kept alive until the mother was secured and then killed like-wise[.][2] Hoisted the Young one on Deck preserved the cranium on account of the organ of hearing for [Ed^d?] Holme Esq. Having removed what little fat surrounded it threw the Carcase [sic] overboard and took its mother along side kept the Ship under sail to weather a Patch of Ice and then lay too in pretty open water. The young Whale was in colour of a Bluish Black on the Back some parts of the head and part of the Belly: on the Back it was marked with deeper spots of Black like the Narwhale some-what especially the Young Narwhale on the belly also some deeper spots[.] we observed: the skin was 1⅛ inches thick, the Blubber on the body 3½ to 4 inches[.] The Skin of the Adult whale is scarcely one inch. The integuments unlike the grand origi-nal were coarse and rough[.] the mother was a pretty fish fine bright skin on the Belly much mixed with white[.] several sail in sight to the W^d chiefly or S^d[.]

Sunday June 16th
Var Inc to calm

Light breezes or inclinable to calm. In the Bottom of a bight formed by loose streams and open passages where were seen several whales particularly to the SE^d or ESE^d[.] Having flinched the last fish made sail towards a patch in that direction and in the Evening struck a whale presently killed it. Sent one Watch to bed flinched with the other two again made sail to Windward and lay too occasionally the watch which

---

[1] Scoresby, *Account of the Arctic Regions*, II, p. 240: 'A whale moving forward at a small distance beneath the surface of the sea, leaves a sure indication of its situation, in what is called an "eddy", having somewhat the resemblance of the "wake" or track of a ship; and in fine calm weather, its change of position is sometimes pointed out by the birds … By these indications, many whales have been taken.' In the climactic final chapters (133–5) of *Moby-Dick*, the role of both wake and birds in the chase was invoked by Melville.

[2] This incident was described again in Scoresby, *Account of the Arctic Regions*, I, 471–2, where the journal's unusual use of the verb 'draw' is clarified: '… a harpoon was hove at her. It hit, but did not attach itself. A second harpoon was struck; this also failed to penetrate …'.

had before slept employed spanning [our?] Harpoons[1] Gumming whale bone watching for fish &c[.] A fog or haze came on in the morning which cleared away about 7 AM sent a Boat after a Fish. The Sarah and Elizabeths boat came on board in the thick informed us they had two Days ago the misfortune to lose a man by the line running foul in a fast Boat which took her away those saved were nearly drowned[.] she had 10 Fish 5 size 40 tons of oil probably more. Gives an account of the W[m] and Ann with 5 fish a week ago Jane of Aberdeen 7 two Days ago and Old Manchester 21 [&?] Lyon Lpool 3 Friday or Saturday last[.]

The last fish we got by a blow with her tail broke the Gunwale and stove the upper plank or streak[2] of our six oared gig. A fish was struck and soon killed (8 AM) and about 10 AM another at some distance from the Ship just at the moment of the commencement of a fog[.] 4 Boats near the spot[.] sent another with a Compass and two Horns with directions how to find the Boats (which bore SbW) and should the fish be killed to tow NbE. The wind a light breeze took alongside the Dead fish and made sail to the SbW sounded a Bugle the Ships Bell and the Men's Voices which were occasionally answered by the Boats[.] At ½ an hour PM got sight of the Boats ['**Monday June 17th Erly**' *in margin*] with a Fish in tow took her alongside employed afterwards flinching[.] Ship reaching by the wind to the S[d] aiming at a Windw[d] situation where we saw a many fish <u>amongst loose Ice lee of a Pack</u>[.] The Sarah and Elizabeth got a fish this Morning[.]

Our success for the last two Days <u>has been wonderful so favoured</u> have we been that every fish was killed with astonishing little trouble[.] No. 17 was a fine fish as well as 20 21 & 23[.] No 20 – 10[ft] 2[in] bone commonly estimated at 13½ Tons was in this Whale supposed to be 16 or 17 Tons[.] No 17 – 13 Tons[,] 18 – 6 Tons[,] 19 – 1 Ton. 20. 16 Tons[,] 21 – 8 Tons[,] 22 – 6 Tons and 23 – 11 Tons thus 7 whales which at a fair estimation might be supposed to produce 61 Tons of oil were captured within 47 hours and all flinched within 57 hours from the commencement during which time also most of the sailors had had 4 or 6 hours rest! The Old Manchesters Boat was on board in the Evening they have 23 fish (10 size) supposed to produce 110 or 120 Tons of oil[.] They accomplished their passage to the North[d] in a Day or two's run About 25th Ap[l] having just come from the Sea close by the Land and run or bored amongst slack Ice to the NE and N[d] and at length E[d] into into [*sic*] the land water from whence they went shortly to the head land saw Fish but were frozen up amongst Bay Ice[.] Two Ships the Guilder and Perseverance accompanied them partly thro' the Ice and then steered off to the NW[d] to us[.] About 1 AM wind increasing and the haze clearing which of late had been in thick frequent showers amongst loose Ice to leeward of a Patch struck a Fish killed it and Flinched with Top sails lowered down Ship drifting to leeward. Finished made sail to windward several sail in sight. Chiefly to leeward some fishing Lively Henrietta Enterprize working up towards us[.]

---

[1] Smyth, *Sailor's Word Book*, s.v. 'Spanning a harpoon': 'Fixing the line which connects the harpoon and its staff … on striking the whale the staff leaps out of the socket and does not interfere with the iron, which otherwise might be wrenched out.' The foreganger is that connecting line.

[2] Smyth, *Sailor's Word Book*, s.v.: 'Strake': 'One breadth of plank in a ship, either within or without board, wrought from the stem to the stern-post.'

Tuesday June 18th

NE NNE

Fresh breezes the fore part clear[,] the latter cloudy with showers of prismatical snow. Plying to Windward amongst loose Ice open Patches and streams to the E and SE open pack to the N^d to the W^d a pack apparently close. Several fish seen. Could get fast to none until about 2 AM when one was struck and presently killed, whilst employed flinching it (the Top sail clewed up & two Boats on the Bran[1] for watch another was struck and killed in about 2 hours got it alongside flinched and then began to ply to Windwd[.] About 20 sail in sight many of them flinching or fast[.] Having now the <u>flinch gut</u> in the Main Hold and twin decks from Main mast to after part of the Hatchway full of Blubber and about 10 or 15 tons in the After Hold sought for a piece of Ice to moor to. The ['**Wednesday June 19th** NEbN' *in margin*] Ice about us being small and light did not succeed until 5[2] PM when we met with a small Floe to which was already made fast the Lively, Fountain and all making off. Made fast to it furled the sails and began to make off in the Fore Hold about 8 PM intending to clear the after hold of Blubber and then <u>start</u> therein to make off. A few hands employed gumming whale bone to be ready to stow in the After hold. Towards noon the weather which had been cold, cloudy, and windy, cleared up and became fine and moderate[.] Employed making off in the After hold stowing whale bone in every vacancy[.] Mr Barton of the Fountain Breakfasted with us they have about 120 tons of oil 17 Fish, were unfortunate in coming thro' the Ice broke the rudder to pieces and were stove in two different Gales of the 15th and 20th May. The Lively of Whitby with 12 fish 60–65 Tons of oil[.] Mr Barton complains of having a discontented disrespectful crew Many ships in sight 25 sail[.] Chiefly Fishing[.]

Thursday June 20th

NNE

Fresh to moderate breezes employed making off made fast as above. 37 sail in sight. The Aimwell worked up from to leeward[.] Mr Johnstone came on board they have 25 fish (13 size) about 130 tons of oil. He gives account of the Henrietta having [*blank space*] Fish Tuesday last about 160 Tons when he had about 100 Tons of oil we had 20–25, we calculate now at [*blank space*] Tons[.] About noon cast off from the Ice the piece we were moored to drifting upon a Patch to the SE^d. The wind falling to a light breeze worked a little to Windward amongst much loose Ice and floes and then lay too in a small opening[.] Had a Boat in pursuit of Whales of which we saw several. Thick fog Showers in the Morning and Afternoon[.] About 5 PM completed three tiers of the hold fore and aft[.] Began to stow and fill the 4th by the main hatch way[.]

---

[1] 'During fine weather, in situations where whales are seen, or where they have recently been seen, or where there is a great probability of any making their appearance, a boat is generally kept in readiness, manned and afloat … the "bran-boat" as it is called ….': Scoresby, *Account of the Arctic Regions*, II, pp. 237–8.

[2] Possibly '3'.

Friday June 21st Lat 78°10N Long 5°E
North
In the morning light airs, various, inclinable to calm: made sail to windward amongst very heavy cross Ice[.] The Sea seen to the SW^d or SSW, still making off 4th Tier. Had account that the John <u>was</u> sailed for home <u>full</u>[.] Here news of the success of several Ships viz Aurora 36–37. = 150–160 Tons Henrietta 35 = 170 Tons. Volunteer 18 (9 size) 100 Tons Euretta[1] 19 Augusta 27 Fish Lively (Whitby) 60 Tons Sarah and Eliz 14 = 70[.] The <u>Ocean</u>[2] we learnt got dreadfully abused by the Impetuosity of the Ice in the Gale of the 7th of June she had been making off at the field edges (or rather Floes) had finished 12 hours before the Gale came on yet did not cast off when they wished to clear some patches to Windward of them which seperated them from the water[.] The [sic] got entangled amongst pieces and the Ship [sore?] <u>stove</u> they were obliged to force into the Ice as far as possible where they received such blows from the Ice agitated by the swell that most of the Timbers they believe in the Ship are broken[.] the pumps are kept constantly going, they have several fish and still persevere in the object of their voyage[.] The Aimwell near us fished as before.

Saturday June 22nd
SW
While working to windward soon in the Afternoon a thick fog commenced we made all haste amongst cross Ice that we could: Cooper & Carpenter employed setting up Shakes[.] At 10 PM finished making off having filled 193 Casks. Having filled and completed 3 Tiers, the 4th Tier from the Fore part of the Main Hatch Way to after part of the after Hatch way together with 5 or 6 casks farther aft. Draught of water of the Ship Forward 13^ft 10^ins and Aft 14^ft 8^in (by the new marks)[3] met with the Fountain still made fast in the thick to the same piece of Ice from which we cast off[.] the fog clearing away we saw the <u>Sea</u> at 3 or 4 miles distance to the S^d[.] Many Ships in sight worked into open water communicating by a sinuosity to the Northern water to the S^d and SW^d[.] An open Pack to the W and N^d[.] Some Ships in it calm or very light airs towards noon with small haze or Rain Showers[.] A few whales seen[.] Cooper setting up shakes took packs of Casks upon Deck stowed others in Twin Deck at hand[.]

Sunday June 23d
Serly
Calm or very light airs in various directions[.] Ship situated as before mentioned.

---

[1] The *Euretta* was mentioned by Lubbock, *Arctic Whalers*, as sailing from the Tyne in 1799 and again in 1801. In the contemporary list for 1811 it was shown as the *Ewretta* and this appears to have been its last whaling voyage from Newcastle; in 1812 and 1813 the *Eweretta* joined the London whaling fleet. Its master in 1811, Captain Boswell, transferred to the Newcastle whalers *Eliza* in 1812 and *British Queen* in 1813.

[2] A London whaler of this name, Captain Westwater, was included in the contemporary list of *Greenland & Davis's Streights Whale-Fisheries, 1811*.

[3] Before the Plimsoll Line was made mandatory by the Merchant Shipping Act of 1875, it was normal to mark the draught required to float a ship on the stem and stern. Apparently it had been necessary to adjust these marks on the *Resolution*. See Smyth, *Sailor's Word Book*, s.v. 'Draught, or draft'.

Many Ships in sight. A few Whales seen one of which we struck and presently killed[.] It was remarkable for the size of its Fins and Tail being large enough for a 10 or 11 foot fish. Having flinched it plyed about in the same <u>bight</u> of Ice surrounded altho' at some distance by loose patches. Mess.rs Kearsly and Johnstone breakfasted and dined on board[.][1] Henrietta 35 Fish (14 size) 150–160 tons of oil Effort – 28 nearly full Volunteer 80 or 90 Tons Old Manchester nearly full. Saw but a few Fish during this Day some were captured by Ships near us. A ship yesterday lost a boats lines which were to Day we believe found by the Effort on a Fish she killed.

Monday June 24.th
SW

Light or moderate breezes with Fog Showers. In the evening ran a little to the N.d in search of Fish saw two had boats in pursuit then lay too[.] much water appeared to the NNE which in the morning had closed from the Eastern patches joining the Pack to the Westward[.] Very few fish seen those were seldom got on account of the number of Boats in pursuit which generally alarmed them. Our Surgeon of whom I have said something before[2] an easy credulous good natured Soul had lent a Book to the Aimwells Surgeon and having lately much wanted it was constantly repining when the Ship was in sight at having parted with it since it contained some information he was very anxious to be acquainted with[.] he pressed me repeatedly to allow him to take a Boat and a Man or two to fetch it[.] I not finding it convenient deferred it at length he contrived to get into a Boat going on Bran and prevailed on the Harponeer to put him on board the Aimwell not far distant with some reluctance he consented and the Doctor obtained the much and long wished for Book. he brought it on board and carefully put it in his <u>Medicine Chest</u>[.] M.r Johnstone understanding he had got possession of it and wishing to teaze him sought for and found the Book in his absence on the Deck which he gave to the care of Capt.n K who concealed it. The

[1] In *Sabbaths in the Arctic Regions*, pp. 57–65, Scoresby used the events of this day and the following week as 'Indications of a Providential Rebuke for Sabbath Violation'. He noted that '... we fell in with two ships from the same port as my own, and commanded by personal acquaintances. After some hesitation and scruples of conscience about breaking in upon the sanctity of the Sabbath and Sabbath-day duties, I was led to invite the Captains on board to breakfast. Being all, on this occasion, successful fishers, the excitement of social intercourse provoked further departures from duty; the Sabbath seemed forgotten, and the conversation, which I had not resolution to attempt to divert, proved worldly and vain, and, on the part of one of my visitors still worse, besides being altogether unsuited for the sacredness of the day. And although I felt conscience-stricken and unhappy, even in the height of our self-indulgence, yet from a foolish and mistaken politeness, I asked them, as they were preparing to retire, to prolong their stay until after our usual early dinner. As they unhappily acquiesced, the religious duties of the day were, for the most part, prevented, and the best of the Sabbath passed away, not only unsanctified, but desecrated ...'. Scoresby then went on to note that, when, compared to other ships in the vicinity, the *Resolution* was during the next week markedly unfortunate in regard to both ice navigation and whale capture. Even the whale that was killed on 27 June 'was in reality a mortification, for instead of yielding the considerable produce which its ample size seemed to promise, it proved lean, meagre, and singularly unproductive!'.
[2] See entry for 11 May 1811.

Doctor presently afterwards went to see if his charge was safe and found it astonishing to behold it removed he knew not whither; he burst out in an exclamation of surprise and partly taxed Capt[n] J with having got which of course he flatly denied persuading the Surgeon he had laid it somewhere else. M[r] J again took it on board the Aimwell whilst the Doctor repeatedly expressed his <u>wonder</u> that the book should be missing and his grief lest it should be lost[.] He had not seen[1]

In the Morning being little wind with fog or snow Showers began to ply to Windward around a SEern patch of Ice. In the Afternoon it fell calm several sail in sight[.] Effort 29 Fish (6 size) 120–30 Tons Volunteer 18 90–100 Tons &c[.]

Tuesday June 25th
Werly

In the Calm cleared away and began to make off (below) in the Forehold[.] . Light various with showers of snow made sail to the SE[d] but in the night falling in with several large fish in a very open patch of Ice by the SW Pack made a loose fall[2] and sent away 6 Boats as likewise did the Aimwell. Many of the Whales were playing near pieces of Ice and would have been good to come at had not the Boats of the different Ships interfered with each other which failed not to alarm the Fish. Thus we spent several hours in active pursuit and got nothing[.] Lay too employed making off the rest of the Day. Several sail in sight[.]

Wednesday June 26th Lat 78°35 Long 5°54E
NNW

Fresh breezes with Snow Showers the beginning of this 24 hours began to ply to the NNE seeing much water in that direction. Finished making off having filled 25 casks with Blubber and completed the lower hold Casks[.] On the snow clearing away I observed Several Ships fishing in the direction at which we aimed and about 10 PM could distinguish that they lay at the clear edge of a large Field of Ice many ships making for it all of which made fast as they got up[.] We reached to the NE[d] a considerable distance amongst loose Ice when we found ourselves seperated the Field by a neck of Ice not much more that [sic] 1½ miles through and which at the times was impervious[3] to the Ships for plying though not to the Boats[.] hence sent 5 Boats off with orders to range the edge of the Field to the W[d] &c[.] In about 4 hours the wind still blowing fresh found the Ice so much slacked that I thought a passage practicable[.] Made sail and after a good deal of anxiety and care accomplished the passage and worked up towards the Field[.] the Boats met us as we got out[.] They brought a bear had mistaken the orders and ranged the Field E[d] instead of Westward[.] Stood to the E[d] few fish seen the wind then Southering began to ply along the field edge in that direction towards the place we left yesterday. The Aimwell to Windward got two Fish

---

[1] In the original this sentence appears to be complete, but is illegible.

[2] '… when the whole of the boats are sent out, the ship is said to have "a loose fall"': Scoresby, *Account of the Arctic Regions*, II, p. 237. This was the situation on 25 June 1811, and Smyth (*Sailor's Word Book*) therefore seems mistaken in his definition: 'LOOSE FALL. The losing of a whale after an apparently good opportunity for striking it.'

[3] A transcription error; the original is '… not much more than 1½ miles through & which at that times was impervious …'.

most of the Ships about us made some captures and some several. The Henrietta and Active (Peterhead[)] bore away with colours flying[1] the wind towards noon again increased to a fresh breeze accompanied with Fog Showers[.] several Ships in sight[.]

Thursday June 27th
SSW
Fresh breezes variable accompanied with Fog[.] Afterwards snow Showers the Fore part[.] Worked up until we came to much loose Ice at the Field edge where seeing several fish called all hands and just afterwards struck one. This was soon killed but got beset by the loose Ice drifting upon the Field made the Ship fast a little to [windwᵈ?] of it altho' the wind blew partly upon the Field[.] Took two whale lines which reached the Fish to the capstern and by many men clearing the Ice away hove her up along side[.] the Boats then went off again in pursuit. The rest of the men flinching. The Effort hoisted his signal whilst flinching. Having flinched the Fish cast off and by a warp out of the Quarter backed the Ship round and sailed off the Ice. Saw a few fish amongst loose Ice. The wind fell and afterwards again increased to a strong breeze. Towards noon reached in to the field from along the edge which had cleared to the Wᵈ and made fast near the Neptune with 24 Fish 130–40 Tons Wᵐ & Ann 19 (14 size) 110 Tons[.] 10 or 15 sail all made fast to this field it drifts very fast to the SSW or SWᵈ[.] 3 Boats on Watch[.]

Friday June 28th
NWbN
Fresh breezes to light airs snow Showers occasionally mostly clear. In the night the field ceased to drift so rapidly to the SWᵈ the loose Ice then set directly off and cleared the edge of the Field far to the SWd so that in the Mornᵍ the loose Ice was 10 miles off. Many ships about us got fish the Neptune two[.] One of our harponeers made a bad heave at one and missed another struck one which ran out 10 lines and escaped[.] The Neptunes boats crew were [civil?] enough to pull up to our Boat and bend on[.] Got a bear[.]

Saturday June 29th Lat 77°59 Long 5°16E
W to SW
Many Narwhales seen in the Evening began to make off in the hold having filled 10 casks with Blubber which together with what was filled before make in all 382[2] = to 190 tons of oil. About 4 Tons remaining to be made off. Draught of Water Forward 14ᶠᵗ 5ⁱⁿˢ aft 14ᶠᵗ 9ⁱⁿ (new Marks[)] About 3 AM made sail 20 miles NWbW fell in with heavy Ice and floes in the thick no fish seen tacked and ½ an hour afterwards tacked again lay SbW[.]

---

[1] 'When this flag is hoisted at the mizen peak, or mizen top-mast head, in the latter end of the fishing season, it indicates that the ship carrying it is "full", and homeward bound.': Scoresby, *Account of the Arctic Regions*, II, p. 523, where Scoresby uses the term 'ancient', i.e. 'ensign', as a synonym for the national colours.
[2] See the journal entries for 12 February 1812 and 26 May 1813, in regard to cask capacities and equivalents.

Sunday June 30ᵗʰ Lat 78°50″ [*sic*] Long 6°40″E [*sic*]
SSE

About noon tacked amongst loose Ice stretched several miles to the ENE when it clearing up worked to the ESEᵈ between Patches of Ice into open Ice[.] At the Sea edge by a Patch of Ice saw a Fish had two Boats in pursuit it appears several had been here by other Ships. Snow Showers commenced with a strong breeze of wind steered away to the NE or NEbE. Spoke the Enterprize with 20 Fish 130–40 Tons gives account of Perseverance of Peterhead having 160[.] [then?] two Ships with the 2 Peterhead <u>Brigs</u> and the Aimwell followed us continued our reach about 8 hours sailing 30–40 miles when we fell in with a Patch of Ice and few Fish[.] the Enterprize struck one[.] worked to Windward (having missed the whales and seeing no more) round the Patch and then sailed about 15 miles further ['**Monday July** 1ˢᵗ Lat 78°40 Long 7°18E' *in margin*] NE into an open Patch of Ice being then a thick Fog and wind having fallen to a light breeze tacked. Before we entered the Patch saw two fish and 4 or 6 Ships[.] reached out to the SSEᵈ amongst open pieses [*sic*] and floes of Ice in a thick constant Snow for about 12 hours the wind being very light saw many Unicorns and heard the Blowing of 2 or 3 fish[.] About 5 AM having come near a floe and hearing the blowing of a whale tacked and sent a Boat to seek it[.] They continued to lie in wait 4 or 5 hours seeing the same fish occasionally which at length was struck near a close patch of Ice to the Nᵈ of a Floe the Boats spreading themselves judiciously soon got to her on coming up and in due time killed her[.] took her along side and flinched as we lay too or reached to the WSW amongst open Ice[.] 5 sail in sight running to the SWᵈ between a pack on the NE and Patches on the SW side of them[.]

Tuesday July 2ⁿᵈ
NbW

The Crew now seemed satisfied with our success as a signal brought the Fish to the Ship with flying Jacks. Finished flinching made a short board to Windward and then reached by the wind to the SWbW fine weather Fog Showers constant fog commenced which continued until (Wednesday) at intervals very thick could not see 100 yards[.] The Fog was such that the decks were quite dry but the rigging became coated with glass. The wind coming WSW about mid night worked about SWbW tacking to the Nᵈ for heavy and apparently partly packed Ice[.] Saw two or 3 fish running very fast to the Sᵈ[.] Fog clearing away at 2 PM found ourselves approaching a patch of Ice extending to the SE of us and in a line about NW and SEᵈ loose patches were ['**Wednesday July** 3ʳᵈ Lat 78° Long 6°E WSW' *in margin*] also seen to the SW of us but an open passage between them[.] made all haste to the SWᵈ. Several Ships seen amongst the Ice to the Wᵈ and NW of us some apparently fishing. Saw a fish had a Boat in pursuit[.] At Mid night 20 sail in sight scattered all round and mostly 10 or 20 miles off. Working to Windward saw no fish during the night towards noon saw one running towards the Wᵈ[.] Employed rigging long FTG Mast.[1] Enterprize Aimwell &c to leeward[.] An open Pack to the Wᵈ at the edges within a Ship apparently beset[.] At noon moderate breezes fine cloudy weather a small shower of Rain[.]

---

[1] In preparation for the homeward journey. See entry for 16 March 1811 and footnote.

Thursday July 4th Lat 77°56 Lon 5°46E
S to SE

Moderate or fresh breezes with astonishingly fine weather for the Season[.] Thermometer 36° at Mid nt[.] working to Windward on the E side of a Pack seemingly consisting of large pieces and floes of Ice some of which are of considerable magnitude[.] loose patches and streams to the E^d of us laying too occasionally on seeing Fish. Saw 5 or 6 they all held a course about W and a velocity of 3 or 4 knots when under water but less considerably when blowing. I observed them as they came to the loose Ice or patches they [***] or tarried a little[.]

About mid night one came up near the Ship which we struck[.] She went very little downwards but running about the surface making sudden turns and moving at the rate of near 5 knots the Boats had some difficulty in coming up to her[.] At length a 2nd Harpoon was struck in and immediately afterwards the first broke in the shank (The Iron broke cold Short or Shot) as the Smiths term it.[1] The Harpoon was of [Flinn's?][2] construction the only one of 12 which had been very much used that stood not the test[.] In a moderate time the Fish was killed. In the Interim of getting her to the Ship &c we divided the Twin Decks into partitions that we might more conveniently make off by emptying only one of them. The Bulkheads were made athwart by the Iron stantions they were 3 or 4 in number formed of spars and hatches supported by them. Flinched the fish under easy sail and then made way to Windward keeping the pack to the W^d aboard[3] when practicable. Two Ships got a fish hereabouts[.] 4 sail in sight Viz Perseverance Peterhead Hope Sarah & Eliz and Prince Brazils[.]

Thursday[4] July 5th Lat 77°46 Long 5¾E
SE

Having now by the kind assistance of Divine Providence obtained a good Cargo suppose upwards of 210 Tons of oil we purpose to proceed homewards taking the Ice along as we go that we may have the chance of obtaining another Fish or two in our way having sufficient convenience for 20 or 30 Tons more could we obtain it. In the night had a Boat in pursuit of fish of which we saw several. Continued plying to the S or SSE along the edge of loose Ice with a moderate or light breeze of wind and Fog Showers towards morning. The Hope got a Fish. Sent a Boat to a patch edge for fresh water Ice got as much as filled about 6 Casks have altogether about 9 Casks Ice 2 of water and 2 of Beer for the passage homewards[.] 5 Sail in sight.

---

[1] *OED*: 'Cold-short ... Said of iron: Brittle in its cold state.' Apparently caused by phosphorus content.

[2] See p. 31, n. 4.

[3] Here apparently used, relative to the ice-edge, in the sense of 'to hug the land in approaching the shore': Smyth, *Sailor's Word Book*, s.v. 'Aboard'.

[4] *Sic*. The column on this page of the transcript was headed, as usual, by the date of the log entry that was in progress. However, this date was inserted incorrectly as 'Wednesday July 4th'. This apparently caused the writer or copier of the log to indicate this next entry, lower down the page, as 'Thursday' instead of 'Friday'. The error was corrected at the head of the next page.

Saturday July 6ᵗʰ
SW

Light to moderate breezes in the night fog Showers. The Ice trending more to the Eᵈ steered about ESE and at 10 PM came up to the Volunteer laying too for us he has 23 fish (15 size) = 150 Tons of Oil he informed us that Captⁿ Cutter[1] had been seeking a passage to the NE of this in an Erly direction out of the Ice and had been obliged to return and seek it more Southerly[.] Mʳ Dawson[2] says he wants a Fish or two more before he goes home[.]

    Reached under easy sail to the ESEᵈ soon fell in with pieces of Ice in a thick Fog proceeded until the Sailing became troublesome then tacked and lay too[.] Employed making off in the Twin Decks upon the Casks in the lower hold[.]

Sunday July 7ᵗʰ
Serly

In the Afternoon the Fog cleared away and we saw an opening to the ESE made sail with a light air of wind followed by the Volunteer whose Captⁿ Came on board. Saw a whale at the edge of a loose pack which now lay all round us but the direction in which we came[.] on the fog clearing up saw about 20 Sail of Ships[.] All but the Volunteer amongst the Ice to the SEᵈ of us made all sail that way but calm and fog stopped us towards morning. towed a little with one or two Boats[.] Finished making off having filled all our Blubber Casks several Beer and Fresh water Casks and 3 or 4 Beef or Pork Casks[.] Number of casks &c as per margin.[3]

    At noon the Aimwell a head hoisted his pendant to us we answered.[4] The Enterprize Hope Volunteer Active Perseverance Fountain &c in all 24 sail in sight all following the same course amongst cross Ice not very heavy in direction by the wind to the SE or SEbS obliged to tack occasionally for close patches the clearest lead being about SbE to SSE. Found more room at noon than we had in the morning. Saw a Finner (Razor Back[).]

Monday July 8ᵗʰ Lat 76°36 Long 9°10E
SW

Light to fresh and afterwards moderate Gales, charming weather favoured our passage thro' a pack of open but cross Ice until about 7 PM when a thick fog commenced accompanied with a great increase of wind which rendered the sailing very dangerous[.] however we reached at the rate of 5 or 6 knots to the SbE SSE &c for 4 Hours when the Fog somewhat thinned and we found ourselves coming to open Ice in which we sailed several miles and then hauled up SSW having found ourselves in the morning apparently at Sea. Several Sail in sight the Enterprize Aimwell and Perseverance in Company[.] employed flinching and making off the Blubber of 6

---

  [1] Master of the London whaler *Reliance*.
  [2] Dawson was the master of the *Volunteer* of Whitby.
  [3] This refers to a list in the original but not transcribed. The 'margin' in the original is extended along the bottom of the page, to include also a diagram described as follows: 'This Figure shows the stowage of the Resolution's Twin Decks or the 5ᵗʰ & 6ᵗʰ Tiers of Casks …'.
  [4] See footnote p. 48, n. 1.

whales Tails cut in pieces and [strewed?] upon the Casks as far aft as possible rigged the long TG Masts Mizen Top Mast &c[.]

Tuesday July 9th Lat 75°30[1] Long 11¾E
W
Moderate or fresh breezes foggy or hazy weather under all sail running to the SSW or sailed by the Wind to the S[d] in Company with the Enterprize and Aimwell which Ships nominated us Commodore[.] Several Ships in sight[.] the Aimwell has 30 fish (18 size) one of which is in bulk therefore favoured him with 4 Provision casks of 180 galls each[.] Employed rigging passage masts &c[.] The Enterprize 31 (22 size[)] about 170–80 Tons of Oil[.]

Wednesday July 10th Lat 75°30 Lon 12°E
SW
Continued our Course to the SSW or S[d] generally by the wind which throughout the Day continued a moderate breeze except for about 2 hours Calm in the Evening until 3 AM when we tacked then lay WNW to W sailed under all canvas 4 to 5 knots P hour[.] At noon 5 sail in sight[.]

Thursday July 11th Lat +74°52 Long 10°E
SWbS
Moderate breezes fog or haze showers little wind towards noon[.] At 8 PM having passed several disseminated pieces of Ice and seeing much loose Ice a head (NW[d])[2] tacked our example was followed by all Ships in sight (viz 7 in sight[)] as well as our Convoy[.] In the Morning fell in with loose pieces of Ice and met a swell SWerly which encouraged us to proceed in a SSW direction[3] and not to bear away SSE as an apparent blink shewed to be the most prudent course. All hand [sic] clearing the Decks of lumber[.] Stowed 3 Boats in the Twin Decks having in stowing the Blubber contrived to leave room for them[.] Placed the Guns scraped Ships sides &c[.] Carpenter employed making new Top Gallt Masts Crosstrees, Royal Masts and Poles[.] At noon much Ice seen to Windw[d] scattered pieces a head and to leeward[.] 9 sail in sight 7 in Company[.] Saw several Bottlenoses and some Finners[.]

Friday July 12th Lat +74°10 Lon 10[¼?]E
Westerly
After a few hours calm a light breeze sprung up which continued the Day accompanied with fog Showers in the Night[.] steered all night SbW amongst scattered pieces was encouraged to steer a little from the wind on account of the Increase of swell a

---

[1] A transcription error; the original is 'Lat. 75°46''. In Scoresby, *Account of the Arctic Regions*, I, Appendix 1, which uses civil days for the records after 1809, the latitude at noon on 9 July 1811 is given as 75°40'N; on the 10th as 75°15'N. Both these were estimates, extrapolating from the celestial determination of 77°56'N on 5 July The value for 11 July of 74°52'N was also a measurement.

[2] *Sic.* 'SW' may have been intended, but the original also appears to be 'NW'.

[3] Scoresby may have assumed that if there was a swell from the SW, there could not be significant ice in that direction.

head[.] got a little fresh water Ice at Noon very little Ice to see except to the E and S^d[.] The Enterprize Aimwell Perseverance Volunteer and Lively in Co[.] at 8 AM steered SSW at 10 SW. 2 Ships to the W^d of us[.]

Saturday July 13th Lat 73°12 Lon 9°¾E
Erly
Light or moderate breezes fog Showers[.] Under much sail steering to the SW or SWbW at the rate of 2 to 3½ knots[.] In the Evening passed several pieces of Ice a strong head swell encouraged us to keep to the SWbW[.] In the Morning no Ice to see washed and scrubbed the sides with sand and urine then soap and water[.] Rigged the TG Masts and sent up Royal Masts[.]¹ Aimwell Enterprize Lively and Volunteer in Company[.]

Sunday July 14th Lat 72°17 Lon 8°27E
SEbS
Fresh breezes in the Evening calm after 4 AM steering to the SW½W or SWbW thick fog showers or almost constant fog. The above Ships in Co[.] Two strange sail in sight[.] Set main <u>Sky Scraper</u>[.]²

Monday July 15th Lat +72°10 Long 6°57E
NW
Moderate breezes to light airs and afterwards moderate breezes[.] The fore part fog Showers[.] In the Evening 9 PM saw a strange Ship astern on the clearing up of the Fog[.] She appeared to be a Ship of War called all hands to quarters loaded all the guns put up breast and quarter cloths³ <u>exercised the musquets</u> &c[.] The Ships in Company shewed their alarm by hoisting Flags &c[.] The Enterprize hauled close by the Wind and parted some distance to Windw^d notwithstanding we shortened sail to concentrate our little fleet. The Ship in Chase fired several Guns[.] at length we hove too took in Top Gallt Sails Stay S^ls &c. She proved to be an English Frigate stationed in high Latitudes to protect the Greenland Ships[.] we alone were boarded by a Lieut^t in a jolly Boat he particularly enquired after the number of Ships left in the Country &c[.] They had seen my Father 18 Days ago with 16 Fish <u>Chock</u> full the Henrietta the Lion and James they had also seen. They had no intention of impressing men. The Lieut^t after making his remarks inquiring respecting all the Ships in Company and drinking a glass of wine left us and presently afterwards their ancient was hauled down as a signal for us to depart when directly we down tacks up T G Sails Flying Jib &c and made all sail. The Niobe is the Frigates name⁴ Captn James Baton⁵ Esq Lat

¹ Opposite this page of the original journal there is a full-page scale drawing of the main mast and rigging, with dimensions.
² Smyth, *Sailor's Word Book*, s.v.: 'A triangular sail set above the skysail.'
³ Smyth, *Sailor's Word Book*, s.v. 'Quarter-cloths': 'Long pieces of painted canvas, extended on the outside of the quarter-netting, from the upper part of the gallery to the gangway.'
⁴ HMS *Niobe* (38 guns) was originally the French *Diane*, and had been captured in the Mediterranean in 1800. Earlier in 1811 she had been on patrol off the Cherbourg peninsula: Phillips, *Ships of the Old Navy*.
⁵ *Sic*, but actually 'Katon', in his last command and acting during the indisposition of Captain Loring, the *Niobe*'s regular commander (loc. cit.).

72°59 Lon 5°28E according to their estimation at noon[.] they had seen North cape a Fortnight ago[.] The Niobe had been so far as 76½°N had seen several Whales[.] The Officers desired I would report having seen them all well on our arrival at England[.] He entrusted me with some Letters from the Officers. Continued our Course SWbW until 2 AM. At 4 by the Wind to the WNW[.] The morning being fine lashed spars upon the rigging called all hands and placed about 44 whales lines on to dry. The Day however unfortunately did not prove very favourable. Completed our new Top Gallt and Royal Masts the Ship much improved in appearance by it[.] About noon Mr Johnstone visited us gave him <u>Signal</u> Instructions. The Enterprize Aimwell Volunteer and Lively in Company.

I continue my Longitude from my former estimation since I suspect the Niobes Reckoning to be too far Westerly they having had no Lunar observation or Correction of Timekeeper since they saw the North Cape[.][1] They sailed from England in May little or no news[.]

Tuesday July 16th Lat 71°24 Lon 4°57E
SW
Light or moderate breezes cloudy at mid night the wind veered to the SSE made sail on a SW½W course.

Wednesday July 17th
ESE
The Wind increased to a Fresh Gale. The Clouds to Windward predicting rain called all hands and hurried the lines into the Gun Room and Cable Tier[.] We had scarcely got them down before the rain in a moderate Shower commenced which in the Evening turned into a thick fog. A strong SE Swell came on about Mid n^t when the wind fell to near calm and Shifted to the NW[.] From the prevalence of an Erly current or else the Compass being attached[2] by the Ship in those Latitudes we allow 2¾ or 3 Pts variation to compensate for it this when sailing on a Southern line brings the accounts more correct[.] Course SW Distance run 87 miles[.]

Thursday July 18th Lat 70°30°+ [sic] Long 3°35E
NW
Light breezes to calm[.] Strong Serly Sea. Occasionally foggy various courses were steered and little progress made[.]

---

[1] At 72°N latitude, the difference of almost 3 degrees in the longitude estimates of the *Niobe* and the *Resolution* is equivalent to about 55 nautical miles (100 km). See Introduction, p. lvii.

[2] *Sic.* In the original the phrase 'or else the compass being [***] by the ship' is a later pencil addition. 'Attracted' is more probable than 'attached'. See Introduction, p. lvii. In the paper on magnetic variation presented to the Royal Society in 1819, and reprinted as Appendix 9 in *Account of the Arctic Regions*, II, pp. 537–54, Scoresby noted (p. 543) that 'ever since the year 1805, I have been in the habit of allowing only 2 to 2¾ points variation on the passage outward to Greenland, with a northerly or north-easterly course, but generally three points variation on the homeward passage when the course steered was S.W. or S.W.b.W. Without this difference, a Greenland ship outward bound will be generally found to be several leagues to the eastward of the reckoning, and homeward bound will be as much as 4 or 5 degrees to the eastward of it.'

Friday July 19th Lat 70°12 Lon 0 53°E [*sic*]
SW
Moderate to fresh breezes clear about noon an hour or two afterwards fog showers frequently very thick[.] Courses WbSW, NW SEbS &c velocity 2 to 4 knots[.]

Saturday July 20th Lat 69°31 Lon 1°35 W
SWbS
Moderate or light breezes occasionally foggy steered WbN to SWbW close hauled by the wind[.]

Sunday July 21st Lat 68°43 Lon 2°5 W
SEbS
Fresh gales rain or Fog showers. Performed Divine Service as usual[.] Towards Noon the weather cleared[.] Courses SW to NWbW and SE[.]

Monday July 22nd Lat 68°28 Lon 2°1 W SWbW
Fresh to moderate or light breezes with Fog Showers and high Sea[.] At 7¼ AM fired a Gun as signal to tack. The Aimwell answered the [Ent*erprise*?] within 50^{yds} of us[.] Fresh breezes impenetrable Fog[.] Courses WNW to SE[.] Velocity only 2 knots[.]

Tuesday July 23rd Lat 66°48 Long 2°26 W
SSE
Clearing up about 6 PM saw the Aimwell Volunteer and Enterprize all joined Company[.] Strong or fresh gales in the Evening in the Morning More Moderate [***] with heavy rain[.] Steered SWbW & by the wind[.] Made 90 Miles Southing[.]

Wednesday July 24th Lat 66°12 Lon 4°57 W
SWbS
Fresh breezes chiefly foggy[.] on account of the scarcity of Coals the fire is extinguished immediately after the Dinner is cooked. From the long continuance of wet and foggy weather find several of our Sails touched with <u>Mildew</u> loose them at all opportunities[.] About 10 AM Fog cleared away and a fine Day commenced[.] The above Ships in Company[.] Var[?] compass observed [3⅛?] Pts Westly[.] Loosed all sails to dry began to suspend two Boats lines in the Suns rays[.] Courses WNW and W[.]

Thursday July 25th Lat 65°30 Lon 5°28 W
South
Fresh breezes fine clear weather having dried 15 lines coyled them away upon the commencement of a Fog[.] Fresh Gales squally with Rain or Fog. Fixed a Mizen stay and bent Mizen Stay Sail[.] at 12 Thick fog with rain 4 PM Much rain[.] Calm short time in the Morning Light to moderate or fresh breezes fog or haze[.] Have had all Day a strong SWerly Swell. The Aimwell Enterprize and Volunteer in *Company*.

Friday July 26th Lat 63°3 Lon 4°16 W
NbE
Hazy weather or Rain wind increases[.] SWerly sea very high[.] Made signal for the

Convoy to continue their same course whilst we hauled to the SW then S bringing the Wind at each time on the Quarter to try if we could sail faster than before the wind[.] we headed them very little[.] Set two lower steering sails afore but were soon obliged to take them in from the great increase of the SWerly swell. Saw some fresh birds viz Arctic Gulls[1] and Looms[2] which shews our approximation to some Land probably Farao [sic][.] Strong gales squally and high Sea reefed Top Sails our Compass differs so much that we cannot tell exactly how we steer sometimes 2 p^{ts} in the var^n of 3 more made made [sic] s^l set TGS^{ls} &c Towards noon Fine Weather sea high[.] The Above Ships in Co Aimwell and Vol inclined more to the E^d[.]

Saturday July 27th Lat 61°33+ Lon 4 43W
NbW

Fresh gales fine weather sea high[.] At 3 PM descried land (which we expected to be near both from our Reckoning and the appearance of Birds such as Arctic Gulls and a kind of [***] <u>Goose</u> a Brown Bird with a White spot on each wing[3] [)] bearing SbW½W Distance about 34 miles[.] It proved to be the high black barren Cliffs of Farroe. The NE^{rn} point was a remarkable high perpendicular Cliff[.][4] At 5^{h}30′ 44″ PM apparent time by the angular distance of the Sun and Moon (several Sets of obs) found the Long of the Ship 7°9′45″W being at that time in Lat reduced from meridian observation of the Moon 62°45N[.][5] A strange sail in sight at dusk[.] Swell very high turning round the N end of Farro and altering from a W to a NE direction on leaving the land it fell[.] In the Morning the Enterprize hoisted her Ancient and [parted Co?] with an intent to go to the W^d of Orkney and thro' Pentland Firth[.] Charming weather suspended the rest of the whale lines to dry[.] At noon Ronaldsha[6] SSE½E 147 Distance[.]

Sunday July 28th Lat 60°58 Lon 3°48W
WNW

Moderate breezes fine weather having got the lines in good order at 4 PM took them down and coyled them away[.] Light airs very variable cloudy with a strong SWerly swell.
Fresh or moderate breezes foggy or small rain[.]

Monday July 29th Lat 60°0 Lon 1°56W
SW

Moderate breezes squally sea turbulent[.] Mr Johnstone visited us[.] At 2 AM

---

[1] In *Account of the Arctic Regions*, I, p. 532, Scoresby defined the arctic gull as 'Larus *parasiticus*', which is not the name of any present *L.* species. Linnaeus applied this term to the arctic skua, now *Stercorarius parasiticus*.

[2] The journal clearly indicates 'looms', as distinct from 'loons' (see *OED* on the varied ornithological meanings of both these terms.) In *Account of the Arctic Regions*, I, p. 532, Scoresby distinguished 'COLYMBUS *Troile*. – Foolish guillemot or Loom' from 'COLYMBUS *grylle*. – Tysté or Doveca.' From his descriptions, however, it appears that the latter bird is the black guillemot *Cepphus grylle*, and his loom is the common murre *Uria aalge*.

[3] Possibly the greylag goose (*Anser anser*).

[4] Villingadalsfjall on the northern tip of Bordoy reaches an altitude of 844 m (2,769 ft).

[5] If these coordinates were accurate, the *Resolution* would have been only about 25 nautical miles (46 km) due north of the Faroes archipelago.

[6] North Ronaldsay, the northernmost island in Orkney.

descried land and presently saw a rock above water and about a mile and ½ distance found it to be the Voe Skeery (The Voe Skeery is the most dangerous spot on this Coast to make lying surrounded with sunken rocks very low and 10 miles from the main deep water (45 Fathoms) at 1½ miles distance.[1] The Aimwell Aimwell [*sic*] supposing we did not see the land hoisted a light and fired 2 or 3 musquets [.]) Foul Isle was seen afterwards 3½ AM bearing SW distant 25 miles[.] The Wind being *Souther*ly tacked[.] The Aimwells Shetland men left them in a Boat of the Ships. Sea high a [freer?][2] wind commencing at 6 AM made sail followed by the Aimwell to the SSW between [Fula?] and the Main[.] passed [Fula?] in 20 to 25 Fathoms water 5 miles Distant[.] At noon Foul Isle bore NWbN and Fair Isle SSW[.]

Tuesday July 30th Lat 58 39+ Lon 1°30W
WSW
Moderate breezes fine cloudy weather[.] Employed in sundry necessary work[.] several strange sail seen two Ships of War[.] About 8 PM passed fair Isle on the East side 3 miles distant had several Boats on board to truck for fish eggs Fouls &c[.] One man had sailed in the John they got 16 10 feet fish and passed Fair Isle 22 Days ago sailed from Shetland in May[.]

Wednesday July 31st Lat 58°14 Lon 1°45
WbN
Light or moderate breezes charming fine weather[.] Employed painting Ship &c.
   Painting Ships Starboard side, leaving the other untouched[.] Therm*ometer* 10 AM 72°[.] The Two Peterhead Brigs and Volunteer in sight[.]

Thursday August 1st Lat 57°37+ Lon 1°51W
SSE½ S
Moderate to fresh breezes fine weather[.] at 6 PM saw[3] but did not get near enough before night to distinguish suppose it to be the coast somewhere near Kinnairds head[4] or further W[.] Courses SW, W ESE &c[.]

Friday August 2nd Lat 57°9N Lon 1°44W
SbE
Moderate to fresh breezes or brisk gales and squally from the S or SbE[.] At the top of the Flood fetched in with the land close by Peterhead saw the En*terprise* and two Fishing Brigs in the Roads one of them went into the Harbour. It appeared they had but just arrived[.] Several small vessels and some Fishing Ships in Sight[.] tacked at 10 PM stood off 5 hours and tacked to the SE of Girdleness[5] at 9½ AM having realized a distance of 25 miles to Windw^d in 11½ hours[.]

---

[1] Almost certainly the Ve Skerries, off the west coast of Shetland (60° 22′ N 1° 49′W).
[2] If this reading is correct, Scoresby was stating that the wind had shifted further abaft the beam.
[3] Transcription omission; '… saw land but …' in original.
[4] At Fraserburgh, Grampian.
[5] Aberdeen, Grampian.

Saturday August 3ʳᵈ Lat 56°37 Lon 2°17W
SbE
Brisk winds from the S to the SbE or SWbS tacked in the Offing[1] at 3 PM to get in
Shore by the latter end of the Flood and carry it off with us[.] At 9 PM being near the
Lime kilns by Red head[2] the SW appearing showery and squally tacked lay SEbS or
SE[.] During the night moderate or fresh breezes cloudy or showers of rain sea high so
that we got very little or no ground[.] At noon tacked not far from where we fetched
last night[.] Several Ships in sight[.]

Manifest of the Cargo of the Ship Resolution of Whitby British built admeasuring two
hundred ninety one 50/94 Tons William Scoresby Junʳ Master from Greenland for
Whitby

250 Leagers	Blubber containing five hundred seventy Butts of ½ a Ton each[.]	
140 Butts		
18 Puncheons	Six tons of whale fin	T Brodrick
6 Barrels		
	Greenland Seas	W Scoresby
	13ᵗʰ July 1811	

		tons	Galls	
1811 Sepᵗ paid duties for		214	72	procured from the cargo
1812 Janʸ Sold		218″	50	

Sunday Augᵗ 4ᵗʰ Lat 56°14 Lon 1°33W
The fore part moderate breezes and various from the Southward SW &c plying off
Montrose a few miles distant gaining very little ground. Several fishing Ships came

[1] Smyth, *Sailor's Word Book*: 'OFFING. Implies to seaward; beyond anchoring ground. – *To keep a good offing*, is to keep well off the land, while under sail.'
[2] Red Head is the promontory on the south side of Lunan Bay, between Montrose and Arbroath, Tayside.

within sight[.] In the Evening calm with heavy rain[.] In the morning a light breeze of wind accompanied at first with heavy rain sprung up from the N[d] made all sail S and the [sic] SbW. The weather[1]

Cheviot hills at WbS S[t] Abb[s] head[2] at WbS at noon[.] The Leviathan[3] came up from astern got a list of the Streights Ships from him he has 10[.] on the whole the fishery in that quarter has been very bad many Ships having but one or two fish each[.][4] Two or three clean. One lost[5] and another under the Ice three Days and got into harbour where a piece of Ice 10 Tons in weight was taken out of the hold[.]

Monday August 5th Lat 55°30 Lon 0° 54W
The Sun shining remarkable hot overcame the wind which about 4 PM fell to calm[.] A SSW breeze about 6 sprung up[.] All the Ships in sight lay starboard tacked we lay larboard tacked W, WbN or WNW conceiving there was a probability of the wind Westering after a hot Day also from the quality of the clouds which arose in that quarter[.] as we expected so it proved for at 8 AM[6] we tacked and lay SSW made all sail to the S½W[.] At 9 saw the Fern lights[7] which we passed about 11PM[.] The Vol Lively Leviathan &c in sight all to leeward. The Situation of the Sun and Moon being favourable for very high springs at this full we were very anxious to gain our port[8] for 17 or 17½ feet water was expected in Whitby bar about Wednesday Morning. Last year in this very spot we met with winds in the full Moon very much similar to those we have now the same direction and of like strength[.] The wind failed tow[ds] Morning fell nearly calm[.] Light airs from the SWbS at noon charming fine weather[.] Thermometer 73° Coquet Island[9] 20 miles distant employed ornamenting the Ship with a head[.][10]

---

[1] Transcription error. This sentence in the original, a pencil replacement for a similar log entry, is 'The weather then cleared up & became charmingly fine.'

[2] North of Eyemouth, Borders.

[3] According to Credland (*Hull Whaling Trade*, p. 125), this was the second *Leviathan* among Hull whalers, built in 1803, 410 tons, and first registered at Hull in 1817. However Lubbock (*Arctic Whalers*), though agreeing on the construction date and size of the ship, identified her as the third Hull whaler of that name (the two previous vessels having made their first voyages in 1754 and 1759 respectively) and indicated (p. 160) that the third *Leviathan* sailed as a Hull whaler from the time she was completed.

[4] Lubbock, *Arctic Whalers*, p. 188: 'The year in Davis Straits was not so good, only 3 ships making over 400 butts.'

[5] The original has a marginal addition 'Koningsberg lost'. The *Konigsberg*, Captain Kirby, was a Hull whaler 254 tons; Credland (*Hull Whaling Trade*, p. 125) noted that the vessel was 'Always listed in the customs registers as Koningsberg'.

[6] A transcription error; 'Pm' in original.

[7] There has been a lighthouse on the Farne Islands since 1673. In 1811 those built in the 1770s on Farne Island and Staple Island were being replaced by new lights on Farne and Longstone, though the latter light was itself replaced by the present structure in 1826: Trethewey and Forand, *The Lighthouse Encyclopaedia*, s.v. Longstone.

[8] ?Possibly 'pos[n]'.

[9] South of Alnwick, Northumberland.

[10] Smyth, *Sailor's Word Book*, s.v.: 'an ornamental figure on a ship's stem expressive of her name, or emblematic of her object, &c'.

Tuesday August 6th Lat 54°48 Long 0 28W

Light to moderate breezes variable from S to WSW or WNW in the Evening tacked and stood in at 3PM at 8 tacked again and made all sail to the SSW or S^d[.] At 10 PM Tinmouth?][1] light bore W½N 10 or 12 miles distant[.] In the morning the wind came more Serly[.] At 6 AM were off [Hindcliff?][2] 10 or 15 miles distant[.] The Ebb tide set us across the Tees to the N^d[.] At 11 AM tacked near Hartlepool lay SSE to SEbE[.] The Aimwell and Lively to the N^d Vol to the S^d[.]

Wednesday August 7th

SbE

Fresh breezes cloudy weather in the afternoon plying to Windward with a flood tide got a pilot on board off Staithes and at 6 PM got into Sandsend roads when the wind presently shifting round to the N^d and blowing hard with heavy rain lay too[.] At Day break began to get out the boats spars and davits[.] At 4 AM weighed anchor and when all the Ships had got within the Piers made sail for the Harbour[.] We were somewhat too late for the tide and soon aground near the scotch head on the SE side[.][3]

Thursday Augt 8th

In the afternoon tide got the Ship opposite Mr Martines where we moored[.] I wished to proceed thro' Bridge but was overruled by the managing owners[.]

Saturday Augt 10th

About noon a heavy NE gale of wind commenced which soon caused a very high sea to roll into the Harbour every Person now much regretted that we had not gone above Bridge[.] Every tide for 2 or 3 Days the Ship struck an hour or two with such violence as to shake the masts exceedingly[.] No <u>evident</u> damage was sustained.

[1] The light at Tynemouth was established in 1540. By 1811 there were twin towers, lit by oil since 1773. These towers had been rebuilt in 1805-8 and lit in May 1810: Trethewey and Forand, *The Lighthouse Encyclopedia*, s.v. Tynemouth.

[2] Presumably Hunt Cliff, near Saltburn, North Yorkshire. See journal entry for 12 August 1812.

[3] Scotch Head is on the western side of the harbour entrance. Scoresby presumably meant that the *Resolution* grounded in the lower harbour opposite Scotch Head. Even today this area is dry at low water. See United Kingdom ... Admiralty Chart 1612.

Journal for 1812

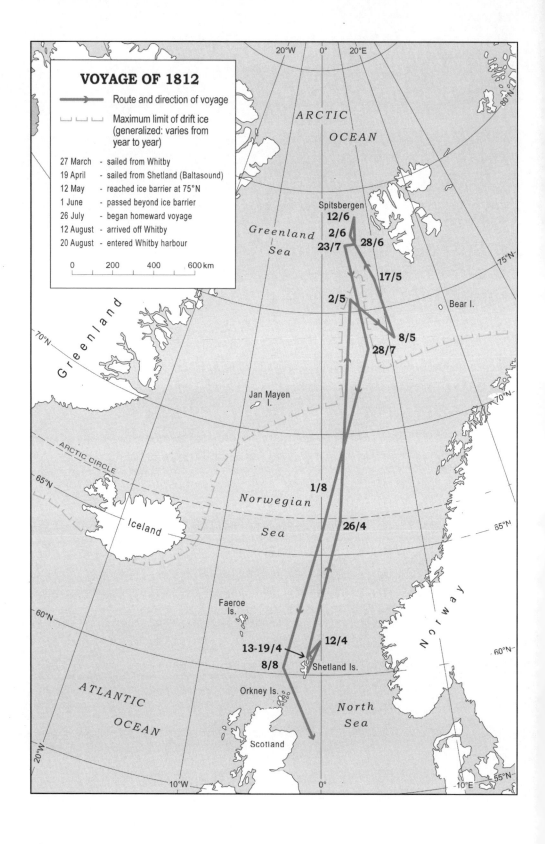

VOYAGE OF 1812

Route and direction of voyage

Maximum limit of drift ice
(generalized: varies from
year to year)

27 March   - sailed from Whitby
19 April   - sailed from Shetland (Baltasound)
12 May   - reached ice barrier at 75°N
1 June   - passed beyond ice barrier
26 July   - began homeward voyage
12 August - arrived off Whitby
20 August - entered Whitby harbour

0   200   400   600 km

ARCTIC OCEAN

Spitsbergen
12/6
2/6
23/7   28/6

Greenland
Sea   17/5

Bear I.

2/5

8/5
28/7

70°N

Greenland

Jan Mayen
I.

ARCTIC CIRCLE

65°N

1/8

Norwegian
Sea   26/4

Iceland

Faeroe
Is.

13-19/4   12/4

8/8   Shetland Is.

Orkney Is.

North
Sea

ATLANTIC
OCEAN

Scotland

Norway

Ship Resolution fitting for Tenth Voyage for Greenland 1812

1812 January

Early this month we salted and packed 26½ pigs weighing with lard deducted

Tons	cwts	qrs	lbs
2	18	3	26[.][1]

We cured 18 Hams and hung 7 rounds[2] leaving other 5 to be taken from the next lot making in all 12 our usual stock[.]

In salting [we?] Corn[3] all the meat touching every part at the time the Butchers cut it up into 8 or 10 lb pieces[.] We allow it to stand 2 or 3 Days when all the Blood settles to the bottom of the Casks which we throw away as useless and then giving it a hearty salting we pack it closely in casks filling them above the top and placing weights upon them which when come down we head up <u>and pickle</u> by pouring into the Bung holes water and salt mixed or dissolving salt in by pouring water upon it when laid on the bung hole dry. This operation we continue until no more can be got in. Into the Pork Casks we put ½ lb to ¾ each of salt Petre[4] (the Casks are 170 or 180 Galls Guage [*sic*]). We apply to each of the Hams about 2 oz of Salt Petre and allow them to lay 10 or 14 Days in pickle or with frequently renewed <u>salt</u> upon them. The rounds are cured in 4 or 6 Days and are lightly Petred[.]

The Ground Tier of the hold Casks, was stowed in [***] and filled with water.[5]

13th Jan[y] Began to stow the 2nd Tier with 2 men and the Boys[.] we left off on the 25[th][.]

27th to 31st Stuffed[6] Decks with warmed Tar. Tarred rigging. Painted Waist and Quarter Boards &c. Carpenter employed in sundry jobs[.]

---

[1] 6,606 lbs, or 2,996 kg.

[2] *OED*: 'a large round piece *of* beef, usually one cut from the haunch'.

[3] Smyth, *Sailor's Word Book*, s.v. 'Corn, To'. '… To preserve meat for a time by salting it slightly.'

[4] Saltpetre, or potassium nitrate (KNO_3).

[5] Scoresby credited his father with this practice of ballasting whalers as far as and into the icefields. 'The whalers … at my Father's commencement … went ordinarily ballasted, or, sometimes, "flying-light," not only because of this being accordant with the practice of merchantmen, but with the view of lessening the concussions against the ice when coming into violent contact with it. My Father, on the contrary, adopted a totally different system. He caused such a large quantity of the lower and second tier of casks to be filled with water (to which he subsequently added ballast of shingle or iron in the interstices of the casks of the "ground tier"), that the ship became as deep as with the third part of the cargo … His deeply ballasted ship might have struck heavier against the ice than others, but she was rarely *allowed* to strike heavily.' This was one of the techniques through which the elder Scoresby 'was enabled to make a progress, in "windward sailing" among ice, which, during a long period of years, defied all competition.': Scoresby, *My Father*, pp. 196, 198–9.

[6] Smyth, *Sailor's Word Book*: 'STUFF. A *coat of stuff*, a term used for any composition laid on to ships' spars, bottom, &c …'

Tons cwt qr lb   T cwt

13th Feby Had 7 oxen weighing 3   1   1   15 which with 1 15 got before makes about 8 Tons[1] leaving about an ox to complete our stock of 8¼ or 8½ Tons[.] this ox we purpose taking out fresh. Boys employed rattling the rigging[.][2]

21st March[3]

Got 3 Chaldron of Coals and on Monday 24th 2½ more from the Phoenix which makes up our stock of 5½ chaldrons[.][4] Filling water in the hold and stowing 2nd Tier[.]

27th

Got Provisions on board[.]

28th

Got 3¼ Tons bread of T Nettle ship[5] together with a 2nd load of Potatoes which makes us 80 Bushels.[6] Prepared to remove the Ship, she did not float out of her Dock until top high water and even then we were obliged to heave her out stern first up the Harbour. By the time we were half-way down we ran foul of an anchor and ere we got the Ship well a Stern the tide had so falled that we grounded upon three Ships Cables. Tried in the morning tide of the 29th but did not succeed[.] in the afternoon however we got the Ship into the Bridgeway birth where we moored. The Mate (Mr Stanger) 3 men and the Boys had to attend on the Morning of Sunday 1st March to

---

[1] Scoresby appears to have included the almost 3 tons of pork mentioned in early January. His total of meat on 13 February, excluding the fresh beef yet to be acquired, would therefore have been 17,401 lbs (7.77 tons) or 7,893 kg.

[2] Smyth, *Sailor's Word Book*: 'RATTLE DOWN RIGGING, To ... To fix the ratlines in a line parallel to the vessel's set on the water.' The ratlines, or ratlings, are small lines fastened across ship's shrouds like ladder-rungs: ibid, s.v.

[3] *Sic*. This is clearly an error for 'February', confirmed by the remark in the entry 'and on Monday 24th'; as 1812 was a leap year, 24 March was a Tuesday.

[4] Smyth, *Sailor's Word Book*, defined a chaldron as 'A measure of coals consisting of 36 bushels; a cubic yard = 19 cwts. 19 lbs.' (i.e. 2,147 lbs or 974 kg). However an 1851 citation in *OED* states that 'The Newcastle [upon Tyne] chaldron is a measure containing 53 cwt. [5,936 lbs. or 2,693 kg.] of coals ... It has been found, by repeated trials, that 15 London Pool chaldrons are equal to 8 Newcastle chaldrons.' This indicates that a London Pool chaldron represented 3,166 lbs. or 1,436 kg. In Salisbury's paper 'Early Tonnage Measurement in England ...' there is the statement that 'An earlier note by Brockbank, in November 1795, referred to the lading of colliers in north-eastern ports. 100 tons register was equal to 6 keels of coals at Newcastle, to 7¼ keels at Whitby, and to 8 keels at Stockton.' This implies that the weight of a chaldron of coals, 'Whitby measure' was 6 ÷ 7.25 = 0.83 of a Newcastle chaldron, so that 1 chaldron Whitby measure = 5,936 lbs x 0.83 = 4,927 lbs, or almost exactly 2 tons, 4 cwt. Chaldrons, like bushels, were however an inherently imprecise unit of measurement, based on volume as much as weight.

[5] Correctly 'Nettleship'. A transcription error; in the original the name is broken at the end of a line.

[6] The imperial bushel was not legally established as a volumetric measure until 1826, when it was defined as 128 cubic feet, or the volume occupied by 80 lbs of distilled water at 62°F. *OED*: 'The bushel had a great variety of other values, now abolished by law, though often, in local use, varying not only from place to place, but in the same place according to the kind or quality of the commodity in question. Frequently it was no longer a measure, but a *weight* of so many (30, 40, 45, 50, 56, 60, 70, 75, 80, 90, 93, 220) pounds of flour, wheat, oats, potatoes, etc.'

carry out the one fluked anchor with the Chain fastened to the Ships heel which served to keep the Ship from off the Shore[.] we affixed the other Chain to the Posts under the Bridge to keep the Ships head off[.] On Monday 2ⁿᵈ We had about completed the hold got the Beer on Board and stood it[.] On Wednesday got Shakes[1] and Guns into a lighter to bring down the Day following[.]
Thursday Got Hams and hung beef[.]

Friday 6ᵗʰ [March] At 11 AM mustered the crew[2] all hands on board viz. self the Mate and Surgeon 5 Harponeers 5 Boatsteerers 5 Linemanagers 14 protected Seamen[3] Carpenter and mate Cooper and Cooks mate Armourer 7 Landsmen and Seamen and 6 apprentices.[4] At 12 began to pay each man his hand money Harbour Pay and Months advance which amounted to £165.9.8 finished before one and dined at ½ past the owners and two or 3 Friends present[.]

Saturday 7ᵗʰ Got Boats on board and stowed them Viz 4 in the twin Decks 3 on Deck and one over the Stern in all 8[.] Bent the sails also[.]

Monday 9ᵗʰ
to
Wednesday 11ᵗʰ Wind N or NE fresh or moderate Gales which at length veered to SW or WSW fine smooth sea and good tide 14½ feet water all the Ships but ourselves got to sea being the beginning of the Springs we were not very anxious expecting to get out on Friday the 13ᵗʰ the Day of the change[5] or New moon the wind however in the night had shifted to the Nᵈ or NE increased to a strong gale and accompanied with much snow hails and sleet[.]

14ᵗʰ to 17ᵗʰ Wind constantly from the N or Eᵈ sea high sometimes blowing a strong gale at others moderate and often accompanied with snow hail or Sleet[.]

Sunday 15ᵗʰ The Sea was so high we got our preventers[6] to our Chains &c[.]

---

[1] The unassembled timbers of casks. See journal entry for 11 May 1811.

[2] The legal requirements of the muster are set out in Appendix 4 of Scoresby's *Account of the Arctic Regions*, II, pp. 513–14. It could only take place when the ship was fully equipped and manned, and therefore ready to sail.

[3] Scoresby noted in *Account of the Arctic Regions*, II, p. 504, that whereas the legislation on impressment was specific in regard to the number of harpooners, boatsteerers and linemanagers who could be protected, there was no similar specificity in regard to ordinary seamen. It had therefore become the practice for customs officers 'to assume the number of common seamen required by law to be on board each ship … as the amount to be protected; that is, 16 men in a ship of 300 tons or upwards, and two men less for every fifty tons smaller burthen'. The *Resolution* (291 tons) was therefore entitled to 14 protected seamen.

[4] See below, after entry for 28 March 1812.

[5] *OED*: 'the passage from one 'moon' (i.e. monthly revolution) to another, the coming of the 'new moon'. *Brewer's Dictionary*, s.v. 'Thirteen' noted that 'It is traditionally regarded as unlucky for a ship to begin a voyage on the 13ᵗʰ, especially if it happens to be a FRIDAY.' Smyth, *Sailor's Word Book*, however, noted that any Friday was regarded as 'The *dies infaustus*, on which old seamen were desirous of not getting under weigh, as ill-omened.'

[6] Smyth, *Sailor's Word Book*: 'PREVENTER. Applied to ropes. &c., when used as additional securities … during a strong gale.'

18th Wind moderate but Sea high the Storm anchor in the Evening tide having come home[1] allowed the Ship to range so much and unobserved that the head chain broke and immediately the Ship fell alongside the houses we had but few hands on board and it was a considerable time before we could get an hawser out to heave the Ship off[.] at length we succeeded and also took a tow line to the Dolphin[2] across the water by means of which we again steadied the Ship we were much alarmed in the interval when the Ship ranged lest the stern junk[3] which was only an old rope should give way[.] if it had we should have inevitably injured the Bridge as well as seriously the Ship for she ranged with a velocity of at least 4 or 5 knots and a distance of 10 or 15 feet[.] In the Morning we carried the small Bower anchor thro' the Bridge not thinking the Posts secure[.] the wind now came from the SE but Sea was high and tides fallen off we found ourselves neaped.[4] The Bar*ometer* fell to 29.47 after which a very heavy fall of snow was experienced showers of Hail fell so large and firmly that several windows were broken thereby[.]

The Carpenters employed in preparing Harpoon and Lance stocks Boat hooks &c[.] the Cooper pails Piggins[5] &c. The rest of the Crew variously employed.

We were congratulated on our fortunate escape of the late tempestuous weather we felt happy in the contemplation and shall continue to think ourselves fortunate or favoured provided we succeed in getting to Sea[.] the next Springs which bring in the Apogee of the Moon are likely to produce lower Tides; the Ship being much by the Stern and drawing near 13 feet water we emptied 8 casks in the after Hold which were filled with Salt water for ballast[.]

Saturday 21st March

Strong or fresh gales of wind from the E[d] accompanied with Snow or Sleet. The Sea very high. The Agriculture (Sloop) came on Shore behind the West Pier close to the Battery[6] about 10 AM. The men easily got on shore; if the weather becomes moderate the vessel may also escape without serious damage[.] At Noon borrowed a mooring Junk of M[r] Agar as a further preventive to the Stern junk and hawser already out lest they might lest they might [sic] give way on the melting of the Snow which in the

---

[1] Ibid.: 'The anchor is said *to come home* when it loosens, or drags through the ground, by the effort of the wind or current.'

[2] Ibid. (among several other definitions of the term): 'a stout post on a quay-head … to make hawsers fast to.' Young, *History of Whitby*, II, p. 540n: 'Above the bridge are fixed *dolphins*, in the middle of the harbour, to which vessels are made fast.'

[3] Smyth, *Sailor's Word Book* also defined 'junk' as 'any remnants or pieces of old cable, or condemned rope' but stated that these have been 'cut into small portions' for various uses, whereas Scoresby here, and again in the next day's entry, used the uncut old rope as a mooring device.

[4] Smyth, *Sailor's Word Book*, s.v. 'Neaped': 'The situation of a ship which … is left aground on the spring-tides so that she cannot go to sea or be floated off till the return of the next spring-tides.'

[5] Smyth, *Sailor's Word Book*, s.v.: 'A little pail having a long stave for a handle; used to bale water out of a boat.'

[6] Young, *History of Whitby*, II, p. 541: 'Since the erection of the quay, the battery near the Scotch Head has been strongly rebuilt, in the form of a crescent, with a small tower at each angle, and is furnished with 8 guns.' Young also noted that there was a another battery at the pier head, with six guns, and that 'The guns are all 18 pounders.'

Country is said to be very deep. Already a considerable fresh[1] is observed in the Harbour.

Sunday 22nd
Fresh or strong gales continued all this Day accompanied with Showers of Snow or Hail and Fog occasionally[.] At 10½ AM a Sloop in the offing was observed to be making for the Harbour the Flag was hoisted on the Cliff as a signal for plenty of water[.][2] afraid however at the dread full surf which broke on the rock she steered so far to Leeward to get round it that she could not fetch they ran on Shore close by the Agriculture the surf on the beach was not so high as might have been expected[.]

Monday 23rd The wind now veered from E to SE or SSE the weather became fine and moderate. Some slight showers of Snow preceeded [*sic*] the Suns transit across the Meridian. The fresh water which comes down in the river was not by far as considerable as was expected especially since the quantity of Snow that fell in the Country was. Most of the moor roads were impassible some lanes completely filled the height of the edges. In the Afternoon the weather was moderate – sea much fallen[.]

Tuesday 24th Wind E to ENE fresh breeze accompanied with much Snow and an increase of swell. Frosty in the Evening[.]

Wednesday 25th Early in the morning wind veered to the NW[d] commencing a furious storm accompanied with uncommon Showers of Hail and Snow[.] After Day light almost constant Snow[.] Sea high all the roads about impassible [.] At noon wind at NNE or NEbN. From the Winds we have had for this last Fortnight it is highly probable the Whitby Fishing Ships have not yet reached Shetland. The various stormy weather and unfavourable winds they have had to contend with renders all the concerned anxious for their Safety.

By the Post which arrived about noon this Day accounts were received from the *Willia*m and Ann at queens Ferry Firth of Forth having experienced much severe weather and sustained some damage in her rigging and sails[.] They expect the rest of the Ships were at Sea the 24th Inst. and not farther North of the Firth of Forth[.]

Thursday 26th In the morning early the wind had fallen and Westered the Bar*ometer* had risen from 29 to 72 [*sic*] to 30.46 in 12 hours[.] the Sky cleared and the Weather became charmingly fine[.] Sea much fallen. The roads in the Neighbourhood from the drifting of the Snow have become worse than yesterday[.] All communication by

[1] Smyth, *Sailor's Word Book*, s.v.: several meanings including 'an overflowing or flood from rivers and torrents after heavy rains or the melting of mountain snows'.
[2] Young, *History of Whitby*, II, p. 540n: 'On the western cliff there is a flag-staff, where a flag is hoisted at high water, to intimate that ships may enter with safety: at half flood, when the depth of water on the bar is only about 7 feet, the flag is half hoisted: when the harbour cannot be entered without great danger, a fire is made near the staff, and the flag is not hoisted.'

coaches is stopped at present[.] Becoming fine weather in the afternoon the mail was forwarded by a chaise and four horses[.] Sister Arabella with 3 other Passengers[.][1]

Friday 27th (Good Friday) The wind in the night came round to the South[d] and in the morning blew a fresh gale at SbW. Took on board some extra ropes[.] Slung the Anchor by a lighter and took the Cable on board[.] Hoisted Flag No 2 (Blue Peter) and unfurled the fore top sail as signals for sailing. This being the Day of full Moon we expected near 15 feet water in the Bar[.] As soon as the Ship floated began to heave her across the Harbour into a fair way for the Bridge but it was not until 3 O clock PM before she came off[.] Passed the Bridge and took a tow line end to a Post near it to take sail from and in ½ an hour we were out of the Harbour[.] We had some confusion in getting out the tide being quite at its height [,] the Channel narrow the water not much more even in mid way than the Ships draught however we got safely out and at 4 PM parted with the Pilot Rich[d] Theaker and the Fog Boat and immediately made sail to the NNE½[2] P compass the wind a fresh breeze at SSE and South some small rain in the Evening[.] The Agriculture Sloop came on Shore on Saturday last has since been staked to the ground with stones and scuttled hence saved from material damage[.] with the lift of the Sea this tide (the Stones having been thrown out and the hole patched up) we observed her move off just as we were preparing to make sail[.] During the night we had moderate or fresh breezes accompanied with much heavy rain[.]

Saturday 28th Wind veered from SSE to WSW after day light had fine weather[.] Cloudy at noon by Indifferent[3] obs Lat 56°18[.] By account Lat 56°10″ [sic] N Long 0°44W.

Distribution of Resolutions Crew 10th Voyage. 1812.[4]			
No.	of Men's Names	Station on Board	Station in Harbour
1	Will[m] Scoresby	Comm[r]	
2	W[m] Stanger	Mate	
3	Christ. Crawford	Surgeon	
4	John Trueman	Speck & H.	

[1] Arabella Scoresby (1792–1881) was William Scoresby's younger sister. This mention of her is especially interesting because the *Life* of Scoresby by Robert Scoresby-Jackson (Arabella's son) quoted (p. 85) from the unpublished autobiography as follows: 'The only passing event of the year 1812, of a personal or family nature, that remains to be noticed, was the marriage of my third and youngest sister, Arabella, with Captain Thomas Jackson, Merchant-navy, of Whitby. This marriage took place about the end of March.' Although Scoresby gave him the title of 'Captain', he was the mate on Scoresby's father's ship, the *John*, in 1813: see journal entry for 29 April 1813. Arabella's aunt Sarah had married Thomas's uncle Robert in 1792, and Jane, another aunt, had married William Jackson, possibly another relative of Thomas, in 1788. (Stamp, *The Scoresby Family*, pp. 10, 20, 26–7.)

[2] *Sic*. A transcription error: 'NNE¼E' in original.

[3] Although 'indifferent' was used in several scientific connotations, it seems more probable, given the cloudy weather at noon, that it was used here in the sense of 'Not particularly good; poor, inferior; rather bad' (*OED*).

[4] This is part of a table that appears in the original; in the transcript the fourth column was omitted. There are three additional columns in the original: 'Station in Action', 'Boat' and 'Watch'. The latter two of these are however blank, and the Stations in Action are indicated only in pencil. A further version, down to No. 45 (Beeforth), with signatures or marks, the 'quality' (i.e. status in the crew) and categories of wages, is in the Scoresby Papers (WHITM:SCO624) on the reverse of the ship's articles. The latter states 'Seas of Greenland or Davis's Streights' as the *Resolution*'s destination.

5	John Farfar [Farrar?]	H.	
6	Willm Harrison	H.	
7	John Dunbar	H.	
8	Willm Rippon	H.	
9	Willm Wellburn[1]	Boats & Skee.	M. Top = L
10	John Hirst	B.	Cap.F top = S
11	Robt Nicholson (1)	B	Cap. M Top = S
12	Robt Nicholson (2)	B	M yard = S
13	Willm Ross	B	F Top = L
14	Thom. Wellburn	Lineman	M. yard = L
15	John Richardson	L.	M Top = S
16	Joseph Clark	L.	Miz. Top = S
17	John Smith	L.	F. yard = S
18	James Anderson	L.	M. Top = L
19	Richd Slytom	Carp^r	M y^d = S
20	John Webster	Cooper	M y^d = L
21	Rich^d [Vipond?]	Armourer	
22	Richd Simpkin	Steward	M^n Y^d = S
23	Willm Smith	Cook	M. Y^d = L
24	Pearson Campion	Carp. Mt.	
25	Anderson Graham	Cook's Mt.	F Y^d = L
26	John Shinfield	Seam^n	F Y^d = S
27	David Chicken	do.	F. Top = S
28	Joseph Britain	S.	F. Top = L
29	Thomas Parsey	S.	M. Y^d = S
30	Joseph Botton	S	M Y^d = L
31	Willm Barker	S.	M. Top = L
32	James Storm	S.	F. Y^d = L
33	Willm Burnicle	S.	M. Top = S
34	John Hall	S.	M. Top = L
35	Wm Thos Gray	S.	F. Top = S
36	John Lee	S.	F. Top = L
37	Willm Standen	S.	M. Top = S
38	Richd Francis	S.	F. Y^d = S
39	Henry Coates	S.	F. Y^d = L
40	John Thompson	Lanm^n [2]	
41	Richd Tindale	S.	F. Top = S
42	Willm Simpson	S.	F. Y^d = S
43	W^m McKie	S	M^n Y^d = S
44	Francis Robinson	L^d	F. Y^d = L
45	Wm Beckforth	L^d	M. Y^d = L
46	John [Parsey?]	App^ce	Miz. Top = L
47	Willm Lawrence	A^e	Miz. T. G. = S
48	Wm Clark (Seam^n)	A. S	F. Top = L
49	Arthur Mills	A.	Miz^n Top = L
50	Willm Hayes	A.	Miz^n Top = S

[1] This surname, like that of No. 14, is 'Welborn' in the version in WHITM:SCO624.
[2] 'Landsman' in the transcript, which has other minor differences from the original.

Sunday 29th Light breezes or inclinable to calm until 4 PM when a fresh breeze commenced accompanied with rain which soon increased to a strong gale.

For 12 hours before this gale commenced (from the state of the Bar*ometer*) I expected it hourly and mentioned my expectations to the Mate and other Officers and the moment the East wind began to blow we began to prepare for the Expected blast[.] The Sea did not rise very high[.] Towards noon more moderate at 10 wind to the NWbN Lat 56°27. Long 0 54W[.]

Monday 30th Fresh gales hazy or snow showers 8 Sail in sight reduced sails and tacked at 10 PM the land in sight at 8 PM bearing NW distant 7 leagues suppose to be Red Head[.][1] Towards morning the Wind increased to a hard gale accompanied with Snow rain or Sleet obliged to carry sail to keep off Shore. At noon Land in sight Sea high and still blowing hard[.] Lat 56°45 Lon 1.27W[.]

[Journal now assumes usual format]

Tuesday 31st March Lat 57°4'34N Lon 1°36'W
East
Strong gales some small Showers of Snow, several vessels seen[.] Carried all sail we could with safety to get of [*sic*] the Shore[.] Being about mid way of the Firth of Forth at mid night wore. Towards morning weather more moderate[.] Sea high[.] At 8 AM saw the land about Aberdeen[.] At noon Girdleness[2] at WNW distant 20'[.]

Wednesday 1st Ap[l] Lat 59°19'N Long 0 40'W
SEbE
Fresh Gales fine clear weather strong NErly swell. About 3 PM a large vessel was seen a stern of us and coming very fast up with[.] observing her with a head copper bottomed[3] and a tier of Cannonades being very suspicious we called all hands to quarters and made ready the Guns[.] He came under our lee and hailed us with "from whence came you" &c[.] We understood she was called the Defiance[4] from Leith to Greenock he wanted to know if we were bound thro' the Pentland Firth seemingly being a Stranger to that Navigation[.] We had fresh Gales all night steered NE to get a good offing in case the wind should eastern[.] At 8 AM we bore up made all sail Studding sails &c to try if possible to gain Shetland before dark[.]

NB We steered NE all night to get a good offing in case the long prevalent E Wind again commences and at 8 bore up with the view of making land to the S[d] and thereby run no risk of passing our port[.]

[1] See journal entry for 3 August 1811.
[2] See journal entry 2 August 1811.
[3] Copper sheathing of the hulls of arctic whaling vessels was unnecessary, because the teredo worm was much less of a problem in colder waters. The copper-bottoming of the unknown ship was therefore a potential danger signal to Scoresby and the *Resolution*.
[4] HMS *Defiance* (74 guns), built in 1783 and a participant in the Battle of Trafalgar, was in her final year of service. In 1811 and 1812, she was mainly on station off the Dutch coast: Phillips, *Ships of the Old Navy*.

Thursday Ap^l 2nd
SEbS
Fresh gales cloudy weather expecting to reach our Harbour before dark we carried all the sail we could crowd[.] At 1 PM we saw land. Fair Isle it proved bearing NW Dist 20 miles[.] Towards Evening whilst running up along the land Snow Showers were observed and the wind abated somewhat[.] we were however enabled to reach the entrance at 6½ PM and got a Pilot and at 7 or soon afterwards brought up near the S end of the Town in a birth rather too near the Shore[.] it was however the only one which presented itself from the Number of Ships (viz 23) which already occupied all the good Births. We found Volunteer Lively and Henrietta here the latter arrived Thursday and the 2 others Friday last. The *William* and Ann is in Scalloway and the Aimwell was left by the 3 Ships in Deer Sound Orkney. They give such an account of the passage as was scarcely ever heard 14 or 16 Days and constantly storms they sheltered themselves in Orkney[.]

Friday Ap^l 3rd
This Day commenced with fresh gales of wind from the SE or SEbE accompanied with rain[.] 2 or 3 Ships came in the Prince of Brazils with her mainmast sprung[1]. Since Morning we have been employed filling water in the hold to trim the Ship unbending some sails &c and making such alterations in the masts rigging and [canvass?] as may best suit the Fishing Country[.] In the Evening the wind increased to a heavy gale accompanied with heavy rain or snow[.] Dropt the best bower anchor[.] The wind continued all night and in the morning veered round to the [E?] then ENE and NE when the Snow ceased. The hills adjacent are all covered with the Snow fall.

Saturday Ap^l 4th
We had strong gales from the NE or NNE the fore part accompanied with Showers of snow or Hail[.] Riding near the Shore with 2 anchors[.] In the Evening the Packet made signal for sailing; we were in haste to prepare our [L^rs?][2] had several Passengers on board for Leith[.] In the Morning moderate Gales with snow Showers hove up both anchors and warped by the Ships into a fairer Birth and then came too again with the small Bower[.] My predictions of the weather from observation [*sic*] the changes of the Bar*ometer* have been astonishingly correct since we left Whitby the Erly gale of the [*blank space*] March I foretold 10 hours and the Gale of Yesterday 6 or 8 hours before hand not only gave an idea of the Strength of the wind but also of its direction and continuance.

Sunday Ap^l 5th
The wind still blowing from the N^d with little variation except strength which actually increased to a moderate breeze[.] At Noon suns altitude by false horizon 71° 57.

---

[1] Smyth, *Sailor's Word Book*: 'SPRING. A crack running obliquely through any part of a mast or yard, which renders it unsafe to carry the usual sail thereon, and the spar is then said to be sprung.'
[2] Presumably 'Letters'.

Monday Ap¹ 6ᵗʰ

Moderate or fresh breezes cloudy weather but fine[.] Bar*ometer* 30"23 having gradually and slowly risen from 29 we may expect for a season moderate and settled weather[.] Employed renewing our Stock of water fitting Greenland rigging and sundry necessary work.

This being the memorable Day of the Nativity of Mʳˢ S Jun and Senᶦ was kept as a Day of sociable Mirth increased by the extra allowance of a Mess bottle of Rum for the Sailors in lieu of British Brandy[.]

In the Morning the Mate Surgeon and Steward with myself set out in a hunting or rather Shooting excursion in the Brassa and Noss side[.]

Tuesday Ap¹ 7ᵗʰ

NE ENE or E

We had fresh breezes of wind all this Day fine weather some Showers of Snow[.] We just landed on the Isle of Brassa at Noon and the shooting party set out straight forward across the heath Clad hill for the Ferry across the Sound of Noss[.] All the way the land held a very barren appearance some small spots of ground however had evidently undergone the various operations of cultivation and had obtained a different hue from the rest. We passed 3 small lakes in which we saw several Ducks but could not get within Shot of them. At length after walking about 3 miles on roads of natures forming across heather and beds of Peat we came to the House at the Ferry: [Eunster's?] or the [Eunsters?]² are the inhabitants 3 maiden women and 2 or 3 young men relations. Tho' unacquainted with them on my part they treated us with the highest hospitality and with such cheer as it [*sic*] to be met with on but few parts of the Island fine fresh milk <u>little</u> tainted with the Peat [Reek?] and new Eggs Rum Brandy, White Bisquit, &c were all liberally laid before us, a Description of the House can scarcely be conveyed by means of words alone[.] It is what's here called a good home possessing both Windows and a Chamber or second Story. We went stooping in at the outer door then proceeded along a dark passage ascending several Steps and turning to the left when we found ourselves in the Kitchen as black as a coal house[.] Here were nailed up or slung the various utensils for fishing and farming. We were desired to walk up Stairs and ushered in form into a kind of Chamber with a Bed in it: their best lodging room one window and ¼ a dozen small squares and situate in the farther corner allowed but a few rays of light to penetrate its sooty surface[.] 3 old arm chairs an aged table 2 or 3 chests and some other trifling things was the chief of the furniture[.] the floor inclined like the Deck of a heeling Ship[.] After refreshing ourselves we had a fund of amusement in the conversation of the women[.] we desired them to procure us a boat to cross the ferry, theirs was <u>at the fishing</u> "Had <u>awa Laddie" says Maggie "to the South [Croar?] an blow the Horn[.]"</u>³ The Lad sped away and makes the signal for the Boat a Neighbour coming up however with his

---

¹ This presumably refers to Scoresby's wife (née Mary Lockwood) and her mother.
² These appear to be the names in the original.
³ In the original, the text is 'to the Sooth Croeu an blaw the Hoorn'.

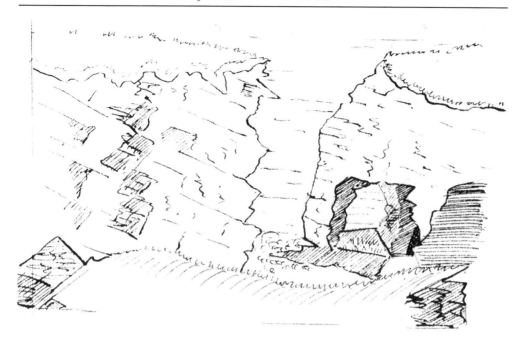

Plate 4. Holm of Noss. Drawing by Scoresby. (Original Log SCO651, 7 April 1812).
Photograph courtesy of the Whitby Museum.

[Cagey?][1] we did not wait but immediately crossed over to the Isle of Noss[.] this Ferry is the narrowest part between Noss and Brassa the Distance not above 150 yards sandy bottom and water shallow[.] A large bay called Noss sound is found between the Sern extremities of the two Islands and runs in Navigable to the Ferry a Distance of 1½ to 2 miles the sides are bounded by [hard?] Sandstone Rocks from the declining strata of which numerous angular parts are exposed highly dangerous to Shipping. This Sounds [sic] is never entered by Ships unless on mistaking it for Brassa which mistake has several times occurred. Some years ago an Old Whitby Fishing Ship ran in here and was lost with all her crew except one or two. Several others have been lost in a similar manner others again have escaped by the timely dropping of an anchor and favourable weather.

The Laird of Noss M[r] Couplen or Coply, requires the tribute of every Stranger visiting Noss asking his leave, this we neglected from ignorance to comply with and he sent a Boy after us with his Compliments saying if we had called at his House he would have sent a Boy with us to show us the famous Cradle of Noss[.] We had a guide however and replyed we would call on our return we now hasted across the Hill towards the remarkable Head Land of [Hangcliffe?] a little to the S[d] or SE of which is this famous phenomenon of nature a Chasm between the rock and across which the cradle forms a passage. The Rock has a perpendicular front a stone dropped to the bottom into the Sea (which comes up between) was 4 seconds of time

[1] Or cazey? Perhaps for 'coggy, coggle', a type of small boat. OED gives coggle in this sense as a Yorkshire term.

in its descent hence the height must be about [*blank*] feet.[1] It appears as if this small Island or Holm had original [*sic*] been united <u>with</u> Noss since on every part of the inside both the form of the rocks and strata correspond. The breadth of the Chasm is about 20 or 30 yards[.] altogether it forms one of the grandest specktacles I ever beheld. The [Massy?] rocks towering 200 feet above the level of the Sea the dark appearance and confirmed hardness the immense overhanging lumps of stone the dreadful abyss the foaming sea below [roaring?] with terrific noise form together one of the most sublime specimens of natures productions. I was charmed with the Romantic Spot and with some regret left it[.] that peculiar effect of the mind which is wrought up by the contemplations of natures sublime I was particularly conscious of and indulged myself for long on the pleasing sensations it produced. It was alarming to move near the precipice it was dreadful at a distance[.] completely seperated from the Main by its perpendicular Chasm the Holm stood single[.] The furious tempest risen surge rushed round its base. In one place a beautiful appearance was produced when a rock was excavated through and the ocean seen thro' it whilst the foam of the surge was pouring into it[.][2]

The Cradle by which a Communication to the Holm is obtained formed by 4 square posts connected by 4 deals which form a kind of long square box without a bottom[.][3] the Posts are all perforated near the top and a tow line rove in the holes hence it is serving two purposes[.] when used the cradle has a bottom formed of ropes passed over and over the deals and crossing in the bottom[.] It is about 4 feet long 2 broad and 2 high[.] The bight of a tow line is passed over a large stone on the Holm [shielde?] by stakes of wood. The two ends are fastened on the Main to a number of stakes in a line so that one giving way the others may hold[.] One end is first belayed and the other hauled tight after the cradle is slung and by means of two hauling lines is traversed backwards and forwards[.] To get the Hawser across and behind the stone they use the following method. They have a long piece of tow line a Person holding each end seperate themselves 20 or 30 yards from each side of the cradle stakes a third stands in the middle and fastening a stone to the bight throws it across until the bight gets behind the stone which accomplished they draw round a piece of Log line then a small rope and lastly the Tow line. The Holm being lower than the Main it slides easily down the man in it is landed then awaits with a hauling rope any thing that may be sent across which is generally Sheep for fattening[.] There is upon the Holm excellent and rich pasture sufficient to keep 20 Sheep from July or August to December when they are generally sufficiently fat. A lean sheep put upon it dies the food being too strong for it[.] a good sheep gets exceedingly fat in a Short time[.]

---

[1] '... the holm of Noss ... with sheer sides of 150 feet surrounded by water': Butler, *Isle of Noss*, pp. 13–14 (who also noted that Cradle Holm was reunited with Noss through a cliff fall in 1968).

[2] At this point in the original there is an ink sketch of the scene, reproduced on p. 73, with a pencil instruction in the margin, addressed presumably to the transcriber, 'leave half a page blank for this sketch'. The space is there in the transcript, but the sketch was not copied into it.

[3] Butler (see n. 1 above) provided a detailed description of the cradle, its construction and operation, that is consistent with Scoresby's text, and included an illustration dating from 1785. The original stakes on the Holm were placed there in the 16th century, by someone who scaled the cliff (and died from a fall on the descent). 'Sadly, the cradle was removed in 1864, though some of the stakes are still visible.' (p. 14).

when they wish to recover those sheep again they proceed as follows[.] several men go upon the Holm[.] two stand across the N or narrowest end at ⅓ distance from the edge and stretch a cord completely across[.] the rest proceed to the S end and walking abreast drive them up Nward when come to the line the two men trip them up and before they can recover themselves secure them and fasten their legs[.] occasionally some are driven over the cliff into the Sea. The rock of noss next the sea we found to be [*blank space*] feet above the level of the Sea. From Hangcliff in clear weather Fair Isle at the Distance of [*blank space*] miles[1] may be clearly seen[.]

We left this interesting spot about 3½ PM and proceeded back towards the Ferry[.] we encountered the laird [***] but whose broad and black front at once told us we had highly offended him in taking that liberty without his leave. We made what we thought every necessary appology but he exclaimed in a surly tone "ye are nea Chields, ye kend the rules[.]" we left him as much disgusted with his pride as he appeared offended at our want of submission[.] it seems he had some idea of bringing us to his terms for without his assistance we could not get across the Ferry having returned the Boat we came in[.] Our Surgeon however being acquainted with Old Lady and having been thoughtful enough to carry her some eye water which she much needed she was pleased to release us from the necessity of forcing a boat by sending us across with 2 Young Girls one of them a Daughter thus after all were [*sic*] honoured by being rowed across by females. I rewarded them with a trifle of silver which amply recompensed them[.]

We now returned to our old resting place the House of the [***][2] where we found prepared for us Plumb Cake[3] and Tea in a much better stile than I could have supposed it was in their power to prepare. This with a few fresh Eggs made us a pretty good repast[.] The furniture of the house was all curious being good specimens of the Antiques[.] An old arm chair of respectable bulk and carved with the names of its first possessor the Grandfather of the present inmates and dated 1698 this was the year the house was built[.] We had the honour of drinking out of Glasses at least 100[d] years old. The Tea Cups we used held about 1/6th part of those now in fashion[.]

A Dog we had with us entered a hole in the Ground near the Cliff edge on the Isle of noss and had pushed so far forward that he could not return[.] we could not see him neither feel him with the ramrods of our Guns. Having no fit instrument to extricate him we were obliged to leave him to his fate.

In the course of our passage we saw very few Birds until come near Noss when we met with a number of Pigeons some Ducks Plovers Willocks[4] many Gulls &c we shot some few which served us in making a Sea Pie for Dinner the Day following. We quietly retraced back [our?] steps to the Lerwick side of Brassa and were just about hiring a Cazey[5] to get off to the Ship when we observed our own Boat coming round

---

[1] The actual distance is about 50 statute miles (80 km).

[2] 'Yeunston's' in the original, written quite differently from the 'Eunster's' earlier.

[3] *OED* recognizes this as a variant of 'plum-cake': 'A cake containing raisins, currants, and often orange-peel and other preserved fruits.'

[4] Probably the common guillemot, *Lomvia troile*, although Wright (*English Dialect Dictionary*) noted that the term has also been applied to the puffin, razor-bill and young heron.

[5] See p. 73, n. 1.

the point having observed us descending the Hill[.] We got on board the Ship about 7 PM having spent 7 or 8 hours in this interesting jaint[.][1] We found it necessary to Shift our stockings notwithstanding we were all Booted the moisture of the ground penetrating the thickest sole of Leather[.]

This being the Evening of the Day (6th Apl according to civil reckoning) on which Mrs S Junr and Senr first breathed the Atmosphere Air as I have before observed the Sailors were allowed an extra Mess Bottle of Rum and so elated were they with it that the music of the Violin Fife Tambourin and Drums at once united to celebrate their pleasure to which they danced with glee extreme from 8 till 10 or 11 PM[.] the excelled music drew crowds of men on board from Ships in all directions. We are fortunate in having several performers on the different Instruments[.]

In the morning weather still moderate and fine the stubborn Northern clouds by their rising shew no sign of any particular change of wind[.] all the Ships begin to anxiously expect a favourable breeze[.] Last year long ere this we cruised off the Ice and soon afterwards penetrated into its inmost recesses[.]

Wednesday Apl 8th
Erly
Moderate or fresh breezes Slightly variable fine weather[.] The crew employed in various necessary work. Carpenter and Cooper employed in preparing Stores and geer [sic] for the Boats[.]

Thursday Apl 9th
NErly
Light or moderate breezes fine weather in the Morning several of the Ships fired Guns and made other signals of sailing notwithstanding the wind was directly a head and before noon 12 or 14 had gone out of the South entry they consisted of the Margaret of London and all the Hull ships but two (The Vigilant of London arrived last night.[)] The occasion of the above Ships sailing was owing to Captn E[2] of the Margaret having by an error in his reckoning his Crew engaged two men above his number two of his Shetlanders being absent in the Country contrary to duty they by sailing left behind and got rid of them[.] like as one sheep followeth another to a Waterpool soon one starting 12 or 13 followg least [sic] by any advantage of wind the Ship should gain an earlier passage & succeed in getting Fish before the others come up[.] The wind towards noon was very moderate and veered to ENE[.] some vessels seen off the Harbour a Brig arrived to take in the Cargo of Timber of a Water logged and dismasted vessel which was towed in here[.]

Friday Apl 10th
NEbE
Light moderate breezes or calm all this 24 hours. Calm towards mid nt[.] In the afternoon the Ipswich came in[.]

[1] *Sic* in both original and transcript; 'jaunt' presumably intended.
[2] A transcription error. The original is 'K' and the contemporary lists show Captain Kay as the master. Another Captain Kay was master of the *Vigilant* from London.

In the morning made the sailing signal and at 10½ AM got underweigh and made Sail out at the South Entry[.] At Noon the Pilot left us 9 Ships preceeded or followed us[.]

Saturday Ap^l 11th Lat 61°15+ Lon 0°11E
NW
Moderate or fresh breezes with Showers of Snow or Rain[.] At 2¼ PM passed Hang-cliff[.] The Land by the Cradle of Noss was at equal distance with Hangcliff at 2 PM the angle formed by the former was 3½° by the latter 7½°[.] Hence if the height of the Cradle be … feet that of Hangcliff will be about … feet perpendicular[.][1]

Most of the Ships which sailed Yesterday were in sight at 3 PM all of them to the S & E ward of us[.]

In the night the wind increased to a hard gale. Close reefed Top Sails and after-wards stowed the F T Sail[.] Showers of Hail accompanied the wind[.] About 8½ AM we experienced a Shower of astonishing large Hail the globules were ¼ Inch and some ½ Inch in diameter[.] At noon several Ships in sight[.]

Sunday Ap^l 12th Lat 61°5 Lon 0°6'
Variable
The wind continued to Blow exceedingly hard in the squalls and particularly in the afternoon when we were obliged to furl the F T Sail[.] At 8 PM [wore?] further reduced the Sails steered to the SE until 4 AM when we again [wore?] At 5 AM saw the N end of Shetland bearing W Dist 20 miles[.]

Having contended now two Days amongst the winds and Sea and no signs of a change of wind notwithstanding it has considerably abated at noon bore up WSW for Balta Sound[.]

Monday Ap^l 13th
The wind blowing a fresh gale from the E^d with showers of rain we continued our course for Balta about SWbW. The Eggington[2] of Hull seeing us bore up with us at 2 PM[.] About 5 PM we saw a Boat making for us on which we lay too and took it alongside notwithstanding I was better acquainted with the Harbour than any of the Pilots[.][3] Abreast of Alwick we met a strong Nerly tide being close in we steered

---

[1] If the height at the Cradle of Noss is taken as 150 ft (see p. 74, n. 1), then by simple trigonometry using Scoresby's angles, the *Resolution* would have been about 2,453 ft (748 m) from the base of these cliffs, giving an estimated height of Hangcliff of 323 ft (98 m). The name 'Hangcliff' does not appear on the 1:50,000 Ordnance Survey sheet of the area, but the pattern of contours indicates cliffs in the vicinity of the Holm of Noss with heights between 50 and 110 metres. Noss Head, the highest point on Noss, is 181 metres.

[2] Correctly the *Egginton*, named for the family that owned the largest number of Hull whalers: Credland, *Hull Whaling Trade*, p. 50. The name of the ship is consistently misspelled in this transcript, but is correct in this entry in the original.

[3] Scoresby-Jackson, *Life*, p. 35, quoting from Scoresby's manuscript autobiography for the year 1807: 'In the progress of this voyage, whilst the vessel was delayed in Balta Sound, Mr. Scoresby employed his time in "making a survey of the harbour, of which there was no chart, and in drawing up directions for the navigation". "The original map", he continues, "and six views of the land, with observations on Brassa Sound, Lerwick, Balta Sound, and the Zetland Islands in general, I

WSW to open the Harbour and then SW into it[.] Hauled up SWbS to clear the Muckle Skerry which was dry being low spring ebb and then about WNW into the inner harbour and brought up in 3½ Fathom water sandy ground[.] In the Morning the wind veered to NW or WNW and we prepared for sailing but just as we were about starting the wind again came to the North and blew Fresh[.] Five or seven Fishing Ships[1] in the Offing running to the S^d probably to Lerwick[.]

Tuesday Ap^l 14th

In the afternoon and night we experienced strong gales squally from the NNW to NNE accompanied with Showers of Sleet or Rain[.] We think it probable that the Ships which sailed in Company with us from Lerwick are not much if any thing to the N^d of us and as seven were said to have been seen running to the S^d yesterday probably more may have bore up for Lerwick[.] I had a specimen of native copper given me to Day which was found on the S of Halswick Bay a mile hence in a vein of the rocks by the Sea side[.] In the Morning the wind was more moderate weather yet cloudy finding the Ship too far to leeward (S^d) we carried out a Kedge weighed the anchor and moored about 60 yards to the N^d.

Wednesday Ap^l 15th

In the Evening we had moderate breezes weather still cloudy and subject to Showers[.] Towards morning the wind again increased to a strong Gale accompanied with much Snow[.] Another Fishing Ship was seen yesterday running to the Southward[.] The ground this Morning was completely covered with Snow[.] some of our Sportsmen went on a Shooting[.] They took several Plovers[.] Two Otters were seen amongst the rocks in the SE Sound. This Storm as well as every other change of the weather was duly Foretold by the falling of the Mercury in the Barometer[.]

Thursday Ap^l 16th

Hard Gales the whole of this 24 hours still from the N^d to NE^d[.] Showers of Hail or Snow being upon the Ground at this Season[.] The winds for this 5 Weeks past have constantly blown from the E^d to N or NW varying in the limits several times a week the Meterologists [sic] here say whe [sic] shall have no real change until it either falls calm or comes round by the way of Sun[.] I observed when we ran down to this Harbour on Sunday that as we approached the high land the wind decreased[.] I believe this is as generally the Case as for the breeze which blows from the Land to be strongest in Shore[.] Towards noon we observed the Barometer to rise being then at 29″59[.][2]

Friday Ap^l 17th

The Barometer gradually arose to 30′.05 which it reached at noon[.] the wind continued from the NbE and gradually moderated to a fresh breeze[.] The Showers became

---

inserted in my journal of this voyage. This survey I accomplished by means of an azimuth compass, quadrant, and Gunter's chain. I afterwards proved it by means of a theodolite, but found it so accurate that I could make no alteration to it."' At the time of the 1807 voyage, Scoresby was seventeen years of age. The plan is reproduced in Stamp and Stamp, *Greenland Voyager*, opposite p. 176.
   [1] I.e. whaling vessels, as is evident from the journal entry from the following day.
   [2] A transcription error. '29.59' in original.

trifling and the clouds instead of the Stormy Cumulus assumed a milder aspect. We trust the forerunner of a favourable change[.] The Ships Decks were found crowded with live stock – consisting of Cocks Hens Geese Oysters Clams Cockles &c&c

Saturday Ap^l 18th

Moderate breezes from the NE to NNW[.] towards noon the wind veered more west-ward became very variable[.] The Therm*ometer* rose to 48°[.] We have acct that 2 Ships put into Lerwick on Monday last[.] Hove short at noon found some small Chafes in the Cable[.] I went in the morn^g to see the Spot from whence the Copper was taken that I received a specimen of[.] found it to be a vein in the rocks down nearly at low water mark[.] the vein is small and not extensive contains besides the Copper the soft green stone like gypsum so abundant here particularly in the vicinity of the [***] [.]

Sunday Ap^l 19th Lat 60°50 Lon 5°0W

In the Evening the wind veered to W and afterwards SWbW but too late in the night and too little wind to attempt to put to Sea. however at Day break in the Morning we began to prepare the wind blowing strong at SWbW with heavy constant rain[.] having reefed the Top Sails we hove short¹ and the anchor started before we loosed a sail[.] we brought the Ship up and once more hove short and on loosing the Top sails it again started. We then veered² out Cable until we had again stopped her[.] being near a lee shore by this time we took out the large kedge and Towline and hove in the Hawser with the Cable[.] having taken up the Anchor we made sail and cast with the Kedge. This operation detained us so long that we did not get clear of the N Entry until 6½ AM[.] From thence made all sail in Co with the Eggington[.] For some time the wind came to NW but at 9 AM fixed at WbS a Fresh Gale accompanied with constant rain[.] A strange Sail to the NE[.] At 10 AM the N end of Shetland Dist 12 miles[.]

Monday Ap^l 20th Lat 62°37 27 Lon 1°8E

WbS

Fresh or strong Gales with constant rain sent down Top Gall^t Yards[.] The Eggington to leeward sails heavy[.] courses NEbN to SEbE rate 1½ to 2 knots var 2½ pts [***][.]

Tuesday Ap^l 21st Lat 62° 54+ Lon 2°9E

NNE

Strong gales flying clouds corrected the watch by means of the mean of 5 Alts of the Sun at 3^h 10' 2" Mean time of Greenwich the true altitude being then 28° 15" 6[.]

   Unbent the cables and hauled the wet parts on Deck to dry[.] Eggington in C°[.] Courses Erly[.]

---

¹ Smyth, *Sailor's Word Book*: 'HOVE-SHORT. The ship with her cable hove taut towards her anchor, when the sails are usually loosed and braced for canting ....' Scoresby was here presumably describing his attempts to turn the vessel towards the harbour mouth, in a confined space.
² In this context, 'veer' means to let out or pay out: Smyth, *Sailor's Word Book*, s.v.

Wednesday Ap^l 22nd Lat 63°16+ Lon 2°23E
[NNW?]
Fresh or strong gales cloudy increased towards mid night to a hard gale accompanied with Snow Sleet Hail or Rain very thick Sea high Ship laboursome. Expecting the Ship to be within 40 miles of the Norway coast we wore at midnight least we should by an increase of the wind be reduced past our sail and be driven too near the land[.][1] The wind fortunately Shifted at 6 AM[.] At noon more moderate weather[.] Sea high and cross[.] made sail Eggington in Company Courses ENE, E & WNW[.]

Thursday Ap^l 23rd Lat 63°35+ Lon 0°9E
NE
Strong or hard gales squally Showers of Snow rain or Sleet the fore part the latter more moderate and clear made sail Eggington in C^o[.] Courses steered NW and WNW Bar*ometer* 30°26 shews better weather.

Friday Ap^l 24th Lat 64°32 Long 1°44E
NEbE
Charming fine weather. The Evening closed with a most beautiful tinge of Crimson in the Clouds a mild sky now prevailed[.]

 The following incident occurred whilst we lay in Shetland[.] M^r [Frier?] the Mate of the Eggington came on board to invite me to dine with Mr Pinkney.[2] I consented whilst he stopped I asked him how his Master liked the Feathers he had purchased on Shore at Balta Sound. "Not very well", he replied, "they were full of dirt[.] " "were they weight" I asked No sir they were not much wet they were a little damp[.] 'Were they weight" I asked again "Yes Sir some of them. Were they weight enough No Sir he again answered they were not white some grey ones were amongst them" Did they weigh heavy enough I lastly asked him <u>and laughed</u>. O yes Sir they were good weight[.]

 At noon Charming fine weather[.] Eggington in C^o. Courses NW to N. Bar*ometer* 30°19[.]

Saturday Apl 25th Lat 65°54+ Long 1°37W
E to EbS
Moderate or fresh breezes the whole Day occasionally squally in the Showers which prevailed now and then. Sailing at the rate of 2½ to 4 knots p hour by the wind to the NNE or NE^d[.] We spliced the Forgangers [*sic*] on the Harpoons selected those Harpoons fit for use &c[.] In the Morning delightful fine weather Therm*ometer* 54° Sun bright[.] Some Finned whales were seen[.] <u>Spanned on the Harpoons</u> (that is secured them by the Foregangers and small cords or <u>foxes</u>[3] to the Stocks ready for

---

[1] Between 60° and 62°N, the islands along the Norwegian coast are close to the longitude of 4°30′E. Further north, however, the coastline turns northeastwards. The length of one degree of the parallel at 62°N is 32.6 statute miles or 28.3 nautical miles.

[2] Robert Pinkney was master of the *Egginton* from 1810 to 1815: Credland, *Hull Whaling Trade*, p. 138.

[3] Smyth, *Sailor's Word Book*, s.v.: 'a fastening formed by twisting several rope-yarns together by hand and rubbing it with hard tarred canvas'.

use)[.] Eggington in C°[.] At Sun set variation of the compass by Suns amplitude 23°50W[.]

Sunday Apl 26th Lat 66°34 10+ Lon 1°30W
Erly
In the afternoon we had a gathering of Clouds which proved themselves Showers on the whole fine weather. Greased Top Masts &c[.] Towards morning it fell calm and so continued save a light SWerly Air which occasionally sprung up and then died away again[.] The Day was delightful like a fine Summers Day in England Bar*ometer* 30°[*sic*] 16 and the Therm*ometer* in the shade stood at 52°[.] The Eggington near us[.] A number of Fulmars about us[.] The Clouds assume an appearance predicting a Serly or SWerly wind the Bar*ometer* and Therm*ometer* seemed to confirm it[.] At 5 PM in the full Moon. the Full change of the moon is generall [*sic*] supposed to have favourable or unfavourable effect on the weather or any great change which takes place within the month is generally about the time of the Full or Change. The winds now for upwards of 6 weeks have not blown a Day together from the SW but generally from the ENE to N or NW. Hope now for a propitious breeze the Season is fast advancing to the common time of the Fishery indeed many Whales have been caught before this time[.]

Monday Ap[l] 27th Lat 67°57+ Lon 0°26W
Calm
Calm until 2 PM when a light air of wind sprung up from the SW[d] it continued and kept increasing until Evening it then fixed. The Ship made a progress of 3 to 4 or 4½ knots P hour to the NE[.] Set Studding Sails[.] the Eggington sail heavy shortened sail for her. In the morning we had still fine weather. Called all Hands at 8 AM and put the Guns in a favourable situation for fishing. Thus 4 of the carriage Guns by the Main mast in the half deck[,] 2, 4 lbers in the Galley and two 6s under the Bowsprit on the Forecastle the Cannonades[1] were lashed in different suitable places about the Decks[.]

Tuesday Ap[l] 28th Lat 70°0 Lon 5°1E
SWbS
Fresh breezes and squally with some Showers of Sleet in the Evening[.] In the Morning cloudy but fair weather[.] Steering NE[.] The Temp*erature* of the air since Sunday had changed from 52 to 26 or 27[.] A brightness and cleanness of the atmostphere [*sic*] beneath the otherwise cloudy atmostphere had every appearance of a <u>blink</u> of a solid body of Ice[.] to confirm also further also a proximity to the Ice or Land we saw a Reddish Brown Duck also a Cetaceous animal apparently of the <u>Common Whale</u>[2] description. The Sea also continued very slight notwithstanding the wind blew fresh[.] At noon fine <u>clear</u> weather the atmostphere near the horizon causes objects to appear tremulous[.] Eggington in Company[.]

---

[1] Correctly 'carronades'. See journal entry for 12 March 1811.
[2] This term was used by Scoresby as an alternative name to 'Greenland whale', i.e. *Balaena mysticetus*, the bowhead: Scoresby, *Account of the Arctic Regions*, I, p. 449.

Wednesday Ap¹ 29ᵗʰ Lat 71°54+ Lon 9°E
NNW

We had fresh or strong breezes with fine clear weather continued¹ our Courses to the NE at the rate of 5 to 8 knots p Hour[.] At 9ʰ 5 PM p Watch Suns Mag [ampᵉ?] at Setting in Lat 70°40 was W70°N the true [Amplᵉ?] is W48°47 hence the Variation 21°13 & true time 9h 9′ 47″ PM[.]² At 3 AM being in Lat 71°10 and Lon 6°31E I was informed by the officer of the Watch that a Quantity of Ice was in sight it consisted of several patches and some detached pieces[.] bore away EbN until we had passed a point end and then hauled up again NE. The Morning being exceedingly fine we called all hands and took two of the Boats out of the twin decks two of the oldest we hoisted up at the Quarters and getting all the lines on Deck assorted them and coyled those of the new Boat in the Chocks a Quarter and the Stern Boats together with those of the two Boats below making in all 5 the rest (three in Number) were left empty for any servile purpose which might be wanted such as milldolling³ &c[.] We saw several finners but no Seals[.] the wind [being?] favourable and the Season too far advanced to think of hunting for those animals of the West Ice. Accordingly we shaped such a course as might be most likely to lead us into Fishing ground[.] The Eggington astern we increase our distance from her under an easy sail without Main sail or Studding Sails when she has two or three Studding Sails and every other sail serviceable[.]

Thursday Ap¹ 30ᵗʰ Lat 73°04N Long 12°E
WSW

We had strong gales towards Evening accompanied with Sleet or <u>Mist</u> which made our progress somewhat dangerous reduced our sails therefore so that occasionally we might haul to the wind in a moment. We continued running NE at the rate of about 6 or 8 knotts until 8 PM when seeing some pieces of Ice we steered NEbE[.] Had a Man constantly watching at the Mast head. At 8 AM tacked lay NW[.] Towards morning the wind veered about hauled close by the wind[.] Towards noon we had it nearly calm. The Eggingtons Boat came on board bringing us a taste of Fresh Fish and salted Fish they were by their reckoning in Long about 8 East[.]

Friday May 1ˢᵗ Lat 74°30+ Lon 15°15E
Calm WNW

About 4 PM a Westerly breeze was observed which gradually increased to a Fresh Gale[.] propelled by it at the rate of 4 to 8½ knotts we steered NEbN until 4 AM when

---

¹ Transcription error: original is '… fine clear weather this day. Continued our course to the NEᵈ at the rate …'.

² Some transcription errors here have been corrected from the original. Captain Barritt has commented that 'The time of sunset can be used to deduce an approximate value for longitude, and thus time, but the main purpose of the observation was to check the compass. This process is problematic in high latitudes because of the rate of change of amplitude.'

³ Scoresby, *Account of the Arctic Regions*, I, p. 310n: '*Mill-dolling*, consists in breaking a passage through thin ice, for a ship, by a sort of *ram*, let fall from the bowsprit; or by one or more boats attached to the jib-boom, having several men in each, who move from side to side, and keep them in continual motion. As the ship advances, the rope by which the boats are attached to the jib-boom, draws them forward, and prevents them from being run down.'

it veered to NbW the remaining part of the Day sailing by the wind to the East^d[.] At 4 PM we had the Sea of a particular Blue colour and at 8 AM in lat 73°21 Long 12°02 East has changed to a deep <u>Bottle Green</u>[.] This remarkable change of colour in a distance of a few miles is not uncommon[.] At mid night or the approach of Morn^g being 1st May the usual ceremonies were gone through in the suspension of a Garland formed of 3 hoops crossing each other at right angles and clothed with ribbands[.] on the Top was a large whale as a vane and beneath it 5 small vessels placed in a circle the action of the wind on the Sails caused them to obtain a constant rotary motion. The crew with blackened faces fantastically dressed and [variety?] and grimace and action amused themselves according to the accustomed form for about an hour. The man on board who has the most recently entered the marriage State suspends the Garland on the Main Top Gall^t Stay – the Music of Drums Fife horns Mess kettles and Frying Pans aid their performances and ridiculous dance[.] No Ice seen this Day. Eggington in C^o[.]

Saturday May 2nd Lat 75°23 Lon 14°25E
North to NE & SSE
Fresh gales and squally until night when we had a moderate breeze of wind. Weather generally cloudy[.] Several circumstances now tended to Shew that we were farther to the E^d than shewn by our reckoning. A great number of Looms and [Roches?][1] were seen[.] Several Ducks were seen swimming in the water (this is almost a sure prognostic of being near Land). I therefore supposed we were near Cherry Island[.][2] to ascertain the truth of this supposition I took an Azimuth of the Sun and found the variation only about a point which corresponds with about 20° East Long[.] My surmizes were further corroborated by a particular character in the appearance of the swell[.] I found Yesterday Morning that the swell came freely from the North or NbW towards Evening altho the wind did not change it keeps drawing from the W^d until about 6 PM when it came from the NWd a round Short swell[.] from this peculiarity I judged we were approaching the Eastern Ice and that it lay in a direction NW or NWbN or[3] SE or SEbS[.] While I was engaged calculating the time from the Azimuth observation which gave P Watch 12° E Long whilst my reckoning was only 9½ E the clouds cleared away in a SE direction and Land was discovered Cherry Island bearing P Compass SEbS and Distant about 33 miles[.] at the same time a strong blink of Ice was seen stretching from NNW to SEbS[.] At 8½ PM we came in with a firm pack of Ice laying exactly in the direction I had supposed. Perceiving the Water look greasy I tried the Temp*erature* found it 29½ shewed it was freezing[4] therefore tacked least on the failing of the wind we might get frozen up[.] We steered off by the wind which veering to ESE we came again up to the Pack steered by the blink NWbW when having passed a point of heavy Ice at 10 AM steered NNW under

---

[1] Perhaps the Little auk, *Alle alle*, which Scoresby also termed the 'Roach': *Account of the Arctic Regions*, I, p. 528.
[2] Bear Island. See journal entry for 16 April 1811.
[3] A transcription error. The original is '&'.
[4] The freezing-point of seawater varies with its salinity. At a salinity of 35‰, the freezing point is −1.9°C., or 28.6°F.

square sails a Studding Sail &c[.] The blink now showed the Ice to lay SSE and NNW and no appearance of any opposition to the Westward[.] At 10¼ AM saw Point look out[1] bearing P compass at N¾E and Distance 8 Miles[.] Eggington in Company[.]

Sunday May 3rd
SSE
Continued our Course along the edge of the Ice from Point to Point guided by the blink which directed us to the NWbN[.] The wind increased to a Fresh or Strong gale and the Sky thickened to the S[d]. The Sea rapidly increased and the Mercury of the Barometer fell. I dreaded a Gale in this critical situation for at such a time as this when about to take the Ice a storm is more dreadful than almost in any other situation[.] To increased [sic] my anxiety a kind of haze commenced which prevented us from seeing a boat 1½ or 2 miles: in case we should have to haul by the wind we double reefed the Top Sails Took in Studding Sails Top Gall[t] Sails mizen and main Sail and thus ran under easy Sail until 6½ PM when being in Lat 75°49 and Long 12°9E I judged it prudent to haul by the wind to the W[d][.] The Eggington came up and followed our example but an hour afterwards the wind having somewhat abated She bore away[.] at this time we had thick Showers of roughly crystalized Snow and haze at the same time Thermo*meter* 30° [.] When the Eggington had sailed about 1½ Mile from us I judged we might with propriety follow at that distance so that on meeting with any opposition we should be so much to Windwd of danger besides the distance he could see. The Snow increasing at 11 PM we both hauled by the wind to the W[d] at that time being close to the Pack edge having since our former bearing steered NWbN¼W Distance about 12 miles so that we expected now to be in Lat 75°33. We reached off under easy sail the Sea increasing and the Barometer having sunk within 16 hours from 30.37 to 29.40[.] The Thermo*meter* in 6 hours from 30 to 15°[.] I dreaded a severe storm[.] By the way of preparation as the ship already pitched very heavy we lay her too under close reefed main Top sail and double reefed Troy sail[.] The wind now increased to a heavy gale was attended with severe frost and a most tempestuous high Short and dangerous Sea.[2] Our situation was alarmingly critical for we knew not the distance of the Ice to the N[d] and W[d] until the wind veered to the EbN[.] I then feared we should scarcely weather the Western Ice since the wind blew so furiously and the sea was so high that we could not carry more sail than what would merely keep the Ship near the wind[.] The fury of the tempest continuing our efforts were entirely set aside our duty led us into the situation and we had employed all our art and means in securing as good a drift as possible under the peculiar circumstances so that we could but rest on the Mercy of a kind Providence who often watches us when we sleep and who many time has shielded us from the fury of the Elements and directed our escape from such dangerous situations as no human wisdom could have availed against[.] we drifted about SWbS p compass and at noon according to estimation were in Lat 75°35 and Lon 10°43E[.]

---

[1] See journal entry for 19 April 1811.
[2] Smyth, *Sailor's Word Book*: 'SHORT-SEA. A confused cross sea where the waves assume a jerking rippling action.'

Monday May 4th Lat 74°36 Lon 10°E
EbN
The wind continued to blow from the EbN to ENE with unabated violence the whole of this Day[.] the Sea in the afternoon was tremendous the Ship laboursome and wet. So thick was the Atmostphere with Snow and <u>Frost rime</u> that the eye could not penetrate above ¼ of a mile. The Therm*ometer* continued at 13° and Barometer never rose until morning[.] About 5 PM I had just gone on Deck and walked a few turns a good deal alarmed with the dismal prospect at the same time could not but be thankful that we had in all probability a good drift[.] had the Storm with equal violence prevailed from the SW[d] or even S[d] I know not what recourse we could have had[.] the same Merciful God that now overrules our safety could alone have preserved by supplying us with extra wisdom or some other means peculiar to his Mercies. I repeat I had been but a few minutes on Deck when I observed a <u>fury forwarded</u> wave topping and raised to the very Heavens close to the Windw[d] of the Ship[.] I ran aft caught hold of a rope. The Sailors had stretched along the Deck for supporting themselves and called out "<u>hold fast[.]</u>" in the same instant the ruthless surge struck the yielding Ship she turns upon her side the Sea uplifted flies over us all and tears away whatever cannot resist its power[.] one man was within a hair of being washed overboard the Waist Quarter Boards were mostly washed away the <u>ruff Tree</u>[1] rail of <u>Fir</u> 6 inches by 4 was broken an 18 lb cannonade weighing upwards of half a Ton was lifted up from between two high <u>cleats</u> and turned aside[.] the half deck hatch was washed off and forced to leeward. I with the rest of the men on Deck was completely drenched and sprained my arm in securing my hold. – Such were the effects of the Sea it had scarcely passed when it was followed by another nearly equally as strong but which did little further damage. – I was particularly anxious for our safety the whole night afraid least we should meet with Ice[.] if we should what could be done our means were weak[.] The Ship in her Hull resembled an Ice berg so completely clothed with congealed sprays that scarcely any of the original was to be seen. She supported some Tons of Ice: About noon the weather was somewhat clearer than it had been and the wind had sensibly abated. The Eggington not seen[.] Barome*ter* had risen to 29.89 the Therm*ometer* still at 13°[.] A Small piece of Ice was seen near the Ship the news was alarming. I found it to be a very small and thin piece I therefore judged it might have come from to Windward and drifted far[.] I should expect that any Ice which had been left by a lee pack or stream should have been in roundish deep lumps such as roll over with the force of the Sea and drift but little[.]

Tuesday May 5th Lat 73°31 Lon 10°40E
NEbE
Hard gales some Snow Showers thick Frost rime. Fell in with several pieces of Ice in the Evening[.] At 7 PM set reefed Fore Sail to put the Ship under command[.] The Therm*ometer* all Day at 12° or 13[.] Ship a complete Ice berg. The Eggington was

---

[1] Presumably a variant spelling of 'ROUGH-TREE. An unfinished spar: also a name given in merchant ships to any mast, or other spare above the ship's side; it is, however, with more propriety applied to any mast, &c., which, remaining rough and unfinished, is placed in that situation.': Smyth, *Sailor's Word Book*, s.v.

seen towards night to Windward of us – suppose she wore early in the morning as she was not seen after 3 AM. At Mid night we were clear of all Ice[.] The Bar*ometer* stationary at 29.89[.] By the intensity of the Frost almost every thing of a liquid nature is congealed in the Cabin. The ale Freezes in the casks[.] With a good fire the Temperature 3[ft] from it is 29 to 31°. The Sea so high are obliged to have the Dark lights[1] in – the light by which this is written is ushered through three Patent light Glasses.

There is sufficient for almost any purpose[.]

Wednesday May 6th Lat 73°16 Long 10°18E
ENE

Hard gales squally Snow Showers. The wind was somewhat more moderate than yesterday until night when it again commenced with its former violence. The Ship drifting fast to the S[d] we wore at 8 PM but at 4 AM were obliged from the increase of wind and beam Sea which frequently came over the Decks to wear again to the SE[d] and take in the Fore sail. The Eggington was seen about 3 miles to leeward[.] At 4 AM the Therm*ometer* was at 10° before 9 it had risen to 20°[.] The Bar*ometer* had fallen since yesterday noon to 29°60 [.] at noon a slight rise was again noticed[.]

Thursday May 7th Lat 72°58 Lon 10°19E
NE to NNE

The wind continued with little intermission until Morn[g][.] At 7 AM being considerably moderated Set Fore Top Sail Main and Fore sails Mizen and Jib and wore because the Sea met the Ship Larboard tacked and she made bad progress but standing to the NW[d] she made considerable way[.] People employed clearing away the Ice from the Ship some Tons in weight, hauling out two of the Boats lines coyled on deck repairing damages of the Storm. Carpenter refitting waste [*sic*] and Quarter Boards &c[.] Eggington in sight 6 AM but not seen at noon – Bar*ometer* 29 89[.]

Friday May 8th Lat 73°33 Lon 10°21E
NNE to NW

Exceedingly variable winds. Fresh breezes and squally accompanied with Showers of snow[.] At 9 PM tacked continued the rest of the Day steering by the wind Larboard tacked. The Mate employed making a Canvass for a tracking[2] Machine for mooring the Ship in a Calm or light breezes to Windw[d] it is stretched by 2 Iron bars crossed within a Foot of their ends being 7 feet in length so that the Space occupied by the canvass is an equivalent triangle of 5[ft] 6½[in] each side.[3] The bars are kept asunder by a

[1] A variant of 'deadlights', see p. 11, n. 7.
[2] Smyth, *Sailor's Word Book*: 'FLOATING ANCHOR. A simple machine consisting of a fourfold canvas, stretched by two cross-bars of iron, rivetted in the centre, and swifted at the ends. It is made to hang perpendicularly at some distance below the surface, where it presents great resistance to being dragged through the water, diminishing a ship's leeward drift in a gale where there is no anchorage.' Scoresby evidently transferred this device to the *Esk* in 1813, where it proved invaluable; see journal entry for 19 April 1813.
[3] From the illustration of the device that is included in the journal entry for 19 April 1813, it is clearly diamond-shaped, i.e. a regular quadrilateral with two acute and two obtuse angles. It can also be seen as two identical isosceles triangles, with their shortest sides in common, and that is perhaps what is meant by the term 'equivalent triangle'.

Short bar screwed upon their Shorter ends and spreading them. Carpenters repairing the Wreck occasioned by the late Storm[.]

Saturday May 9th Lat 74° Lon [11?]°20E
NE to W[1] var
Exceedingly variable fresh or moderate breezes squally and much crystallized Snow [.] Chiefly of [I₁?] and the [Spinous Mod?] [.][2] Steering by the wind on the tack which seemed the most advantageous the wind veered from NWbW to NbE frequently in the space of a few minutes. Saw several scattered pieces of Ice and at 3 AM tacked near a stream supposed to be the Ice which lay near Cherry Island before the late Storm[.] Saw a number of Ducks Roches Fulmars Seals some Unicorns &c[.] At noon steering to the Wd by the wind[.]

The Armourer employed executing an invention to answer the purpose of a Steer thole for a new Boat which has too light Gun wales to admit of a hole sufficiently large for a thole according to the common method[.]

Sunday May 10th Calm NW var Light or moderate breezes variable accompanied with much Snow. Occasionally calm[.] Plying to the Nd loose streams of Ice seen to the Eastd of us[.] In the Morning saw a Ship running to the SEd on seeing us she hauled by the Wind[.] At noon fine weather cloudy[.]

Monday May 11th Lat 73°36 Lon 8°8E Calm var Calm until evening[.] at 8 PM a light air of wind sprung up preceeded by a very heavy SSW swell[.] persevered to the NNE North or NNW along the outside or West side of Streams and patches of Ice[.] towards Morning we had fresh gales of wind accompanied with Showers of Snow[.] At 7 PM we found the Ice tended more to the Westwd. being already too far in that direction we hauled up to the NE in a bight of the Ice chiefly consisting of patches and pieces of late formation[.] seeing some prospect of getting a few miles to the NEd we bored thro a Stream run a little to the Nd and then turned up to the ENE in a comfortable opening. The Ice seems open to the NW very close to the Nd and a watery Sky to the NEd and Ed tho' the Ice in the vicinity is mostly cemented together by Bay Ice and but few openings to be seen[.] It seems to be opening however towards the Ed. We lay too at the Weather side of the opening and coyled the lines of 3 Boats – Filled also several Casks of water for trimming the Ship being 6 or 8 inches by the Stern[.] At 17'33" PM Lat by double altitudes of the Sun two Sets 74° 28'N[.][3]

---

[1] A transcription error. 'NE to NW. Var.' in original.

[2] This terminology was accurately transcribed from the original. It is not easy to relate these comments to Scoresby's discussion of snow crystals in *Account of the Arctic Regions*, I, pp. 427–31.

[3] 'Given two altitudes of a heavenly body and the interval of time between the observations, the latitude may be computed by the so-called direct method of double altitude. In using the direct method, the latitude is computed by the rigorous process of a spherical trigonometrical calculation.': Cotter, *History of Nautical Astronomy*, pp. 145–6. Cotter devoted considerable space to the double altitude problem, including indirect solutions devised both before and after the time of Scoresby's voyages.

Tuesday May 12th Lat 75°37 Lon 8°20E

Erly

In the Afternoon we had fine moderate weather little frost a whale was seen. Three vessels in sight all followed thro' the Ice they proved to be the Euretta of Shields Captⁿ Kellick and the Aurora of London Paterson a Brig unknown supposed to belong Aberdeen. Two of the Capt^{ns} above named came on board from whom we had tidings as follow[.] Several Ships have got Fish the Henrietta two Sarah and Eliz*abeth* one [***] &c &c[.] the Euretta at the Commencement of the late Gale was caught at the bottom of a <u>bight</u> a sinuosity down which we essayed[.] she was driven upon the lee Ice by the Violence of the tempest and almost stove in pieces[.] death stared them in the face all hands were engaged introducing fenders (for which purposes they cut up a new cable) between the Ship and her varied blows[.] her rudder was broken, sails rent and the Ship dangerous by stove. The Aurora was better off but got some severe blows likewise. Most of the Ships are said to be to the SE^d of us[.] the Aurora parted with a considerable fleet four Days ago in that direction they had very heavy Ice here we have only Shallow light pieces and from the Masters account it would appear we are nearly in the division between the two different kinds which is the most likely situation for obtaining a speedy passage Northward. The Prospect at present does not seem exceedingly favourable for obtaining a speedy release thro' the Ice[.] Two methods offer for [pursuit?] the one to content ourselves to search a Fishery to the Southw^d and be exposed to every Storm which may occur, the other to contend for a passage thro' this Ice into an opening of water which is almost universally found between the Land and the Ice about this Season. the Fishing here obtained is generally pretty free from that risque of storms which is the danger of the Southern Fishery at the same time commonly affords a greater abundance of the Cetaceous tribe.[1] To obtain this situation we have concluded to attempt[.] this probably may be effected by great perseverance and industry taking advantage of every opening which offers in a direction between North and East to realize a distance[.] Eastward is very advisable when possible otherwise the natural set of the Ice to the W^d will retard your progress[.]

I was roused in the Morning at 6 oclock with the tidings of closing Ice where we lay and opening to the Eastw^d[.] I instantly arose and found three Ships in a small awkward spot not sufficient to turn one Ship round in[.] I observed slack Ice to the Eastward and a very large opening about three miles off to the Eastw^d which led away as far to the NE as could be seen from the Mast Head[.] We plyed amongst very cross and close Ice for 2 hours when we obtained a small opening separated from the large hole before mentioned by a thick set patch of Bay and heavy Ice intermixed. At 9 AM conceiving it possible to bore thro' it we made sail and by the aid of all hands in about an hour accomplished our end in an ESE direction[.] the Ships in C^o immediately followed[.]

---

[1] Scoresby, *Account of the Arctic Regions*, II, p. 206: 'If a barrier of ice prevents the fisher from reaching the usual fishing station, he sometimes perseveres in search of whales on the southward margin of the ice, but more generally endeavours to push through it into an opening, which is usually formed on the west side of Spitzbergen in the month of May, where he seldom fails of meeting with the objects of his search.' See Introduction, p. liv.

Wednesday May 13th Lat 75°52 Lon 8°18E
NE, NNE to NNW

Towards afternoon the wind increased to a Fresh breeze[.] we made great progress in plying to windward found much water in which however were a number of pieces of light Ice disseminated throughout[.] At 2 PM we saw 4 Ships at least 10 miles to the NE of us they had apparently obtained a passage from the SE of where we took the Ice[.] We continued under a press of Sail plying up this opening to the NE or NNEd[.] At 7 PM we had come to the top of the bight lay too. At Mid night I was told an opening had appeared to the Ed I arose we bored thro' several Streams[.] and made considerable progress to the Eastwd and NE[.] we used every endeavour to get through the varied streams we were followed by the Aurora the other two vessels lay still[.] At 9 AM we had passed several openings and patches of Ice and came to a very open pack where the Ice chiefly light at first was disseminated regularly abroad and offered us sufficient room by using the necessary precautions to realize a rapid progress to the NEd we passed a large Iceberg[.] Saw 2 or 3 Whales[.]

Thursday May 14th Lat 76°12 Lon 10°E
NNW to WNW

About 4 PM we lay too in a Slack place the Ice Eastwd seeming close[.] At 8 I was informed the Ice lay very cross[.] I observed they struck several pieces and was alarmed on discovering our dangerous situation the Ice close and heavy about us and the wind blowing very fresh the Ship was constantly in danger. We attempted the NE and on sailing in a very difficult passage for some time we found it more open and discerned a considerable roomy spot to the Nd of us we worked up amongst very heavy and cross Ice and in about 4 hours obtained it[.] lay too for some time but it closing we made fast to two of the heaviest pieces of Ice we could meet with. At noon light winds. The Situation of the Ice within sight of us at this time was as follows. To the Westwd in open light Ice to the NE a close heavy pack to the Ed within a few yards in a close pack of light Ice[.] It seems probable we shall have to steer NW or NNWward from hence to get round this Eastern pack and then away again NEward[.] I fancy our situation for obtaining a quick release is pretty good since we seem to lay nearly between the body of heavy Ice to the Eastwd and loose light Ice to the Wd which now with a Wrly wind sets down upon us and in a great measure besets us. I expect the first change of wind will set us at liberty as it may be supposed with any [Erly?] wind the light Ice will seperate from the heavy and leave us in the opening[.] We saw the Land in the Morning from about ENE to East the nearest part Distant about forty miles[.] three Ships seen to the Westward dodging about the Aurora near us[.]

Friday May 15th Lat 76°15 Lon 9°40E
WNW to SW

The wind fell to near calm was very variable in the afternoon. About 6 PM a slight Serly swell was observed the lee pack setting up to the NWd and the Thermometer having arisen from 22° to 26° predicts a likelihood of a Southerly wind[.] A Whale and several Narwhales seen[.] About 10 PM the wind had veered to the South. The Ice closed us being chiefly heavy we secured by means of warps several thin light pieces alongside as fenders in case of a heavy swell[.] this I conceive to be the best plan possible for the heaviest pieces coming in contact with those will little affect the Ship – secured a piec [*sic*] also near the rudder. In the Morning the wind had veered to the SE[d] the weather was clear[.] The Ice all close packed from SE to E, N and NW. Two Ships seen to the SSE under way and the three ships to the NW all beset. The Ice slacker to the W[d] and SW. The Aurora near us[.] Wind strong breeze[.]

Saturday May 16th
SE to E
The wind increased in the Evening slipped our pieces of Ice drifted a little to the NW into a clearer spot and took hold of another piece and in the night a third which was the heaviest. In the morning Fresh or Strong Gales with constant thick Snow. Ice slack to leeward as before but not yet very cross and heavy[.]

Sunday May 17th Lat 76°07+ Long 9½E
NE to NNW
Strong or hard gales the whole Day accompanied with thick and constant Snow until mid night when it cleared up and continued free from Snow the rest of the 24 hours[.] a very considerable opening to the ENE otherwise to Windw[d] a close pack of very heavy Ice. A small opening close by us to the W[d][.] Slack Ice. Ships in Sight as above[.]

Monday May 18th Lat 76°37 Long 10¾E
NbW to NW
The Ice had opened in a very narrow lane to leeward of us about 6 PM which communicated with the water to the ENE before named. The Wind blowing strong reefed the Top Sails and called all hands up[.] we cast off from the Ice and allowed the Ship to drift out of the Patch in which she lay this being soon accomplished we bore up along the opening to the SE first then E and afterwards working up to the NE[d][.] in about 4 hours we had obtained a very extensive opening which led to the NE as far as could be seen from the Mast head. This led us into more room we made rapid progress to the NE and ENE[d] amongst very open patches of Ice and at length came to large extensive floes[.] The Aurora we left not being then able to get out of a lee pack into which he had drifted[.] The three other Ships in sight all on the way and believe likewise got into open water[.] At 9 AM we had come to a closer body of Ice consisting entirely of large heavy floes. We run down in a narrow space and then got a little further Eward and lay too being partly at the extremity in a large hole of water[.] About noon a light breeze of wind and showery weather[.] at that time having since we started viz 18 hours come about 60 miles to the NE or ENE[.] The Aimwell came up to us Capt[n] Johnstone came on board he has no fish has been beset several Days Far to the W[d] with the Aurora of Hull &c[.]

Tuesday May 19th Lat 76°27 Lon 10¾E
NW to WSW
Took the Ice May 2[nd][1] just before the heavy gale of the 3rd and following Days lay

---

[1] This is apparently a continuation of Johnstone's account.

secure in smooth water[.] Gives account of several Ships having got Fish. The Wind in the Fore part of this Day being very light with Showers of Snow and seeing much water to the NE[d] we lay too until some opening should break out. In the Evening saw a clear lead into it made all sail with a light breeze of wind [at?] East and fine weather. We worked up between two floes in a narrow passage[.] At 7 PM we were coming into a narrow opening between the Points of two floes which seemed somewhat closing yet room enough to get thro' and apparently with safety the wind being come to NE which close hauled would admit us to sail thro' NbW or NNW[.] The Winds still being very light we sent two Boats to assist in the Narrows – –[1]

At length we came to the Straightest spot and passed it, when lo! at this moment a blackness was observed on the water and showers at a small distance, the sails shook the <u>vane</u> whirled round and in less than 15 seconds of time a heavy gale of wind right a head at NbW fell upon the Sails the Ship got Stern way a rope could not be got out she must go back[.] she ran astern 100 yards and fell against one floe with her rudder which broke the wheel ropes but did not injure the helm[.] her Bow then fell off and she was caught between the meeting floes; our situation was most dreadfully alarming, Nothing could be done, the Ship lay on her Broadside the Sails could scarcely be got down, the men were all confusion. We had every sail exposed to this rough blast. Top Gall[t] S[l] Stay sail Jib &c &c[.] in a few minutes the floes overlapped each other on their point the pressure was heavy but Providentially we were to leeward of the main Stress. The Floes twisting the Ship in about 5 or 10 minutes was turned before the wind with her bow and her sides to the Ice[.] I saw she would be stove by running against the leefloes if we did not get out a rope[.] a Hawser was quickly fastened to a Hummock and as quick the Ship

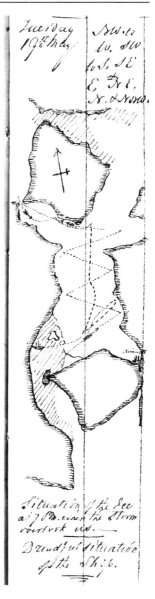

Plate 5. 'Dreadful situation of the ship'. Drawing by Scoresby. Whitby Museum (Original Log SCO651, 19 May 1812, margin). Photograph courtesy of the Whitby Museum.

[1] Here follows a blank half page, suggesting the use of two transcribers. In the original there is no such break, and the text continues in the same paragraph. It is possible, however, that the space was left blank to enable the inclusion of a sketch that appears in the margin of the original, entitled 'Situation of the Ice at 7 Pm. when the Storm overtook us.' This sketch shows the track of the *Resolution* from its position at 7 pm in the narrows until it moored to the floe among bay ice. The position of the *Aimwell* is also shown. Note that the winds indicated on 19 May in the original (Plate 5) differ from those in the transcript.

started from between the Points[.] she got considerable way but brought up by the Hawser which was like to <u>fire</u> the bit head[1] by its friction[.] The Top Sails by this time were cleued up we braced the yards to turn the Ship to Port and when her Bow cleared the point of lee floes we let go the Hawser[.] she then scudded some Distance and on hauling her too met with the weather floes even on the lee bow, we had great difficulty in saving the Ship here again for it may be observed the Snow was so thick that we could not see above 50 yards[.] I never saw so thick a Shower. We fortunately however got clear of this Floe also by very slightly striking it[.] in a minute we hauled to the wind larboard tacked and lay too until we reefed the Sails[.] We still found ourselves very critically situated for we lay between two heavy floes with only a breadth of about 200 yards[.] In a very Short time I saw the Floes had met to leeward and formed a semicircular bight, what was to be done? I very fortunately observed a considerable patch of Bay Ice astern united firmly to the Western floe[.] I conceived it to be an excellent situation were it possible to <u>stay</u> the Ship (there was not room sufficient to <u>wear</u>) by a rapid celerity we filled all the Sails in a moment and stayed the Ship in good stile and run the Ship into the Bay Ice which we cut with a Boat and entered 100 yards and moored to the Floe[.][2]

The Wind continued with little abatement until noon and accompanied with frequent thick showers of Snow[.] At this time we found the Ice cross and connected in all directions except to windward where seemed a large open*in*g. The points of the 2 Floes we lay between united [to?] Windw[d] of us consequently barring the passage in that direction. From the state of the Bar*ometer* which sunk from 29 85 to 29.75 I expected an increase of wind which came in a wonderfully sudden manner. It is worth remarking that with 12[hrs] of its continuance the wind had regularly veered about from NW to W, SW to NW again[.]

Wednesday May 20th Lat 76°36N Lon 10½E
NbW
Fresh gales or Fresh breezes accompanied with much Snow and frost rime. In the Evening saw 8 sail of Ships within 3 miles to Windward of us on the clearing away of the Snow[.] At 3 AM the Floes between which we lay having separated to windw[d] we cast off sailed the Eastw[d] and lay too. Saw much water to the ESE but not accessible. The Ice being open to the N[d] we made Sail with a strong wind and plyed up amongst large heavy floes seperated to the SE[d] S[d] and W[d] but closely connected to the NE and East[d][.] We worked passed every Ship in Company many Miles amongst which were the Augusta Laurel Aurora (Hull) James Brittania [*sic*] &c[.]

---

[1] Smyth, *Sailor's Word Book*: 'BITT-HEADS. The upright pieces of oak-timber let in and bolted to the beams of two decks at least.' Smyth noted that the phrase 'to the bitter end' originally referred to that part of the anchor rope or chain that was closes to the bitts to which it was secured.

[2] Scoresby, *Account of the Arctic Regions*, I, pp. 271–2: 'Bay-ice is sometimes serviceable to the whalers, in preserving them from the brunt of heavy ice, by embedding their ships, and occasioning an equable pressure on every part of the vessel …' Scoresby then went on to explain why in other respects bay-ice 'is the greatest pest they meet with in all their labours'.

Thursday May 21st Lat 76°30 Lon 10°E
NbW

At 8 PM we lay too having sailed and plyed to the NWbN about 14 miles. We then [found?] ourselves to the S^d of a heavy Body of Ice consisting of Fields and Floes with scarce a lane of water to be seen in it. Heavy Floes likewise surrounded us but considerably disseminated[.] The wind blew a strong gale the rest of the Day accompanied with Snow Showers and Frost rime the effect of a Temperature of 19°. Saw a Whale. The Aimwell near us[.] The situation of the Ice is very remarkable this Season – to meet with heavy Fields and Floes in the Lat of 76½ is very uncommon in the month of May[.] how to obtain a passage amongst them to the Eastward and Westward I cannot devise. It seems improbable that they will speedily admit thro' the midst of them and at best the navigation is exceedingly dangerous the motion of the Floes being frequently so rapid [various?] and dangerous a Ship being caught between any two of them is crushed to pieces in a moment. I think it likely a better passage might be obtained further to the Southw^d provided we can get round these Floes and keep out of the Ice which [sets?] round <u>Point Look Out</u> to the W^d. Doubtless there is much Water in with the Land and very likely an easy Fishery would be the result could we obtain it[.]

Friday May 22nd Lat 76°20 Lon 10°E
NbW

In the Evening we had still a strong gale of wind. Frost rime and much Snow the Ice unaltered. during the Day we had worked into a pretty large opening to the NE but being surrounded by Floes and leading nothing further to the NE^d I thought it prudent to run out[.] At 6 PM I determined to explore the situation of the Ice to the S^d to clear the Floes therefore steered first WbS 6 miles then SW, SSW about other 10 miles when we found ourselves embayed amongs [sic] Floes[.] between the Showers we saw much Ice still to the W^d and no passage to the S^d hauled therefore by the wind. In about 4 hours we had returned to the place from whence we started it being the largest opening near and there awaited expecting from the State of the Barometer (29.66) a more severe gale of wind. In the night it commenced and continued blowing exceedingly hard and attended with almost constant thick Snow and severe Frost[.] Thermometer 19° [.]

Saturday May 23rd Lat 76°10 Lon 10°E
NbW

Very strong gales with Snow & Frost rime [.] Continued Dodging about under the lee of some heavy Floes in the same large opening as yesterday under close reefed Top Sails &c[.] The Aimwell Elizabeth Augusta &c near us several sail to leeward 14 sail in sight[.]

Sunday May 24th Lat 76°5 Long 10°E
NbW to NWbN

Two strang [sic] Ships seen plying to Windward to the W^d or NW of us. The James of Liverpool took the advantage of a small opening and joined them. In the Afternoon the [sic] were seen to the N^d of us in much water but inaccessible to us[.] At 3 PM made fast to a heavy Floe at the Top of the bight with several Ships[.] Wind still blowing a strong gale but accompanied with little Snow. The Floes closing a stern of us at 10.PM cast off and after a few hours proceeded to explore an opening which led a few miles to the East^d[.] we found the extremity nearer than expected[.] on the entrance closing we ran out and in the Forenoon worked up a lead to the NW^d with a Moderate breeze of wind. Weather [fair?] Bar*ometer* 30.00[.] About noon made fast to a floe our example was followed by 6 or 8 Ships. Much water appears to the W^d and various lanes in other directions but from the connected state of the Floes are inaccessible to us[.] the Ice here is lighter than we have had it since we entered amongst the Floes[.] 13 sail in sight[.]

Monday May 25th Lat 75 58 Lon 10°E
NWrly Various

Light or moderate breezes[.] in the Evening cast off the Ice closing[.] Dodged about in a small opening until Morning when seeing a lead into open Ice and great Sea room to the W^d we began to warp [tow?] &c but we got sufficiently to Windward to take sail[.] two points of Ice closed and we made fast [.] 8 Ships which we left were in a great measure beset[.] many Ships in sight[.]

Tuesday May 26th Lat 75°30+ Lon 9°40
Nerly Var Nerly

Light airs all Day variable fine clear weather[.] In the Evening we set to work with all Hands to endeavour to cut thro' a Bay Floe followed by the Aimwell. One Ship the Aurora of London which was near us by a favourable turn of the Ice got away. We warped and cut [with Boats?] for several Hours[.] At 1 AM on the Ice squeezing we desisted for a while. We observed the Floe to press and open within the space of a few minutes sometimes running at the rate of 2 knots. We were easy as regarded our safety having the precaution to lay the Ship amidst the lightest Ice[.] At 6 AM the Ice again slacked another Ship got off we towed and sailed to the SW^d about a mile and were again stopped by the re-closing of the Ice. We pushed the Ship in a stern of the Aimwell and lashed our Bow to her Tafrail and sent our crew on board. some were employed cutting or breaking Bay Ice and then warping[.] ['**Wednesday May 27th** Lat 75°57 Lon 9°E NNE' *in margin*] We had a severe job of labour for about six hours and at 2 PM got clear of the points. We had now to warp to Windward and after hauling the Ship up 6 lines length (say 700 fathoms) we took sail and just passed a narrow place lately opened between two floes at 3 PM and sailed into loose Ice and much water[.] 24 Ships in sight chiefly to the W^d none E^d of us[.] We saw two or three Fish after reaching a few miles to the NW but could not come near them[.] Four Ships in sight got Fish to Day[.] The wind continued very light sometimes calm. The Ice slack all round but not sufficiently so to risque a passage to the NE amongst the heavy neighbouring Floes[.] here we find ourselves amongst very open Ice[.] At noon 36 Sail of Ships in sight most of them with Fish[.] The remarkable situation of the Ice confounds the Oldest Captains they are all at a stand and despair of making any Fishing worth while. So many Floes so far South at this Season was never before known[.]

some it is true have got 2 or 3 Fish but those are more by chance than management in general for the Fish which have been seen and got were chiefly stragglers from the main herd. The chance of making a good voyage thus circumstanced is very precarious especially since so many Ships are collected <u>en masse</u> and when a Fish is seen probably 20 boats are in pursuit[.]

Thursday May 28th Lat 75 50° Lon 9½E
Serly
Light airs inclinable to calm. We ran several miles into a bight to the W^d in search of Fish seeing none worked out again[.] At 7 PM we saw a Whale and had two Boats in chase. I believe we should have got fast had it not been for the interference of two Boats belonging a London Ship[.] from this time we plyed to the SE^d amongst loose Ice and floes in C° with a Fleet of 34 sail of Ships. The Ice to the E^d and NE a firm Body of Floes cemented together apparently with Bay Ice[.] 2 Ships in sight got Fish to Day[.] Spoke the Volunteer with one Fish Lively clean Eggington clean Zephyr 3 Fish Aurora Hull one several others with one two and 3 each[.]

Friday May 29th Lat 76°6 Lon 9°20E
S & SW
Light airs still continued very variable from the S^d or SW[.] In the Evening all the Ships lay too in an Erly bight of the Ice between 2 Floes[.] Seeing a deep sinuosity leading to the ENE and a Dark Sky shewing much water in that direction if we could pass the floes within sight we ran down it almost 3 miles but found our progress bounded by light Floes and much Bay Ice E^d of us[.] I could perceive much water at about 8 or 10 miles Distance to the ENE^d of us and have little doubt but if we were so far thro' this Ice we might get as much Eastering and Northing as we pleased or in other words I believe we might sail without obstruction into the expected NEern water[.] I should imagine those light [***] winds were very favourable for the Ice seperating[.] the Bar*ometer* being high having very gradually arose from 29.60 to 30.28 in 7 Days we have some reason to expect still a continuance of the fine weather we now enjoy[.] If it produce not the desired effect I am at a loss to judge what can do us any service save the favouring hand of Divine Providence[.] We worked out of the bight and lay too at 9 PM[.] We have been engaged these 30 hours framing a small crows nest on my Fathers principle for the top Gall^t mast head to be used when a more distant prospect is wanted or When the Top Gall^t Sails are set[.][1]

Saturday May 30th
Werly
In the morning we saw little alteration in the Ice worked up to the SSE^d by the Floe

---

[1] In *My Father*, pp. 135–9, Scoresby recognized that a makeshift crow's nest had been used 'From time immemorial … on the main top-mast "cross-trees".' At its best this was uncomfortable and unsafe and 'when top-gallant sails were set, this contrivance was all but useless'. His father's invention, 'The greatest boon, therefore, of modern times, ever given to the Arctic navigator, it may be safely, I think, said' was a well designed structure 'perched, like a rostrum, on the head of the main top-gallant mast, with nothing whatever above'. See Introduction, p. xxvi.

edges towards an opening leading SE^wd. did not like the prospect lay too[.] At noon 37 sail in sight.

Still light airs and charming fine cloudy weather[.] Whilst we lay too some of the Ships to leeward bore up to the N^d run a considerable distance and were followed by the whole fleet[.] we being amongst the weathermost of course were left far astern. I observed the headmost Ships got fast away to the NE therefore at 6 PM we made sail after them[.] By this time all the fleet had set every sail possible Studding sails below and aloft[.] We set Top mast and lower studding sails as well as every other sail that we had bent[.] We first ran to the NbW about 8 miles then came to very cross Ice which we passed slowly on account of the Wind failing us amidst the Ice (this is often the cast [sic] almost constantly in light winds)[.] We then hauled up NE at 1 AM in a considerable opening amongst heavy Floes and much water to be seen to the NE^d of us[.] This Spot two Days ago was quite close as far as could be seen to the E^d and N^d and ESE was a solid Body of Packed or aggregated Floes[.] thus it is that an apparently solid and impervious body of Ice frequently within a few Days or even hours so seperates that it is in every direction possible especially in light variable winds such as have of late prevailed. We continued our course during the rest of the Day to the ENEward tacking occasionally as the leads amongst the floes and slack Ice directed[.] the head most Ships get fast away[.] At noon we found ourselves the Sternmost of 36 sail except two or three[.] Five Ships a head keep their course about 14 sail are seen stopped in a great measure between two floes or warping in the very narrow passage a¹ towing head a wind. At this time we came within 2 miles of those 14 or 16 sail and found the passage by which the 5 headmost Ships had sailed quite closed we with about 15 sail left behind[.]

Sunday May 31st Lat 76°20 Lon 10¾E
SE
Light airs inclinable to calm[.] occasionally I observed a narrow opening between two Floes to the S^d which seemed to lead afterwards into much water Eastw^d we bored towards it and found it filled with Bay Ice[.] another was seen more to the East^wd leading head a wind[.] We sailed and towed towards it[.] when under its lee cleued up the Sails and by the Efforts of 6 Boats well manned effected a passage through in some 2 hours (the distance was about 2 miles) the rest of the Ships near us followed [two?] just preceeded us. This obtained we still used two Boats to work to Windw^d in the light variable wind which prevailed seeing a lead first between two Floes again head a wind and then to the NE^d quite out by a narrow passage in a large hole of water to the ENE^d of us. Come to the Narrow place between the Floes we made a <u>guess warp</u>² of a Boats lines (which is a warp or lines or assemblage of warps and lines first taken into a Boat and then made Fast to the Ice at a Distance and then brought on board the line being thrown overboard as they row[.] this is the most expeditious method of taking ropes a great Distance[)]. By means of this and two Boats towing we just

---

¹ A transcription error: 'or' in the original.
² Smyth, *Sailor's Word Book*: 'GUESS-WARP, OR GUEST-ROPE. A rope carried to a distant object, in order to warp a vessel towards it, or to make fast a boat.'

effected a passage as the opening closed[.] one Ship only got after us[.] we then used 5 Boats to tow along the ENE narrow but notwithstanding our utmost efforts two points had met before we got through[.] we pushed the Ship into a piece of Bay Ice and by means of two active Boats Crews and Boats cutting the Bay Ice we got thro' in about an hour[.] All the rest of the Fleet were left behind[.] About 3 PM we obtained the before mentioned large ENE opening. The Fleet which was stopped a head of us between the Floes got out near about the same time[.] In the morning we met with very heavy cross Ice and in many places cemented together with Bay Ice[.] slack Ice seen further Eastw^d. we made sail winding in the clearest tracks occasionally cutting thro' Bay Ice but avoiding it whenever practicable. At noon 13 of the 14 Ships we left yesterday were seen at least 15 miles to the W^d or SW of us[.]

Monday June 1st Lat 77°14 Lon 9°5E
SErly
Light variable breezes fine cloudy weather. In the afternoon whilst continuing our routes to the E or EbN we met with very light Ice much Bay Ice and but few Floes[.] we carried top mast and lower studding sails[.] Saw several whales at a Distance[.] One Ship had a <u>loose fall</u> but we did not lower a Boat thinking a Fish at this crisis might very probably be in the end a loss by preventing or retarding the now seemingly likely to be obtained passage through the Ice. Yesterday I observed we were Sternmost of the Fleet except two[.] to Day at 7 PM when we were immerged from out the Ice into the Land water we were head most except three and an hour afterwards we were the most NEernmost of the whole fleet of 37 sail. Thus, favoured by Almighty Providence we have at length realized this long wished for passage and trust a favourable result will be the Consequence towards a propitious voyage. The Land was seen at 7 PM bearing from E to NEbE Distance probably 20 to 25 Leagues[.] Since entering midst these Floes &c and at 6 PM on the 30th we have made about the following traverse viz (p compass) NbW 8 miles ENE½ N 20 NEbE½ E 8 miles ENE 4 miles E½[N?] 30 miles making a difference of Lat 47 N miles [***] 35 miles and Diff Long 2° 30 E Variation of the Compass 2¼ Points Werly[.]

   For this week past we have experienced remarkable fine weather it is probable that nothing but such variable light winds could have so seperated those Floes as to afford so quick a passage. Propelled by a light favourable breeze we made all sail to the NE N & NNE or NNW at the rate of about 3 or 4 knots p hour except for 2 hours calm amongst scattered brash and bay streams of Ice[.] At noon Point Look Out bore SE Distance 25 Leagues and the Middle Hook of the Fore Land faintly seen NEbN [*blank space?*] Leas[.] 22 sail in C^o mostly astern all carrying studding sails some to the number of 5 or 6[.]

Tuesday June 2nd Lat 78°15 Long 6°E
Swerly
Light or moderate Breezes cloudy with Showers of Haze or Snow[.] continued steering to the NNW or NW until mid nt when falling in with much loose Ice had to bear away NbW a few miles after which steered NWbW NW or NNW the rest of the Day

amongst loose Ice patches and Floes[.] we passed between several large and heavy Floes much Ice appears to lay between us and the Land[.] About thirty Sail in sight[.]

Wednesday June 3rd Lat 78°50 Lon 7°0E
SWerly

Fresh breezes cloudy weather[.] At 3 PM had run into the bottom of a bight in a NNW Direction here we saw 2 or three whales had 2 Boats in pursuit but succeeded not[.]

From hence went round some floes and came into a very large opening to the NW which communicated with an immense hole of water to the W[d] save the intervention of two bay Points of Floes[.] Two Ships attempted to cut thro' it one stuck in the very beginning the other made some progress but was not seen to get thro'[.] We then sailed by the Wind to the E[d] about 30 miles and got into very open Ice[.] Heard news of the John of Greenock[1] thro' the Enterprize of Peterhead and at 8 AM saw a Ship answering her description which proved to be her[.] we ran down and I went on board found her clean[.] She is furnished with a great variety of apparatus for Skinning Chopping boiling and readily making off the blubber which may be captured. At noon many Ships were running to the E[d] near the Land[.] the John had been to the 7 Ice bergs near the Land[2] and found the Ice united united [sic] in the Lat of the Head Land never saw a Fish the whole season[.] Was in Londonderry Lock May 1st got thro the Ice 2 or 3 Days before us[.] N end Foreland at E Distant 25' [.]

Thursday June 4th Lat 78°30 Long 5½E
SSE

Strong breezes cloudy or foggy weather[.] Steered back again partly from whence we came to the WSW 5 hours and then meeting with impenetrable Floes we worked to Windw[d] the John struck and got a sucking Fish its mother was laid in wait for 2 or 3 hours by ours and the Johns Boats but without success[.] The Aimwell passed us has got a small fish[.] At noon somewhat clearer 4 or 5 Ships seen[.]

---

[1] Commanded by Scoresby's father.

[2] Scoresby, *Account of the Arctic Regions*, I, pp. 101–2: 'One of the most interesting appearances to be found in Spitzbergen, is the Ice-berg. ... I speak not here of the islands of ice which are borne to southern climates on the bosom of the ocean, but of those prodigious lodgements of ice which occur in the valleys adjoining the coast of Spitzbergen and other Polar countries, from which the floating icebergs seem to be derived. Where a chain of hills lies parallel to the line of the coast, and within a few miles distance of the sea-beach, having lateral ridges jutting into the sea, at intervals of a league or two, we have a most favourable situation for the formation of icebergs. Such is precisely the nature of the situation a little to the northward of Charles' Island, where the conspicuous bodies of ice noticed by Martens, Phipps and others, and known by the name of the *Seven Icebergs*, occur ...'.

'The Seven Icebergs are each, on an average, about a mile in length, and perhaps near 200 feet in height at the sea-edge; but some of those to the southwards are much greater.'

From this description, and the position of the *Esk*, Scoresby appears to have been referring to the glaciers descending to the sea from the Lilliehöökbreen on the western side of Albert I Land.

Friday June 5th Lat 78°40 Lon 5½E
SSE
Strong to light breezes with very thick hazy weather which covers the rigging and masts with a thick coat of transparent Ice much rain at one time. In the night we reached in to the W^d amongst Floes and loose Ice where we met with an old and young whale[.] the Johns Boat got fast to the former and we assisted in killing her she fortunately ran no distance and was soon overcome[.] The John made fast to a floe to flinch whilst we dodged about to the Eastw^d near her[.] My Father liberally rewarded our Seamen for their assistance by giving them their loved [Totol?]¹ Grog & also sending us for all Hands <u>Mess Bottles</u>[.] No fish seen the rest of the Day[.]

Saturday June 6th
Serly
Fresh to light breezes and constant impenetrable Fog or Rain[.] worked up to the S^d in much water occasionally seeing pieces of Ice and Floes but never a Fish or Ship[.] We begin to get anxious about the Fishing the prospect at present is certainly very unfavourable[.]

Sunday June 7th Lat 78°00 Lon 5¼E
Serly
Light breezes calm constant thick fog[.] plying a little to Windward or dodging about but seeing no fish indeed the Fog was so thick that a fish could scarcely have been got had any been seen[.] Open Ice as before. Saw some white whales[.]² Got a Seal[.]

Monday June 8th Lat 78° Lon 6¾E
Nerly
The wind increased to a Fresh or Strong gale and the Fog cleared away[.] seeing a deep sinuosity of the Ice to the W^d of us we reached into it then ran before the wind a few miles but seeing no fish we began to work back again[.] At Mid nt tried a NWern bay but saw no fish[.] The rest of the Day plying to Windw^d to the E^d of a Body of Floes and loose Ice[.] only 2 Ships in sight[.] The Middle hook of the Foreland at noon ESE Dist 9 or 10 Lea*gue*s[.] No fish seen[.]

Tuesday June 9th Lat 78° Lon 6½E
Nerly NW
Fresh gales to light breezes[.] At 2 PM the John [bored?] into an opening of the Ice to the W^d between two Floes we followed and found much water and saw some Whales[.] The John struck one which I believe died upon one Harpoon[.] we reached

¹ *Sic.* A transcription error for 'tot of'.
² The Beluga whale, *Delphinapterus leucas*. In *Account of the Arctic Regions*, I, pp. 500–501, Scoresby remarked that 'I have several times seen them on the coast of Spitzbergen; but never in numbers of more than three or four at a time.'

and plyed still more to the NW^d amidst Floes and much loose Ice and in the Evening
fell in with several small Fish[.] Whilst cruising about we struck one at 1 PM it got
into the midst of a Floe where several holes all accommodated it whilst we could
not come at it. It was not until six hours afterwards that we killed it[.] it always
evaded the Boats and sunk on their approach until after 5 hours pursuit. We
flinched it drifting to the E^d and then worked up to the place we left[.] here again
we met with several Fish and struck two one we killed. The line of the other was cut
suppose by the Harpoon which might be hanging only by a <u>Wither</u>[.] Whilst we
flinched this we made fast to a large piece of Ice, when finished we made a loose
fall[.]

Wednesday June 10th Lat 77°54 Lon 6¼E
NW to WNW
Seeing several small and sizable Fish and at 3 PM we found ourselves engaged with
two both of which we killed at a Floe. Cast the Ship off and worked up to the said
Floe then made her fast to it and got both the Fish alongside[.] The John Fishing 4
miles to leeward another Ship to the E^d of us. The weather charmingly fine and clear.
Having flinched the two Fish seeing none at the Floe we cast off then sailed to the E^d
and run down two or three miles to the South^d amongst loose Ice and scattered Floes
and during our progress we saw several Whales and came [5?] times within 10 or 15
y^{ds} but the clearness of the water and stillness of the weather could not succeed in
getting fast. A body of fast Ice appears to lay 6 or 8 miles to the NW^d as we
approached it met with but few fish they seem to prefer the loose Ice to leeward[.] At
noon upwards of 20 sail hove in sight all but two from the South^d and the fleet we
came through the Ice with[.] they met with Fish several miles to leeward of us[.] The
Henrietta appeared from amongst the Floes to the NW^d running towards us[.] lay too
to Windw^d having met with Fish[.] at this Time Showers of small prismatic Snow
wind a moderate Breeze[.]

Thursday June 11th Lat 78°44+ Lon 6½E
NNE to NNW
Light to fresh breezes – showers of Snow – on the whole very fine fishing weather[.] In
the afternoon we began again to ply to the NE^d partly from whence we came[.] We
entangled a small Fish which was presently killed[.] at the same time a sizable whale
was struck and never afterwards appeared alive she took out seven lines[.] We lay in
wait upwards of two hours[.] the Crew of the Boat got the 6 lines and then could
[heave?] no more with the winch, supposing the Fish dead at the bottom (which from
the length of [tight?] perpendicular line would be 4200 Feet) we made the Ship fast to
a piece of Ice near the Boat and [slacking?] her a warp's length to leeward we took the
lines on board to the Capstern and never ceased or slacked heaving at a regular pace
until the Fish appeared on the surface and we presently secured her[.] We used every
precaution for heaving steadily and without [jerks?] relieving the Men one by one
every 20 minutes on every line so that from beginning to end the Capstern never
stood one moment. The Flinching being finished we cast off and made sail to Windward[.] Spoke the Henriettas Boat – has 9 Fish had the misfortune to loose four men

suppose by a Fish amongst whom was Ben Gamerson[1] Harponeer and late Boat-steerer of the Resolution[,] the Boatsteerer and other two Seamen[.]

Friday June 12th Lat 78°58 Lon 6¼E
NE
Fresh to strong gales at first Showers of Snow latterly fine clear weather with severe Frost Thermometer 23° [.] Spoke the John with 9 Fish about 65 tons of oil. A number of the Ships had by this time [worked?] up to us we understood that none of them had got more than a single Fish since they got through the Ice and many of them none[.] In company with the John we worked briskly to the NE[d] on the East side of a Body of clagged[2] Floes and amidst Floes and loose Ice. We soon changed the colour of the blue water to a deep thick green far more favourable for Fishing[.] Observing a narrow opening extending far to the NE[d] and between Floes we worked up in a very streight passage and coming into more room saw several Fish lowered a Boat and presently struck[.] Notwithstanding the Sea was so agitated with the wind that the Boats with great difficulty made any progress to Windward yet the Fish was killed in about an hour. Just as we took her alongside another was struck and [behold?] the Shank of the Harpoon broke[.] the next minute a third was struck very shortly (say 1 AM) afterwards[.] sent three Boats to assist whilst the rest of the hands flinched the Fish alongside the Ship in the mean time drifting to leeward[.] finished worked up to the Boats and found the Fast Boat with 9½ lines out and as much strain as she could sustain[.] made fast the Ship near her took the lines to Capstern thro a Snatch Block abaft the Fore chains and leading in at the Gangway Sheeves[.][3] in 3 hours hove the Fish up notwithstanding the Ice drifted to the SW at the rate of 2 knots P hour[.] Flinched the whale about noon. The Ice we find closes fast about us the opening where we entered is now close for a mile thro'[.]

Saturday June 13th Lat 78°56N Lon 6¼E
NNE to NNW
The wind being now moderate cast of [sic] and plyed to Wind[d] up the opening – saw several Ships fast to the NE and others flinching at 4 or 5 miles distance[.] The John got a Fish yesterday and the Mary and Elizabeth another which was all that was got I believe of the Fleet of near 20 Sail[.] As we worked to Windward we struck a small Fish which was very soon killed[.] whilst we flinched her another was struck[.] after an hour and a half supposing her to be dead on the hook we sent three Boats to assist in pulling it up being at the edge of a Floe that had considerable drift and to which the Ship was moored. All the lines being quite slack we now imagined she had slipped[.] began to wash the Decks and hoist up the Boats when the crew who hauled in the

---

[1] Or Garnerson. In the original it appears to be 'Gammerson'. None of these names is among the crew lists of the *Resolution* reproduced in Stamp and Stamp, *Greenland Voyager*, pp. 172–7, though these lists are incomplete, especially for the 1811 voyage.
[2] *OED* indicates the verb 'clag' as chiefly northern dialect and cites Robinson's *Whitby Glossary*: 'to adhere as paste; also to cling as the child to the mother …'.
[3] *OED* indicates 'sheeve' as an obsolete form of 'sheave', i.e. a pulley.

lines were heard to give three Cheers a signal that the Fish was not only dead but actually secure in their possession at the surface. It would appear that the Fish in approaching the Surface being considerably fat and eased of the great pressure to which she was subjected at a great depth the expansion of the air vessels &c caused her to [blank space][1] up and come to the surface with little or no strain upon the lines. Having completed the Flinching we cast off and made sail with an increase of wind towards the NE^d[.] Dodging about the rest of the Day at the edge of several heavy Floes to the W^d N^d and E^d of us to which many Ships were made fast. Spoke the Volunteer with 6 Fish Lively 2 Aimwell 4 Henrietta [blank space] &c[.] The Land in sight[.] Thick Frost rime in the morning clear towards noon[.] Saw a great number of Razor Backs but no whales except one[.]

Sunday June 14th Lat 78°30 Lon 6½E
NNW to ENE
The wind increased now to a Strong gale clear weather[.] plyed about to leeward of a Body of Floes to which were moored a number of Ships[.] Whilst I was at my dinner, the Officer of the Watch Wm Harrison through negligence or error in judgment ran the Ship foul of the John by filling the yards when we lay very near the above Ship and under her lee quarter. The Consequence was we got entangled [crushed?] off the Fore end of one of the Johns Boats carried away a Davit and stove other two Boats[.] On our part we had a six oared Gig crushed to pieces and rendered entirely useless. We saved all the lines and materials. We being liable to all expenses I sent a Boat to the John and took board hers to repair being new last year[.] At the same time renewing her tackle falls[2] which were out and broken[.] the John supplied us with <u>Deals</u> for the repairs and when finished we are to exchange for our own Boat again. We found the Ship in a dreadful unsafe trim[.] she refused to [wear?] except under circumstances the most favourable possible[.] we could not prevent her running against some pieces of Ice in consequence of which we made fast to a Floe and notwithstanding it was Sabbath Day At 1 AM we began to prepare for making off in the After hold to remedy the fault of the Ship which was upwards of 14 inches by the head considering it actually as a case of necessity for the Ship was every moment exposed to danger when under way. The John Aimwell Dundee William and Ann &c made fast near us[.] The W & Ann has 2 fish Dundee 7 – 40 Tons[.]

Monday June 15th Lat 78°48 Lon 6¼E
NE to NNE
Strong to fresh Gales fine weather but Frosty employed making off[.] All the Ships Cast off and worked to the E^d or NE during the night and was [sic] seen to fall in with fish[.] At 8 AM we cast off also notwithstanding we had not finished our making off and made sail after them[.] Before we started we Shot an old Bear and took two cubs that She had with her alive[.] About noon left off and began to clear all up having completed two tiers of the Hold from the after part of the Main Hatch way to Chock

---

[1] 'buoy' in original.
[2] Smyth, *Sailor's Word Book*, s.v.: 'The part hauled upon in any tackle, simple or compound.'

aft[1] together with the third tier of wingers[.] At noon we began to draw near the Ships seen to be well employed[.]

Tuesday June 16th Lat 79°24 Lon 6[¾?]E
NNE

Strong gales the whole Day[.] plying to Windward under a brisk sail amongst Floes and loose Ice but much water[.] did not see a single Fish the whole of this 24 hours. During the Day most of the Ships run off before the wind or to the South[d][.] The Ice lays very close to the W[d] consisting of impenetrable Floes it trends about NEbN and SWbS and continues that direction far out of sight by the blink[.] The blink also shews many openings within it which is probably the reason we have no fish here since it is likely quite open within for 100[ds] of miles[.] The Henrietta indeed been 100[d] miles[2] and saw very few Fish met with large Fields – there he lost his Men[.] they had struck a fish <u>very</u> near the Ship which stove a small hole in the Bow[.][3] on receiving the Stroke all the Crew leaned and Shifted to the opposite side which caused the Boat to upset[.] they all got upon the bottom but unfortunately very shortly afterwards the line had run foul[4] and the Boat suddenly disappeared together with the 4 men who were lost. In the interim it need not be doubted they made every exertion to get a Boat to their assistance but in the confusion every thing seemed to retard their celerity so that it was not until some minutes after that a Boat could clear the Ship[.] the[5] had a very small distance to row but only arrived in time to save the two survivors.[6] Yesterday we saw the Margarett one of the Ships which stuck in some Bay Ice endeavouring to obtain a large hole of water to the W[d] she I understand met with few or no fish. The other Ship the Royal Bounty of Leith we have not since seen or heard of[.]

The two Bears we took Yesterday seem pretty contented one of them walks about at large and is quite harm less the other somewhat larger seems not quite so inoffensive. When the Mother was shot and our Men went towards them they did not retreat but ran round and round the Mother first looking at her then at the Men[.] The [sic] sat down reared up and placed their fore paws on the dead. They moaned whilst the smallest licked the wound[.]

---

[1] Smyth, *Sailor's Word Book*: 'CHOCK-AFT … as far aft … as possible ….'

[2] The original is also incomplete: 'The Henrietta indeed has been 100 miles from & saw very few fish.'

[3] I.e., the bow of the whaleboat, not the *Henrietta*.

[4] In chapter 60 of *Moby-Dick*, Melville emphasized that lines were never attached to whaleboats: 'This arrangement is indispensable for common safety's sake; for were the lower end of the line in any way attached to the boat, and were the whale then to run the line out to the end almost in a single smoking minute as he sometimes does, he would not stop there, for the doomed boat would infallibly be dragged down after him into the profundity of the sea …' The term 'smoking' is literal: Scoresby noted that when the rope is paid out through several turns on a bollard in the whaleboat, 'To retard … as much as possible, the flight of the whale … Such is the friction of the line, when running round the bollard, that it frequently envelopes the harpooner in smoke.' He too stressed the danger involved 'When the line happens "to run foul", and cannot be cleared on the instant, it sometimes draws the boat under water ….': *Account of the Arctic Regions*, II, pp. 245, 246.

[5] *Sic*, but possibly 'She'.

[6] Scoresby described this incident again in *Account of the Arctic Regions*, II, p. 363.

Wednesday June 17ᵗʰ Lat 78°40 Lon 6°E
NE to NNW
Fresh Gales to light breezes fine cloudy weather Showers of Snow[.] In the Evening still meeting no Fish neither did the Ships 6 or 8 miles to Windward we bore up to the SWᵈ and ran about 9 hours suppose about 36 miles we very soon got into the land water where was considerable swell[.] steered along by the edge of the Ice which was chiefly quite loose except here and there a kind of Sea Stream but plenty of water within[.] At the end of 9 hours we observed 13 of the Ships which started some 12 hours before us as laid too a head[.] we hauled by the wind and followed the John thro' an opening of the Sea stream and reached several Miles into the Wᵈ by the Wind (at NNW)[.] fell in with some Ships and a few Fish[.] amongst the Ships before mentioned was the James of Liverpool Clough with 10 Fish near 100 Tons of Oil two Brigs well fished the Latona clean and the Margaret of London unknown how fished. Laid in a Stock of Fresh water Ice[.] Several Ships in Company and in sight scattered about 4 Sail <u>fast</u> or <u>flinching</u>[.] A close body of floes and loose Ice lays to the NWᵈ of us[.] To the Wᵈ much open Water[.] Fine cloudy showery weather at noon[.]

Thursday June 18ᵗʰ Lat 78°30 Lon 6°E
NNW
About 5 PM a Fish was seen playing about the point of a Floe[.] I directed two Boats how to proceed and one of them at 6 PM struck it. It was presently killed flinched it plying to Windwᵈ[.] This is the first Fish I have seen since Saturday last. Just as we had finished washing the Deck we entangled another Fish which we also presently killed flinched it also in about an hour. Lay too then run before the wind or to the Sᵈ or SWᵈ at an easy rate for 5 hours got into transparent Blue Water fish exceedingly scarce[.] Snow Showers prevalent[.] At noon lay too sent a Boat on board the John for a Cask of Coals the 2ⁿᵈ this voyage our Coals being all expended but those in Casks and which being stowed low in the Fore hold cannot be come at without Starting a great deal of water[.] could we get a few more tons of blubber might make off in that part and then should get at them in the process of the work and save the labour of refitting[1] the emptied Casks with salt water[.] Some Ships in sight.

Friday June 19ᵗʰ Lat 78°13 Lon 6°E
SW
Light airs variable or calm Fog Showers occasionally[,] and occasionally or chiefly charming fine weather Thermometer 34°[.]
Dodging about not far from the same place in search of Fish saw very few and these on account of the clearness of the water and stillness of the weather could not be come at. The John and Eggington got a Fish each[.] At noon plying about amongst Floes and loose Ice[.] 30 sail of Ships in sight scattered around us in almost every direction.

[1] *Sic*; 'refilling' intended?

Saturday June 20th Lat 78°87[*sic*]¹ Long 6°E
NErly NNE

Light to fresh breezes with frequent showers of Snow in the night[.] worked a few miles to the N^d after plying about in every direction and exploring any situation near us likely to afford Fish without success[.] we ran to the W^d into a bight of the Ice where we met a number of small patches of Ice and playing about which we saw four different whales one we got two others we frightened and the Prince of Brazils got the other[.] made fast to a small Floe flinched cast off and began to ply to Windw^d[.] Many Ships in sight chiefly plying to Windward few of them doing any good. The John left us in the night passing thro' a narrow opening which closed immediately[.] at noon she was got out of sight suppose to the WSW or SW^d[.]

Sunday June 21st Lat 78°27 Lon 6½E
NNE

Fresh breezes to strong gales[.] Plying to Windw^d till mid night when we came to a NWern bight by some heavy Floes where 4 or 6 Ships were all either fast to Fish or flinching we saw 3 or 4 but could not come at them[.] Made fast to the Floe sent a letter on board the James she being near full[.]² At 4 AM cast off and worked up to several Ships 6 miles to Windward all which had got Fish but when we arrived they all had disappeared[.] At noon lay too in a N sinuosity of the Ice amidst Floes and loose Ice[.] 10 Ships in sight[.]

Monday June 22nd Lat 78°32 Lon 6½E
NNE

Strong gales cloudy weather with Fog or small snow Showers[.] At 5 PM seeing no Fish and supposing they were to the NE we made sail to the SE until we passed a train of Floes laying N & S and connected the weathermost which was impenetrable Ice[.] we then hauled by the wind and plyed up all night amongst numerous Floes and loose Ice under a press of sail. The water now assumed a Dark Green Hue & was thick and very favourable for Fishing had there been any whales[.] we explored now every bight or Sinuosity every opening cavity patch point &c which was accessible and at noon having come to a kind of ragged Field which lay ENE and WSW solid all over save some small holes and connected apparently with the solid Ice to the W^d this according to common experience was an unexceptional situation and seldom fails to afford Fish[.] here however were none[.] We traced it to the W^d with the wind a beam two or three miles in a very narrow opening of the floes to leeward[.] we pursued the break as far as possible but ['**Tuesday June 23rd** Lat 78°30 Lon 6¼E NNE to NW' *in margin*] seeing no signs of fish returned. The wind was now more moderate the Showers continued. The Aimwell in Company having followed us this two Days has yet but 4 Fish 20 Tons of Oil[.] In the Evening we made sail and ran to the WbS into a deep bight amidst a small number of Floes and loose pieces of Ice apparently a most likely spot for whales[.] so it proved for as soon as we entered a small but fresh opening we saw three one we struck and another we frighted. The Fish was killed very soon[.]

---

¹ 78°17 in original.
² And therefore likely to return to Liverpool in the near future. See journal entry for 30 June 1812.

made fast at the outside of the narrow to a small Floe flinched it and in three hours from the first we reached again in the same opening saw 4 or 5 Fish came very near but could not entangle any[.] In the Morning the Flood setting together we [reached?] out and went a distance to Windward where several Ships had worked up within 12 hours[.] At noon no fish to see[.] The Eggington near us with 9 Fish 45 or 50 Tons of oil[.] 15 sail in sight[.]

Wednesday June 24th Lat 78°5 Lon 6°35E
W to WSW to SbW
Fresh breezes to Strong gales with showers of small prismatic snow. made all sail and worked up a very narrow and awkward passage leading to the WSW into much water[.] after 6 hours obtained it and continued still plying to Windw^d or to the S^d amongst disseminated Floes and scattered Patches of heavy Ice[.] In the midst of and under the lee of several of these Floes and patches we saw heavy Fish[.] had two Boats away two or three times came very near several Whales but had not the fortune to entangle any[.] 22 sail in sight situated all around us chiefly plying to Windw^d some however fishing[.] Passed the Experiment with 8 Fish 80 Tons of oil[.] At noon we were plying up close by the Sea edge or just within the Sea Stream[.] sent three Boats away in pursuit of sev^l Fish which were seen sporting about a small patch of Ice[.]

Thursday June 25th Lat 78°8 Lon 6°45E
SbW to SErly
The wind now became moderate in the Evening decreased to a light breeze[.] we had a number of very near and good chances for Fish but none succeeded until Wm Harrison followed close on the track of an eddy by which he was directed to very near the Spot where the Author rose and ere he sunk struck him[.]¹ It was very easily killed and flinched in about 2¼ hours in the midst of a thick fall of Snow which commenced. The same Harponeer when his lines were hauled in got on the back of a very large whale and lo! by some fault missed his mark[.] he struck with all his might but the Fish [shrunk?] at the same moment he did not know but he was well fast otherwise he might have easily struck again to greater advantage when the whale rose its back to depart[.]

In the thick we reached to some Floes and loose Ice by the wind which had by this time (1 AM) come to the NE[.] fell in with 2 or 3 Fish could not entangle[.] From 4 AM plying easily to the NE^d by the edge of the sea Ice. At 11 AM having met with 2 or 3 Fish under the lee of a small Floe one was presently struck by a heave from the hand of Robt Nicholson (loose Harponeer)[.] In a very short time all the lines (6½) of his Boat were run out and those of another Boat fast followed so that in less than half an hour he shewed signals for more line by the [overending?]² of 2 oars[.] no boats being near having all left him to follow the Fish which had taken to the E^d and partly to windward of the Floe under which he lay we happened to be at least ½ a ['**Friday June 26th Lat 78°10 Lon 6°40E NNE**' *in margin*] mile from his [*sic*] also with the Ship

---

¹ See journal entry for 15 June 1811.
² Scoresby, *Account of the Arctic Regions*, II, pp. 245–6: 'The approaching distress of a boat, for want of line, is indicated by the elevation of an oar, in the way of a mast, to which is added a second, a third, or even a fourth, in proportion to the nature of the exigence.'

we immediately made all sail towards him with a fresh gale of wind[.] I presently observed 4 oars erected in the Boat some of the crew placed on the Stern and the Boat fit to sink with Strain[.] we fortunately had a Boat by the Ship with lines[.] we lowered it ready manned and oars shipped but too late the Crew were seen bundling their Pea jackets &c upon the Ice[.] the Boat according to the Greenlander phrase was Head sheets under when we were yet but 60 yards from them[.] in a moment the Boat was drawn under the Ice the Crew leapt into the water towards the Ice which by a tongue (or projection under water) prevented them stepping upon it[.][1] two or three were swimming but all got safe on the Floe and were presently picked up[.] The moment they were on board we made all sail and worked up amongst some very rank[2] or close heavy Ice and then reached to the E^d in the direction I had seen the Fish take[.] the other Boats were in pursuit and erelong a second Harpoon was struck and about 2 PM a third and soon afterwards a fourth[.] we were yet at a distance the Ice all around as was the most favourable possible for Fishing being any where penetrable for Boats except a new broken up Floe to E^d of the Boats at least a mile[,] and three from where the fish was struck[.] into this she took with her former strength and velocity[.] The Boats of the 2nd Harpoon being in a patch found line wanted[.] they made the end fast to a Hummock of Ice and the line broke ⅔ from the Boat. By this time 3½ PM we had got up to them with the Ship we run round a patch [towed?] a Boat and searched every corner but could not find the fish[.] I then went to the two supposed fast Boats which had already penetrated and beset themselves in the thick heavy patch before mentioned. I supposed the fish was dead but to my surprise found her taking from the 4th as fast and as freely as at first and him in want of line[.] he held such a strain that Pieces of Ice sufficient to hang a Ship were turned round and in every vacancy the Boat flew with the velocity of an arrow[.] I found that the third fast was loose the Fish therefore rested solely on the 4th[.] We again searched the Patch on the East side and at length got sight of the Fish[.] by this length all the Boats except one were dismantled[3] or engaged[.] with this one and an empty Boat we gave chase to the Fish making rapidly to the E^d we set all sail on the Ship and towed the Boats[.] into those emptied of lines we put two in the rough and a Harpoon[.] I judged the Fish by her distance from the Boats must be loose this promoted the Chase[.] I found we gained fast upon and allthough [sic] she went occasionally down yet we had some near chances of entangling her[.] All the Boats were observed now to be making for the Ship[.] one soon arrived and informed us to our regret that the Fish had taken the lines of two Boats and was proceeding with the 3 when the line ran foul and broke. Alas our labour seemed thus to have been most unprofitably thrown away and attended with serious loss that of a Boat and 28 lines in length 6740 y^ds or nearly four English miles and in weight upwards of one and a half Tons. The wind was fortunately moderate and weather charmingly fine therefore we determined to continue

[1] Scoresby appears to mean that the underwater projection prevented the crew from stepping directly from the boat on to the ice.
[2] *OED* cites Scoresby, 'Endangered, while among rank ice, by a gale of wind' (*Voyage*, p. 240), in its definition of 'rank' as 'In close array, crowded together; thick, dense.' This meaning is regarded by *OED* as obsolete, except in northern dialect.
[3] Here presumably meaning 'lacking additional lines'.

the chase though with little hopes of succeeding in completing the Capture[.] with three Boats therefore and directed by my best judgment with the Ship close at hand we pursued the direction the Fish took which was about East P compass and in clear water and very Providentially at length having followed 5 or 6 miles from the patch other two Harpoons were struck by <u>Heaves</u>[.] on the other Boat coming up one more was struck as well as one of the former renewed which had drawn and soon afterwards fully fatigued with the draught of so many lines and harassed with so many wounds of Harpoons and lances her activity and strength only yielded to her fleeting life[.] at 10 PM three huzzas announced the death indeed to us it was a joyous sound eleven hours constant and anxious labour had been spent in the Capture of this wonderful whale[.] It may be worth while enumerating the quantity of line ran out which exceeds by ½ or more anything I ever before witnessed[.] From the first fast Boat were taken 13 lines 3120 y^{ds} and the Boat drawn under the Ice[.] from the 2nd Boat 6½ lines 1560 y^{ds} and for want of more the line was broken[.] from the 3rd 3½ lines then drew[.]^1 from the 4th 14 lines or 3360 yards in length and then broken close by the Boat by the line running foul[.] from the fifth 3½ line [*sic*][.] from the 6th 2½ lines[.] from the 7th 2½ lines and from the 8th Boat which struck about 1 line. Thus the whole length of lines run out of the boat [*sic*] was 100,40^2 y^{ds} or 6 miles besides what was hauled in and repeatedly drawn out again. We immediately took the Fish alongside searched for the lines found the last 14 and 1½ from the 2nd fast Boat all still connected though [most in in?] only slightly but the 13 lines together with the Boat which went along with them had parted and were consequently lost[.] the 13 lines were new this Season and in value [*blank space*] £[.] The Boat was the same we had repaired for the John but had no opportunity of returning her. Many Ships in sight fishing many Fish seen[.]

By the time the Fish was flinched we had continued to get all the lines on board which were fast to her immediately made sail and reached over to a patch W^d and then sailed 2 hours to the NE^d to a quantity of loose floes where we saw two or three Fish[.] we had coyled the lines and fitted 4 Boats and just afterwards an old fish having a young one with her was struck[.] We put rough lines and two which were in a tub into the two empty Boats[.]^3 The Fish was seen to lay a long time in a hole of a floe and could not be come at[.] presently however she came to the leeside we struck

---

^{1} I.e. the harpoon was dislodged from the whale.

^{2} *Sic*. In *Account of the Arctic Regions*, II, pp. 276–82 Scoresby recounted this episode, evidently based on this journal entry. The total length of line drawn by the whale was again given as 10,440 yards. However the individual lengths per boat in the journal entry total 11,160 yards (1 line = 240 yards). In *Account of the Arctic Regions*, this error was corrected by reducing the length of line drawn from the fifth fast-boat from 3½ lines to half a line. Scoresby also clarified (p. 282) the reason why the 13 lines and the first fast-boat were lost: 'the harpoon connecting them to the fish having dropt out before the whale was killed'.

^{3} 'Rough' lines, here and elsewhere, appear to mean uncoiled. In chapter 60 of *Moby-Dick*, Melville noted that 'In the English boats two tubs are used instead of one; the same line being continuously coiled in both tubs. There is some advantage in this; because these twin-tubs being so small they fit more readily into the boat, and do not strain it so much; whereas, the American tub, nearly three feet in diameter and of proportionate depth, makes a rather bulky freight for a craft whose planks are but one half-inch in thickness.'

other 3 Harpoons and several lances[.] in the agonies of death she ran down near two lines length and died after an hour and a half[.] she was hauled up[.] Made the Ships fast to a fine flat Floe near cleared the main hold of blubber started a great ['**Saturday June 27**th Lat 77°59+ Lon 6°07E NWbW' *in margin*] quantity of water having the united objects of getting coals which were stowed in casks next the ground tier (of which necessary article we had but a Days stock) and of making a larger <u>flinch gut</u> by removing many of the Casks of the 3rd tier so that should we be favoured we shall be enabled to take in such a quantity as would make us a good voyage say 150 to 170 tons of Oil and since the Season is so far advanced it is absolutely necessary as far as possible to prevent any stoppage in the Fishing concern. This work finished and three Casks of coals obtained we began to flinch and were soon obliged to cast off from the rapid and dangerous motion of a circular nature which the Floe we lay moored to commenced which brought towards us several pieces of Floes – One of the Bears I mentioned taking alive (16th Inst) we gave to Mr Johnstone the other we kept and while we lay at the Floe we put him overboard with a long rope to his neck he swam to the Ice presently got upon it ran to and fro growling in a very angry manner seemingly at his <u>yoke</u>, the rope was fastened to a <u>grummet</u> which was slipped over his ears as tight as possible so that by his increase of size cannot now be removed without cutting[.] he showed wonderful sagacity in endeavouring to extricate himself: he went to a piece of Ice which was rent through the midst and at the top was about 18 inches or 2 feet wide and about 3 feet to the water in depth[.] by means of a hinder foot upon each side of the rent he suspended himself and dropped his head and most of his body down the opening and then with his <u>fore paws</u> tried for some minutes to push the <u>grummet</u> off his neck[.] finding this impracticable he removed growling all the time to the main Ice and then set off in full speed to try to break it[.] being checked he turned back and then run as before repeatedly[.] finding it all to no purpose he lay down. Having flinched the Fish we made sail and began to ply to the NNW in much water and with no Ice to the SE of us[.] Saw but one whale the rest of this Day[.]

Sunday June 28th Lat 78°0 Lon 6°E
NNE
Moderate breezes showers of Snow in the night or thick haze[.] Worked up to a fine field of Ice amidst several Floes and loose pieces of Ice[.] made fast to it with 8 or 10 Ships[.] some fish had been got as we worked up – we saw but one in the morning[.] near noon all the Ships run off to the Southd we soon followed as the Ice to the Wd and Ed set rapidly together[.] as we ran out saw two Fish two Ships got a fish each not far from the field edge[.] 37 Ships in sight to the Ed Sd & Wd[.] The Aimwell by us with 6 Fish 30–35 tons of oil Dundee [*blank space*] Fish 50–60 Tons – Mary and Elizabeth 8 Fish 60 Tons[.] Mr Johnstone sent me the head of a [Hornless?][1] Narwhale[.]

---

[1] Scoresby, *Account of the Arctic Regions*, I, p. 490: 'this external tusk … is peculiar to the male'. Modern research suggests that a small number of females also develop a thin tusk.

Monday June 29th Lat 77°40 Lon 6¼E
NNE to NW
Moderate to fresh or strong Breezes fine clear weather until mid night when a thick fog or haze commenced which continued several hours[.] at noon it began to clear away[.] having run out of the bight annexed to the Field we steered to the E or EbN for about 16 miles and on account of the thick fog lay too amongst loose Ice and but few pieces of Floes. During this Day we saw no less than 44 or 46 Sail of Ships in every direction of us. Finding our Blubber waste very rapidly after mid night we began to make off in the After hold[.] By noon had completed the third tier to the Main Mast[.] A few Ships in sight[.] No fish to see.

The following anecdote of Capt[n] Blate[1] of the Volunteer of Whitby so tickled my fancy that I thought it worth communication. The Ship being beset and the vessel of a Friend laying in the same predicament about two miles off he conceived the Idea of a journey across the Ice. A Boat was manned with a double Crew and M[r] B took his seat in the Stern. From some adventitious circumstance he was obliged to quit the Boat and walk the rest of the distance – shortly he came to a flat of Ice which was covered with water a few inches deep[.] not wanting to wet his feet he put himself on the back of a stout man of the name of John Robinson to be carried across[.] they had proceeded but a few yards when crash goes the Ice and through they drop up to the Shoulders[.] "My <u>Pores</u> (Pow'rs)[2] are you going to drown [me?] John" cries out the drenched Capt[n][.]

Tuesday June 30th Lat 77°30′ Lon 6¼E
NWerly to N
Moderate breezes of wind accompanied with thick Fog Showers the fore Part the latter part almost always constant thick snow[.] Lay too and drifted almost all the Day amongst loose Ice and [bits?] of Floes. The Henrietta worked up to us in the Evening has 17 Fish 11 size about 120 or 130 Tons of Oil. Gives the following news John 4 Days ago with 12 or 13 Fish 80–90 Tons. Lively and Volunteer each about 100 Tons W[m] and Ann 40 or 50 Tons Sarah and Eliz[h] 80–90 Tons [Walker?][3] 13 large Fish. The Lion of Liverpool bore up to Day for England with 120 or 130 Tons of Oil[.] The James[4] bore away last Friday (26th Inst) quite full about 130 Tons of oil by this Ship I forwarded a letter to my Dear Partner my beloved Wife I put it on board on the Sunday preceeding the (21st Inst) giving the news to that time and requesting Capt[n] Clough to enclose it in a list of the Ships as far as he was able to give their success at the time of his departure – I was on board the Henrietta. Capt[n] K[5] gives the following account of the first voyage he took to Greenland in the old Resolution

---

[1] *Sic.* Probably a transcription error. In the original, it appears to be 'Captain B. late of the Volunteer'.

[2] These alternative spellings, and the parenthesis, appear in both original and transcript.

[3] The *Walker* (Captain Harrison) was a Hull whaler of 335 tons: Credland, *Hull Whaling Trade*, p. 128. See also the journal entry for 9 July 1812.

[4] The *James* (Captain Clough) and *Lion* (Captain Hawkins) were the two whalers sailing out of Liverpool. The former is not to be confused with the Whitby *James* (Captain Smith), which was whaling in Davis Strait. See Introduction, p. xxxvii.

[5] Kearsley.

Capt[n] Steward in 1785[.][1] They sailed from Whitby 7th of April fell in with fields and Floes in a low Lat something similar to this Season got through in Lat 77°½ or 78 keeping to the W[d] of the Fields and then clearing them and got in the Land water[.] fell in with several Fish got one of about 9[ft] or 9½ bone[.] they had previously taken 600 Seals[.] they then went to Magdalena Bay[2] to make off[.] lay a week with several Ships then got off to the W[d] to look at the Ice find a field, one Ship get[?] two Fish wind comes to the S[d] they try for a harbour cannot fetch Magdalena Bay bear up for the Norways[3] and moor there in Company with a number of Ships[.] lay there a Fortnight never look for Fish but go on the Land and chase the Deer, one is caught and a feast made of it[.] they see willows growing[4] – A ring of Iron is fixed is fixed [sic] in a rock (by the Dutch) for mooring to[.] an extensive burying place is seen and many graves. The Wind coming Nerly set the Ice down upon the Islands they were obliged to quit their Harbour and steer out to the E[d] within Land had to bore thro' some Ice and then bear up in the thick fog which prevailed to the S[d] run 100 miles then heave too and visit 12 or 24 hours[.] most of the Masters get intoxicated and are carried insensibly to their Ships – bear away again run into 73° or 74 of Lat and then have another visit or <u>Mallemuching</u>[5] as it is termed by the Fishers. At every opportunity during the passage they repeat those excesses while ever any spirits are amongst the Fleet[.] At this Season 40 or 50 Tons was always well thought of and 100 was sufficient to cause the Bells to be rung for Joy.[6] The Masters had considerable privileges [sic] which are now abolished from Whitby and most other ports of Britain. They had all the Blubber &c of the Fins Tails and rumps and the Pairing of the Jaw bones with the Oil which ran from them so that it was not uncommon for them to obtain near two tons of oil from [a?] large fish and worth £60 they had likewise 10/6 Per Ton on the whole cargo and similar hand money and I believe Fish Money that is now given but no fraction of the net [produce?][.]

Wednesday July 1st Lat 78°0 Lon 6¼E
SW, S and SE
Moderate breezes thick showers of Snow or Fog. Dodging amongst disseminated pieces of Ice and small patches[.] About mid night finished making off having

---

[1] This was the first whaling voyage of the *Resolution*, 379 tons, built in Whitby in 1766. The smaller *Resolution* that Scoresby commanded was Whitby-built in 1803: Lubbock, *Arctic Whalers*, Appendix F. Meanwhile, William Scoresby Senior was also making his first whaling voyage in 1785, as a seaman on board the *Henrietta*: Scoresby, *My Father*, p. 37.

[2] Magdalenafjorden, Albert I Land, Spitsbergen, 79°35′W 10°50′E.

[3] The Norways is mentioned in Scoresby's *Account of the Arctic Regions*, I, pp. 115–16. From that context, it appears to be one of the channels between the small islands that shelter the sound of Fair Haven, on the north coast of Vasahalvøya, 79°50′N 11°30′E.

[4] Several willow species, including *Salix polaris* and *S. arctica*, grow as dwarf species several hundreds of miles north of the conventional tree-line.

[5] *Sic*. Smyth, *Sailor's Word Book*: 'MALLEMAROKING. The visiting and carousing of seamen in the Greenland ships.'

[6] This general statement was confirmed by Lubbock, *Arctic Whalers*, pp. 122–3. He noted that in 1787 the Hull whaling fleet, over thirty vessels sailing both to the Greenland Sea and Davis Strait, brought back 110½ whales and 3,583 butts of blubber and oil, 'the average for the period'. The four most successful Hull ships in the Greenland Sea shared a catch of only 28 whales and 806 butts.

completed two tiers as far forward as the after part of the Fore Hatch way the third tier of wingers the same space and the third 'tier' complete in the after hold[.] 118 casks were filled with Blubber which with 83 before make together 201 casks of Blubber and 2 of crang suppose 100 or 110 Tons of oil[.] [Stowed?] the third tier complete as far as the 2nd was filled and then began to ply to windward. A Pungent <u>Gass</u> which arises from the Blubber casks on being emptied of the water which has been filled about 7 or 8 month ago and which resembles the Gass evolved on distilling whale oil so affects the <u>fauces</u>[1] of the eyes that 6 or 8 of the men were partially blinded who wrought in the hold, some did not recover for several hours and in the interim were assailed with very acute pain. In some Ships it has been known so pungent and deleterious that the labourers have been drawn up with ropes almost insensible and have remained blind for several Days.[2] All brasswork about the Ship exposed to this effluvia is turned to a bluish black colour on the surface. Silver the same and Gold in a great measure. Diacylon plasters[3] are turned a complete lead colour and where any water is thrown on the painted ceiling it assumes a deep brown or blownish [sic] black colour. The <u>Bilge</u> water itself is in colour like the water which has been kept in new casks that have been burnt internally[.] It has a deep bluish black tinge[.]

The Heads of three Narwhales represented in the ensuing page[4] two females and a male show the variety of form towards the front[.] In N° 1 the facial angle (the ∠ formed by the roof of the mouth and a line drawn from the upper lip toutching [sic] the forehead) was 72° in the 2nd 92° and in the third 67° [.] The Craniums of each were very similar and the variety of form arises from a greater or lesser quantity of adipose substance on the forehead which in some is 6 inches in depth and in others 8 or 9 inches. The dimensions of No 1 are as follows. The Facial ∠ 72° the ∠ of the lower lip 45° ∠ at a 91° from A to B 12 inches from A to C 20 Inches from A to D 12 Inches from D to the eye 14[.] In length of the Mouth 6[.] In <u>depth</u> of <u>adipose</u> substance at E 6½ In [.] from B to the eye 16 Inches[.] In the ears and about them were an innumerable quantity of worms like eels about an Inch or two Inches in length very slender and white[.]

Thursday July 2nd Lat 78°9+ Lon 6°20E
SE to NEbE
Moderate breezes occasionally snow or Fog showers on the whole fine fishing weather. Saw several whales had Boats constantly in pursuit but could not entangle tho' every Ship around us but one did ([Seven?] in No). The Henrietta got a Fish and

---

[1] If this reading is correct, Scoresby appears to have used an incorrect anatomical term. The fauces is the cavity at the back of the mouth. Perhaps 'focus' was intended.

[2] See Introduction, p. xlvi, n. 3.

[3] Correctly 'Diachylon plasters'. *OED* records various spellings of diachylon, though not the one in Scoresby's journal. 'Originally, the name of a kind of ointment composed of vegetable juices; now a common name for lead-plaster … an adhesive plaster made by boiling together litharge (lead oxide), olive oil, and water; prepared on sheets of linen as a sticking-plaster which adheres when heated.'

[4] The three sketched heads appear in the original, but were not copied to the transcribed journal although, as noted later, the next page but one was blank. See plate 6.

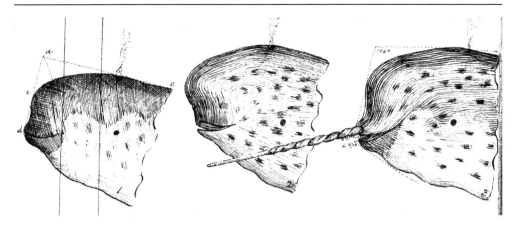

Plate 6. Narwhal heads. Drawing by Scoresby. Whitby Museum (Original Log SCO651, 1 July 1812). Photograph courtesy of the Whitby Museum.

hoisted his ancient.[1] Spoke the Enterprize with 16 fish 160–170 Tons of Oil[.] Plying to Windward or laying too close by the Sea stream amongst loose Ice and small patches[.] 15 or 20 Ships in sight[.]

Friday July 3rd Lat 78°20 Lon 6°30E
ENE to NE
A Fresh breeze of wind in the fore part increased to a very strong gale accompanied latterally[2] with very thick showers of Snow[.] Plying to windw[d] laying too occasionally on seeing Fish were in pursuit of several but were particularly unfortunate almost every Ship around us made some capture to Day or Yesterday nay I may say every one succeeded to the number of 10 or 15[.] In the height of the Gale being in such clear water and at a distance from scattered Floes to Windw[d] we saw several Whales but could not lower a Boat on account of the strength of the wind and <u>lipper</u>[.][3] At noon began to work up amongst Floes and loose Ice towards the N or NbE[.] Saw but one whale from 6 AM[.]

Saturday July 4th Lat 78°20 Lon 6°40E
NE to NNW
Having worked up to the top of a bight having an impenetrable Body of Floes to the W[d] of us seeing no Fish and the weather still continuing thick with constant Snow we steered Eastward two or three miles met with much Ice lay too and took on board the half of a piece of fresh Water Ice which ½ had the following dimensions 10f[t] in length 3[f] 9[in] in depth at one end 5 and the othe [sic] 2 feet broad hence the solid content (being of regular surface) 131[ft] 3 in[.][4] Now Fresh water Ice when very dense floats

---

[1] Indicating that the ship was full and homeward-bound. See journal entry for 26 June 1811.
[2] *Sic*; 'latterly' presumably intended.
[3] Smyth, *Sailor's Word Book*, s.v.: 'A sea which washed over the weather chess-tree, perhaps *leaper*. Also, the spray from small waves breaking against a ship's bows.'
[4] Correctly, the volume was 131.25 cubic feet.

with a quantity above to that below Water as 16 to 137 (in salt water at freezing point) and as 1 to 15 in fresh water at freezing point[.] now 1/15 deducted will give its weight in fresh water or the N° of f^t to be multiplied by 62½^{lb} (the weight of a Cubic foot of Fresh Water) for ascertaining the whole weight now 1/15 of 131$^{[***]1}$ = 122½ which x by 62½^{lb} = 3 Tons 7 cwt 3 qrs 7 lbs[.][2]

After this ran out from amongst the Floes in the thick getting into much water searched W^d and the [sic] E^d for fish saw none until morn^g when being moderate weather we reached to the E^d amongst loose Ice and met with 2 or three[.] Spoke the Volunteer with 12 fish (8 size) 90 Tons oil and the Lively with 9 Fish (8 size) 85–90 Tons oil. Heard news of the John having 5 Days ago 175 Tons of oil. Several fish got around us 10 or 15 sail in sight[.][3]

Sunday July 5th Lat 78° 10 Lon 6⅔E
West to SW
Fresh breezes to fresh gales accompanied with snow Showers occasionally[.] Saw several Fish amongst the loose Ice had 3 Boats in pursuit they wounded two and scared a dozen or more[.] we were particularly unfortunate almost every Ship around us got fish as before[.] a certain fatality prevented our succeeding for we had equal chances with any Ship near us and some got 2 or 3 even to Day[.] neither could it be attributed to mistake or want of judgment but merely ill fortune or bad luck. Finding we could not succeed amongst the Ice we reached out to Sea to the SE^d and worked up or lay too the rest of the Day from Midnight in clear water[.] We have lately filled up a Harpoon Gun saved from the wreck of the Rodney[4] to Day I tried the effect the first Shot the ring of the only Harpoon we had on board accommodated to a Gun broke and we lost the weapon thus the Gun was rendered useless[.] Had we been provided with Guns and good careful skillful Harponeers we might have Shot at least 50 Fish which we have missed[.] even to Day one man was within shot of two or three [.] Seeing straggling Whales in clear water we had a Boat in pursuit notwithstanding a strong wind lipper prevailed[.] At 3 PM John Dunbar struck a Fish she run him out 9 or 10 lines and was presently killed by the activity of the other Harponeers[.] we took her alongside to flinch cleued up the Sails &c but the swell increased so rapidly that we could not get even started all our [Strop?][5] gave way nothing could sustain the Effect of the turbulent wave[.] finding it impracticable flinching in the Sea we set the

---

[1] This superscript is obscure also in the original, but might possibly be read as '¼', which would yield the correct answer to Scoresby's calculation, i.e. 122½.

[2] This final calculation appears to be incorrect. Multiplying 62.5 lb by 122.5 gives 7656.25 lb, or 3 tons, 8 cwt, 1 qr, 12¼ lb.

[3] This is the foot of a manuscript page. The next, right-hand, page is blank, as is the following left-hand page.

[4] The *Rodney* of Dundee was lost in 1810: Lubbock, *Arctic Whalers*, p. 186.

[5] Smyth, *Sailor's Word Book*: 'STROP, OR STRAP., a piece of rope, spliced generally into a circular wreath, and used to surround the body of a block, so that the latter may be hung to any particular situation about the masts, yards, or rigging.' What Scoresby was probably referring to was the rope suspended from the ship and fixed to the kent of blubber, enabling the whale to be turned as it was flensed alongside the ship. See Introduction, p. xliv.

sails and wore but first clinching[1] a 9 Inch tow line to the rump as well as the rump rope[.] very shortly it with the rump rope broke and the fish only hung by the nose and the rump tackles[.] we very readily however got the y^{ds} and sails aback and the Fish rescued by a 7 inch Hawser and a 5 inch warp & allowed the fish to drop astern whilst we towed her by the wind W^d to endeavour for Shelter amongst the loose Ice in that *quarter* 15 or 20 sail in sight.

Monday July 6th Lat 78°5 Lon 6½E
SWbS
Fresh gales cloudy and accompanied with Fog or snow Showers[.] after sailing about 10 miles to the W^d we came in amongst loose Ice and got Shelter cleued the Sails up and flinched the Fish then made sail and began to ply. About 5 AM after having been in pursuit of a number of fish we again had the good fortune to get fast and very soon killed her[.] being close to the sea edge we reached a little within to the W^d and made fast a Floe which an hour afterw^{ds} broke up with the swell drifted to leeward until we had flinched the fish which was accomplished in 2½ hours then made sail and began again to ply to Windward[.] Several Ships have fish to Day near us[.] A great number of <u>Razor Backs</u> have been seen at intervals for this several Days past. They are easily distinguished from the common Whale by their Strong high <u>Blast</u>[2] and bluish black Skin and ridged Back[.] About 20 Sail in sight[.]

Tuesday July 7th Lat 77°58 Lon 6¾E
WNW to Werly
Light or moderate breeze thick fog Showers occasionally[.] on the whole however most uncommon favourable weather for the Season[.] in general it is very rare to see a clear Day in July or even a clear hour.

Having worked a distance to Windward amongst very open Ice loose pieces patches and Floes at mid night we reached out to the Southw^d into the Sea or Land water where we saw several fish but withal so active and wild that we could not come at any[.] The Armourer having made another Gun Harpoon we began to fit up that weapon about noon and prepared for using it in the Boat on trial it carried out 20 fathoms of line when fired in an horizontal position. Harpoon Guns are uncommonly dangerous if carelessly or ignorantly managed too great a charge is sufficient to tear every fastening away by the violent reaction indeed when moderately loaded the reaction is amazingly great. The swivel of a Gun fixes into the Stem of a Boat when built for the purpose but when not a <u>bollard</u> is firmly bolted to the Stem which answers the purpose, the Gun is likewise lashed securely down to the Boats ring to prevent its rising. Many accidents have happened with these Guns by carelessness or ignorance and generally in the quantity of powder which is required to be very small[.] having a contracted Barrel a little more than a Soldier's musket takes is required[.] 19 sail in sight[.]

---

[1] Smyth, *Sailor's Word Book*: 'CLINCH. A particular method of fastening large ropes by a half hitch ....'
[2] Scoresby, *Account of the Arctic Regions*, I, p. 479: 'Its blowing is very violent, and may be heard in calm weather, at the distance of about a mile.'

Wednesday July 8th Lat 77°40 Lon 6¼E
WSW or SW
Moderate or fresh breezes the fore part clear the latter impenetrable Fog[.] plying to Windw^d in clear water off the edge of a <u>very</u> open Body of Ice saw during the Day several Fish were very near some had a loose fall after one which had to be chased 3 hours by two Boats but could not entangle[.]

Thursday July 9th Lat 77°30 Lon 6°E
SWbW
The weather continued as above until about 10 PM when the Fog rather thinned away at which time we saw two whales[.] being near a small patch of Ice we sent away two Boats which scared both of them[.] an hour or two afterwards the Gun Boat was within 4 yards of a Fish and the Gun missed Fire thus the very weapon which was expected to gain fish otherwise inaccessible was the means of losing the first chance for there was nothing to prevent the hand Harpoon from being hove into the Fish[.] The Volunteer and Prince of Brazils each struck a fish near us[.] Passed the Walker with 23 Fish. In the morning we made a <u>loose fall</u> after several fish seen seperated from the Sea by only a stream or two of Ice to the S^d and SW^d[.] A fish was struck at a great distance from the Ship and a mile from any Boat[.] the nearest Boat hoisted his jack as a signal to the Ship which on account of the haze or Fog showers could not be seen[.] he held such a strain that the Harpoon drew[.]

Having hoisted up all the Boats but two we reached to the SW^d and there struck a fish in a most unexceptionable spot, when lo! The Harpoon of Flinns <u>Make</u>[1] broke thus ill fortune seemed to chase us in every form we even despaired[.]

Friday July 10th Lat 77°30 Lon 6°E
NW to NNW
Moderate breezes hazy or towards noon thick fog showers[.] plying too [sic] and fro just within a few streams of Ice near the Sea to the SW^d but much Ice to the E^d NE^d N^d and NW^d of us[.] Saw straggling fish in the midst of a thick fog one was struck and was easily killed[.] in 4 hours she was in the Hold tho' very fat and 8½ feet bone. Just as we finished a second was struck[.] being some distance from the Ship, the Harponeer had as near as possible lost his lines. I verily believe our new six oared Boat saved them and the Fish for she rowed ['**Saturday July 11th Lat 78° Lon 5°40E NNW'** *in margin*] past another of our quickest Boats at the rate of a knot and when she arrived there was not line to [serve?] 5 seconds[.] This fish like the last was killed in about an hour and a half[.] just as we took her alongside a third Fish was struck[.] we sent two Boats which had a [severe?] row to save his lines tho' at no great distance from us[.] we detained one Boat to secure the fish already captured then sent her after them with a quantity of Provision and Beer[.] by this time the Boats engaged with the former fish had about got their lines in and proceed to assist in killing this which we were highly favoured in effecting in the space of about an hour or an hour and ½ [.] we worked up to the Boats with the Ship and Fish alongside and

---

[1] See journal entry for 4 July 1811.

stayed on each tack with equal facility as with no incumbrance[.] Having gained the Boats with with [sic] the third fish we took a warp to her and cleuing up the sails began to flinch[.] 16 hours from the first fish being struck we had completed the capture of three and the flinching notwithstanding there was a considerable swell towards the latter end and the Blubber of the whale[1] being equivalent to 30 Tons of oil[.] Set the sails and worked to the NNW^d partly in clear water many open Floes to the Eastw^d none to the Westw^d[.] At noon 5 or 6 Ships in sight no fish to be seen. Several Ships were near us when we got the last two Fish[.] I did not observe any of them get any save one by the Inverness thus have we this Day been as much favoured above our fellows as heretofore we have been by ill fortune cast below them. At mid night Land at ESE Dist 50 or 60 miles[.]

Sunday July 12th Lat 77°56 Lon 6°60E
NNE to E Var
Strong or hard gales with Snow Showers[.] seeing no Fish at 2 PM made fast to a heavy floe cleared the forehold started the remnant of water and completed making off in the 2nd tier and 3rd of Wingers Fore and aft together with the 3rd tier before filled in the after hold[.] having filled by mid night 48 casks on the commencement of the Sabbath discontinued our work[.] Several Ships in sight dodging near us[.] Many Razor Backs and some Narwhales seen but not a single Mysticetus[.]

Monday July 13th Lat 77°46 Lon 5°40E
NE to NbE
Fresh gales to moderate breezes Fog Showers[.] on the whole fine weather for the season. Loose Ice and Floes setting around us we were obliged to cast off worked to Windw^d up to a Body of heavy Floes saw one or two Whales. The Sabbath being ended after mid night we recommenced our labour of making off while the Ship drifted under two treble reefed TSails to the SW^d. Two Ships in sight each got a Fish we saw but one during the latter part[.]

Tuesday July 14th Lat 78°20 Lon 6°20E
N to NEbN
Moderate breezes Fog Showers the fore part[.] at 9 PM finished making off having filled 80 casks with Blubber and 2 with crang which together with 48 and 2 [of c?] = 329 of Blubber and 4 of crang.[2] This Blubber completed 3 tiers fore and aft together with 3 or 4 longers[3] of the 4th from the main mast forward[.] The wind increased to a hard gale the latter part[.] when reaching out to Sea we encountered a heavy swell. Thick fog Showers prevailed. Saw 2 whales could not lower a Boat for Sea[.]

---

[1] *Sic.* It is possible for a single whale to yield 30 tons of oil (Scoresby, *Account of the Arctic Regions*, I, p. 462) but here 'whales' was presumably intended.

[2] Scoresby was calculating from the entry of 1 July, in which 201 casks were accounted for.

[3] Smyth, *Sailor's Word Book*: 'LONGER. Each row of casks in the hold, athwart.' Scoresby may, however, here mean that the casks in the 4th tier were stored on their sides, because of a lack of vertical clearance.

Wednesday July 15th Lat 77°59 Lon 5°40E

NE

Very strong gales with Fog Showers[.] the Ship pitching heavy we tacked reached in amongst loose Ice streams and floes and found Shelter[.] working about 20 miles to the N^d we lay too seeing no fish and after drifting about 25 miles to the S^d we saw 2 or 3 whales[.] No Ships in sight[.]

Thursday July 16th Lat 77°40 Lon 5 35E

NE

Strong or fresh gales thick fog or Snow Showers[.] Saw several Fish by the scattered patches of Ice arounds [sic] us could not entangle[.] In the night reaching to the W^d fell in with the John with 9 other Ships we joined Company[.] they have 23 Fish about 180 or 190 Tons of oil[.] left the Aimwell and William and Ann 2 or 3 Day since both <u>near full</u> the Aimwell of late has been wonderfully successful. We worked a little to windward in search of Fish saw none but 1000^s of seals[.]

Friday July 17th Lat 77°50+ Lon 5°7E

NE to E [&?] SE

Fresh to strong gales with fog or snow Showers[.] plying about all Day not far from the Sea edge in search of fish had near chances after 2 or 3[.] About noon had a Strong Serly swell penetrated beneath the lee of a heavy stream and lay too in Company with the John The Eliza with 23 Fish 180 Tons and Margaret (Kay[)][1] with 170 Tons of oil. At noon very strong gales[.]

Saturday July 18th Lat 77°59 Lon 5°E

SE to ENE

Very strong gales to fresh or moderate breezes[.] laying too until near noon when reaching to the N^d we fell in with several Fish and made a loose fall[.] at noon 6 Ships in sight[.]

Sunday July 19th Lat 78° Lon 5°

NE to NNE

Moderate or fresh breezes of wind the fore part. At 1 PM we struck a Fish at a great distance from the Ships[.] one of the Johns Boats bent[2] on or they would have lost the lines. Immediately a thick Fog commenced which we were afraid would prevent us finding the Fish[.] we were much favoured however for tho' a very thick patch[3] lay by the Fast Boat to leeward and the Fish took into it on being struck but shortly she came out at the weather side near the place where struck and the Johns Boats struck 2nd and 3rd Harpoon before any of our Boats could get up – so favourably was she handled that we killed her close by the Ship (in the Fog which the eye could not penetrate above 100 or 150 yards) in about half an hour[.] we took the end of the first fast lines to the Ship so that Boats (having 9 lines out) would draw themselves to us and

---

[1] The *Eliza* (Captain Boswell) was the only Newcastle whaler in the Greenland Sea. The *Margaret* (Captain Kay) was the London whaler mentioned several times earlier in this journal.

[2] I.e. added its lines to those extending from the *Resolution*'s whaleboat.

[3] Of ice, presumably, not fog.

prevent the danger of losing the Ship. Thus we were much favoured in securing with the prompt assistance of the Johns Boats the finest fish we have taken this Season[.] she measured only 9ft 3in bone and would produce apparently 15 or 16 tons of oil. Before the fish was flinched the Fog cleared away saw 3 Ships fishing or flinching to Windward[.] Finished in 3¼ hours made sail worked up to the John when again coming in thick lay too in a bight of the Ice[.] an apparent pack to the N^d and W^d of us[.] At noon light breezes cloudy haze or snow Showers[.] Seeing a number of Fish near an open pack edge sent all the Boats away in pursuit which at the end of 6 hours returned ['**Monday July 20th** Lat 78°N Lon 5°E NW' *in margin*] as they went save with a little fresh water Ice[.] the weather was so very calm and still that altho' they came very near for several successive times they could not get fast[.] Calm the while with Snow Showers. The Watch had been set about an hour only one Boat was down when She got upon the back of a whale which they struck[.] it was very favourably at a distance from the pack to Windw^d a mile, it took right down ran out 5–6 lines remained 30 minutes concealed and then came up exhausted[.] it was killed without much trouble and flinched in about 4 hours. The John stood out to Sea in the Springing up of a Serly breeze but reached back again and soon afterwards struck a fish in the midst of a thick fog[.] we sent two Boats to their assistance she was soon killed[.] At noon charming fine weather loosed all sails to dry employed Gumming whale bone setting up shaked Casks making off Fresh Water Ice &c[.] No fish to see[.]

Tuesday July 21st Lat 78°0 Lon 4°40E
S to SE
Light or moderate weather and chiefly clear amazingly favourable for the Sea[.] Having followed the John thro' a stream to the S^d we fell in with a number of Fish made a loose fall but could not get fast. The John having struck a fish which took towards our Boats we sent three to assist in catching and killing her[.] they pursued her about an hour when the Harpoon drew[.] she then took to the SW and W^d the Boats all in chase this was almost 3 miles from the first fast Boat. The Fish was then killed when a query arose whose Fish was it. According to Greenland laws established by Custom <u>a loose fish is fair game to any person</u> hence legally the Fish was ours but on the other hand it is urged <u>by the laws of honour</u> that it was the Johns fish because we went with the intent of killing the fish for them and not for ourselves and because we should not have got the Fish if they had not struck her first. in reply our men say the Johns Boats could not keep pace with her therefore they would never have got her. This unfortunate circumstance would of necessity cause a breach between My Father and Myself were I to persist in taking the Fish and since honour spoke in favour of him I earnestly wished him to have her but lo! our men towed her alongside the Resolution whilst the Johns Crew quietly retired to their Ship. My Father was wroth I argued with our Crew but they (according to the law) were stubborn for their right and [swore?] the John should not have their property. As there might appear to be some partiality towards My Father or that I was awed by his influence I could not exert that authority which I could command in any other Case. I argued the dishonourable case but without effect. In this dilema [*sic*] placed between the duty as a Master and duty as a Son which had opposite actions I was in an unhappy strait. I went on board to

endeavour to conciliate matters and I thought by dividing the Fish all parties might make themselves content. My Father was long before he would consent to any such measure at length appeared to agree to it when the moment I had left the Ship he made sail and worked away to Windward nearly out of sight. Thus was I left by my Father in the heat of his displeasure threatening to enforce the law on the Ships arrival &c and very harshly attributing all the blame to me. I was so agigited [sic] and hurt by these Circumstances that I arose from my bed in a very unwell state. Had I found it possible to have given up the Fish, the Resolutions owners knowing their legal claim would doubtless find fault and attribute either to the influence of my Father or my partiality[.] Thus it would have been no credit to disgrace us both. I certainly should under the same circumstances have insisted on the Fish being given up to any other Person then the motive would be evident.[1] The fish being flinched we worked up towards the John made fast to a floe watering[.] The Ice seems to have quite enclosed us[.]

Wednesday July 22nd Lat 78° Lon 4°30E
E
Fresh or strong breezes fine weather. Reached out to the Sd amongst very cross Ice loose pieces and floes. The John struck and killed a fish which they hauled from under the Ice where she died and made fast to trim the Ship by making off in the after hold[.] The loose Ice setting round us were obliged to cast off lay too. A swell which breaks up the Floes[.]

Thursday July 23rd Lat 78° Lon 4°30E
Erly
Light breezes cloudy or foggy weather tho' not very thick[.] followed the John thro' very rank Ice to the ENEd plying to Windward when she entangled a Fish by two Harpoons notwithstanding which they lost the second Harpoon drawing and the first line breaking. We both made fast to a small but heavy piece of Ice. Employed making off.

Friday July 24th Lat 78°6 Lon 5°¼E
SE to S
Light or moderate breezes fine weather[.] The Ice closing arounds[2] us we cast off at 2 AM to attempt to get thro' an apparent Sea Stream to the ENE[.] after 3 hours and enduring two or three smart strokes of the Ice we accomplished the wished for end and found ourselves at Sea tho with streams of Ice to the Ed SE and Sd of us and apparently quite free to the NEd. Saw 3 Ships before we got on the way which stood in to the edge of the Sea stream tacked and were seen no more having kept their reach to the Ed. We took them to be the Dundee[3] Margaret of Hull and another[.] At noon delightful weather employed in making off whilst laying too[.] completed the [hold?] save 1 Cask by filling 74 casks with Blubber and one with crang[.] Saw 2 Whales[.]

[1] Not surprisingly, Scoresby made no explicit mention of this incident in either *Account of the Arctic Regions* or *My Father*. In *Account of the Arctic Regions*, II, pp. 324–5, however, he argued, about loose whales in general, for what was essentially the view adopted by the *Resolution*'s crew.
[2] *Sic*: 'around' in original.
[3] All six of the whalers operating from Dundee in 1812 were in Davis Strait; this refers to the *Dundee* of London, mentioned again in the journal entry for 28 July.

Saturday July 25th Lat 78°20 Lon 6¼E
S to SSW
A very thick fog commenced in the Evening just as we were aiming at the narrow part of a Stream of Ice apparently the only Ice to the E[d] notwithstanding which being very little wind we fell in fortunately and thro' in about an hour without much trouble[.] The John in Co with 25 Fish whereof 20 are size about 200–210 Tons of oil. To our disappointment we fell in with Ice again in 2 or 3 hours[.] had to run ENE or N for 8 hours at the rate of 2 knots P hour[.] at last went thro' an open patch to the E[d] and met a strong Erly Sea and an open Sea of water but steering too far Serly we fell [' **Sunday July 26** Lat 77°44 Lon 6°39E N to NE' *in margin*] in with heavy Ice again and which we did not clear until mid night at which time we judged ourselves in the Land water from the quality of the Swell &c[.] Finished making off having filled casks as below[.] Steered SSW the rest of the Day[.] The John in Co constantly thick fog[.] Wind fresh Breeze at noon[.]

Quantity of blubber filled 419 casks supposed to produce 201 tons .. 200 Galls[.]

Monday July 27th Lat 76°4 Lon 6°48E
Strong to fresh breezes constant thick fog impenetrable frequently 100 yards[.] Running under brisk sail with the wind at NE to the SbW½ W or SSW at the rate of 4 to 4½ or 5 knots p hour[.] Fell in with several scattered pieces of Ice in the Evening but saw none after mid night engaged cleaning the Ship rigging Jib Boom &c &c[.]

Tuesday July 28th Lat 73°26+ Lon 6°45E
Fresh gales fine weather clear the latter part[.] steering under all sail to the SSW or SWbS with the wind at ENE[.] In the Evening saw two Ships a head which proved to be the Neptune and Dundee of London[.] we came up with them by 11 PM and spoke the former with 28 Fish 150 Tons and the latter with 130 Tons of Oil. They with us suppose we are the last of the Fleet all the rest being further on their way homewards[.] In the morning employed all hand [*sic*] rigging Mizen Top Mast sending down crows nests Dismounting Boats placing the Guns rigging Royal Masts &c John in C°[.]

Wednesday July 29th Lat 71°18 N Lon 3°45E
ENE
Fresh or strong gales from the ENE accompanied latterly with rain. In the afternoon judging ourselves clear of all Ice we began to steer SWbW and towards noon WSW thereby to get quickly into the meridian of London and guard against the SErly winds which generally prevail at this Season and likewise to avoid any way laying Privateers of our Enemies which may be out on the Watch for Fishing Ships[.] what a wonderful change has taken place in the site of The Ice within a short space of time[.] Less than two months ago a body of Ice penetrable only by the most arduous labour and industry is now dissipated and scattered so far that in its very place an ocean of water is found so considerable that by steering in a chance course our progress has not been at all impeded nor indeed (save a few scattered pieces of Ice seen the 27th) has any Ice at all been visible since we first cleared it in Lat 78½° [.] This quality or motion of the Ice whereby it allways seperates itself from the Land towards the end of the Fishing

Season is very advantageous and providential for were it otherwise or had we the same difficulties to encounter in accomplishing our egress as we meet in the access the whole of such as [sic] Season as this would be spent in the passages since we should not dare to await the setting of the thick weather which would highly endanger the safety of our Ships. By 8 PM we had finished our labour as mentioned yesterday in rigging Masts and also bent large Mizen[.] took all the Boats in without lowering them down by hoisting all those aft [over?] the quarters (except the Stern Boat) and put three below the two remaining we secured in the Chocks. A strong SErly swell[.] The John in C°. At noon wind more moderate[.]

A Manifest
of the Cargo of the Ship Resolution of Whitby British Built admeasuring Two hundred ninety one 50/94 Tons Wᵐ Scoresby Junʳ Master from Greenland from Whitby.

275 Leagers	Blubber containing 530 Butts each	
140 Butts	Five tons of Whale Fins one seal skin	
17 Puncheons	on [sic] Bear skin and one living Bears	Thoˢ Brodrick
5 Barrels	Cub	
———	The produce of twenty five	
In all 437 casks	whales one seal two Bears	

Greenland Seas 27ᵗʰ July 1812   Wᵐ Scoresby Junʳ

Thursday July 30ᵗʰ Lat 70°3 Lon 2°3E
E & SSE
Fresh gales the fore part with rain[.] The latter light air haze or Fog[.]
Having on board but a small quantity of coals we filled two Casks thereby to know

what quantity was constantly left for the passage [.] One of those Casks we to Day started into the Coal hole[.] John in C⁰[.] Courses SWbW 6 to 2 knots[.]

Friday July 31ˢᵗ Lat 68°24+ Lon 1°7E
SSE
Moderate or fresh breezes generally thick Fog[.] Courses 1 to 5 knots.

Saturday Augᵗ 1ˢᵗ Lat 67°44 Lon 1°38E
W
Light or moderate breezes thick fog at night[.] Had all Hands employed cleaning and washing the Guns at the same time stationed every man to a post at Quarters[1] in case of action[.] Steering by the Wind to the Sᵈ or Wᵈ[.]

Sunday Augᵗ 2ⁿᵈ Lat 66°40+ Lon 0°32W
SbW
Light to moderate breezes squally occasionally all Day[.] Delightful weather. Gave the John a Bear and old Studd*ing* Sail [boom?] for a Boat load of Coals[.] Courses WbS and SWbW[.]

Monday Augᵗ 3ʳᵈ Lat 65°15+ Lon 2°17°W
SE
Moderate or fresh breezes delightful weather[.] At 1ʰ 26′ 49″ PM seeing the Sun and Moon took 16 sets of altitude and distances from the mean of the best we determined the Longitude of the Ship to be 1°17′37″W differing but 37 miles for my reckoning with a departure 3 months ago[.] Regulated the watch at the same time and set it to the mean time of Greenwich suspended 3 Boats lines to endeavour to dry them[.] The rest in a heap are kept wet with Sea water[.] Courses SW[.]

Tuesday Augᵗ 4ᵗʰ Lat 64°35+ Lon 2°42W
SE
Light breezes Inclinable to calm[.] At 6 PM took the lines down into the Gunroom they were very nearly dry[.] Steered SWbS to WbS by the wind[.]

Wednesday Augᵗ 5ᵗʰ Lat 64°19 Lon 4°1W
WbS
Light or moderate breezes foggy weather the fore part[.] The latter part fresh gales with strong head Seas[.] Steered by the Wind S to NW.

Thursday Augᵗ 6ᵗʰ Lat 63°23 Lon 3°16W
W
Towards morning the wind increased and the weather became fine[.] At 8 AM suspended three Boats wet lines on the Booms to dry[.] Courses WNW to S[.]

[1] Smyth, *Sailor's Word Book*, s.v.: 'The several stations where the officers and crew of a ship of war are posted in time of action.'

Friday Augt 7th Lat 62°8 Lon 3°6W
NW
Inclinable to calm[.] Fine clear weather[.] After noon set up the rest of the whale lines
to dry[.] being favoured with a hot Sun at 6 PM we began to coyl those of three Boats
away in small coyls. The rest we run down into the line room in case of Rain or Fog's
[sic] they being also very nearly fit for coyling[.]

By equal altitudes of the Sun found the watch too fast 18′ 43″ which gives Long
4°40′45″W[.] Saw several signs of proximity to Land such as Molluscous animals
land Birds &c[.]

At 10 PM a breeze sprung up accompanied with thick Fog which continued all
night[.] At 8 AM fine weather very cloudy[.] Courses SWbS and SSW[.]

Observed var at noon 2¾ Pts Werly

Saturday Augt 8th Lat 60°13+ Lon 2°26W
NNE
Light to fresh breezes cloudy weather. Ever since noon we had a Strong SSE to SE
swell[.] at 8 AM a heavy swell commenced from the WbN or WNW both the swells
might be clearly distinguished together[.] Now having Yesterday a heavy Werly swell
and whilst we passed the Lat of Faroe we had it smooth I thence have a presumptive
proof that we are to the E^d of Faroe and not far distant and that the swell which
commenced at 8 PM came immediately round the S end which would from it appear
to bear WbN or WNW which accords very correctly with our reckoning supposing
our distance 50 to 60 or 70 miles[.] Several [***] Roches Gulls &c but no Molluscus
or Sea Weed inclines me to suppose we are as far to the W^d as the Longitude shown by
the Watch. Courses SSW & S[.]

Sunday Augt 9th Lat 58°57+ Lon 1°55W
NE
Fresh gales cloudy weather Strong NE swell[.] seeing no signs of Land at 3 PM hove
too and struck soundings 73 Fathoms Gravel water blue. I was much astonished at
this for it is generally or universally supposed that no soundings are to be met with to
the W^d of Shetland out of sight of Land. I confess if it had not been for the Lunar
observations the great variation[1] the stoppages[2] and the swell in the Lat of Faroe with
the Symptoms of Land then seen I should almost have concluded we were on the East
side of Zetland. Indeed it is a rule with most Greenland Commanders and the only
rule for their guidance Viz that if you strike soundings you are on the East side not on
the West[.][3] We hauled up then as P Log carrying a press of sail[.] At 6 PM sounded in
45 Fathoms hard rock and Shells water deep bottle green[.] We now saw several
Solan Geese[4] or Brown Gull and some Fulmars but no Mollusca. I suppose from these
signs and from a decrease of swell we have [sic] approaching Land[.] At 10 PM being

[1] Presumably magnetic variation.
[2] This is not a technical term. Scoresby appears to have been referring to the changes in swell
noted in the journal the previous day.
[3] See Introduction, p. lviii.
[4] Gannets (Sula bassana): OED, s.v.

dark tacked sounded in 60 Fathoms all Shells the Water smooth and of a deep green colour[.] By account from the Lon shewn by the Watch we were at this time we were [*sic*] in Lat 59°57N and Lon 2°11 W[.] Foul Isle[1] P Compass NNE Distance 10 miles[.] At Day light saw Foul Isle bearing NE p Compass Distance 20′. Sun rose at 4h 21′ AM p Watch[.] At 7 AM N Ronaldsha light bore NWbW½ W Dist 6′[.][2]
   Courses SbE SE S &c

Monday Aug[t] 10th Lat 56°56+ Lon 0°42W NErly Fresh gales &c[.] Charming fine weather with very heavy ENE swell[.] At 4 PM a man of war Brig was descried a head which hove too in our hawse[3] and hoisted English Colours[.] We ran under her lee with all hands at Quarters[.] The Commander hailed had we seen any men of War? any Americans &c! I told him his was the first Ship we had seen since leaving L 74°N[.] He informed us the Americans have declared War[.] The Brig is called the Nightingale[.][4] Very dark and warm in the night with lightening to the SE[d] wind light[.]At 10 AM suspended the whale lines to dry[.] Bent cables &c &c Courses S and SSW[.]

Tuesday Aug[t] 11th Lat 55°8 Lon 1°12W
NE
Moderate breezes fine cloudy weather in the away the lines[.][5] At 5 PM being in the opening of the Firth of Forth 50 or 60 miles from Land a <u>Fulmar</u> flew on the Ships decks and was taken alive[.] At 4 AM saw Land. Descried Fern Island light[6] bearing NW Distance 5 miles[.] At noon several Foreign vessels in sight either licenced Ships or Prizes[.] Tinmouth castle at West Distance 2 Leas[.] Courses SWbW½ W and SbW[.]

Wednesday Aug[t] 12th
Light to moderate breezes charmingly fine weather[.] Winds NNE to NE NW and N[.] At 5 PM passed Hartlepool fired 3 Guns and hoisted our Ancient to our Cousin Lieut[t] Quelch[.][7] At dusk passed Huntcliff fired Guns hoisted lights &c but were not noticed from Whitby[.] At 11 PM hove too[.] At 2 AM Day break reached towards the Land and at 3½ AM were in Sandsend Roads[.] At 4½ a Pebble[8] came alongside with Pilots they told me there was no chance whatever of getting into the harbour without lightening[.] The height of [our?] [*blank space*] springs being past therefore

---

[1] Foula (60°8′N 2°5′W).
[2] The present lighthouse on North Ronaldsay, Orkney (59°23.4N 2°22.8W) was built in 1809: Trethewey and Forand, *The Lighthouse Encyclopaedia*, s.v. North Ronaldsay.
[3] Smyth, *Sailor's Word Book*, s.v.: 'This is a term of great meaning. Strictly, it is that part of a vessel's bow where holes are cut for her cables to pass through … Also, said of a vessel a little in advance of the stem; as, she sails *athwart hawses* ….'
[4] HMS *Nightingale*, 16 guns, Captain Christopher Nixon, spent most of 1812 on the Baltic station: Phillips, *Ships of the Old Navy*.
[5] A transcription error. Original reads 'in the afternoon coyled away the lines'.
[6] See journal entry for 5 August 1811.
[7] No relative with this surname is mentioned in Stamp, *The Scoresby Family*.
[8] Small coble, boat used on the Yorkshire coast and favoured by pilots for their sea-keeping abilities to lie off and wait for vessels in heavy weather. Staithes yawls, fishing on the Dogger Bank, carried a pebble on deck for handling the longer lines. Information kindly supplied by the Whitby Museum.

anchored in 7 Fat*hom*s[.] At noon fine cloudy weather swell considerable from the Eastward[.] I went on shore and had the happiness to find all Friends in good health all anxiously looking out for us[.] all the Greenlandmen belonging our port having arrived with the following success Aimwell [*blank space*] Fish about 120 Tons *Willia*m and Ann [*blank space*] 140 Volunteer [*blank space*] 100 Tons Lively [*blank space*] Fish [*blank space*] Tons and Henrietta [*blank space*] Fish 160 Tons[.] on enquiry it was ascertained that we took 50 Tons of oil after the rest of the Ships of our Port sailed for home[.]

Thursday Aug[t] 13th
Light or moderate breezes of Wind from the NEd which caused an awkward swell in Sandsend Ness[.] the Winds somewhat freshening at noon weighed the anchor which in the act [parted?] with one of the Flukes[.] I went on shore to get another which we thought of taking off in a long Boat but having met with a suitable place for lightening the Ship we put an anchor belonging to the Aimwell on board her and awaited the tide to get her out[.]

Friday Aug[t] 14th
Still moderate weather but strong Erly swell[.] At 8 PM got the Brig Three Brothers T Clark Master out of the Harbour the wind falling to a calm or inclinable to the Wd it was not until 8 AM we could get the Ship into a Road Stead again brought her up with a kedge until we bent the small bower cable to the anchor[1] and then drop our hove in the kedge and rode by the anchor[.] Toward noon charming fine weather[.] Wind SW and swell much fallen[.]

Saturday Aug[t] 15[th2]
Charming fine weather wind from the SSE or South a moderate or fresh breeze[.] At 6 PM completed the loading of the Brig by 10 casks upon deck 111 in the hold and a quantity of whale bone which done she left us and with the Assistance of six of our men she gained the harbour at 8 PM [.](Sunday) The weather still fine and winds variable[.] Barometer at 30.14[.]

Being now the dead of the Neaps the Ship 13 feet of water and scarcely 12 feet upon the Bar we were obliged to continue in the roads[.] we still found ourselves highly favoured in a continuance of fine weather moderate winds and smooth sea. Many Coasters in the offing.

Monday Aug[t] 17th
Calm most of the Day weather sultry hot Therm*ometer* in shade 68° and in the rays of the Sun 102°[.] We had three Ministers of the Gospel dining with us on board who

---

[1] Several words omitted here from the original, in which the rest of the sentence reads: '... to the anchor in the Brig which done we hove the Brig near to our Ship to clear his anchor & then drop ours, hove in the kedge & rode by the anchor'.

[2] In the original, '& Sunday' and '16' have been inserted, but the transcriber either missed these or the insertions took place after the transcription. This clarifies the parenthesis '(Sunday)' in the journal entry.

seemed highly delighted with the Calm Serenity of the glass like plane of the unruffled ocean[.]

Tuesday 18th

Light breezes from the S[d] or SE[d] or calm charming fine weather and remarkable smooth sea[.] At 12¼ AM (Wednesday) had 12½ feet water on the Bar at full tide[.]

Wednesday Thursday Aug[t] 19th & 20th

Light or Moderate breezes fine weather until 11 AM (Wednesday) when a fresh gale of wind from the SE[d] opening up we got under weigh and made sail with the wind at SE for the Harbour[.] before 12 having to make 2 or 3 tacks we were overtaken with a violent thunder storm thunder and lightning Rain and Wind[.] we close reefed the Top Sails struck Royalmasts and yards and waited till tide time off the Harbour mouth[.] At ½ an hour PM (Thursday) the Flag was hoisted on the cliff[1] a signal for 13 feet water when we made all sail out 3 reefs in the Top Sails and steered thro' the <u>Sledway</u>[2] for the Harbour and at 1 PM just passed the entrance of the Piers and stuck fast[.] began immediately to deliver casks and guns into the three lighters which we loaded with all the Guns and about 35–40 casks and awaiting the next tide to get the Ship further up the Harbour[.] . In the Morning tide got up above the Scotch Head[.] At 7 A M loosed all sails to dry and (at ½ PM Thursday 20th Civil Day) unbent them and sent them to T Chilton's sail loft and at tide time 1½ PM got up to the [*blank space*][3] side[.]

Friday Aug[t] 21st

In the afternoon got above bridge 200 yards to near the Bell gates[.]

Saturday Aug[t] 22nd

Paid men 5 mo[s] 16 Days[.]

---

[1] See journal entry for 22 March 1812.

[2] The Sledway was a narrow navigation channel between Whitby Scar and Whitby Rocks, east of the harbour entrance.

[3] 'Staith' in original.

Journal for 1813

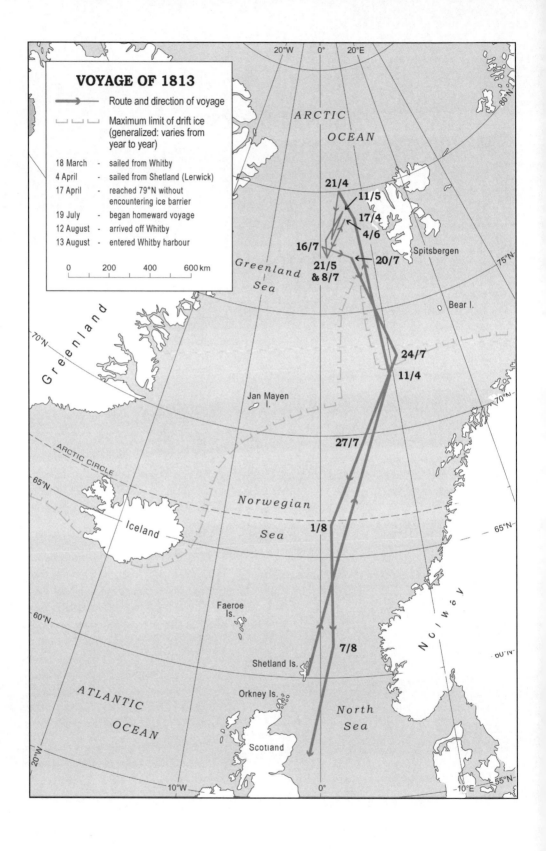

VOYAGE OF 1813

➤➤➤	Route and direction of voyage
⌐ ⌐ ⌐	Maximum limit of drift ice (generalized: varies from year to year)

18 March	-	sailed from Whitby
4 April	-	sailed from Shetland (Lerwick)
17 April	-	reached 79°N without encountering ice barrier
19 July	-	began homeward voyage
12 August	-	arrived off Whitby
13 August	-	entered Whitby harbour

0   200   400   600 km

ARCTIC OCEAN

21/4
11/5
17/4
4/6
16/7
21/5 & 8/7
20/7
Spitsbergen

Greenland Sea

Bear I.

Greenland

24/7
11/4

70°N

Jan Mayen I.

27/7

ARCTIC CIRCLE

65°N

Norwegian Sea

Iceland

1/8

65°N

N o r w a y

Faeroe Is.

60°N

7/8

Shetland Is.

ATLANTIC OCEAN

Orkney Is.

North Sea

Scotland

20°W   0°   20°E

80°N

75°N

70°N

65°N

20°W   10°W   0°   10°E   55°N

JOURNAL
OF A
GREENLAND VOYAGE
UNDER DIVINE PROVIDENCE
in the New Ship
ESK of and from WHITBY
for the purpose of capturing
THE CETACEA of the NORTHERN OCEAN
by
William Scoresby Junr M.W.S.[1] Commander
1813.

In the Summer of the Year 1812 a Keel was laid down by Messrs Fishburn & Brodrick Ship Builders of Whitby upon which the superstructure considered as best adapted for a Whale Fishing Ship was erected. The qualities which are of particular advantage to Ships in this trade run somewhat as follow. The vessel should admeasure 300 to 400 Tons; built of the best & strongest materials; flush decked; hold Beams laying low the better to resist a pressure of Ice, also to allow a great height in the Twin decks; a flat floored burthensome hold, for good stowage and carrying a large Cargo; the height of the hold adapted for containing three tiers of Ton Casks say 10^{ft}..6^{in} to 10^{ft}..10^{in} clear of the Beam. &c. &c. these with many ['more' *deleted*] smaller, but useful peculiarities of structure were united in the Building of the ship Esk.[2]

   In the Month of September I engaged with my worthy Friends Messrs F & B the sole proprietors to take command of the Ship Esk on a Greenland Voyage and from that time had the direction of the preparing and fitting of the various compartments and

---

[1] Presumably an abbreviation for 'Member of the Wernerian Society.' See Introduction, p. xxxi.

[2] In *Account of the Arctic Regions*, II, pp. 187–9 and 506–7, Scoresby provided detailed arguments for his belief, based on experience, that 'a ship of intermediate size between 300 and 400 tons, is best adapted for the fishery. And, on the whole, perhaps, a roomy ship of 330 or 340 tons, possesses more advantages, with fewer advantages, than a vessel of similar build of any other capacity.' An important consideration was the ability of a ship to receive the blubber flensed from captured whales: 'a ship of 330 tons burden may receive on board about 150 tons of blubber at once; a ship of 250 tons scarcely 100'. The smaller ship, 'soon crowded with blubber, … the fishing is necessarily suspended, until the blubber obtained is packed in casks, an operation requiring so much time, that a favourable opportunity, such as a run of fish, rarely continues until it is completed, nor often recurs in one season' (p. 506). The *Resolution* was 291 tons, the *Esk* 354 tons. See Introduction, p. lii.

extra materials a Fishing Ship needs.[1] I likewise engaged a Crew of good officers, consisting of Six Harpooners, Six Boatsteerers, and Six Linemanagers, together with Surgeon, Carpenter, Armourer, Cook, &c. – At this time the <u>Hull</u> was nearly completed, the hold & Deck Beams were laid, the hold Beam [*blank space*] feet abaft the Main Mast for the Orlop Deck[2] were placed [*blank space*] Inches higher than those for the Twin decks; thereby admitting of <u>four</u> Tiers of Casks of 180 Gallons each in the after Hold – An apartment was likewise taken from the hold, laying beneath the Orlop Deck [*blank space*] feet before the Mizen Mast: it was 6 feet long, the width of the Ship & four feet in height for the convenience of holding the Cables in the Fishing Country where they are not needed – A Gun-Room, or Provision & Line<u>room</u> was framed beneath the Cabin Deck passing forward [*blank space*] feet before the Mizen Mast. that is, as far as the <u>Cable Stage</u>: a portion [*blank space*] feet Broad in the Middle was partitioned off for Provisions & the sides were allotted for Whale Lines. Beneath this again lay the Magazine, a small platform was erected on the Kilson,[3] the Roomiest or middle part ceiled off for the Powder Room; the sides and other vacancies annexed were united as a receptacle for Potatoes. The Cabin was fitted up in the best style by the ablest Ship Carpenters in the Town, – about three feet on each side & a large space before it[,] was adapted for Sail, Bread, & Store<u>rooms</u> together with various convenient Lockers as p plan. About the same time <u>fortification</u>[4] timbers were applied within the Stem & Bows for the purpose of resisting Blows from Ice, they consisted chiefly of four large straight Timbers called <u>Ice Beams</u> about 13 In. square & 26 feet in length: they all <u>butted</u> with their Foremost ends against a Strong Fore Hook, laying immediately below the Beams of the 2^d Deck . Where they touched the Hook their ends were about [*blank space*] feet asunder from thence they diverged so that their after ends divided a Beam which they just reached into five equal parts: they were notched into each of three Beams which they passed beneath, and to each were fastened by two, <u>one Inch</u> Bolts, & particularly secured by Cleats & Bolts to the last or aftermost. – The next important part of the Fortifications consisted

---

[1] Scoresby-Jackson, *Life* (p. 88) quoted from the unpublished autobiography: 'My reasons for changing my ship were, I now perceive, not absolutely justifiable. I was partly influenced by private pique towards one of the owners of the *Resolution*, partly by ambitious motives to obtain the command of such a large and finely equipped ship as the *Esk*, and partly by an increase in my wages which, however, had previously been as good as were paid to any captain from the port, and had returned me £912 for my two voyages as commander.' The sum of £912 in 1812, during a wartime period of relatively high prices, was approximately equivalent in purchasing power to £34,627 in 1998: Twigger, *Inflation*, Table 1. See journal entries for 8 and 10 August 1811 concerning Scoresby's disagreement with the owners.

[2] Smyth, *Sailor's Word Book*: 'ORLOP. The lowest deck, formerly called "over-lop", consisting of a platform laid over the beams in ships of war, whereon the cables were usually coiled, and containing some cabins as well as the chief store-rooms.'

[3] Smyth, *Sailor's Word Book*: 'KEELSON, OR KELSON. An internal keel, laid upon the middle of the floor-timbers, immediately over the keel, and serving to bind all together by means of long bolts driven from without, and clinched on the upper side of the keelson.'

[4] 'S' of plural ('fortifications') deleted. Scoresby described the 'additional Strengthenings requisite for resisting the Concussions of the Ice' in *Account of the Arctic Regions*, II, pp. 191–4. Smyth, *Sailor's Word Book*, includes such terms as 'fortifications' and 'ice beams', apparently based on this passage in the *Account*.

of ['four' *deleted*] timbers ['on each side' *inserted and deleted*] fitting the Curve of the Ships Bows, were laid upon the Ceiling inside and nearly parallel with its planks. Some <u>butted</u> with the ends of the Fore Hooks, others passed between, there lay four on each Side and about [*blank space*] Inches asunder, they were firmly trenailed & bolted to the timbers of the Ships Bows. – Across these curved timbers or <u>Pointers</u> four or five <u>Riders</u> were made to pass nearly at Right Angles, or in the same direction as the Ships [<u>Truttrek?</u>] <u>Timbers</u>[1] – Now from each of the points of Section of the <u>Riders & pointers</u> proceeded a smaller timber or <u>Shore</u> joining ['the' *deleted*] Some one of the Ice Beams & secured by a Rabbit[2] – Five [<u>Shores?</u>] proceed from the upper pointer to the Side Ice Beam, five from the lower pointer to the Second Ice Beam & the Remaining ten from the two Middle Pointers equally divided between the two Ice Beams on each side of the Ship. Strong pieces of Timber or <u>Carlines</u>[3] connected the Ice Beams together in various places; so that a Blow on any part of the Stem or Bows must be Communicated by the pointers & [Riders?] through the Medium of the lateral timbers or shores to the Ice Beams, and each part through out must bear mutually owing to their Strong and intimate Connexion. The vacancies amidst the lateral timbers or Shores being Ceiled off formed an excellent Coal Hole fit to contain near seven chaldrons of Whitby Measure.[4] – As a still greater defence from the Ice the Ship was <u>doubled,</u> as it is termed, that is, an additional thickness of [*blank space*] Inch Oak Plank was applied upon the outside of the Ship from the Wales down to the Six Feet Water Mark, from one end of the ship Completely to the other. – Ice Knees[5] were as usual also affixed, to preserve the sides of the Stern & Front of the Bows from being Cut or Shattered by strokes from Ice: the Stern by the Ice Knees was likewise protected by being covered with half Inch Iron plates, which plates, as well as the Ice Knees extend from the [*blank space*] feet water line up to the [*blank space*] feet mark. – Davits for the suspending the Whale Boats were likewise fixed: these consisted of four Beams of Fir 8½ to 9 Inches square & about 27 feet in length, supported 6 feet above the Deck by Oaken <u>uprights</u> on the sides, they were placed the length of a Boat as under beginning from Close by the Ships Stern, say 25 or 27 feet apart & passing directly across the Deck.[6] An Armourer's Shop Seven feet square was erected on the Larboard side of the Foremast in the Twin Decks – it was completely lined with Sheet

---

[1] Probably the 'Futtock-timbers, futtocks, or foot-hooks' of Smyth, *Sailor's Word Book*: 'The separate pieces of timber which compose the frame. There are four futtocks (component parts of the rib), and occasionally five, to a ship … Those next the keel are called ground-futtocks or navel-timbers, and the rest upper futtocks.'

[2] Smyth, *Sailor's Word Book*: 'RABBET, OR REBATE. An angular incision cut longitudinally in a piece of timber, to receive the ends of a number of planks, to be securely fastened therein.'

[3] Smyth, *Sailor's Word Book*: 'CARLINES, OR CARLINGS. Pieces of timber about five inches square, lying fore and aft, along from one beam to another.'

[4] See journal entry for 21 February 1812. This suggests that the capacity of the *Esk*'s coal hole was close to 15 tons (15,000 kg).

[5] Smyth, *Sailor's Word Book*: 'KNEE. Naturally grown timber, or bars of iron, bent to a right angle, or to fit the surfaces, and to secure bodies firmly together …'. Smyth listed several types of knee, but did not include ice-knees.

[6] In *Account of the Arctic Regions*, II, p. 196, Scoresby noted that this arrangement of whaleboats was a novel one, initiated in 1813 both on the *Esk* and on his father's ship, the *John* of Greenock.

Iron thereby to prevent any danger from the Forge. The Half Deck on each side was supplied with Cabins for the Sailors, two heights: on one side six Cabins intended for 3 Men each being 6 feet by 4¼ broad, & across the after end were 4 Cabins: 6 feet by 3 feet adapted for two Men each, thus affording accommodation for 44 Men to rest at a time. A Bulk's head separated the Half or Orlop Deck from the Twin Decks, two sliding doors, one on each side, four feet wide, open to communication when necessary. [*Rest of page blank, followed by diagrams*]

JOURNAL

The whole <u>Hull</u> of the Ship being completed and every article in tollerable state of forwardness on the 2ᵈ of February 1813 the Esk was launched into the water: the following day she was hauled up on the South side of the <u>Bell</u> and [***] : shewed no leak of importance. From here she was taken to the side of Brown's Quay.

On the 4ᵗʰ received Certificates of Protection[1] for 14 Seamen at the Custom House, on an owner making Oath that ['the' deleted] each Man should proceed in the Ship Esk to the Fishing Country & the Men each signing a Bond of [*blank space*] Pounds that they would proceed accordingly.

On Monday the 8ᵗʰ Febʸ Commenced the Masting, owing however to a Ship being laid aground alongside the lower [Masts?] were with difficulty got in. These Masts were rigged on the 9ᵗʰ & in the Course of the week most most [*sic*] of the other Masts & Yards were Rigged in their places.

On the 10ᵗʰ Received the Beef of 11 oxen weighing 4 tons 18 Cwt 3 qr. 27 lb which we cut up & Corned in F & B.'s Wharehouse.

12ᵗʰ Began to stow the Hold according to the following Method: viz; – It may first be necessary to premise that to make the best Stowage the Casks in general should be precicely of a length however variable their capacity: hence the Casks we built were

---

'Prior to the year 1813, a ship having seven boats carried one at each *waist*, that is between the main-mast and fore-mast, two at each *quarter*, one above the other, and one across the stem. The disadvantages of this were that 'it was necessary that the under quarter boats should be taken upon deck in every storm, accompanied by a high sea, – an operation which, on some occasions, was scarcely practicable. They were, likewise subject to be damaged by the passing ice. The Scoresbys' arrangement also enabled 'any particular boat of the seven to be lowered by itself, or all the seven boats at the same time', and the system was immediately copied by other whalers, both for new and existing ships.

[1] Footnote in journal text: 'The officers before mentioned were <u>protected</u> & thereby bound in a Bond of [*blank space*] £ at the time of their being engaged; on the Owners giving a Considerable bonded security & on making oath likewise that these men were intended as part of the Crew of the Esk, & that she should proceed to the next Fishery on penalty of forfeiting the Money thus bonded.' See note to journal entry for 6 March 1812, which suggests that the *Esk* would have been entitled to protect 16 ordinary seamen. See also the entry for 12 March 1813.

formed 4 ft 11 In in length & consisted Chiefly of Tons: about 80 Tons however of second hand Casks were purchased in London, the Contents of each near about a Ton but their lengths were almost as variable as their Numbers: this made some difficulty attendant in the operation, however I remedied the inconvenience by adopting the following plan, that is, we stowed most of these old Casks in the Floor of the Ship & keep the lengths regular put two together whose united lengths should make 9 ft 10 in or twice the length of ['the' deleted] any of the new Casks, thus we were enabled make as good stowage as if that had been all precisely of the wished for dimensions. We commenced at the [pump?] well & stowed Ton Casks next the Kelson 6 lengths forward, then added three other Casks each of which was about 15 Gall[s] smaller than the one preceeding it, the last one just reached the <u>foremast</u>. The next [Row?] commencing Half a Cask farther forward consisted of five Tons to which were added 4 Casks diminishing in size agreeable to the before mentioned proportion. Along the Sides of these were stowed (likewise Bilge & Head) beginning half a Cask still farther forward a row consisting of 6 Casks from 215 to 200 Gall[s] & continued by two smaller before them: these Casks Covered the Floors of the Ship from the [Pump?] Well to the Foremast – The first tier of [***] Casks, resting on the last Mentioned Row, consisted of 6 of 300 Gall[s] finished forward by two Tons. Upon the Kelson we stowed such sized Casks as best suited the situation of the Stantions, that is exactly to fit in length & about $4\frac{1}{4}$ feet wide in the Bilge or <u>Bouge</u>[?],[1] Seven lengths completed the distance between the two masts: Now the rest of the 2[d] Tier beginning to stow next the <u>winges</u> [sic], consisted entirely of Ton Cask stowed Bilge & Head with the [wing?] Casks, two Rows on each Side, making altogether Seven Rows. – The third Tier, owing to the Ship being a very trifle wider at the plane of its Site, was an exact counterpart of the Second Tier. – After this part of the Hold was finished I found that the only improvement that could well be made would be to have in the lower Tier 300 Gall[n] Casks next the Kelson & Casks about 4 Inches or 6 Inches large[2] diameter in the Bouge upon the Kelson, thus a little Room which was lost between the upper Tier & Hold Beams would be fully occupied. – The Casks on different Sides of the Kelson (ground Tier), were stowed Bouge & Head, I think however they would have answered full as well or better to have been exactly similar on both sides, that is, the Casks next the Kelson to have lain <u>bouge</u> & Bouge, or exactly abreast of each other. The after Hold was stowed different, the ground Tier consists first of 5 Short Ton or 230 Gall[n] Casks 2[dly] 5 Casks diminishing from Tons to 180 Gall's & 3[dly] 6 Casks from 200 to 100 Gall[s] diminishing as they passed aft. The Wing Commenced with a 300 Gall[n] Cask, next 200, 180, 180, & lastly, against the Bulk's Head a 300 Gall[n] Cask. On the Kelson lay 3 Tons & one 300. Two rows of 180 Gall[s] Casks or smaller filled between on each side & completed the 2[d] Tier. In the 3[d] Tier the Wings were composed of 180 Gall[n] Casks Chiefly & were filled up between with first; 6, 180's next the Bulk's Head aft stowed Bilge & Bilge, & 4 f[t] [7?] in. in length, & 2[dly] two

---

[1] Smyth, *Sailor's Word Book* defined 'bouge or bowge and chine, or bilge and chimb' as 'The end of one cask stowed against the bilge of another.' Scoresby appears to use the phrase 'bouge and head' to mean the same thing.
[2] 'larger' intended?

[longers?] Consisting each of 7 Beer Casks of 126 Gall^s 4 f^t [9?] in. in length likewise stored Bouge & Bouge & which third longer reached nearly to the [***] . The fourth Tier filled up with chiefly 180 Gall^n Casks, smaller towards the stern. Owing to a want of some Casks agreeable to the above mentioned dimensions this plan of stowage could only be partially complied with, so far however as we had Casks we complied with & I believe it to be the best method for stowing the largest Cargo in a Ship of the Esk's Dimensions: at least so far as my experience in this art leads me, or allows me to judge.[1]

February 13th Finally Salted and packed the beef in Casks of 180 Gall^s[.] On the 17th Received on board Seven chaldrons of Coals (Whitby Measure). Filled the ground Tier of Casks in the Hold with water as Ballast & likewise the Second Tier from the Bulk's Head in the after Hold to the Fore part of the Main Hatch way. On the 18th had Strong Gales of wind accompanied with Rain: the 19th fine weather wind SW. Riggers put up all masts.

25th of February. The Ship was Registered on the proprietors Messrs Fishburn & Brodrick making Oath that they were sole Owners of the Ship called <u>Esk</u> of Whitby, agreeable to the following characters & descriptions certified by Isaiah Moorsom Surveyor at this Port.[2]

That the Said Ship or Vessel is <u>British Built</u>, has <u>Deck</u> & <u>half Decks</u>, and <u>three</u> Masts;

that her Length from the Fore part of the Main Stem to the after part of the Stern Post aloft is – 106 feet 6 Inches;

her Breadth at the Broadest part above the Main Wales is 27 feet 11 Inches;

her Height between decks 7 feet 8 Inches;

and admeasures 354 73/94 Tons;

that she is a Square Sterned, Flush Decked Ship, has no Gallery & <u>Carved Head</u>.

---

26. A Gun adapted for Shooting a Harpoon at a Whale, arrived from the Maker W. Wallis of Hull.[3] It cost 25 Guineas & six Harpoons Nine Guineas More. See drawing page [*blank space*]

[1] This stowing presumably took several days. The journal entry for the following day (13 February) implies that the water-filled casks in the lowest tiers were filled and stowed at this time.

[2] Presumably a member of the Moorsom family of Whitby, the best-known member of which was Admiral Sir Robert Moorsom (1760–1835), commander of HMS *Revenge* at Trafalgar. The latter was the second son of Richard Moorsom (1729–1809), who in the 1770s was 'in partnership with Thomas Scarth and John Yeoman who between them owned eight whaling ships.': Ventress, *Admiral Sir Robert Moorsom*, p. 3.

[3] 'The ultimate development of the flint-lock harpoon gun was achieved in the workshop of George Wallis Jnr (d. 1833, aged 63), an outstanding Hull gunsmith. In his design two large flint-locks were placed one on either side of the breech, housed under hinged covers to protect them from wind and spray. By pulling a lanyard tied to the end of the trigger lever directly behind the breech, and threaded through a hole in the wooden stock, the two locks were fired simultaneously to ensure the rapid and efficient ignition of the main charge.': Credland, *Hull Whaling Trade*, p. 25. The gun

On the 1ˢᵗ & 2ᵈ of March we got on board 20 Casks Containing 10 Tons of Beer & 8 Casks about 300 Gallons of Ale.

3ᵈ Received 80 Bushels of Potatoes: [*blank space*] Sacks or One Ton of Flour 30 Stones of Oatmeal, together with sundry other Stores.

4ᵗʰ Took the Provisions on Board: Say, 7 Casks of 180 Gallˢ of Beef Containing 4 Tons, 18 Cwt, 3 qrs, 27 lb & 4 Similar Casks of Pork Containing 30 Pigs or 3 Tons 2 Cwt & 17 lb. Took in likewise the Guns Consisting of 8 Carronades of 18 lbs weighing each about 10 Cwt: & 2 long [***] Guns weighing each about [*blank space*] Cwt.

5 & 6. The Gunner fitting Guns, &c. Received 4½ Tons of Ship Bread¹ and 15 Tons of Fresh Water.

8ᵗʰ & 9. Got [60?] Whales Lines, 1 Coil of <u>Foregangers</u> – Seven Whale Boats and my own Stern Boat. Four were stowed in the Twin Decks[.]

On the 10ᵗʰ was the National Fast Day:² on the 11ᵗʰ Bent Sails.

12ᵗʰ Mustered the Ship's Crew according to the usual forms in the presence of the Owners by Isaiah Moorsom Survey & Mustering Officer: those men who it is required by the act to Muster are the 18 officers before named, & 16 Seamen whereof 6 are Greenmen or have not been to the Fishery: together with 6 Apprentices, Surgeon, & Master: & thus for <u>every</u> Ship of 300 Tons or [upwards?].³ After the Mustering paid the Men each his Harbour wages due to him, one month in advance Sea pay, & Handmoney to the Harponeers, each Man being bound with his Master under articles of agreement on a Stamp of [*blank space*] Shill*ing*s: penalty of non-compliance One Month's Imprisonment I believe – with the forefeiture of all wages due, Clothes, &c. each man signed these Articles, on condition of receiving wages, [Tin?] Money, & perquisities According to the following Scheme.

---

and harpoons illustrated in Plates 18 and 19 of Scoresby's *Account of the Arctic Regions*, II, were Wallis designs.

¹ Presumably 'BISCUIT. ... Bread intended for naval or military expeditions is now simply flour well kneaded, with the least possible quantity of water, into flat cakes, and slowly baked': Smyth, *Sailor's Word Book*, s.v.

² In 1813 this was the Wednesday after the first Sunday in Lent and therefore an 'ember day' of fasting in the church calendar.

³ The Act of Parliament referred to was that providing for the payment of bounties on whaling, 26 George III, c.41, as subsequently amended. The relevant provisions, including those for mustering, are set out in Scoresby, *Account of the Arctic Regions*, II, pp. 491–505.

Stations	Sea Pay p Month	Striking Money	Fish Money p N° of size	Oil Money p Ton	Hand Money
Harpooner – Single Stⁿ	— — — —	0 . 10 . 6	— — — —	0 . 6 . 0	7 . 7 . 0 .
Boatsteerer	3 . 0 . 0 .	1 . 1 . 0	— — — —	0 . 1 . 6	— — — —
Linemanager	2 . 17 . 6	1 . 1 . 0 .	— — — —	0 . 1 . 6	— — — —
Seaman	2 . 15 . 0	1 . 1 . 0	— — — —	0 . 1 . 6	
Landman	2 . 5 . 0 / 2 . 10 . 0	— — — —	— — — —	0 . 1 . 0	— — — —
Carpenter	4 . 15 . 0	— — — —	1 . 1 . 0	— — — —	— — — —
Cooper	4 . 6 . 6 .	— — — —	— — — —	0 . 1 . 6	— — — —
Surgeon	4 . 0 . 0	— — — —	1 . 1 . 0	— — — —	— — — —
Armourer	3 . 0 . 0	— — — —	— — — —	0 . 1 . 6	— — — —
Carpenter's Mate	3 . 5 . 0	— — — —	— — — —	0 . 1 . 6	— — — —
Cook	3 . 0 . 0	— — — —	— — — —	0 . 1 . 6	— — — —
Chief Mate (Single)	3 . 3 . 0	1 . 1 . 0	1 . 1 . 0	0 . 2 . 0	— — — —
d° with Harpooner Extra	2 . 2 . 0	— — — —	1 . 1 . 0	— — — —	— — — —
Spicksioneer Extra	— — — —	— — — —	0 . 10 . 6	0 . 0 . 4	1 . 1 . 0
Sec^d Mate Boatswⁿ Skeeman	1 . 1 . 0 extra				

The Sea Pay or Monthly Wages of the above different Ranks of Men & Officers advance 5/- p month each, provided the Ship produces 100 Tons of Oil. Those likewise who have Monthly wages receive ['d' *deleted*] a Note from the Captain whereby their wives or other person they may leave it with becomes entitled to the Sum specified therein (which in general is One Guinea tho' to some few more) on its becoming due two months after the payment of the Month's advance & continues to be repeated the corresponding day of each succeeding month whilst the Ship remains at Sea.

Monday 15th of March. Took on Board two Cables 15 Inches circumference;[1] the one 95 the other 110 Fathoms in length: likewise an Ice hawser 9 In. 90 Fathoms these with a Towline 7 In. 95 Fathoms & two warps one of 5½ In. 120 Fathoms the other 4½ In. 90 Fathoms Constitutes our stock of Ropes for mooring or transporting the Ship in Harbour & in the Fishing Country. About 60 Blubber Casks put up in a small Compass for Stowage, denominated <u>Shakes</u>, were likewise received on Board. – The wind this day blew lightly[2] from the westward, owing to this probably was the high tide which we observed with some surprize. According to the Shields tide tables[3] which are calculated on astronomical principles, regarding the Apogees & Perigees of the Moon, the Moon's Latitude, the Conjunction or Opposition of the Moon & Sun: the Earths distance from the Sun, the Sun's declination, &c. &c. from which date[4]

---

[1] 'diam' deleted immediately before the word 'circumference'. Smyth, *Sailor's Word Book*, clarified the hierarchy of ropes: 'HAWSER. A large rope or cablet, which holds the middle degree between the cable and towline, being a size smaller than the former, and as much larger than the latter ....'

[2] 's' deleted, changing the word from 'slightly' to 'lightly'.

[3] Presumably tide tables for the mouth of the Tyne estuary, at North and South Shields.

[4] *Sic.* 'data' presumably intended.

assisted by [various?] Observations, & Experiments, they are enabled in circum-stances where the tides are not affected by the winds to shew the rise of the water in feet & Inches in many of the principal ports of Great Britain to a remarkable degree of nicety. – By these tables now & by common observation we were led the [*sic*] expect that from Saturday the 13th the tides would gradually & daily increase until Thursday the 18th when they would attain their maximum this being near two days ['past' *deleted*] or about 40 hours past the time of Full Moon – this was not the Case however for owing to the effect of perhaps distant winds the tide on this day was as high within a few Inches as the best tide was expected to be and it so proved that the 5 following tides were all beneath the mark of this by several Inches. This Circum-stance of the tides running much out of Course, especially in [apoge?] Springs has been known to take place frequently before though very seldom so remarkably particular. It is perhaps not so singular as it appears to be on the first consideration, for the attraction of the Moon & its corresponding effect in elevating the water being much less considerable now than on a Perigee falling in with the Full or Change, hence the effect of the wind is rendered more striking. In very high tides a foot more or less water is not much noticed but in bad Springs, a foot lower than what might be calculated on must be very striking, especially in a tide & bar Haven like this where on an Apogee Springs at the best a large Ship well ballasted can but barely find water to proceed in safety to Sea. – Having no idea of the great tide we had in the afternoon we were neither prepared for Sea, nor [even?] to remove our Birth to a situation more ready and convenient for the first opportunity, otherwise we might possibly have got down to the Bridge through a space of 400 yards where, in the Channel, is scarcely water enough for to float the Ship down, which, would have a great advantage to us. The rest of the Ships had water sufficient to have taken them to Sea, but they like us were not ready.

On Tuesday the 16th Wind variable [Werly?], Northerly, or Calm; we got all ready for Sea, in the Morning we received the Beef of Two Oxen killed the 15th for our Sea Stock of Fresh Meat & to make up our usual quantity of about 8¼ or 8½ Tons of Beef & Pork – The Legs being covered with Canvass & several of the finer parts were just corned with Salt & suspended under the Tops & other convenient places, the coarser parts were cut up into 8 or 10 Pound pieces & salted & packed in a Cask. – At 2½ or 3 Pm, the tide was high water, we have a Considerable strain on a Hawser but could not get the Ship over the bank which she had raised without her by the pressure of laying aground. The Aimwell however & the William & Ann & the Lively & Henri-etta being of lighter draught of water and in more convenient situation, got to Sea. At 4 Am. on Wednesday, being Calm weather, we tried again but found less water by 4 Inches than on the Evening before. During the Next Ebb we get 6 or 8 of our men to dig away the outside raised part of the ground which prevented the Ship moving out of the Dock she had formed by her weight, at 4 Pm. by mere strength of power we drew this Ship forward & get her into the deepest water or the Channel – about 100 Yards past Allen's warf she took the ground, the tide was fallen 8 Inches. After or about this time the remaining two fishing Ships the Volunteer & the Resolution sailed to Sea & we were left alone. The owners began now to be very anxious least the Ship should be neaped in the Harbour more especially after we had again attended in the morning of Thursday the 18th & though the Ship was drawn about 20 yards forward she was never clear of the ground. I was requested to lighten the ship, this however could not possibly be effective before the time of tide, the only thing we could do was to lash a couple of lighters by ropes under the Ship's keel & by confining them down, their buoyancy would assist in lifting the Ship from the ground at an earlier period of the tide of flood – this was accordingly effected by obtaining the lend of two [vessel?] ropes upon which our ship fortunately lay. Thus prepared & having two ropes out in a [fair?] & long lead ahead of the Ship we anxiously awaited the flooding of the tide which seemed to come in rapidly & promised to be the highest we had yet experienced. At 4 Pm we began to heave, the Ship presently moved & was drawn by the [press?] and power of our Engines¹ forward with a slow motion – in about half an hour we got into deeper water & the Ship was afterwards hauled freely away, we passed the Bridge in about two Minutes without touching either side: hauled down near the Scotch Head, Set the Sails, & by the assistance of a rope to the Pier, two [Tug?] Boats & a light breeze of wind from the SEᵈ we were safely drawn without the Piers at 5 O'Clock Pm. At 5½ Pm. the Pilot & [Tug?] Boats left us; falling Calm the Ship drifted rapidly to the Northward towards the Rock,² we hoisted a boat out & put a Kedge into her; a breeze of wind opportunely springing up from the westward we were shortly afterwards clear of danger & did not use the Kedge, we were obliged to pass over the N.E.ernmost Corner of the Rock – had plenty of water however, so that the Ship was not critically situated whilst the Breeze continued or the Boat could tow her ahead.

Whitby Abbey in Latitude 54° 28'½ Longitude 32' W, at 7 pm. bore SSW p Compass Distance 2 Miles. Wind a light Breeze at North steering to the NEᵈ[.]

Friday the 19th Delightful clear weather; wind moderate at West to South steering NbE½ E under all the Sails we could display. Loaded eight of the Guns, the other two were charged the preceeding Evening.

Saturday 20th. The wind at SSW increased to a Strong Gale. In the Morning the weather was fine but at Noon became hazy & unpleasant, it was followed with Rain. We steered NNE from 5 to 9 Knotts p hour.

Saturday 20th March 1813³
SSW to WSW
In the afternoon a strange Sail appeared on our Larboard Quarter which gave Chase to us, we continued under easy sail expecting to make the Land before Morning. This

¹ Presumably capstans.
² 'Whitby rock – Whitby Scar and rock extend from the east cliff, and are covered with kelp, visible at low water. The rock has 2 feet on its outer edge, situated 4⁷⁄₁₀ cables, 41° true, from East pier lighthouse, but its extremity, as defined by the 3-fathom contour, extends 6 cables northward of the lighthouse': *North Sea Pilot*, p. 116.
³ This heading is on a new page. From here onwards the journal is set out in the standard form: basic facts of date, wind directions, latitude and longitude, etc. in a narrow left margin; text on remainder of page. Unlike the journals for 1811 and 1812, it appears to have followed civil time (midnight to midnight) throughout.

vessel soon came up with & hailed us, enquiring whether we had seen any ships or vessels of suspicious appearance, I told him none – He replyed, "they were out in pursuit or search after two American Schooner Privateers which were said to be cruizing between Shetland and Norway", probably laying in wait for Greenland Ships. The Oberon (for such was the Brig) Sloop of War of 16 Guns had sailed from Leith two days before, in consequence of the report of these Americans[.][1]

When the Wind & Sea were <u>right aft</u>, or when we Run before the Sea I had an opportunity of judging with tollerable accuracy of the velocity of the waves in the ['Velocity of Waves' *in margin*] direction of the wind. I observed that when a wave first came the length of the Ship's stern, & when it quitted the bow – the interval was 7 and sometimes 8 seconds the distance in which it run the length of the Ship or say 100 feet: the Ship at the same time was sailing in the same direction, at the rate of 8 Miles an hour from which

	ft		ft	miles
As 8″:	100 :: 1 hour or 3600″:		45000 =	7.45
Add Ship's velocity			8.00	
	Nautical Miles		15.45	

	ft		
Or, as 7″ :	100 :: 3600″ ; 51286 or		8½ Miles
	+ Ship's velocity [.]		8
			16½ Miles

This last is probably the most accurate which shews that could a Ship have sailed at this time with a velocity of 16½ Miles, she would have been borne on the Top of a single wave for any distance, or in the hollow between two, so long as the wave kept its form & relative situation. After the Rain the wind moderated & shifted to the westward, this change after rain is not uncommon. At 8 Pm. shortened sail & proceeded under two reefed Topsails NbE, supposing ourselves not far from Fair Island.

Sunday 21st March
WSW to S variable
Fresh Gales of wind prevailed in the Morning. The Moon having risen & the sky become clear & light at 1 Am made sail steering North to Make the Land afraid of being too far to Lee-ward which would have Cast us past Lerwick had the wind continued. Ships coming out to Shetland are commonly to the Eastward of their Reckoning. At 4[?] Am however we descried Fair Isle bearing about NW p Compass & 10 miles distant. Set all Sails & steered NNE or NEbN & at 6 Am saw Fitfil[2] Head bearing NbE. At 8 Passed Sumbro[3] Head. At 9½ Mousa Island & at 10 obtained the

[1] HMS *Oberon*, built in Hull in 1806, spent most of the Napoleonic Wars searching for privateers in the North Sea and adjacent waters: Phillips, *Ships of the Old Navy*. Appendix H in Garitee, *The Republic's Private Navy*, is a list of 124 privateers with Baltimore owners operating during the War of 1812, though most of them were active along the eastern seaboard of North America or in the Caribbean.
[2] *Sic.* Fitful Head, on the west side of the southern peninsula of Shetland mainland.
[3] Sumburgh Head, the southern tip of the peninsula.

S. entrance of Brasse Sound [***] , shortening sail as we approached the Harbour & at 10¾ Pm [*sic*] anchored in the midst of about 15 Sail of Ships. Owing to the Stupidity of the Pilot who directed us to a berth where there was no room to swing or bring up we gave the Aurora of a London [*sic*] a Foul birth; the wind increasing to a Heavy Gale accompanied with Rain we could not remove but must lay the night. A universal gloom prevails throughout the Town of Lerwick, regret ['is' *deleted*] or mourning is seen depicted in every countenance, on account of the recent Severe loss of the Doris packet with 16 Passengers & a Crew of 6 or 8 all of whom perished. Goods likewise to the value of 12 or 14,000 pounds, not a tenth part of which were insured shared the Common fate. Every individual more or less feels the Shock. Amongst the passengers were 6 or 8 persons of respectable Connexions, one was a Minister of a neighbouring parish another a Writer; 3 or 4 were considerable merchant & five were females. The Doris was originally built for a Privateer, was captured on the Norway Station about two Years ago & brought into Shetland where she sank in shallow water. She was bought by Messr.s Ogilvy & Co. On being condemned was risen upon and fitted out Schooner rigged, as a Trader. She was found to sail fast but proved very Crank or tender at Sea. I think she had made three or four voyages and about six weeks ago took in goods for Shetland at Leith; a large quantity being on hand she was loaded very deep and particularly lumbered upon the Deck[.] the master M.r Craggie was more than once cautioned respecting the danger of making his vessel unsafe or top heavy, he replied, he did not fear, but hoped if the weather continued fine he should make a safe passage as usual. Accordingly on Saturday the 20.th of February about 4 Pm he sailed from Leith, a tremendous gale of wind from the SSW soon afterwards commenced & the following morning the Schooner was seen dismasted off Aberdeen & on the 22.d she drifted on shore on the Rocks near Slaine's Castle[1] between Aberdeen and Peterhead where she was in a few minutes dashed to pieces, not a soul was on board – & for many days none of the bodies were found[.] it was hoped the Crew & passengers might have been taken out by some passing vessel.

The Master Craiggie [*sic*] was considered as a worthy man, serious steady, & clever he was universally respected. It is too evident, that the overloading & lumbering of the vessel was the primary cause of the dreadful catastrophe.

Amongst the passengers who perished in this vessel there were several whom I well knew. M.r R. Sinclair Merch.t & general agent, a M.r Angus, M.r Smith Merch.t & his brother, &c. &c. Little of the property in the vessel was insured caused a heavy pecuniary loss to many individuals; some who had sent their whole Cash to Leith for goods to begin trade were reduced to beggary & want. It is a remarkable and melancholy circumstance that this is the second packet belonging Shetland that has been

---

[1] Now a cliff-top ruin at Cruden Bay, eight miles south of Peterhead, Slains Castle was visited on 24 August 1773 by Dr Samuel Johnson and James Boswell. In Boswell's *Journal of a Tour to the Hebrides, with Samuel Johnson, LL.D.* he noted that 'Dr Johnson observed, the situation here was the noblest he had ever seen.' Boswell however grumbled that 'I had a most elegant room; but there was a fire in it which blazed; and the sea, to which my windows looked, roared; and the pillows were made of the feathers of some sea-fowl, which had to me a disagreeable smell: so that, by all these causes, I was kept awake a good while.' See also Crowl, *The Intelligent Traveller's Guide to Historic Scotland*, p. 544.

lost this winter, the other vessel struck upon upon a Rock in the Neighbourhood of Scalloway, the sloop sunk & all on board perished.

I am informed that a suspicious looking vessel, Schooner Rigged, was seen of the Skerries to the Eastward of these Islands about 8 days ago. There remains little doubt but it was one of those American Privateers which the Oberon was in pursuit of. (*End of a page; next page left blank.*)

Monday 22ᵈ March
SSW. SW.
Fresh Gales prevailed until afternoon, fine light breezes continued the rest of the day. Having fine clear weather we set all the Rigging (after having warped the Ship to windward into a good fair birth.). Most of the Hull Ships came in & anchored in the Sound.

Tuesday 23ᵈ March
SWerly or S.erly.
The remnant of the Hull Fleet, the Augusta, Clapham, &c. &c came in. The [Aurora *deleted*] Nightingale Sloop of War[1] from a Cruize on the Norway Station likewise anchored here: she calls to take in such part of a levy of 100 Men made by Government on the Islands as have been [procured?] & sent to Lerwick by the Landholders. On examining the Esk's Crew I discovered owing to having 6 Raw lads of 12 to 16 years of age that we were on the whole somewhat weaker manned than I had conceived. Men being plentiful I engaged two Sailors who agree that I shall not Land them here on the Ship's return unless it be perfectly convenient, & that if they are carried past their Island they must be liable to dismissed with the rest of the Crew on the Ship's arrival in England. They are to have wages 50/- p Month & 10/6 for every size Fish. All the Hull & London Ships want a Number of Men some to the amount of 20 to 30 – they will all get supplied as it is calculated that not more than 600 will be wanted for the Fishing Ship whilst there are found to be near 800 who are expecting Births.

Employed all hands filling water to bring the Ship deeper making Crow's nest, Matts[2] for Rigging, &c. &c . Wind a Fresh Gale.

Wednesday 24ᵗʰ March
SW. W North
Moderate or Fresh breezes of wind accompanied with much Rain. Finished trimming the Ship having filled all Casks which I judged prudent & suitable. The Ship now [swims?] 12ᶠᵗ 2ⁱⁿ according to the Fore Marks & 12.8 aft. A Brig came in from Scotland which brings an account of the body of one of the Passengers of the Doris having been found, this circumstance blasts the remaining hope of these persons interested

---

[1] See journal entry for 10 August 1812.
[2] *OED*: 'Mat. ... A thick web of rope yarn used to protect the standing rigging from the friction of other ropes.'

who eager to grasp at any [shardow?][1] of comfort fondly imagined their Friends their Relatives, might have been picked up by some passing Coaster.

I had some oysters sent me from the Shore today. I certainly think the Shetland Shell Fish of this description to be preferable to any I have ever tasted, either in London, Ramsgate or Margate. They are well sized, firm, flat, & fine flavoured. The Common rate of sale when no ships are here is one shilling p 100, they are now about double[.]

Thursday 25 March
W.erly SW.erly
The demand of the legislature made on this Country for One Hundred Men for the Navy not having been supplied of a sudden this Evening the Crew of the Nightingale aided by a party of Soldiers rushed armed into the Town to impress Men to make up the deficiency near 50 I believe were caught between 40 & 50 were before obtained from the Landholders so that some were yet wanting: – The form in which this Levy was to be enacted or enforced was this – 100 Men was the whole demand – every Laird was therefore requested by the Sheriffs of Lerwick to supply a certain number in proportion to their quantity of Land or Number of Tenantry, this some complied with, others from carelessness, indolence, or an aversion to Nominating any of their tenantry as suitable for his Majestics Service have either let the request alone or have but partially supplied their numbers. – Now of those men impressed. when regulated, such as belonged to any of the Whale Fishery Ships in the Harbour & stood on the Muster List, or were natives or residents on the parishes which had procured or supplied their full proportion of the demand, were released, the rest were detained & sent on board of the Nightingale. – The Sum of One Hundred Men being furnished will protect all natives of these Islands, for three years, from serving his Majesty, calculated from the time the Levy was first made, which I believe was in the Month of September last.

Came in two or three Ships – 2 or 3 Sailed for Greenland.

Friday 26th March
SW. SSW. to WNW.
To day we had Strong Gales of wind with some Rain. In the morning the Volunteer & Lively of Whitby with 2 or 3 other Ships sailed for Greenland: we should have likewise gone but owing to the quantity of work which remains to be prepared before we come to the Fishery, this work can be done much better here than at Sea. – A great variety of things are yet to fit, prepare, & make for the Fishery [few?] things being done at Whitby which were not indispensibly requisite, owing to the hurry with which the Ship was fit out, & the want of time which produced that hurry, the Ship was launched too lately near a month. Came in the Dundee & Neptune of London &c. &c.

Saturday 27th March
N.erly Variable, WNW.
In the Morning Several Ships of the Feet [sic] made signals for sailing, the wind

---

[1] *Sic*: the transcriber may have been confused between 'shadow' and 'shard'; the latter was probably intended.

however increasing to a Strong Gale accompanied with Rain & hail (Temp^e 45°) & the wind being far Northerly I thought it prudent to content ourselves by remaining in the Harbour. In the Evening wind moderate & heavy rain.

Sunday 28th March
WNW, NW or W.
Blowing very heavy all the day until Night: some Rain Showers. Two London Ships came in which had been blown past the Harbour. The Esk laying near the windward shore I with some difficulty encountering the flying sprays [made good a landed?] & twice attended the Kirk. The Rev^d old Gentleman Mr Menes preached, he very suitably & feelingly dwelt on the Mercies of Almighty God & strove to impress his hearers with the Conviction: that privations, trials, & afflictions were means in the hand of God for producing & calling forth the graces of patience, reconciliation, &c & finally efficatious towards the Sanctification of the Soul. He alluded in the whole tenor of his discourses towards stating & amplifying every means of Comfort which the Christian [possesses?] under severe afflictions [&?] which trials do good to the Soul tho' painful to the flesh & prepare the Spirit for ['attended kirk' *in margin*] the Everlasting Kingdom: Many persons being present who had suffered irreparable losses from the late dreadful Calamity in the wreck of the Doris, would doubtless feel themselves strengthened and benefitted. He likewise laboured to impress on their minds as an additional solace [under?] their afflictions, that we being but sojourners here, this not being our Everlasting rest, we should all shortly (being justified by the Redeemer) meet our friends under joyous circumstances in the Kingdom prepared for the Righteous from the Foundation of the World.

Mr Menes seems a very worthy Man & faithful labourer: his White Locks, & age furrowed cheeks, stamp an impression of Reverence on every mind. Not so his presenter[1] – A Gaping, fat, peculiar looking Psalm singer. The Slow, ill-timed, ill-tuned, coarse music, abounding in discords from every Corner & no attempt ['wretched church: the best in Shetland' *in margin*] towards Harmony is really tormenting to the <u>tympanum</u> of a fine Ear, in fact it is miserable. The Kirk is likewise in a piece with the Singing – slovenly, <u>dirty</u>, ruinous, unpainted, dark, prison like. – Notwithstanding its despicable character it is well attended, even the gallery stairs were clad with women & no admittance could be given to half a Dozen of our Sailors for want of room.

I dined & Tea with Mr Ogilvy's & embarked for the Ship at seven.

Monday 29th March
WSW, NW.
Fresh or Strong Gales with frequent Showers of Rain or Hail. In the morning prepared again for sailing, the wind however suddenly increasing and veering to NW I relinquished the thought. The Resolution got under weigh before the Change and although no ship set sail besides her, she worked out of the S. entry & proceeded to

---

[1] Correctly, precentor. *OED*: 'in churches or chapels in which there is no instrumental accompaniment, the officer who leads congregational singing'.

Sea. – The Nightingale still remains here, I put letters on board on Friday expecting her to Sail the day following. The packet is likewise detained on account of the stormy weather.

Tuesday 30ᵗʰ March
NW to WS.W & variable
Strong Gales, heavy squalls in the Showers which prevailed at intervals throughout the day. Came in the Resolution Phillips of Hull[1] in a state bordering on <u>distress</u> – her jibboom carried away, taff[?] ports leaky, ship altogether bad & ill found. The Margaret of Hull Hewitt sailed alone. All hands still employed in preparing sundry necessary gear for Sea & the Fishery.

Wednesday 31ˢᵗ March
NW to WSW, very Var.
In the morning at 4 O'Clock we had Calm weather for a short time, a furious storm then re-commenced – the wind blew tremendously hard in the Showers of Hail, or Snow that occurred every hour or more frequently. The Barometer yesterday started at 29.72 Inches, to-day at Noon had lowered to 29.17 Inches: thermometer 38° to 36°. A Packet bringing mails from Leith arrived in the afternoon: sailed on Monday last. – Had experienced boisterous weather the wind mostly at NW. I have not yet heard the News.

Thursday 1ˢᵗ April
W.erly, NW to NbE
Hard Gales & squally accompanied with Much Snow. A circumstance highly entertaining occurred yesterday, on the arrival of the Packet from Leith. – Several young Gentlemen anxious to hear the news [hasted?] on board the vessel before she was well brought up – several passengers were seen amongst the rest some Ladies – a Mr Hay went into the Cabin & was surprised on seeing a fine looking well dressed Girl, a stranger to him, having with her a young Child: Mr H. presently understood, that his Companion who had come off with him, a Mr Heddle, Son to the Comptroller of the Customs in Lerwick, was better acquainted with this Girl than himself – he directly ascends the Deck & whisperd Heddle, that a Charming Girl was below would he go down & see her – "Aye, where is she"? "In the Cabin", replied his Friend. They both descended the Ladder: Mr Heddle was pushed into the Front, Mr Hay watching his emotions – "Ugh"! says he, on observing who the Girl was, "<u>how are ye</u>"; ["]What brought you here"? – The Girl blushed, He was Confounded, bit his Lip, and expressed the utmost vexation. Hay retreated & left them together to explain

---

[1] Not to be confused with the *Resolution* of Whitby, Scoresby's command in 1811 and 1812 and mentioned in the previous day's journal. According to Lubbock, *Arctic Whalers*, Appendix D, the Hull *Resolution* was built in Whitby in 1802, 292 tons, and made her first whaling voyage in 1811. However, Credland, *Hull Whaling Trade*, p. 126 listed her as captured as a prize in 1808, 334 tons. His spelling of her master, and that in the contemporary list of whaling ships in 1813, is 'Philips'. As a vessel engaged in Davis Strait whaling, the Hull *Resolution* would not normally have appeared in Lerwick.

Matters. It seems M[r] Heddle got acquainted with this Girl in Edinburgh whilst he attended the Lectures – he became too intimately Connected with her – the consequence was, a child! H. had been very remiss in providing for the subsistence of the Child & the Girl probably not being in Circumstances fit to provide for it & her self, threw herself into the packet & wafted by a propitious breeze, ['was' *deleted*] sooner than she expected arrived at the Birth place & residence of her gay <u>intimate</u> & sooner than <u>he</u> expected or wished was discovered to him – He provides a Lodging for her & support for his Child.

The Barometer in the Evening settled to 28.80 Inches, an altitude compared with the mean pressure very low, hence we may expect a severe storm of wind & moisture.

Friday the 2[d] April
N, NE, NW.erly very Var:
At 2 Am according with my expectations a tremendous squally wind accompanied with uncommon thick Snow at once attacked us. I awoke with the noise of the wind in the rigging & shortly heard the dropping of a second anchor. I arose & before I got upon deck heard our men crying "veer away <u>your</u> Cable" – the Ship was driving with 70 or 80 Fathoms of Cable out on the small Bower – already had she passed the Henrietta not 10 yards. distant & had come within two yards nay as near as three feet to the Resolution of Hull when providentially the best Bower anchor seized the ground & brought the Ship up. The strength of the wind abated in an hour & a strong Gale prevailed the rest of the night. In the morning a very particular scene presented itself – In two places were seen ships lashed together – 6 or 8 Ships lay within a few yards to the rocky shore of Brassa (where some years ago two ships were wrecked by driving, whilst two others drifted quite out to Sea). One Ship had her Bowsprit sprung – others their davits Chocks Cat heads,[1] &c. Carried away – in short of 38 ships which lay moored in the Sound upwards of twenty must have drifted.

After day light the wind moderated. In the afternoon we weighed both anchors & warped into a clear birth and brought up again with the small Bower under 60 Fathoms of Cable. In the Evening a heavy fall of Snow. Weather Calm.

Saturday 3[d] April
W, NE.erly
Most of the day we had a fresh breeze of wind attended with very fine clear weather. In the evening had a party of Ladies and some Gentlemen taking Tea with us on board the Esk – they were highly gratified with the fine Ship & superior Style of her Fitting especially the blacksmith's Shop and Cabin – they seemed to enjoy themselves highly. The Furious Gun Brig[2] came in about 5 Pm. At 10 the Oberon[3] likewise anchored in the Sound having had an unsuccessful cruize. Calm weather in the Evening – Water highly Luminous: beautiful.

---

[1] Smyth, *Sailor's Word Book*, s.v.: 'The cat-head ... is used to lift the anchor from the surface of the water [and] ... serves to suspend the anchor clear of the bow, when it is necessary to let it go.'
[2] HMS *Furious*, 14 guns. Built 1804, King's Lynn, sold 1815. 'She spent most of her active life escorting convoys through the Channel': Phillips, *Ships of the Old Navy*.
[3] See journal entry for 20 March 1813.

Sunday 4th April (in Lat. 60°49 Lon 54'W)[1]
N.erly, Calm, SW.
Very light breezes continued all the Morning with most agreeable weather: At 1 PM a small air of wind from the S^d sprung up which at 2 became a confirmed breeze[.] Most of the Fleet being anxious to be moving proclaimed from the mouths of their Cannon their intention of putting to Sea. A pilot attended us on hoisting a <u>Blue Peter</u>. At 3 weighed anchor, <u>cast</u>[2] with a warp to the Neptune & made sail down the Channel of the North entry. Lay too on the outside until I finished a Letter to Messrs F & B,[3] and another to my dearest Mrs S. then made sail first EbS, then ENE, NE &c – Twenty two Sail accompanied us, most of them ahead – At 8 passed Fetlar Head and at 10 Pm Halswick (the high Land near the North end of Shetl.) ['in Lat. 60° 49 Lon. 54' W *in margin*] bore West Dist. 6 Miles Wind a fresh Gale – Experienced a heavy W.erly swell on passing the North land, the Ship laboured heavily.

Monday 5th April
SSW
Strong Gales of wind with Showers of Rain & high cross swell all the day – Steering NNE½ E at the rate of 7 to 11 Knotts p hour – At noon were in Lat. 62° 30' Long. 42' W. Seventeen Ships in sight all steering nearly the same course. The Mercury in the Barometer sunk to 28.70 In. Thermometer 40°–46° .

Tuesday 6th April At noon Lat. 65.30 0°42'W
SSW or SWbS
Fresh Gales, squally with Showers of Hail, Sleet, or Rain, steering still to the NNE^d under a brisk sail. Henrietta and Leviathan in Company. It is remarkable that the low state of the Barometer has not been indicative of a heavy Storm. I certainly expected it & prepared for it. I suspect however that the wind has been much heavier to the Southward. Sailing from 8 to 4 knotts p hour.

Wednesday 7th of April At noon Lat. 66.30 Long 0°39'E
SW Variable Calm NNE to N. & NE.
The wind died away to a calm at 3 AM – A Breeze then springing up from the NNE, we <u>tacked</u> to the Eastward. It is a circumstance worthy of note that this was the first time the Esk ['has' *deleted*] ever was tacked from the period of her being launched she was never wore nor stayed, nor ever sailed by the wind[4] until this morning though she has accomplished a distance from her port of upwards of 700 Miles: all the way a

---

[1] Parentheses in transcript.
[2] Smyth, *Sailor's Word Book*: 'CAST, TO. To fall off, so as to bring the direction of the wind on one side of the ship, which before was right ahead. This term is particularly applied to a ship riding head to wind, when her anchor first loosens from the ground.' The 'blue peter' was the flag, a white square on a blue ground, flown at the fore-topmast head as a signal that a ship was about to sail.
[3] Fishburn and Brodrick: see the first two paragraphs of this journal.
[4] Smyth, *Sailor's Word Book*: 'BY THE WIND. Is when a ship sails as nearly to the direction of the wind as possible. ... In general terms, within six points; or the axis of the ship is 67½ degrees from the direction of the wind.'

fair wind. At Day Light six sail were discovered near us. At noon all but the Henrietta & ourselves tacked to the W^d & were soon out of sight. Until noon we had fresh Gales of wind, squally with Showers of Rain & heavy Northerly Swell. In the afternoon finer Weather Barom*eter* 29.25. At 10 Pm the wind having shifted to NE. tacked in *Compan*y with the Henrietta.

Thursday 8th April at noon Lat. 67.16 Lon 2°14E
NE to E, & SE. or South.
In the Morning blowing fresh we unbent the Cables, meaning to Coyl them away in the Cable Stage if the day proved fine: the wind however increasing & a heavy NE. swell prevailing Caused the Ship to pitch very heavy & take in a good deal of water – let the Cables remain therefore in their former situation. – At Noon reefed Top Sails: took in Jib, Mizen Top Sail, &c. Wind a fresh Gale attended with Rain. Squally at 4 Pm a strong Gale at 6 steering NE and although the Head Sea was very untoward the Log showed 9 or 9½ knotts p hour. All hands were engaged an hour close ree*fi*ng Fore T. Sail, Main T. Sail, Main Sail, [Steering?] Mizen &c. Split the Cap on the Bowsprit end,[1] hauled down the Jib until it was secured by a lashing and wedges – Passed a Beam of timber apparently 12 Inches square and 30 or 40 feet in length. Sea too heavy to lower a Boat. In the night wind more moderate, Made Sail – Henrietta near us.

Friday 9th Apr Lat 69°39' 4°14E
SW, W WNW NW & NNW
Tollerable fine weather in the Morning: Showers of Rain at intervals. Cleared the Starboard Cable Tier & Coyled in it, the whole of the [Ice?] ropes consisting of a 9 Inch Hawser [*blank space*] Fathoms long; a 7 Inch Towline [*blank space*] Fa*thom*s, a 6 Inch Towline [*blank space*] Fa*thom*s a 5 Inch warp 120 Fa*thom*s & a 4 Inch twice laid warp[2] [*blank space*] Fathoms in length. The Cables remained in the larboard Tier until a favourable day shall occur when they will be dried and Coyled down aft, in the Cable Stage: they consist of one 15 Inch Cable 110 Fa*thom*s & another 15 In. 90 Fathoms. The wind at 6 PM shifted to NW & began to blow strong, the preceeding part of the day we had carried all sails, Studd. Sails, &c. had sailed 7 to 10 knots NEbN we now were obliged to diminish our Canvass, the wind so increased that by 8 Pm we were under sail but the two Close Reefed Top Sails & reefed Main sail. Furled the Fore Top sail at 10 blowing very heavy with Rain or Sleet. The Henrietta near us.

Saturday 10th April Lat 70°54' Lon. 7°10'E
NNW or NWbN
The wind continued to blow a strong Gale all the Day with some abatement however towards Night. ['so that' *deleted*] Set the Main sail, Jib, & Mizen in the Forenoon: the Sea heavy from the NEbN caused the Ship to pitch in an unpleasant degree. The

---

[1] Smyth, *Sailor's Word Book*, s.vv. 'Cap' and 'Jib-Boom'. A cap was a 'strong thick block of wood' used to bind a mast extension to the mast. It was also used when extending the bowsprit with a jib-boom.
[2] Smyth, *Sailor's Word Book*: 'TWICE-LAID. Rope made from a selection of the best yarns of old rope.'

Thermometer at day light stood at 31° & at Sun set 28°: this fall of Temperature though[1] not very great was nevertheless very sensible to our feelings. – Some Hail fell to-day, it was of the opaque description, in composition resembling Snow, except being formed in roundish masses. – Hail is very rarely seen in Greenland & never that I ever saw or heard of does it occur in lumps like <u>grains</u> or [corms?] of Ice, but always of small specific gravity & opaque.

We steered all the day by the wind, laying NE or NEbN.

Sunday 11th April Lat. 72.13 Lon 9.40E
NWbN
Blowing a Moderate or fresh breeze we set all sails which could be of service: the Sea much fallen, indeed quite slight. The Thermometer stood at 22° at 8 AM, the sailors found the change of climate so considerable as to induce several of them, to add an additional covering of a wig to their heads, mitts to their hands, and a Flushing Jacket[2] to their Backs & Shoulders. A pair of capacious Boots were likewise worn by some. There is something ludicrous in the Costume of a Greenland sailor, to appearance. Good looking, healthy, Young Men, clothed in such Coarse Materials ['NNW or NbW' *in margin*] as <u>Cow Tail</u>[3] wigs; Flushing extra jackets; large Fishermen's Boots a yard or More in length & capacious enough for containing a leg & two or three pairs of thick stockings, perhaps ['Seamen's Costume!' *in margin*] two pairs of mitts, one of yarn the other of leather or water proof sealskin – these with some other minor articles form a dress warm & Comfortable to the feelings but odd & fantastical to the eye. – Reefed Top Sails in the Evening – took in T. Gall^t Sails, Jib, Mizen &c. Wind a Strong Gale accompanied with snow & heavy squalls in the Showers. – The Henrietta to Leeward.

Monday 12th April Lat 72°46 Long 11°18'E
North to NNE or NEbN. & NNW
At 3 Am. the wind blew so strong that we thought it prudent to take in all sails but Close reefed Main Top Sail & reefed Fore sail. At 4 making a course no better than ESE wore & set the Mainsail standing to the North Westward. – At Noon two strange sail appeared to windward; supposed the part of the Fleet which sailed from Lerwick with us. – The Sea proves very slight in comparison of the strong wind which lately prevailed; this with the appearance of <u>Snow-Birds</u>,[4] together with the remark-able variableness of the wind & its disposition to heavy squalls in the showers of Snow, seem strongly to indicate our approximation to <u>Ice</u>. – At Noon set the Fore & Mizen Top Sails together with the reefed Main Sail. Thermometer 24°[.]

---

[1] 't' deleted, changing 'thought' to 'though'.
[2] *OED*: 'Flushing ... A kind of rough and thick woollen cloth, so called from the place where it was first manufactured.' *OED* includes several citations for Flushing jackets from the first half of the 19th century.
[3] *OED* does not define this as a type of wig. However 'cow-tail' is 'The coarsest grade of wool, sheared from the sheep's hind legs.' In Scoresby's context, therefore, it may refer to the material of the wigs, not their appearance.
[4] The Ivory Gull, identified by Scoresby, *Account of the Arctic Regions*, II, p. 535, as *Larus eburneus*, but nowadays as *Pagophila eburnea*.

At 9 Pm. the wind was moderate: having veered to NNW we tacked & made sail to the NE^d the Henrietta far to Leeward. A Strange Ship suppose the Will*iam* & Ann of Whitby tacked near us & followed.

Tuesday 13th April Lat 73.13 Lon 10°.58′E
NNW W.erly Var.
Wind very Moderate. Inclinable to Calm about Noon. In the Evening a Fresh Gale. When the wind would permit steered NNE – At 8 am. all hands began to remove the Cables, first hauling them on the Deck to dry. – Two Casks of Provisions which were in the Cable Stage were shifted in to the ['empty' *deleted*] birth of two which have been emptied. The other two were hoisted on deck & lashed on the Quarter Deck. In this conspicuous place should we be so unfortunate as to injure the Ship (which God in his great Mercy forbid), ['they' *deleted*] one month's provisions are always at hand. This was a plan of my Father's I highly approve of it, not being so superstitious as <u>some</u> who suppose that by providing against a misfortune, we encourage the realizing, or invoke the fulfilment of an accident.

The Carpenter at the same time put up & fixed the Boats' Davits. ['South to SSE' *in margin*] The Armourer finished Iron work for Crow's Nest: &c. &c – In the afternoon Coyled the Cables down into the Cable Stage. Put four Guns below & lashed them abaft the Pump Well; &c, &c. &c. Two of the Boats which were on deck we suspended by the Davits at the Quarters. – A Breeze sprang up at South, in the afternoon & rapidly & regularly increased the whole remaining part of the day: it attained apparently its acme about Mid Night blowing a tremendous Gale. The weather was clear until 8 Pm. small granular Snow then commenced which changed into thick flaky particles at 10 Pm. until this time we steered ['until' *deleted*] under a Brisk sail NbE running at the rate of 8 or 10 Knots laterally. Being now in a Latitude where Ice is frequently met with and thick weather pevailing [*sic*] we hauled by the wind to the E^d & lay too under close reefed Main Top Sail. –[1]

Wednesday 14th April Lat 74.°35′ Lon 10°41′E
SE to ESE or E
At Mid Night the Snow cleared away so that we could see some miles (twilight continuing throughout the night)[2] set the Fore Top Sail & reefed Fore sail & scudded NNE for an hour[.] being again thick with Snow we once more hauled too under Main Top Sail. At 9 AM. the wind still Blowing tremendously had veered to the ESE we set Fore Sail & F. Top Sail & steered by the wind under these Sails, the Main T. Sail & double reefed Mizen, the rest of the day. – The Sky was generally thick with Snow, at intervals however so clear that we could see two Miles: at such times were within sight the Henrietta & two other ships unknown. Barom*eter* 28.85.

---

[1] In the transcript, the text continues on the same line: '... Top Sail – At Mid Night ...'.
[2] Scoresby's note is very appropriate. At latitude 73°N 'civil twilight' (i.e. sun not more than 6 degrees below the horizon), is continuous between sunset and sunrise after the middle of April: *Smithsonian Meteorological Tables*, Table 172.

Thursday 15th April Lat.76°02′ Lon. 9°27′E

E to SE.

The Barometer still continues below 29 Inches – the Ther*mometer* 23° the Ship clad with Ice. – The wind even increased & blew so very heavy that we were obliged to Furl all sails but the Main T Sail & Fore sail reefed. – At 9 the Ship <u>rolling</u> very heavily immersed the Lee Quarter Boat under water, rising suddenly, the head ring was torn out of the Stern & the Boat broke completely in two across the [<u>ground tow</u>?] in the middle of her. Fortunately this was an old spare Boat which we took merely as a <u>hack</u> by the way of saving our new Boats, so that we still retain 6 Boats together with my Barge.[1] The Boat on the Starboard Quarter we lashed up to the Top of the Davits thereby securing her against a like fate.

['SE' *in margin*] At 10 AM Snow something less thick, wind nothing abated, we saw a stream of Ice ahead of the Ship, several loose pieces were scattered to lee-ward of us; these apparently heavy & from the high Sea rendered very dangerous to approach: it might be ['Made the Ice: Remarks on the propriety of taking it' *in margin*] that by pushing on, should we run safe, we might find ['obtain' *deleted*] an easier passage northward than can ['will' *deleted*] be afterwards obtained for many weeks, indeed in heavy Gales of wind the Ice is commonly most detatched & pervious especially about this Season before the main obstruction to the Northward is firmly glued together by the formation of Bay Ice: this consideration would seem to warrant some exertion, but on the other hand, the tremendous wind, renders the ship in a great measure unmanageable from not being able to bear much sail – the Snow likewise which has hitherto very rarely allowed us to see two miles & commonly not half a mile renders the attempt still more dangerous, since a ship might easily be lost if so unfortunate as to get entangled in the thick amidst any awkwardly disposed heavy Ice where the Sea still prevailed – these considerations duly weighed determined me to wear which we with some trouble accomplished – At 11 am the Henrietta passed us to wind^d as we did not see her wear we supposed she had taken the Ice. – The Sea continues very heavy, the ship which all along has proved somewhat leaky now shows a rapid increase. The pumps are very wretched, so faulty ['Ship proved leaky pumps wretched!' *in margin*] are they that one good machine of similar dimensions will deliver more water than three such as ours. What the failure is owing too I have not been able to determine: we thought them deficient before we left home, the maker assured us it was want of use & that they were as good as Could be made – It is well known that new ['good' *deleted*] pumps rarely work well, and that a leaky Ship's pumps are commonly excellent, hence I suppose they might improve. The Ship thus leaky & pumps Bad, one of them is kept constantly at work, it is really alarming having only such wretched machines to depend on. – a very trifling disarrangement of the planks or timbers of the Ship from a Blow of Ice or any other Cause would prove fatal to the vessel which in proper circumstances would be perfectly safe.

Wishing to be ready to take the Ice on the least amendment of the weather & dubious whether the Ice we saw might be a detatched patch far seperated from the Main

---

[1] Smyth, *Sailor's Word Book*: 'BARGE. A boat of a long, slight, and spacious construction ... for the use of admirals and captains of ships of war.'

body (in which case we might have proceeded forward) or on the other hand nearly connected with it, to be on the Spot therefore we wore at 8 Pm. & proceeded all night under the Close Reefed Main Top Sail alone. At Mid-Night Bar. 28.97 wind still very severe – Snow prevailing Constantly thick.

Friday 16th April Lat. 76°57′ Lon 8°0′E
SE. to East.
At 6 AM. the weather was somewhat meliorated, still however Thicker than usual with Snow, scarcely being able to see a distance sufficient to wear in; to make the Ship more ready & under better Command in Case of falling in with Ice we set the Fore Top Sail. The Fore Top M. Stay sail would not stand – we set it yesterday to wear & it split & this morning tried it again & the sheet broke.

At noon the Snow cleared away & the wind was sensibly abated, at 2 Pm. the Barom*et*er had risen to 29.20, the weather was so much improved that we set, Main Sail, Fore Sail, Mizen &c. and at 6 Pm out Reefs set Jib, & Top Gall^t Sails steering by the wind about NNE. – Passed two or three Small streams of Ice & through the midst of a Patch of <u>brash</u> Ice – apparently much water to the N^d. At 7 Pm Saw Land supposed to be point Look Out; bearing SEbE Distance 20 Leagues. A fresh Gale prevailed in the Night caused us to taken in Top Gall^t Sails, Reef Top sails, &c A Ship to <u>Leeward larboard</u> tacked.

Saturday 17th April Lat. 78.59 Lon 7°40′E
E SE. South SW.
Steered NNE all night, saw several pieces of heavy Ice & some scattered Streams, but nothing to retard our progress. – It now appears that the Ice we first saw (the 15th) was an isolated patch & might probably have been passed with Safety, had we been assured of this or if the weather had been only tollerably Clear, we should certainly have proceeded. At 8 am. we were abreast of the Foreland the Middle Hook in Latitude 78°46 & Longitude 9°10E[1] bore SEbE Distance about 6 Leagues. The Land as usual at this Season exhibits a dreary, yet picturesque prospect of barren Craggy Rocks, Completely clad with Snow except on such projecting points as the Snow cannot fix itself so firmly as to resist the effect of Strong winds. There is something grand in the view of the Foreland, especially the Middle Hook,[2] it consists chiefly of f [*blank space*] large hills nearly a mile in height having their base at the Sea beach, & from thence rising with an angle of about 45° from an horizontal plane, each side has likewise a similar <u>slope</u>, and the whole of these three inclined planes meet in a ['Description of the Foreland' *in margin*] Common point at the Top. The whole of these f [*blank space*] mountains are very similar in appearance, the [*sic*] are arranged in a line North & South & their bases unite about [*blank space*] feet above the level of the Sea; their form when viewed from the W^d has the figure of several V's reversed, thus ^^^^. This land either from its height or the strong light which it generally

---

[1] Scoresby's value for the latitude of the central area of Prins Karls Forland is accurate, but its longitude is about 11°E.
[2] See sketch in Scoresby, *Account of the Arctic Regions* II, Plate 3, No. 3. The maximum elevation is 3,380 ft (1,030 m).

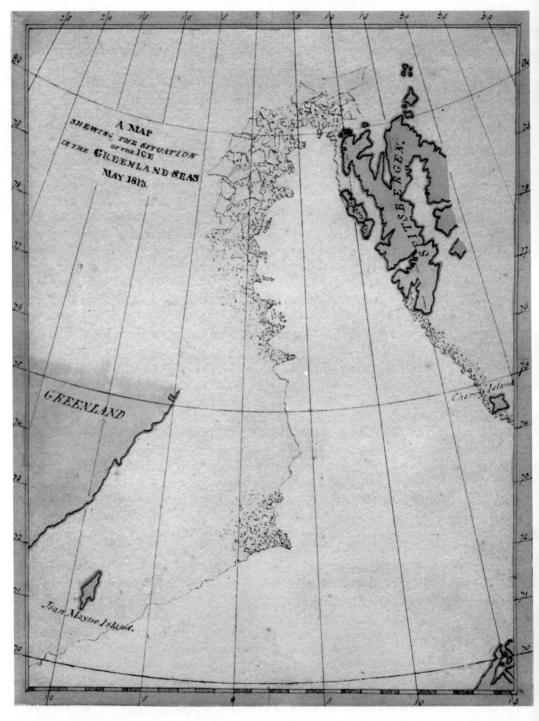

Fig. 4. Map of ice distribution in 1813. Whitby Museum. Photograph courtesy of Whitby Museum.

154

reflects ['upon it' *deleted*] from the presence of such a quantity of Snow, is astonishingly deceiving with regard to its distance a Stranger at 20 miles off would not suppose himself more than two or three Leagues, at 10 miles half that Distance & at 5 miles would actually suppose the Ship was almost on shore – Nay I have heard Men who have been many years in the Country affirm the Ship ['Deception in the Distance of the Land' *in margin*] was not a mile from the Land, though we sailed directly towards it above an hour afterwards at the Rate of 5 Knotts & then were two miles distant. This deception is not peculiar to the Foreland but may be observed throughout the whole of the high Coasts of Spitzbergen, only in this situation the character is the most striking.[1]

At 6 am. all hands set about preparing the Boats for the Fishery, ['Coyl the Whale Lines & fit the Boats for the Fishery' *in margin*] two were taken out of the Twin decks & two left. Into each Boat we coyled 6 Lines (some 6½) each line of 2¼ In. Circumference being 120 Fathoms in length & weighing about 1¼ Cwt. in each strand of the rope are 20 to 22 yarns. – Each Boat has likewise a Harpoon, a spare Harpoon 6 Lances, a Jack or Flag, 6 or 7 Oars, a Snatch Block, Grapnel, Axe, Fid,[2] Fin & after-tows, 2 Boathooks, 5 or 6 spare Grommets for the Oars, Swab, Broom, Snow shovels, Piggin,[3] Mick,[4] *[5]&c. &c. and two of the Boats have winches for heaving the Lines in with when a great many are out. – In the afternoon spanned in several Harpoons, that is a stock of [*blank space*] feet in length was adapted to each & firmly fastened in by the attatched white line or Foreganger, which of 4½ Fathoms in length, is similar to the whale Lines, except the deficiency of Tar whereby it is more supple & better adapted for heaving out. The one end of the Foreganger is spliced closely round the small shank of the Harpoon, the other is spliced to the Whale Lines.

About noon we had Calm weather: by the situation of the Land it is determined that we have obtained a Latitude of about 79° North & Longitude 7°40′E, thus far have we come without any obstruction from Ice worth naming, this free navigation so far North at so early a period of the year is denominated an open Season, it is but

---

[1] Scoresby returned to this difficulty of estimating distance in *Account of the Arctic Regions*, I, pp. 110–13. Though writing in the context of Spitsbergen, he noted that it was a characteristic of the arctic atmosphere, and suggested that it explained the failure of the voyage, in the early 1580s, of Mogens Heinesøn to re-establish contact with the Norse colony in Greenland. As Scoresby described it (p. 112) '... he got sight of the east coast of Greenland, and attempted to get to it; but though the sea was quite free from ice, and the wind favourable, and blowing a fresh gale, he, after proceeding several hours without appearing to get any nearer the land, became alarmed, tacked about, and returned to Denmark. On his arrival, he attributed this extraordinary circumstance, magnified, no doubt, by his fears, to his vessel having been stopped in its course by "some loadstone rocks hidden in the sea."' See also Gad, *History of Greenland*, I, p. 196, where 'a heavy adverse current' is offered as the probable explanation.

[2] Smyth, *Sailor's Word Book*, listed several definitions of a 'fid'; in the context of equipping a whaleboat it was probably 'a conical pin of hard wood, of any size from 10 inches downwards, tapering to a point, used to open the strands of a rope in splicing'.

[3] See entry for 18 March 1812.

[4] Scoresby, *Account of the Arctic Regions*, II, p. 233: 'a "mik" or rest ... , made of wood, for supporting the stock of the harpoon when ready for instant service.' It is illustrated in Plate XX, Fig. 7 of that volume.

[5] The asterisk, and the following footnote linked to it, appear to have been later additions to the manuscript. 'Tarpaulins for the Lines, Tail Knife, Mallet for driving tholls, & spare tholls'.

the third time in twelve years that such a conformation of the Ice & Water has been exhibited so early as the month of April.[1] Commonly the Ice joins the Land by Point Look Out & is likewise intimately connected with the western Ice thus forming an almost impassible Barrier between the Ocean & an extensive, free, & open Space of Water generally lying to the westward of Charles's Island or the Foreland, as it is ofter termed; this opening is rarely wanting in the spot where we now are after the expiration of April, and it is for the obtaining of this situation that the whole of our efforts & labours tend in the first instance, and it sometimes happens that notwithstanding the application of all the arts which human industry suggests we cannot accomplish this object before an advanced period of the Month of May or even the beginning of June – it is remarked that generally the greater the difficulty experienced in the passage through the Ice, the more favourable will be the ['Fishery' *deleted*] opportunities for Fishing when once this difficulty is surmounted & on the other hand, that open Seasons ['are' *deleted*] often afford bad Fisheries – an open Season has this disadvantage, that every strong wind except westerly raises a Swell amongst the Ice & near which is highly ['disadvan' *deleted*] unfavourable for Fishing and dangerous for the Ship, it likewise frequently forms the Ice into impervious packs in which the Whales find refuge & are out of the adventurers' Reach – there is one advantage to oppose however which is one of some importances, that is, as no time is expended in obtaining a passage to the site of Fishing Ground, a much longer time is allowed for accomplishing the object of the voyage, in searching for and killing the Whales.

Before leaving England I ventured to predict, that Greenland the present year would exhibit an open Country, or in other words that there would no obstruction from Ice offer, to the Navigation to a proper Fishing Latitude. I affirmed this to Several of my Friends – I ['The open Country Predicted' *in margin*] drew this conclusion from the following circumstances or data: viz, The winter in England was very mild, Frosts occurred but very seldom, from this I supposed the Ice lay far North that little of it had been [dissolved?] ['Reasons for drawing such a Conclusion' *in margin*] otherwise the heat that it absorbed would have caused a greater Cold in our Latitude. In very cold winters in England I have observed the Ice to lay very far to the southward. – Again, the most powerful agent in performing grand movements and causing the Ice to separate from the Land is a heavy swell, now when no water lays to the Northw^d of the Ice there is no room for the wind to raise a swell, therefore North winds cannot have so great agency as those winds which can bring a powerful Ice with them, the Southerly quarter must be Clear of Ice, the ocean lies for the wind to act upon & the whole power of the waves is exhausted upon the Lee Ice. A natural deep bay in the Ice (from what cause arising I cannot say) almost always lays in Longitude 6 to 15° East,[2] this is the spot where we always attempt our passage; from

---

[1] In *Account of the Arctic Regions*, II, pp. 276–84, Scoresby briefly summarized the ice conditions in each year from 1803 to 1818. From that summary it is clear that the other two years to which he referred in this journal entry were 1803 and 1805.

[2] In *Account of the Arctic Regions*, II, p. 206, Scoresby narrowed this longitude range: '... that remarkable indentation of the Polar ice, lying in 5 or 10 degrees east longitude, which I have denominated the "Whale-fishers Bight"'. At 78°N, the length of one degree of the parallel is 14.4 miles, 12.5 nautical miles, or 21.3 km.

the Converging of it the Sea sweeps down it with increased force, with concentrated effect and finally the long prevalence of such winds and waves, assisted by a Mild atmosphere which they never fail to afford at the same time; forces a passage through the Ice & sweeps one part away to the westward whilst it confines the Eastern part in its place, or removes it Eastward as far the Land will admit. Now the past winter in England has afforded a surprising continuance of heavy Southerly or Southwesterly winds, these winds may have been a primary cause in forcing the Ice from the Land – at least from these considerations I ventured my opinion, & however erroneous the data may be, the result has proved agreeable to my Conjecture.

In the Evening a Breeze [sprung?] up from the NE^d being now well to the North^d probably far enough we steered off NW to find the Ice & search for whales, for they are seldom caught near the Land, but generally near, at the edge, or within the Ice to the W^d or NW^d of the Foreland or Head Land. It depends however much on the disposition of the Main Body of the Ice. 4 Sail in sight one of them the Resolution of Whitby. At Mid-Night we had a Strong Gale of wind, no Ice to see. Snow Showers.

Sunday 18th April 78°59′ Lon [*blank space*]
NE
At 2½ Am. in a shower of Snow we fell in with Ice, apparently a solid pack but could not determine. Wore and stood by the wind under easy sail until 7 am. when we tacked. At 1 Pm. still blowing strong we wore close to the Ice which I found to consist of a pack of heavy Rough Ice – its edge lay about NE & SW consequently could afford no shelter ['Make the West Pack' *in margin*] we saw no living creature near it except Common Birds. At this time we were in Latitude 78°59′N. and Longitude 3°10′E. 70 Miles distant from the N end of the Foreland bearing SEbE. The water [freezes?] near the pack edge. Ther*mome*ter at Noon 15½° Baro*meter* 29.90 Inches. Considerable swell.

Stood to the SE^d until 8 Pm, then tacked, the wind failed us about mid night & fell nearly Calm. One Ship seen to Leeward.

Monday 19th April Lat. 78°51′ Lon 4°30′E
Calm. W.erly S.erly
Weather delightfully fine, clear sky, Sun bright and invigorating, the Temperature rose to 27° the water nevertheless freezes around us. At 10 Am. all hands Commenced work repairing the damages sustained in the late Gales of wind, clearing the Ship of Ice, tons of which are attached to the sides, Bows & decks. Greased the masts, Top Sail Sheets, Boats skeeds,[1] &c. Rove double Foretacks[2] of new Whale Line likewise wheel ropes of the same: spliced in Harpoons, or attached Fore Gangers to make up the Number 24. Spliced likewise straps for 12 spare Harpoons; Splices Eyes in all the Ice ropes, & running Eyes in the two smallest: together with a great variety of other

---

[1] See Smyth, *Sailor's Word Book*, s.v.: 'SKIDS. Massive fenders.' *OED* recognizes 'skeed' as an alternative spelling of 'skid' and cites Scoresby, *Voyage*, p. 303, concerning the passage of an iceberg: 'it cleared all our boats, and occasioned only a trifling injury to some of the skeeds in its progress'.

[2] A tack is 'A rope to confine the weather lower corners of the courses and staysails when the wind crosses the ship's course obliquely': Smyth, *Sailor's Word Book*, s.v. Captain Barritt suggests that what Scoresby was doing was to provide extra strong tacks by using doubled-up tough whale line.

work necessary and convenient. At Noon Eight Sail were in Sight like us apparently taking advantage of the Calm for putting their Ships in order. The pack in sight to the NW^d 8 miles distant. The Breathing, or Blast of a Fish was seen but whether a Common whale or Finner we could not determine.

A light westerly breeze sprung early in the afternoon at the same time a SE swell was observed. Anxious to ascertain the exact situation of the Ice & quality as well as to look for whales we steered about NbW until we came within about two miles of the edge – Newly formed Ice of the description vulgarly called Pancakes (from the resemblance in shape to those articles) lay many miles distant, but were larger towards the Main Ice. This Ice as we observed yesterday was an impervious pack, consisting chiefly of rough looking heavy pieces, the edge as far as could be seen lay nearly in a straight line NE & SW.

The SE swell rapidly increased, the westerly Breeze likewise failed us in a great measure; ['the' *deleted*] heavy clouds began to rise in the S, SE, & East direction of us, these signs were strongly indicative of a ['A heavy SE swell drifts us rapidly towards the Ice' *in margin*] Southerly or SE.rly wind, we therefore turned the ship's head from the Ice & attempted to sail off, the wind being light however & sea very heavy we made little progress. About 6 Pm. it was again Calm we found ourselves rapidly drifting towards the pack, we hoisted out three Boats, but found them, ([***] the intensity of the swell, preventing them keeping the tow rope tight which also several times broke) of little service, the Ship moving stern foremost at the rate of more than a knot – What was to be done? Our situation was truly critical for should we drift into the Ice with such a heavy swell, it would be providential if the Ship did not suffer serious damage, nay it would not by far be impossible but a total loss might be the consequence, ['make use of a tracking machine, or floating anchor'. *in margin*] or at any rate we should be likely to get beset & might be frozen in during the best of the Fishery. It fortunately occurred to me that we had on board, the Iron work of a tracking machine, or Floating anchor[1] which I made last year. It consists of two Iron Bars 2 In by about ¼ or ⅞ thick, each 11 feet in length, a screwed Bolt passed through each of the centres upon which they turned so as to lay parallel for stowage when not used & at right angles when ['by covering the Iron work with a Royal Sail' *in margin, followed by a sketch of the device*] needed for service. We had no canvass however prepared for them, the spoiling of a sail however this Case was not worth a thought, one of the Royal was therefore produced, the head was the right length the foot & depth being more than sufficient we put a lump of wood within the canvass at a proper distance from the head & on the same seam of Canvass & by this Knob lashed each of the lower parts to the two remaining ends of the bars – a rope was then applied to each of the four extremities & another by a hole being made thro' the Canvass to an eye bolt which formed the centre, these at about 10 feet distance perpendicular with the surface of the canvass, from the centre were made to meet in a point, formed into an eye & a Whale Line bent to it. To one corner was likewise attached a Buoy by a rope 16 or 20 Fathoms long whereby the machine was prevented from sinking too deep – all these arrangements were completed within the

---

[1] See journal entry for 8 May 1812.

space of 20 Minutes when one of the Boats being called alongside, the whole apparatus was put into her, together with about 250 Fathoms of line which the Boatsteerer threw overboard as the Boat receeded from the Ship the end being kept on board, according to the technical phrases in ['The machine although very imperfectly prepared & fit is yet highly advantageous' *in margin*] performing such an operation they are said to pay & go, the Boat by this Method being released from the labour of dragging out the weight of the lines. – having got to as great a distance in a SE. direction as the lines would admit the Machine was slipped overboard & the line hauled up on board the Ship, by this means the Ship not only held her ground but advanced somewhat ahead, had we had another machine we could have kept her stationary for almost any length of time, but wanting this we drifted near 100 yards during the time occupied in carrying it out again. Nevertheless it answered the wished for end for in four hours we lost not more than 200 or 300 yards whilst before we made use of this help we drifted in one hour above a mile towards the Ice. – Had it not been for this we should inevitably have been in the pack in two hours from the Commencement ['W.erly' *in margin*] of our operations even with all the Boats towing. At 8 O'clock one Ship was observed in the Ice, clewing up her sails, several others were likewise very near. At 11 Pm. a light breeze from the W^d again sprung up contrary to any persons expectation for the Clouds from the SE had by this time advanced ['at midNight Lat. 78°55' Lon 4°E. *in margin*] into our Zenith and were already pricipitating their Snow [upon?] – aided by this opportune breeze we sailed off about 2 Miles by MidNight, ['**Tuesday 20th April** Lat. 79°05' Lon. 4°0'E South SSE or ESE variable' *in margin*] when it suddenly shifted to South & blew strong: we reached having thick Snow, about 10 miles & then lay too – at 6 am. the wind veered to SE & blew a heavy Gale, we reached to the S^d. under treble Reef^d Topsails & foresail & Fore T.M. Stay Sail – At 9 we wore, the wind blew so heavy & the Sea increased so rapidly we found it necessary to employ all hands in lashing the Boats up to the Davits, & sending down the Top Gall^t Yards – we were obliged to wear again at noon having fallen in with several pieces of Ice & the Snow being so thick that we could not see

Plate 7.
Tracking machine.
Drawing by Scoresby.
Whitby Museum
(Transcripts SCO1253,
19 April 1813).
Photograph courtesy
of the
Whitby Museum.

a distance sufficient to wear in, the wind most unfortunately [southered?] & we lay only the same way back even SW or SWbW not allowing for lee way – At 4 Pm. we again fell in with Sludge and small Ice, blowing tremendously heavy, Sea exceedingly high wore again – lay off ENE this direction I flattered myself would keep us off the Ice, which it [did?] the remainder part of the day.

Wednesday 21ˢᵗ April Lat. 79°42′ Lon 4°50′E
SE to South SW & W
The thick Snow still confined the limits of our vision within a Circle of half a Mile in Diameter, the wind likewise & Sea pressed heavily upon our vessel, a considerable quantity of water came upon the Deck. At 3 am. we again fell in with water having its surface covered with Snow or the small crystals of new Ice (commonly called Sludge) shortly afterwards several detatched pieces Ice, we wore & in the act, saw several very heavy lumps, the Sky likewise seemed to reflect a Strong light thro' the Snow shewing the pack to be near, stood to the SSWᵈ 5 hours & then wore again wishing to keep well to Northward & not too far from the Ice to be ready to search for whales, on the first amendment of the weather – At 10 am. the Snow cleared away & at noon the wind had considerably abated & veered to the SW, wore & made sail towards the Ice. Several ships in sight mostly to leeward. The Barometer during this Gale stood at 29.53 & did not rise in the approach of fine weather, this accounts for the wind westering or perhaps more correctly the wind westering accounts for the Bar. remaining stationary[.] Thermometer 26° Towards Midnight we had Calm weather, some Fog showers passed us coming from the Westward – to the E, SE, & Sᵈ of us cloudy. 9 Sail in sight. Some having Boats down appear to have seen whales.

Thursday 22ᵈ April Lat 80°00′ Lon 4°50E
Inc. to Calm, SSW, W.rly, S.rly Variable. Calm. SW to W. & NE.rly.
The Snow which fell yesterday, we find lies undissolved on the surface of the water & begins to form itself into circular masses of Ice. The pack lays about four miles off to the NWᵈ – the SE swell still keeps up. Very early in the Morning we saw a Whale & shortly afterwards several, first three & afterwards our three remaining Boats were hoisted out and sent in pursuit. At 3 Am. they had the good fortune to strike one of those [greasy?] inhabitants of this Northern Ocean, it run out 6 lines directly downwards & by the prompt assistance of the other boats which struck two more Harpoons

['The Mate G. Sinclair. M.¹  No. 1 = 8 feet Bone' *in margin*]

& multiplied [*sic*] lances, it resigned its Breath beneath the bloody spears of our Hardy Harponeers – Its fleeting Life was to them a cause for rejoicing, & its death was proclaimed abroad by the loud Huazas [*sic*]. This whale Remaining long under water was so exhausted on coming to the surface that it was not able to make any exertion towards making its escape & thus it fell an easy prey to our active <u>Whale Hunters</u>. – A Strong Breeze sprung up just as the Whale was killed put us under some

---

¹ This abbreviation is evidently used to indicate that the whale was a male.

apprehension least a hastily forming swell should yet snatch our Victim out of our hands: we were favoured however for the Snow on the Water prevented the wind from ruffling its surface, so that we effected our purpose without more extra trouble than the prevalence of the SE swell caused. – Finished; we made sail & worked to the SW^d as long as the Wind Continued. At noon 7 Sail were in sight; one of them flinching several miles to the Southward of us. – We find ourselves in a place very likely for meeting Fish: the Ice as hitherto observed has always trended NE & SW; to the Northw^d of us it turns more Easterly so that by the <u>Blink</u> (a bright reflection of the Ice in the Atmosphere near the Horizon) it appears to stretch directly East, towards the Head Land. In the Evening we took several Casks out of the Main Hold, the third or upper tier under the Hatch way for the forming of what is Called a <u>Flinch Gut,</u> or receptacle for any Blubber which may be taken. Towards Mid Night SSE swell very heavy – the <u>Pack</u> in sight from the Deck. – Wind very light from the NE^d Sky very dark to the S. & E.ward the Ships in that direction have a fresh Gale from the same point as the Swell. The heavy S.erly Clouds approach us, Showers are observed in that Quarter which make way until they overtake us, from which I judged a S.erly wind as Certain. Several Ships in sight.

Friday April 23^d Lat. 80°07′ Lon. 5 °E.
NE.erly Calm. E. SE.erly South SW.to W & NW – Calm NE.
The Winds this day blew from every point of the Compass at diff*eren*t times & with every degree of intensity from a calm to a heavy Gale, sometimes accompanied with thick Snow chiefly finely crystallized in <u>Star</u> like forms, at other times Clear, towards Mid Night exceedingly thick with the vapour called Frost Rime.[1] – It is commonly observed during strong winds whenever the Thermometer is below 14 or 12° of Farenheit [*sic*] . It seems to arise from the congealing of the small particles of water dissipated in air by the sprays topping or breaking from the power of the wind. These ['Frost Rime!' *in margin*] frozen particles are excessively minute, they ascend seldom higher than 100 Feet & often not [a?] Quarter of that height – they attatch themselves to every part of the Ships rigging & Hull where they can have access, they lay themselves on the weather side with a ragged or <u>jagged </u>edge towards the wind, when a quantity of them are trod on they produce a [chirping?] acute sound which produces the sensation of <u>edging the teeth</u>. The Frost [hag?] or <u>rime</u> ascends the highest with the heaviest Sea & in a perfect Calm can scarcely be observed however severe the Cold.

   At 1 am. one of our Harponeers pursuing a Fish, got on the spot during the intervals of her disappearance between her <u>blasts</u> & overran her so far

['John [Dunbar?]][2] Harpoon Drew' *in margin*[3]]

---

[1] Scoresby described the weather events of this day, especially the winds, in *Account of the Arctic Regions*, I, pp. 405–6.
   [2] The name is uncertain as written, but see the crew list for the *Resolution* at the beginning of the 1812 journal, p. 69.
   [3] Scoresby drew a black whale's tail to indicate a kill; a blank outline of the tail indicated that the whale escaped.

that striking the Harpoon underwater it fell on some hard part & not penetrating was bent. Shortly after the same Harponeer struck a <u>Sucking</u> Whale (so called whilst under its Mother's Protection) whereby was obtained a considerable chance of securing the Mother, for she is rarely known to desert her offspring whilst life remains in it or herself: thus their maternal affection becomes a snare to them, the [<u>Sucker?</u>][1] not so timid & cautious as the <u>old one</u> fears no danger & is easily got at, on which the <u>old one</u> frequently takes it under its fin & drags it off ['Maternal Affection of the Whale.' *in margin*] several hundred yards, perhaps then quits it, scours the adjacent Sea with great anxiety, resolution, alarm or trepidation, yet inspired with such a courage by its affection that it, hurries onwards, taking huge circuits round the object of its care frequently appearing beside it & dares even to rise amidst the watchful Boats, though frequently wounded – thus it is that by striking the Young the Mother often falls a prey her tender attattchment to her Young – With regard to the Young one we entangled, its Mother frequently appeared close by the Fast Boat, sometimes seeming wishful to entice the Captive off at others dragging it away by force – unfortunately the Boats [were?] a long time before they got up to the one <u>Fast</u> & shortly afterwards, the mother so effectually dragged off the young that the Harpoon was drawn.

I know not whether to rejoice or regret at our want of success in this instance, for we were led near the Ice by the Fish, the swell from the SSE[d] was very heavy, thick Snow commenced & every appearance indicated a speedy confirmation of a Southerly Storm, I was anxious therefore to get off the Ice & at the first appearance of a breeze we made use of every sail to effect our purpose. It was not however until ['Remarkable weather accounted for' *in margin*] two hours after wards that the wind fixed at SSE or S. & speedily increased to a Strong Gale – the Barometer having fallen from 29.74 to 28.98 in about 12 hours I expected a severe storm – we accordingly prepared ourselves by lashing every thing fast, sending down Top Gall[t] Yards, lashing the Boats up to the davits & taking the waist Boats upon Deck. We stood off the Ice until 1 Pm when we tacked – I have before observed that the Sinuosity of the Ice which we left appears to me to be very favourable for attracting whales[.] I wished therefore to keep near the spot so that whenever the weather should amend, we should be at hand. – At 5 Pm. we saw the Ice off the Deck, the Snow clearing away to the NW[d], we immediately tacked & in a few minutes the wind fell to a dead Calm. This change of weather from a Gale to a Calm was truly astonishing – I thus account for it. It is very evident that to the S[d] a heavy Gale prevails this I know from the strong swell & it is likewise evident from the Sky always Clearing over the Ice & from having a Breeze [*next right-hand page blank, except for feint outline of boat, and* 'Scale ¼ of an Inch to a Foot' *at foot of page; next left-hand page is also blank*] at the edge Constantly at NW, N. or NE that within the Ice the wind is Northerly, hence it seems here is a Conflict between two winds we have been Several times between, at intervals we have had a Calm, then first one wind & then the other has alternately prevailed.. I was [now assured?] however that the N.erly wind would finally Carry the superiority from the rapid fall of the Mercury in the Thermometer. At 10 am it

---

[1] Again, there is some doubt arising from the legibility, but *OED* gives other citations indicating that this was an accepted term for whale calves.

stood at 30° & at 4 Pm. at 19° – This was clearly the case for at 7 Pm. a NE breeze sprang up, fortunately we had kept the sails all double reefed, in expectation of a sudden storm, I say fortunately because in half an hour we were reduced to close reefed Top Sails & Reefed Fore Sail. It blew so heavy sometimes that we should have stowed the Fore Top Sail had I not been anxious to keep to windward both on account of having smooth water ['Rapid increase of Cold' *in margin*] & in expectation of meeting Fish in the Bay to the NE^d of us. At Mid Night thick Frost Rime – Therm^r at 10 Pm 12° a fall of 18° in 12 hours!!!

Saturday 24th April Lat. 80°10' Lon. 5°E
NE
At the Commencement of this Storm we reached off & so continued laying ESE, Sea very turbulent owing to the Continuance of the S.erly swell. A most melancholy circumstance occurred this morning which being without remedy or alleviation was truly afflicting; four hands had ascended the Mizen Rigging to furl the Miz^n Top Sail, John Dodds on the weather side encumbered with a Flushing extra Jacket, & two pairs of mitts on his hands besides other clothing adapted for rendering a man inactive, unhappily ['Melancholy accident John Dodd Lineman Drowned! *in margin*] slipped his grasp & was precipitated over the lee-quarter even clear of the Boats into the Sea – in a Moment he was astern. As I lay in my Bed reflecting on my happy home, my affectionate wife & the delights of connubial Love, enjoying the recollection of the past, & anticipating with hopes & fears, the delight of returning if [***] happy circumstances to her my heart holds most dear – at this pleasing moment I was aroused by the noise of rapid steps & a cry of a Man overboard. I leapt from my Bed & ran on deck & to my consternation I found that the poor Victim of the Ocean had already [sunk?] to rise no more – the Ship moving swiftly he was out of the reach of help in a moment, had he indeed been able to support himself by swimming we could not have lowered a Boat, the Sea was too heavy for a Boat to Live, even had the Sea been smoother from the way the Boats were lashed up, we could not possibly have got one from the Ship in less than a Quarter of an hour or perhaps more. – Thus in an unexpected moment was a Soul launched, alas! perhaps unprepared, into the presence of an almighty & just Judge – & may this Soul find Mercy under <u>justification,</u> arising from the [imputed?] Righteousness of the Lord Jesus – may the presence of the Redeemer be his portion for ever. How uncertain is Life! Sailors from their occupation are more exposed to casualties than most other employments – what a trifle separates them from Eternity. – In a moment they may be hurled into the <u>World</u> where time is found no more – at the best but a few planks separate them from death. O that Men would consider, before it is too late: that they would charge their thoughts with the importance of their Souls & the ['early' *deleted*] necessity for seeking an Early Salvation – May the Lord Bless the poor weak means which are in my hands, may the prayers & discourses read to my Shipmates affect deeply their hearts – for who knows – the grace of God assisting the Weakest Means the most imbecile instrument can produce wonderful effects. – John Dodds our poor sufferer was an active, ['quiet' *deleted*] willing Sailor, & an innoffensive [*sic*] quiet Man – He seems to have had some presentiment of his approaching fate having told his <u>intimates</u> that

they need not be surprised if any thing happened to him, he believed he should never Reach home: he had had <u>strange Dreams</u>. – May the Lord receive his Soul in mercy.

We continued our course to the ESE until the Rising of the Barometer ['to' *deleted*] ¾ of an Inch indicated fine weather. This was at 10 am. we then tacked ['Severe Cold & its effects' *in margin*] being in very smooth water we were assured of our proximity to Ice. The Wind agreeable to our expectation abated considerable [*sic*] we set Jib, Stay Sails, &c. & lowered two Boats down into the tackles to be ready for Fishing – Frost rime still very thick. Temperature at noon 5°[.] This intensity of Cold has some peculiar effects. In the first place the Ship at the Bows is quite concealed in masses of Ice – the Rudder would very speedily be frozen fast was the Ice not occasionally cleared away. Any Metal which had attained the Temp. of the Atmosphere if not too thin will by applying it to the ['Thermeter [*sic*] falls to –2° !!' *in margin*] Tongue so attatch itself that on removing it, the skin remains on the Metal ['its removal' *deleted*]. A Peculiar sensation is communicated to the Nose, something similar to that cause [*sic*] by [***] heat or dryness. The mouth is drawn up as by a Sphincter so that words are with difficulty articulated. Iron becomes brittle, fracturing with a compartively [*sic*] small force. The British spirit Brandy at a wholesale strength freezes, &c. At 4 Pm. the therm*ometer* fell to Zero & an hour afterwards to –2 a degree of Cold I never before measured. I be no doubt [*sic*] but at the MastHead it would have been as low as –4 or –5°.[1] – The weather all day continued very thick with Frost rime, so that on Meeting with several heavy pieces of Ice & apparently a pack to wind^d we tacked and lay with the Main Y^d aback. Laying too or plying to windward near the same spot the rest of this day.

In the Evening the Ship being tollerably still I thought a good opportunity for attempting to freeze Mercury.[2] I therefore mixed diluted Sulphuric Acid & Nitric Acid in nearly equal parts, I then exposed this ['Attempt to Freeze Quicksilver: failed' *in margin*] with all the vessels intended to be used to the Cold of the atmosphere in about 2 hours they had their Temparature [*sic*] reduced to about +5°. I had no Snow or Ice therefore used the snow like substance, the <u>Frost rime</u> which covered the vessel all over – a quantity of this I added to the mixture of Acids, stirring it about with the Ball end of an Hygrometer in which I had put about a dram of Quicksilver, occupying ⅓ the Capacity of the Ball – this frozen vapour was instantly dissolved & I added more. I now allowed it to remain 10 minutes, stirring occasionally, the Mercury in the Hygrometer Ball not congealed, unfortunately I had no Thermometer graduated below –15° one of the lowest I put into the mixture it instantly sank below the scale & all the Mercury passed into the Ball, from the Rapidity with which it fell I judged

[1] In *Account of the Arctic Regions*, I, p. 329, Scoresby stated that 'On the 25th April 1813, latitude 80°, the thermometer fell to –4° during a hard gale from the northeast (*per* compass), but, on account of the ship being driven away from the ice, it soon rose to 10° or 15°.' In that section (pp. 328–32) he also described several of the cold-weather phenomena mentioned here, including the brittleness of metal, freezing of 'brandy of English manufacture and wholesale strength', and the effects on the nose and vocal chords. He did so, however, mainly in the context of the period of prolonged cold experienced in April 1814.

[2] The freezing point of mercury is approximately –38.8°C. or –37.8°F.

the Temparature could not be much less[1] than –40° or –45°. I afterwards added more of the congealed vapour but without success. I attributed this failure to the want of Ice – [pounded?] Ice is well ['Supposed cause' *in margin*] known to produce a greater cold than Snow & I fancy Snow would have a better <u>frigorific</u> effect than the substitute I used, this <u>rimy</u> vapour being remarkably light, & in in [*sic*] wonderfully small particles.

['Seamen Frost Bit' *in margin*] Several of our Men this ['to' *deleted*] night had their faces or fingers <u>Frost bit</u>, the inconvenience was speedily removed by the application of friction with Spirits of lime or a hearty rubbing with Snow.

Sunday 25th April Lat. 79.10 Lon. 5°E.
NE to ENE
After Mid Night the <u>Frost rime</u> was so thick that we could no [*sic*] see 80 yards – this being a distance too short to <u>wear</u> in & the wind having increased so that we could not carry sail sufficient to <u>Stay</u> under, the ship being at the same time very unhandy, suppose too <u>much water by the head</u>, this circumstances [*sic*] rendered our approaching the Ice attended with very great danger, we were therefore obliged to keep our reach to the ESE[d] and in a few hours encountered a very heavy swell – the Therm. was said to be at -4 I did not see it however being in bed at the time. – The great intensity of Cold soon clothed the Bowsprit, Head, & Bows with an immense weight of Ice, the Ship straining with the Sea leaked a ['good' *deleted*] great deal, the water ran forward as the Ship dipped with her Stem by the weight of Ice & thus rendered the inconvenience greater, for no water could be [got up?] by the pumps for more than 12 hours, all of it from <u>forward</u>, the Ship at this time exceedingly dangerous, it was really alarming to see the waves break over the Bows, the [lee fore Chains?][2] were scarcely ever out of the water & the Ship <u>heeled</u> in such a manner that no person could stand on the deck without some support. We had hithertoo carried sail (viz, Close reefed Fore Top Sail & Fore sail, & treble Reefed Main Top Sail) wishful to keep near the before mentioned <u>Bay</u> or <u>Bight</u> of the Ice expecting there to find Whales at the Conclusion of the Gale, at the same time having smoother water than ['Dangerous situation of the Ship' *in margin*] farther to lee-ward. I found now however we could not [longer?] with propriety contend, nay not without great danger of the Ship & our lives, I therefore got all hands up, wore the Ship which ['&' *deleted*] took us above half an hour with an abundance of head Sail and nothing abaft the main mast, we then took in all sails but still little water came to the pumps: finding we might fall in with Ice on this tack, whilst Frost rime was thick & the Ship unmanageable, with some difficulty we again wore, removed some Tons of Ice from the Bows, started a Ton of fresh water overboard, passed all our Shot from the Galley to the Mainmast, the waistboats we brought on the Quarter Deck, put the Blubber far aft; &c. &c the water then coming to the pumps we soon experienced a great amendment. – After

---

[1] *Sic.* 'higher' or 'warmer' presumably intended.
[2] Smyth, *Sailor's Word Book*: 'CHAINS, properly CHAIN-WALES or CHANNELS. Broad and thick planks projecting horizontally from the ship's outside to which they are fayed and bolted, abreast of and somewhat behind the masts … they are respectively designated fore, main, and mizen.'

performing Divine Service as usual, agreeable to <u>forms</u> of <u>the Church of England</u>, with a sermon from Burder's Village Discourses,[1] we set the watch.

['Therm*ometer* mid n^t 10°' *in margin*] The wind continued a hard Gale the whole of this day; lay too under the Fore& Main Stay Sails & reefed Mizen with the Ship's head to the SE^d <u>Bar. all</u> day 29.95.

Monday 26th April Lat. 78°15' Lon. 6°0E.
ENE to NE or North.
The Gale continued with unabated violence the whole of this day; in the Morning the <u>Frost rime</u> was somewhat lessened, at the same time Snow showers commenced. At 8 am. being able to see upwards of a Mile we wore & proceeded under three Stay Sails, Fore Sail & Main Topsail to the WNW[.] I felt myself most uncomfortable during this Gale, to [*sic*] motion of the Ship prevented me from walking the deck, at the same time caused the Cabin to Smoke intollerably, we were obliged to keep the doors constantly open, whereby the Thermometer in the Cabin fell to 22° & continued at that point most of the day. I scarcely ever remember such a heavy Gale as we at this time experience with the Mercury of the Barometer so high – 29.95 it stood all the day of yesterday, today at Noon 30.15 & somewhat higher in the Evening. The Thermometer at noon had risen to 15° & continued thereabouts the rest of the day.

Tuesday 27th April Lat. 78.07'+ Lon. 3½°E.
N or NbE.
After Mid Night we observed a favourable change in the weather; at 4 Am. we were able to set & carry the Fore Top Sail. Still [standing?] to the W^d we found the Bolt rope[2] at the Foot of the Main Top Sail quite broken in two in the Middle & nearly in the same predicament in another place: we put stoppers, on the weak parts to serve until the weather should allow us to repair them.
    At 6 Am. we fell in with disseminated pieces of heavy Ice & at ['NNE' *in margin*] 8 several streams, having increased our sail we proceeded amongst streams & loose Ice to the W^d until 10 am. when coming to an impervious pack laying about NNE & SSW we were obliged to tack – A Considerable opening appearing to windward we hasted in that direction – Six sail of ships to lee-ward. One Ship to the ENE of us. All hands began at 9 am. to put the ship to rights, to repair the damages sustained in the late Gale, to [clear?] the Boats, clear the Ship of Ice & water; to <u>trim</u> the Ship by starting 6 or 8 Casks of water near the Foremast (the vessel being unhandy on account of being more water forward than abaft) – A Mizen Top Mast stay sail was bent, & variety of other needful work effected.

---

[1] Presumably Burder's *Village Sermons; or ... plain and short discourses on the principal doctrines of the Gospel; intended for the use of families, Sunday schools, or companies assembled for religious instruction in country villages* which was published in London by Mathews in eight volumes between 1798 and 1816.
[2] Smyth, *Sailor's Word Book*: 'BOLT-ROPE. A rope sewed all round the edge of the sail, to prevent the canvas from tearing.' 'Stopper' is a general term for a rope length used for added security or as a preventive measure.

At Noon Lat. Observed 78° [*blank space*]' N. Lon. Account 3°30'E. Bar. 30.33 Therm. 20°.

By 6 Pm. we had explored this opening until we came to a pack to wind[d] we then reached out to the Eastward amongst a quantity of smallish pieces of Ice, close streams occasionally thwarting us & forcing us to bear up. Towards Mid Night we had little wind, delightful fine clear weather. A large opening appearing to the NNE made all sail to work up – we saw no Whale Fish the whole day, notwithstanding the Ice was apparently very favourably situated for them. Several narwhales & some Seals were seen. At Mid Night the Sun was visible above the Horizon for the first time this Year,[1] we have however, had no appearance of Night for this ten days past.

Wednesday 28ᵗʰ April Lat.78°19'+ Lon. 3°50'E
NNE Variable
A Moderate Breezes [*sic*] of wind with delightful clear weather. Thermometer in the Shade 16° in the sun 26° (10 am.) Barometer 30.35. Unbent the Main Top Sail and replaced it by a Fore Top Sail in the interim. The Sail Maker immediately set to work to repair it, by ripping the whole of the Bolt rope from off the foot & putting a Main [***] (the only suitable piece of rope we had) in its place.

At 10 am. we had again got to the far end having come to a heavy pack, it shews impervious within except near the edge where it seems to be in the act of giving off streams & patches. Searching all around & seeing no Fish or sign of any, except some maneuvering of a Ship 3 or 4 Miles to Lee-ward, & considering it grievous to pass such fine weather in inactivity, I hastened to search the Country more to the Eastward and Northward at every opening. We had at first to run to the SE[d] two or three miles when we hauled by the wind & sailed eight hours without making a tack, amongst much Ice, partly scattered about in the interstices of compact streams to lee-ward & a pack to windward. 8 sail in sight, 5 we left to the westw[d]. One followed us & two appeared a head as we came out to the Eastward. At 10 Pm. we were come so near the outside of the Ice to the Seaward that only a few small pieces of ['N.erly. Calm' *in margin*] Ice widely scattered were to be seen to the SE[d] of us[.] in this situation we saw a Whale & afterwards two more, the first made a very narrow escape, it heard the Boat & received a small wound from the Harpoon. About this time the wind died away to a Calm. To the SE, South & SW[d] heavy clouds seen to rise likewise some observed to the W[d] the Rest of the Atmosphere beautifully clear & serene. The repairs of the Main Top Sail being completed, we unbent the substitute & rebent the proper sail. Thermometer at Mid N[t] 19°.

Thursday 29ᵗʰ April Lat. 78°34+ Lon. 4°50'E.
WSW to SW.
A Fresh breeze sprung up at 2 Am. accompanied by thick Showers of Snow, we reached out to the SE[d] into the open Sea. The Whales hereabout are certainly very scarce, so few indeed that the probability of making a tollerable fishery amongst

---

[1] At 78°N, the sun is continually above the horizon by 24 April; the delay of a few days was presumably due to cloud and weather conditions.

them, is very small, hence it is of importance to search out, if possible a more lucrative spot, farther Northward seems to be the best direction & the wind now suitable, we bore up, first steering SE, 10 miles until we were to the Eastward of all Ice & then, East or ENE for 25 miles further, being constantly within sight of streams & patches of small Ice, broken up Bay Ice & scattered heavy pieces: thick Showers of Snow were frequent. – At 10 Am. seeing no Ice to the N^d we bore up NE an hour & then hauled up North a short time & afterwards by the wind to the NWbN. – Five Ships following us fell in with Fish & lowered several Boats in the very spot we passed at 10 o'Clock, we had a good watch at the masthead at the same time but saw nothing. After sailing 20 miles North we passed some Brash streams & presently saw the edge of a pack laying about ENE & WSW for two miles to the Eastward of it, the Sea was covered with Bay Ice we reached into it, tacked & reefed all TopSails, blowing a Strong Gale of Wind. We worked a litle to Windward & obtained shelter by some Ice which stretched out from the pack in a SSE direction. I had retired to rest & slept two hours when I was informed the John commanded by my Father, was in sight & scarcely two miles off: the officer of the watch assured me it was her – we hoisted a Jack & afterwards an ancient but they were not regarded. When I arose I really thought it must be the John, the Ship had every appearance of her & what was particularly striking ['a Disappointment' in margin] was a Crow's Nest placed on the Top Gall^t Mast Head, no ship had before been seen with such an one except the John, we made sail up to her & hasted to a disappointment, she proved to be the Clapham of Hull.[1] It is a Hackneyed phrase, nevertheless true, that "whatever we anxiously wish to be, that we readily believe." In the present instance this remark was certainly true; the effect was a train of particularly unpleasant feelings[.] When hopes too sanguine are indulged a disappointment is attended with aggravated pain: human nature being prone to this error, I must give myself the Credit of having habituated myself in general to resist these ardent expectations which if defeated are ['attended' deleted] followed by such baneful feelings: many indeed a grateful anticipation have ['Reflections on expectations balked' in margin] I deprived myself of from a too great fear of this error, yet on the whole I cannot regret it since thereby fruition is rendered more complete, seldom failing to surpass any anticipation which I believe is not commonly the case. In the instance now remarked I was not so cautious: I had very particular reasons & multiplied for wishing for the Company of the John, which caused me to freely indulge in the idea and added greatly to the disappointment and its ungracious attendants. In the first place it would have been a high gratification to have seen my dear parent from whom I have been constantly separated since the commencement of August last: my Brother in law Thomas Jackson[2] Mate of the John, an old acquaintance, schoolfellow & playmate, him I have not seen of several years, ['passed' deleted] his presence would likewise be particularly grateful: but above all I am in expectation of a packet from her united to me by the tenderest of ties, whom I

---

[1] The *Clapham*, 374 tons, was making its first whaling voyage in 1813. In 1815 it was destroyed by fire and an explosion in the Greenland Sea: Lubbock, *Arctic Whalers*, p. 199 and Appendix E; Credland, *Hull Whaling Trade*, p. 122.

[2] See the journal entry for 26 March 1812. Thomas Jackson married Arabella, Scoresby's younger sister.

sincerely Love and deservedly esteem – of a most delicate nervous texture & highly refined sensibility, she acutely feels the trials which my situation in Life calls her to bear – aware of her undissembled attatchment, and of the painful feelings to which her susceptibility renders her liable, I am particularly anxious to hear from her – indeed at any rate the traces of the pen from the hand of those we love, especially when it expresses the feelings of the heart, produces sensations too grateful to be expressed. Our Son likewise is an object of great solicitude: infancy is so prone to diseases and afflictions, that it would be peculiarly pleasing to be informed of his welfare & increasing strength. The idea, that every thing connected with human nature is fallible, that Life is a slender thread, liable to be broken by one of a thousand accidents or circumstances, renders all sublunary endowments, possessions, riches, unstable: & obliges us to look up to the God who created such endless variety & forms & qualities of matter, and from him to seek, a situation, possessions, & riches, which have a more firm basis than the Earth we inhabit, which shall continue through Eternity.

Captn Munroe[1] of the Clapham, could give us no news except that of about 40 Sail of Ships which he had seen most of them were <u>clean</u> known by the specktackle[2] Blocks being stopped up to the Guy, this is a practice universally followed which distinguishes even at a distance, the <u>Clean</u> Ships from the <u>fished</u>. – Since 4 Pm. Ships have come within sight to the Number of 40 Sail! We have seen two Fish near the pack edge since our arrival, the quantity of Ships however render this an unenviable spot even were there several Fish in [Stir?], for where so many vessels are collected within so small a Circle, little advantage can be expected. A Fish seen would have 20 boats in pursuit by which the chance of Capture becomes a small fraction & is even reduced by the eagerness of its numerous pursuers. – By the way of an attempt to better ourselves, therefore at 11½ Pm. we made sail once more to the Eastward to clear the Ice in sight, meaning afterwards to explore the direction to the NE.ward or accordingly as the Ice trended. 7 Sail had started whilst I was in bed: the Clapham & 5 others followed us.

Friday 30th April Lat. 79°05′ Lon. 8°15E
SW. to SSW or SWbW at noon.
We had a strong Gale the whole of this day: the weather nevertheless fine, being remarkably Clear. By 4 Am. we had sailed about 30 Miles on an ESE course, patches & streams of Ice deflecting us from our wished Course. We passed through Some open patches, where we experienced a heavy swell. After 4 am. we hauled by the wind & sailed about SE to ESE. At 8 am, saw Land & at 1 Pm. the North end of the Foreland or Charles's Island bore SE Distant scarcely 10 miles. No Ice to be seen near the Land, nor indeed did we see any after 4 am. At 1½ pm. we wore & made more Sail back again to the NW^d. At 10 pm. passed a Stream of [brashed?] Ice & many small

---

[1] 'Captain Martin Munroe, who made a great name for himself as a skilful whaling master …': Lubbock, *Arctic Whalers*, p. 199. This was his first year in command, but he continued annual whaling voyages until 1832: Credland, *Hull Whaling Trade*, p. 138.
[2] Smyth, *Sailor's Word Book*: 'SPIKE-TACKLE AND CANT-FALLS. The ropes and blocks used in whalers to sling their prey to the side of the ship.' See Introduction, Plate 3, p. xlv.

pieces disseminated all round. At Mid N^t no Ice to [see?] a strong <u>Blink</u> however appeared extending from NNE to West. 10 Sail in sight. We saw no whale the whole of this ['day' *deleted*] twentyfour hours. At Mid N^t supposed ourselves 60 miles NW from the North End of the Foreland.

Saturday 1st of May Lat. 79°20′ Lon. 4°25 E
WSW to NW & North
Immediately after Mid Night a Garland formed of three Hoops Clad with Ribbands was suspended on the Main Top Gall^t Stay according to the usual form & accompanied by the established Ceremonies.[1] For what purpose this Garland was first instituted or what ideas superstitious or otherwise were originally connected with the Ceremonies I cannot satisfy myself. Perhaps it may have arisen from a wish to resemble or imitate the May Poles or Garlands of Flowers which are [erected?] & exhibited on May ['Suspending the Garland' *in margin*] day & attended with rejoicings & hilarity in many country places in England. The Greenland Garland is formed ['of' *deleted*] by the intersection of three Firkin Hoops forming the figure of a sphere, these are decorated with Ribbands, above there is frequently fixed some ingenious figure or device such as a whale, a Ship or Ships, Windmill, representation of Whale Hunting or the Fishery, &c, &c. A weight in such Cases is attatched the under part by a long fanciful Tail for the purpose of Compensating the matters above. The Ceremonies ['Various Ceremonies on this Occasion' *in margin*] are Somewhat as follow: the Garland being all prepared, is suspended the moment <u>May</u> Commences by the Man who has the <u>last</u> entered into the <u>Marriage State</u>, immediately all hands assemble upon the deck, draped in the most fantastic manner they can devise, some with [Pig's?] Tail, <u>Cocked Hat</u>, Sashes, imitation swords, epilettes, [revised?][2] wigs, Marks, &c, & the whole have their faces painted with a mixture of <u>soot</u> & <u>grease</u>. The suspension of the Garland is announced by three Cheers followed by a March round the decks to the music of kettles, pans, drums, fifes, &c. wherein every one found unpainted is arrested & forced to submit to the operation. They afterwards play various antics in imitation of the most faceteous of the Crew who in this Case is always the leader, & himself shews first the example, they perform various of the tricks of the men called <u>mountebanks</u> as far as their activity or ability will allow, they engage in mock fights, and various ingenious tricks calculated to unbend the most grave countenance. I have even heard that the force of example has been carried so far, that in a Calm when a Ship lay near some Ice, the leader after having exhausted is [*sic*] stock of wit & varied tricks as a <u>denoument</u> leapt overboard & was followed by every one of the Crew who could swim!![3] Thermometer perhaps 15° or 20°! An

---

[1] In the account of his 1822 *Voyage*, Scoresby devoted several pages (34–8) to a description of May Day festivities, most of it transcribed from his journal of the 1820 season. In 1822, however, he remarked that 'Not having any particular taste for witnessing these scenes, I did not turn out at the time the ship's company were all busily engaged in the performance of their various parts in the humours of the day.'

[2] If this reading is correct, it may be a transcription error for 'reversed' in the original.

[3] This anecdote is also included in the *Voyage* account, though there Scoresby stated that some of those leaping into the sea could not swim.

allowance of Grog exhilerates the spirits & concludes the [scene?] with Singing and dancing.

Still Blowing a fresh Gale of wind at 2 am. we fell in with a patch of heavy Ice, several streams separated us from an opening of water to the [NW^d?] where we could calculate of smooth water & it might chance whales also. A very narrow opening presented itself through which by a press of Sail & prompt attention we sailed within five points of the wind. This large opening lead us to a firm pack – here we [sauntered?] until I taken a little rest. At noon seeing none of the objects of our seach [sic] we bore up East or EbN running close past the points of Ice which presented themselves in that direction & searching every likely spot for Fish; about 20 Sail all seemingly inclined the same way. The Land in sight extending from NE, several points to the East & Southward: the nearest part about 35 Miles distant. Several Ships steered away ESE to try for Fish near the Land, they hauled off again however in an hour or two & steered to the Northward. We passed an extended promontary [sic] of heavy Ice at 11 Pm. & hauled round it NNE as the edge lay – an extent of water appearing in that direction. – At Mid Night a thick Fog commenced which was likely to inconvenience us as I purposed exploring the full extent of the Navigable Seas in the direction of the North or NorthWest. Wind a moderate breeze.

May 2^d Sunday Lat 79°54+' Lon. 7°E
NW to North & NNE
We had a Moderate or Fresh breeze of wind and excepting four hours of thick Fog charming fine Clear weather the whole of this day. At 2 am. we came to a quantity of heavy pieces of Ice laying cross & awkward, by which our sailing was rendered very critical, we made some tacks, on the Fog clearing away soon afterwards we found ourselves aiming at a spot where was no passage. 4 Ships appeared to the NW^d one of them apparently engaged Flinching being made fast to a piece of Ice, the rest (being the Henrietta, Resolution, & another) dodging about – the wind coming to the North^wd we reached out to the NE^d until we came to a firm body of heavy Ice & which seemed to extend in a SE direction quite in with the Land. To the NW^d the Ice seemed rather open but nevertheless lay so unfavourably that the navigation amongst it must be attended with some difficulty, the Ship therein seeming [uningaged?] we lay too on the recommencing of the thick Fog, & tacked about in this spot until Night. Several ships explored the openings to the NW & W^d but seemed to meet with no whales, others ran back to the SW^d or W^d. The Aimwell & Lively of Whitby came near us & both the Masters visited me: I was informed that many Ships have been severely strained by the late tremendous Gales, that the oldest Captains scarcely recollect such ['Loss of the Oscar Melancholy event! Vide May 29th'[1] *in margin*] a continuation of bad weather. I was much concerned to learn a melancholy account of the loss of the Oscar late a Brig but the present year being lengthened and fit out as a Ship: she had sailed out of the harbour of Aberdeen & anchored in the Roads or Bay together with three other Ships[.] a sudden & dreadful storm arose drove the Oscar

---

[1] The phrase 'Vide May 29th' is written in a different hand from both the journal text and the rest of the marginal note.

from her anchors on shore and all hands, except the Mate & a Boatsteerer perished almost at their own doors! The other ships were more favoured, one cut her Cable & by the help of some small sails providentially regained the Harbour, not however without sustaining so considerable damage that Casks & Materials for the Fishery were required to be landed.[1]

The Aimwell & Lively are <u>clean</u> together with most of the Fleet in sight consisting of near 30 Sail of Ships. Mr Johnstone informed me that to the Southward of 78° Lat. he was in so much Bay Ice, which extended so far as he could see towards the Land, that with a fresh Gale of Wind the Ship stuck fast. How is it that to the Northward of this Latitude we have seen very little newly formed Ice whilst to the Southw^d is so much?

Ancient adventurers to this Country tell us that they frequently caught fish very near the Land, that a Foreigner filled his ship in <u>Magdelena</u> Bay whilst he[2] lay at anchor! The Fish must now be somewhere why not there, to ascertain this we made sail at 10 Pm. steering SE closely passing the projection of the Northern pack meaning to approach the Land as near as the Ice would permit.

Monday 3^d of May Lat 79.36+ Lon. [*blank space*]
NE to Easterly, SE.erly ENE
Aided by a Fresh breeze of wind we steered ESE or SE under a Brisk Sail, always within two or three miles of the pack edge & sometimes passing within a few yards of the Points or Promontories – at ½ an hour am. the Aimwell & Lively which had accompanied us since 10 Pm. judging unfavourably of appearances changed their direction to the Westward & left us: we continued; at 1 Pm. we saw a Young Fish & afterwards two large ones, we had three Boats in chase, they were both frightened, a Harpoon was cast at one of them but

['Robt Dowell F. N° 2 = 10 ^ft 2^in' *in margin*]

did not reach her. After this we hoisted up all the Boats but one & reached about 6 Miles more to the SE^d when another whale was seen having a young one with it: after near two hours pursuit she was struck ['upwards of' *deleted*] scarcely half a mile from the pack edge, fortunately she followed a circuitous route & on the whole rather quitted the pack, she shewed great anxiety for her young, she did not descend more than 150 yards after being struck, three more Harpoons were speedily added towards her entanglement and within an hour <u>she died</u>. The young one was allowed to escape, it was remarkably small, seemingly not more than 12 feet in length & might be supposed to have made its appearance in this external world only a few days ago.[3]

[1] 'A severe storm towards the end of March caught the Aberdeen ships in Gray Hope Bay, the *Hercules*, *Oscar*, *St Andrew*, *Middleton*, and *Latona* all dragged their anchors. The *Oscar* was wrecked within 200 yards of the shore and in sight of crowds of spectators, her whole crew of 48 men with the exception of two being drowned, but the other ships managed to bring up in time.': Lubbock, *Arctic Whalers*, p. 192.

[2] Possibly 'she'.

[3] 'Based on all available data, the length at birth is apparently 3.6–4.5+ m [11.8–14.8+ feet] but most new-born calves appear to be larger than 4.0 m [13.1 feet].': Koski *et al.*, 'Reproduction', pp. 239–74 (258). See Introduction, p. xli (re De Jong).

The whale being brought to the Ship we clued the sails up at the Mast Heads & flinched her. – Finished; we made sail & stood with a light breeze of wind with most delightful fine clear weather, amongst open Ice laying off the edge of the pack which now trended to the SSE. At noon the land Seen from ENE to SSE the Seven Icebergs at ESE Distant about 20 Miles. Therm^r about 28° (at mid N^t & even 5 am. it was 13° although the Sun shone clear & bright.) No Ships in Sight or whales to see.

Mr Johnstone yesterday informed me, that the Neptune in Lat. 74° & Lon. 3°E fell in with Ice, they steered from thence ['ENE' *inserted and deleted*] NE or NNE near a pack edge until they ['Situation of the Ice to the Southward' *in margin*] came to 79° from which it appear that the Ice held nearly the same direction to the Southward as we found it here on our arrival at the Northward, that is about NE & SW. Another Ship proved a pack to lay as is Commonly the Case, in a direct line between Cherry Island & point Look Out. Thus the Ice on the West Side & the Land & Ice on the East leave a space of water between bearing some resemblance to a funnel, the smaller end terminating about Latitude 80° where we find it to be very narrow. In the pack lying between Cherry Island & Point Look Out Mr Johnstone in the year 180 [*sic*] saw a great number of large Fish, the main quantity of whales may be thereabouts at this present and it is very probable seeing they are so scarce to the Northward. – I am told that about 15 Sail of ships which sailed for Davis's streights, experiencing dreadful adverse Gales contended two or three weeks & then bore up for Greenland, several of them we have seen.

['SE to South' *in margin*] At 6 Pm. we had reached a considerable distance in amongst the loose Ice, all the way within a mile or two of the main body lying to the Northward & Eastward of us, not a symptom of a Fish could we see, the Land about 12 Miles off, the N. end of the Foreland bearing SSE Distance [*blank space*] Leagues; about this time a Fresh breeze of wind sprang up at SE which before Mid-Night [veered?] to South; under shelter of the loose Ice & streams which lay off the Land we worked to wind^d under a brisk sail least a heavy Storm should drive us up on the lee-Ice. At Mid Night we treble reefed the Top Sails, Snow Showers Commenced, & the Sea made rapidly; this is a ['the' *deleted*] most dangerous circumstance to which <u>open Seasons</u> as the present, are liable; with any wind between SE & WSW we are quite exposed to the swell of the Main Ocean no Ice laying in the way to afford the least shelter – these swells are not only dangerous but inconvenient and materially retard the operation of the Fishery by preventing us from assailing any whales which may be in sight or from approaching the Ice to search for them.[1]

Tuesday May the 4th Lat.78°50′ Lon. 5°E.
South Variable Calm
By two O'clock the Sea had scattered abroad the pieces of Ice forming the Streams, that had hitherto afforded us shelter, we therefore quitted this situation and kept our

---

[1] This is just one of several places in these journals where the importance, and even the danger, of sea swells near the ice margin is emphasized. However there is little or no mention of this in *Account of the Arctic Regions*; swells were discussed by Scoresby in vol. I, pp. 218–23, but not in that context.

reach off to the westward. At Noon Thermometer 32° Bar. 29.95 – a ship passed us Starboard tacked. In the Evening the Gale abated & presently died away to a Calm, at the same time the Snow ceased & the sky cleared. Having no employment we cleared the lumber & Casks out of the Fore Hold & pumped the water out of about 15 of the ground Tier & began the operation of making off, that is the clearing of the Blubber from all extraneous matters such as Skin, Crang or lean flesh, cutting into pieces of about 3 Inches square & the thickness of the Blubber in length, & lastly of putting these pieces into the Casks through the medium of the Bung Hole of 4 Inches diameter. It is a matter of surprize to every ['making off' *in margin*] one unacquainted with the process however a Ship is filled by a method so apparently tedious in the extreme, how 300 Tons of Blubber can be disposed of in the space of time afforded by the Stay of the Ships in the Fishing Country. It is certainly more than could be expected that a Ship's Crew consisting of 50 men & boys whereof two thirds work together will, pump out & start 150 Tons of water out of Casks into the hold & this again overboard & will fill 300 Tons of Casks in this way with Blubber, at the same time stowing them in closed regular order all complete within the space of six days and nights! – At MidNᵗ two ships seen. Calm weather. No Ice.

Wednesday 5ᵗʰ of May Lat. 79°33′ Lon. 3°40′E
E.erly, ENE.
Light breezes to Fresh Gales, fine clear weather. We reached by the wind under easy sail starboard tacked towards the Ice which soon confirmed our proximity by the appearance of a strong blink extending from SW to NE (west about). At 2 Pm. we saw a close pack from the deck & within it about 2 miles from the edge lay two ships beset. Tacked close to the edge where we saw an old fish accompanied by its young, sent a Boat away which rowed after several whales that were seen, the Sea increased so much however that at 7 Pm. we were obliged to take the Boat [up?] – made some sail by the way of keeping our ground. During the day 18 Ships were observed running to the SWᵈ In the Evening finished our operation of making off, the Blubber filling 42 Casks equal to 75 Butts. – At Noon Therm. 30°, at Mid Night 20°.

Thursday 6ᵗʰ of May Lat. 79°29+ Lon. 2°20′E
ENE Calm N.erly
We lost ground in the Course of the Night, seeing no Fish at Noon & the Sea preventing us gaining any advantage in the way of plying to windward we wore round & bore up along the pack edge to the WSW, SW or SSW accordingly as the Ice trended. No ship in Sight except the Resolution the Master of which came on board, informs me he has been as far south as 77° Latitude within a few days & saw no Fish, that there he saw 50 ships the whole in the Country except 25 – Most of them were clean, the Resolution amongst the unfavoured.

I have mentioned in the Introduction to this Journal, that our Boats were to be fixed or suspended on four nearly equi-distant Cross Beams or Davits, as it was a matter of extreme difficulty ascertaining without experiment the exact length some deficiency is observed on the application of the Boats in their places – first as an inconvenience all but the after one are too short, wishing to give them some pressure

Plate 8. Scarf joint. Drawing by Scoresby. Whitby Museum (Transcripts SCO1253, 6 May 1813). Photograph courtesy of the Whitby Museum.

against the <u>Skeeds,</u> it has been overdone – & 2[dly] the uprights if they had borne the Davits a foot higher would have more effectually secured them from Danger in great Swells – the two middle one's [*sic*] likewise having at each end sheeves for ['two' *deleted*] an end[1] of two Boats in the same transverse line the tackle Block interfere with each other, to remedy this each pair of Quarter Boat sheeves should have been without those of the waist – & those of the Second Quarter within those of the first Quarter, to accomplish this end the Davits must be lengthened, the 2[d] from aft two feet, the 3[d] two feet & half, the 3[d] however seems of the most importance, this we therefore remedied in the following manner – we had no timber nearly thick ['NW.erly' *in margin*] enough & no plank longer than 10 feet by 8½ In & 2 In. thick, this plank I found would lengthen the Davit full two feet by cutting the Davit obliquely longitudinally with an 8 feet straight line, & laying the plank between – we accordingly made the cut & applied the plank securing the Scarf[2] by four Clasp Iron hoops, we likewise removed a pair of sheeves at each end a foot inwards for the waist-Boats & then refixed the whole in its place – as p annexed figure. [*Here follows a sketch of the work.*]

In the Evening we had little wind, towards Mid-Night the water shewed its surface covered with crystals of Ice. Weather delightfully fine. Therm. 22° Barometer 30.10. <u>No Fish.</u>

Friday 7th of May at Noon Lat. 78°50′ Long. 2°20′
NW.erly SW SSW WSW
We had little wind inclinable to Calm until about 8 am. a Fresh breeze then commenced at SW by which we attempted to ply to wind[d] along the pack edge first WbS then WSW, we made very small progress however: the Sea near the Ice was of a deep Green Colour, at 15 Miles distance of a transparent Blue – the opaque water is the most favourable for Fishing – We saw no Whales in either – no Ships but the Resolution in sight.

Started two Casks of Bread into the Steerage Locker – Weather fine & clear.

Saturday 8th of May Lat 78°47′+ Long. 2°0′E
WSW WNW NW
Moderate or Fresh breezes with some Snow – at 3 am. three Ships were seen running

---

[1] Originally 'ends'; the 's' deleted.

[2] Smyth, *Sailor's Word Book*: 'SCARPH, OR SCARFING. Is the junction of wood or metal by sloping off the edges, and maintaining the same thickness throughout the joint.'

before the wind to the NE^d on seeing us two of them hauled their wind[1] – at 10 am, spoke the Earl Piercy[2] of Kirkaldy Capt. Cunningham Forth of Firth [sic], she was bound to Davis's Streights, but meeting dreadfully adverse storms bore up for Greenland & had just arrived. They saw several Whales from Lat. 75° to 77° N in clear water but none were observed on approaching the Ice to the E^d or W^d. At Noon seeing several Ships steering to the NE^d & supposing them to be part of the Fleet which had formerly run to the S^d & met no Fish we continued our reach with [free?] wind to the ENE and NE^d accordingly as the Ice trended. Carpenter & Armourer employed Fitting a Machine for working both pumps at the same time. At 8 Pm. we hauled round a point of Ice close by the wind, a deep bight or sinuosity appearing to the NW the termination of which could not be seen – we had clear water of a Blue Colour until this time when we observed ourselves again in that of Deep Green shade – At 9 we saw a Whale & shortly afterwards several more, we made a <u>loose Fall</u>, that is all the ['NW' *in margin*] six Boats were sent in pursuit and continued on the Watch until near Mid Night – several Fish in the mean time were seen but none of them would allow us to approach near enough: they seemed to be feeding, by the long time they remained under the surface & by the distance they moved beneath without any apparent determinate <u>Course</u>[3] – This Colour of the water is understood to be rich with their food & from its opacity favourable for Fishing. At Mid-Night two Boats only remained <u>down</u>: weather fine Cloudy; temperature of the air 19° – A great number & variety of beautifully modified lamellated Crystals of transparent Snow, indefinitely thin, & from ¼ of an inch in diameter to the Smallest discernible particle, all equally finely crystallized, the smaller however the most beautifully marked with great diversity of lines, which as well as every angle exhibited was never found to vary to[4] any other quality than precisely 60°, 120° or their halfs, & very rarely a right angle. Besides the lamellar description some [few?] of the large specimens shewed collateral ramifications, arising from a primitive table, in a great variety of different planes, though always with a regard to the angle formed with the primitive table as well as with each other – I examined many of the crystals and discovered a beautiful diversity of forms, all regularly formed in true mathematical proportion, the <u>hexigon</u> [sic], and <u>stellated</u> or Starlike form having six points radiating from a [common?] Centre in the same plane, formed the basis of most of the particles examined with the microscope. From what I have observed relative to the crystals I suspect, that ['nature' *deleted*] every individual Shape which it is possible for the angles of 60

[1] Smyth, *Sailor's Word Book*: 'HAUL HER WIND. *Haul your wind*, or *haul to the wind*, signifies that the ship's head is to be brought nearer to the wind – a very usual phrase when she has been going free.'

[2] *Sic*, but *Earl Percy* according to Lubbock, *Arctic Whalers* and the contemporary printed list.

[3] '*Water-column feeding* – This category of feeding is the most problematic to describe. Nevertheless it is undoubtedly by far the most common feeding mode, despite the fact that it cannot be seen directly. Water-column feeding is surmised because whales dive for repeated and relatively long times (up to about 30 minutes, usually about 15 minutes) in the same area. They also tend to move slowly while at the surface, staying up only long enough to take a series of breaths between dives. While at the surface, whales often move in a partial circle, diving near the spot where they surfaced.': Würsig and Clark, 'Behavior', p. 168.

[4] Replaces 'from' deleted.

& 120° Combined to produce, that is of simple figures, these Nature exhibits in the Crystals of Snow of high Latitudes & Low temperatures: not simple figures only, such as the hexigon, triangle, stellate, &c, that I confine the term to [but?] the variety of combinations which these form without multiplying the principles more than necessary to complete the beauty & perfecting of the hexagonal crystal. An aggregation of Hexagons, of Spines or hexagonal prisms, or of triangles are not uncommon. The most wonderful circumstance of appearance these crystals exhibit is the constant regard which the form of each spine & appendages bears to another in the <u>Stellates</u>; the mathematical accuracy of the hexagons, their internal lines, & the proper distribution of any attendant Ramifications, & the Constant completion of the regular figure in almost every crystal.

Sunday 9th of May Lat. 79°5′ Lon. 4°0′E
SW.erly variable
We had variable breezes the whole of this day, weather cloudy with some Snow – At 1 Am. we spoke the <u>James</u> of Whitby[1] a Ship which with many others was not able to make a passage to Davis's Streights never in the memory of the Oldest Seaman was such dreadful weather experienced, constant Storms & always from the SW, W. or NW, the James 3 or 4 times was obliged to return to Shetland on account of different accidents & distresses, at one time a Top Mast failed & the last the Rudder was severed by the stroke of a Sea – She drifted so near the Coast of Norway that if the Storm had Continued twelve hours longer the vessel must have inevitably gone on Shore – The … … lost her Foremast & Bowsprit & various distresses assailed other ships, I sincerely wish all the older vessels may have been enabled to endure the stress of weather – The James saw the <u>John</u> of Greenock near the Ferroe Islands on the 19th of May.[2]

We lay too or plyed about near the spot where we saw so many Whales yesterday, we observed different Fish during the day – Towards Night we worked into a deep Bay of the Ice & proceeded amongst a quantity of loose Ice near the edge of a pack laying to the NW^d here we saw several whales, had three Boats down in the Evening. The Earl Piercy & the James each got their first Fish – 4 other ships in sight. We spoke the … .. which had been in Company with the Main Fleet to the Southward, they find no entrance into the Ice & Fish scarce.

Monday 10th of May Lat. 79°12′ Lon [5?]°+E
SWerly S.erly
Remarkably unsettled weather, Strong breezes, or Calms, exceedingly variable, the <u>Nimbus</u>[3] modification of the Clouds constantly observable in different quarters, the aspect of the Heavens very dark & stormy like. The Barometer settled to 29.50; the

---

[1] According to Lubbock, *Arctic Whalers*, p. 192, the *James* (Captain Smith) had been the first British whaler (of a total of 138 to both the Greenland Sea and Davis Strait) to set sail, on 14 February; 'she had also been the first to sail in 1812'.

[2] *Sic*. 'April' presumably intended.

[3] 'Nimbus' was normally a noun, indicating a rain-cloud; nowadays it is used only in association with cloud types, e.g. nimbostratus and cumulonimbus.

strange state of the weather seemed to proceed from contending winds & a <u>brewing</u> Storm which I observed to some of my officers would probably attack us like a Clap of Thunder: in this I was not deceived as will afterwards appear. We often saw Fish whilst we plied about nearly in the same situation as yesterday having Reached from amongst the loose Ice in the above described <u>bight</u>, we had Boats frequently in pursuit from one to three in number. Land seen at 4 Pm. bearing ESE, not distinguishable ['the exact spot' *deleted*]. 4 Ships in sight. Frequent thick Showers of Snow in the afternoon.

Tuesday 11th of May Lat 79°20′ Lon. 5½°E
NE to North
We had no wind an hour after Mid Night, the ambient atmosphere black with Showers – three Boats were in pursuit of a Fish two miles from the Ship, they were in the act of retracing their way on board when a NE breeze sprang up accompanied by thick <u>granular</u> Snow, in ten minutes it was a Confirmed Gale: the Boats were for a while obscured by the Snow, I had carefully marked their direction however & steered by the Compass a Course directly towards them: presently they were seen – we were obliged to employ all hands in taking the Sails in before they could approach the Ship & even after the Ship was laid too we had considerable difficulty in getting them up without injury but at length fortunately succeeded, the Sea accompanying the Gale & the remains of the Southerly Swell not coalescing ['caused' *deleted*] produced a very turbulent effect on the water. I congratulated myself on our not having overtaken the Fish we so anxiously pursued, had our wishes been accomplished near the time of the Gale's Commencement we should inevitably have lost any lines which might have been out, probably some of the Boats & at the same time endangered the lives of ['some of' *deleted*] our Men.

   Having treble reefed the Top Sails we reached off the Ice by the wind, for six hours & <u>in</u> five hours, it was then very thick with Snow, wore therefore & stood four hours off & back again until Mid Night. – The wind had increased during the day which reduced our sails to two Close reefed Top Sails & Fore Top Mast Stay Sail, a Short tumultuous Sea accompanied the wind which obliged us to take the Waist Boats upon the deck & lash the Quarter Boats with their Bows up to the Davits. One Ship in sight. Therm^r 15°-16°. Barometer 29.55.

Wednesday 12th of May Lat. 78°59′+ Lon 5°10′E
NNW to NE or EbN & NEbE
The Force of the wind was lessened for a few hours, but afterwards returned with redoubled violence accompanied with Showers of Snow. At 11 Pm. we reached under the lee of a Stream where finding the Sea Smooth plenty of room, & no appearance of the Ice closing I determined to rest ['the' *deleted*] here during the Night. Seven sail in sight all to windward but one. Saw two whales near the Streams. A pack in sight to the westward or NW^d of us. a Heavy Sea without. Barometer at Mid Night 29.52 Thermometer 21°.

Thursday 13th May at Noon Lat. 78°50 Lon. 2°20′E
ENE, NE, East SE, NE & Variable.
Very Hard Gales the Fore part of the day, afterwards Fresh or Strong Gales, showers

of Snow at intervals throughout. At 10 am. a strong SSE swell assailed us in our retreat notwithstanding the Streams completely sheltered us in the direction of the wind, the clouds heavy & black in the SE[.] I was afraid the wind might be coming from that quarter, made sail therefore & reached out Clear of the Ice, the wind became then moderate & very variable from NE to SEbS – We endeavoured to work to the Eastw^d but made little or no progress. Saw several whales near the edge of the Main body of Ice. 8 Sail in sight. Barometer 29.42 Inches Thermometer 21 to 25°. Heavy SE Swell.

Friday 14th of May Lat 78°45′ Lon. 2°30′E
ENE to NEbN
A Strong Gale all day – Sky almost Cloudless – Very heavy E.erly swell. Working still, off the face of the Ice under a brisk sail, not able however to keep our ground. Several sail in sight some laid too others carrying all possible sail. Meeting a very heavy Sea Larboard tacked the Ship made near four points lee-way. Barometer at noon 29.40 Thermometer 27° .

Saturday 15th of May Lat. 78°10′ Lon. 2°0′E NE to NNE or North Strong Gales, with showers of Snow – high E.erly swell. In the Evening the wind having veered to North we reached in with the Ice in search of shelter, by running a mile or two to lee-ward we hauled up under a heavy stream where we found a very safe & commodious retreat, as the Stream by its outer point projecting far towards the SE afforded us shelter even from the Easterly swell – we had very little loose Ice to incommode us. Saw one whale. No Ships to see¹ – at Mid N^t Bar 29.45 Ther. 13°.

Sunday 16th of May at noon Lat. 77°51′+ Lon. 1°50′E
North to NW
The Ice to the NW^d of us shewed to be a close pack, one opening only to be seen & that small, by 10 am. however it had increased amazingly, a vein of water led into it & the wind having considerably abated we made sail & found more room as we went to the NW^d. At Noon we had abundance of water in which was scattered small streams & patches of very heavy Ice. 5 or 6 miles to the N^d & NNW^d the Ice seemed [unnavigably?] close. We continued our progress towards the NW occasionally tacking & having passed a considerable quantity of closer Ice than we had yet met with, at 6 Pm. we got sight of an opening so large that it appeared like the sea, we now began to find the Ice very heavy – large pieces of Floes scattered all around us, the Water Green but no Fish. – Two ships astern contending in the same direction[.] One of them struck a Fish – we did not see one near the place. Many Narwhales played near us before we entered the Ice. From our observation of the Latitude it appears we have lost a great deal of ground within these two days past. Towards Mid-Night we came within sight of a very large Floe – supposing it might harbour Fish we anticipated the result by forwarding two Boats up to it: they saw no Whale, although we observed several to lee-ward of it, but could not come near them. Much water about us – 18 Sail of Ships make their appearance behind a patch of Ice to the SW.

¹ Possibly 'lee'.

Monday 17th of May at noon Lat. 78°00′N Lon. 1°10′E
NNW to North or NNE – Variable[.]
Moderate or Fresh Gales all day – keen frost Thermometer 17° to 20°. Weather Cloudy frequent Snow Showers in the afternoon. At 1 Am. we got up to the Floe before noticed – it is a very flat piece of Ice, covered with a great thickness of Snow the surface of which in many places has been glazed by the power of the Sun. It seems to be about 20 miles in circumference. We worked up along the west side of it under all the Sail we could set, two boats running up along the edge at the same time. At 3 am. a Fish was observed at some distance from it which we had the good fortune to entangle – it descended on being struck and remained

['Tho[s?] Welburn **M**   No. 3 = 10..8.' *in margin*]

about 30 minutes below the surface, three more Harpoons assailed it on rising[.] it again descended a few minutes & when it rose was presently dispatched by well directed lances. Moored the Ship by an Ice anchor & towline to a flat point of the Floe where we flinched it: the longest lamina of Whalebone measured 10 f[t] 8 in & the circumference of the Body as ascertained by the length of the <u>Cant</u>[1] 25 Feet. The head & the Fins were uncommonly large compared with the Body. Several Fish were seen whilst we were engaged flinching, a Boat on the watch had some fine chances. The Margaret, Kay of London[2] got a Whale & made fast near us, a message came from the Capt[n] enquiring if we could furnish him with a <u>Rudder Pinion</u>: having two spare ones I sent one of them: it appears the Margaret was within some Ice at the time of the commencement of the late long Gale, her main top sail giving way she drifted amongst it & severely injured her rudder, breaking a pinion, &c. with some heavy blows she was extricated from amongst the Ice. the present Captain makes her success four large whales – they report that the John is not far distant to the SE[d] with five Fish! Also that in the late Gale 14 Men were separated from the Volunteer of Whitby & would probably have perished, had not the Lively providentially fallen in with them; they could not inform us how the separation took place. vide May 31st.[3] At 2 Pm. the water around us became frozen on its surface, the loose Ice closing around us likewise, induced us to cast off: we made sail & worked up on the NW. side of the Floe towards a most spacious opening of water – on the western hand we met a body of Ice consisting chiefly of Floes & containing very few & small openings – a Solitary whale seen occasionally. In an extensive opening to windward of the Floe from which we cast off, we saw several Fish, the Strong wind lipper[4] rendered the chase difficult & our Boats always returned unsuccessful. At Mid-Night an appearance of <u>Fast Ice</u> to windward gave us lively hopes of finding whales more plentiful than hitherto. Several Ships in sight some of them clean. 5 or 6 Fish were killed within sight of us during the day. Thermometer at Mid N[t] 16° Barometer 29.60 Inches. Wind a fresh Gale Snow Showers.

[1] See Introduction, p. xliv. Both 'kent' and 'cant' are recognized by *OED* for this whaling term.
[2] The *Margaret* (Captain Kay) was one of 14 London whalers in the Greenland Sea in 1813.
[3] This cross-reference appears to have been a later addition to the transcript.
[4] See journal entry for 3 July 1812.

Tuesday 18th of May Lat. 78°10′ Lon. 1°30′E
NNE or North

Fresh Gales all the day. Snow Showers the Forepart, towards Evening fine cloudy weather. At 4 Am. the officer of the watch informed me that the <u>John</u> was actually passing within a hundred yards of us – after assuring myself of the Correctness of the information, for I dreaded a Second disappointment, I arose: an hour afterwards I went on board & was gratified by a sight of my Father, brother Jackson, &c, all in good health: I was grived [*sic*] to learn however that the report of her success was entirely without foundation, she being yet Clean, having only come into Lat. 78° two days preceeding the late Northerly Gale. They were amongst the Ice laying between Cherry Isl^d & point lookout where they saw an immense number of <u>Sea-Horses</u>.¹ I had the satisfaction of receiving two letters from my beloved wife, ['Meet with the John' *in margin*] the one dated so late as April the 7th, wherein I was peculiarly blest in ['learning' *deleted*] the perusal of their pleasing contents, particularly in the assurance of the continued health & welfare of those most dear to me. The natural, the affectionate, the tender effusions of a heart most abstractedly & unalienably devoted to me, painting the feelings of separation, the hopes & fears of a joyous meeting in the most strong colouring yet refined shading by the pencil of Sensibility, had certainly a more pleasing, delightful effect on my mind, than my feeble powers of application of language would warrant [any?] attempt to delineate or describe. Much was said concerning our Dear Son; a Mother's expression of tenderness & affection to an infant of 6 or 7 months old, with the relation of her delight on discovering his having cut his first <u>tooth</u>, her enjoyment obtained by nursing the object of her solicitude, the pleasure she experiences in marking the development of successive powers of body & mind, with the daily proofs of increasing <u>rationality</u>, are feelings which cannot be duly appreciated by any but a parent. That I received high satisfaction [therin?] I am proud to confess, & I thank almighty God that he has endued me with that susceptibility which enables me to reap enjoyment from a source too much neglected in a general way, tho' to those by whom it is fitly valued it proves one of the greatest blessings peculiar to <u>virtuous wedlock</u>.

By 8 am. we had reached the Northernmost sinuosity of the Ice within sight, formed ['bordered' *deleted*] by heavy Floes on each side & a firm body of Floes from NE to NW. Some Fish were seen here, the John got one as likewise did several other Ships. About 10 Sail of Ships made fast to Floes, we continued plying about amongst them, laying too occasionally & frequently seeing Fish, had sometimes three & commonly two Boats on the watch but without success.

At Mid Night 22 Sail in Sight, 5 or 6 of them running to the Southward; Thermometer 20° Barometer 29.74.

---

¹ The walrus, *Odobenus rosmarus*. Described by Scoresby, *Account of the Arctic Regions*, I, pp. 502–8. He gave the Latin name as *Trichecus Rosmarus*, and 'Morse' and 'Sea-Horse' as alternative common names. He mentioned the use of the tusks 'by dentists in the fabrication of false teeth', but suggested that 'In the present age, the Sea-horses range the coasts of Spitzbergen almost without molestation from the British. … The whale-fishers rarely take half a dozen in a voyage; though my Father, in the last season, procured about 130 in Magdalane Bay.' This incident in 1819 was described by Scoresby at greater length in *My Father*, pp. 191–4.

Wednesday 19th of May Lat. 78°0′ Lon. 2°E
N.erly, Calm.
Fresh to Moderate breezes, very variable; with Snow showers: in the Evening Calm.
All the Fish having been frighted from the spot where we lay, at 6 Am. bore up in
Company with the John & sailed about 15 Miles ESE or SE amongst Floes & loose
Ice. At Noon we fell in with some whales, worked up into a **bight** until we reached the
borders of the Main Ice where we struck a Fish – it ran out 9 lines 1080 Fathoms in a
NW direction & appeared in a small opening between two Floes, twice in about an
hour after being struck, on her[1] sec^d appearance she was so furiously

['Mr Sinclair **M.**   No. 4 = 9^{ft} 1ⁱⁿ' *in margin*]

attacked by one Boat that she sought refuge from the piercing wounds of the lances
beneath the surface of the water: remained concealed about 15 Minutes, and on
again visiting the air was speedily deprived of life by the efforts of the Boats &
Crews. We made the Ship fast to a Floe, & flinched our Capture finished about 11
Pm. About a Dozen Ships in Sight, none observed to have got a Fish to-day – At Mid
N^t calm cloudy weather. Snow Showers. Barometer 29.78 Thermometer [*blank
space*][.]

Thursday 20th of May[2]
Calm N.erly NE.erly
Very little wind all day – weather cloudy with constant flying particles of Snow beautifully crystallized. Cast off from the Ice at 1 am. & drifted a little to the SE^d the water
all round us freezes rapidly. Whales were seen occasionally all the day, in the Evening
many appeared amongst Bay Ice to the W^d of the Floe, which Ice was so tough that
the Boats could with difficulty make any progress through it. At 3 Pm. made fast
again to the Floe in a place where the Bay Ice had set off & left the edge of the Floe.
The John & other four ships in the Same opening likewise made fast. There is no
opening or passage to be seen which can lead us out of the place in which we lay, the
Floes & loose Ice having blocked up the Navigation all round us, leaving us however
several square Miles of open Sea to Fish in. 5 Sail laid too about 8 Miles to the South^d
– one ship to the SWestward apparently Fishing. The day being fine & little employment offering I thought it a good opportunity of performing the experiment
suggested by Sir Joseph Banks of ascertaining the Temperature of the Sea at great
depths in the Greenland Latitudes. To accomplish this he very politely furnished me
with an apparatus contrived by Cavendish[3] &c. some years ago – on trial however it
proved insufficient to bear the pressure of the Ocean at the great depths to which it

---

[1] Scoresby implies a female in this text, but the marginal entry clearly indicates ('**M.**') that this
whale was a male.

[2] Although no coordinates are included in the journal entry for this day, in *Account of the Arctic
Regions*, I, p. 187, Scoresby gave the *Esk*'s position as 77°40N, 2°30′E when the sea temperatures
were measured. See Introduction, p. lx.

[3] Henry Cavendish (1731–1810). In *Account of the Arctic Regions*, I, p. 185, Scoresby
commented that the apparatus was 'made by Carey, under the inspection of Messrs Cavendish and

was sent, being formed of Fir <u>deal</u>, it became so soaked with water & consequently so swelled that two glasses on the Sides were broken by the warping of the wood, the Seams were likewise opened & the Instrument became unfit for the purpose[.][1] To remedy the inconvenience to which this Instrument proved liable I made a Model on the same principle & got a <u>Cast</u> from it in Brass. I applied the valves of the wooden one to the ends and fit it up as represented in Plate ... .;[2] This Instrument must doubtless bring up the water of the lowest depth to which it descends, but on account of the good conducting quality of the materials of its formation it will be liable to have its temperature changed during the time of drawing it up; this apparent defect is remedied by sending down with it an accurate self regulating Thermometer, made by <u>Carey</u> by which the greatest heat & the greatest cold passed through in the descent is <u>marked</u>.[3]

On using this Instrument I first filled it with water from the surface Temperature 29° at which point with a Magnet I drew down the Iron markers ['Temperature of the Sea at considerable depths.' *in margin*] contained in the Thermometer tube upon the Mercury – on sending it down 20 Fathoms no alteration was observed. At 50 Fathoms was nearly the same. At 80 Fath[s] the Temp. was 30° & at 110 Fa[s] 31° . Similar results have always been obtained in all my former experiments, Viz, that the Greenland seas are warmer at great depths than on the surface, which seems to be quite the reverse of what is observed in any other Climate. The instrument was carried by a current from the perpendicular in a direction about East or NE hence the current of an upper motion would seem to set to the West or SW[d]. I have reason to believe that the water drawn from different depths, varies in its specific gravity, I have not however perfectly satisfied myself on the fact.

['Will[m] Watson F. No. 5= 10.. 1 bone' *in margin*]

At 8 Pm. the pleasing object, a Boat's Jack was displayed in our Boat on watch, at some distance from the Ship, a signal of having struck a whale: our Men were quickly dispatched to their assistance, yet were likely to be too late as three oars were seen set over end a signal of [pressing?] want of lines. A Boat which was just passing by, belonging the Thornton[4] very kindly & opportunely bent on & on our Boats coming up made

---

Gilpin, both of whom, it is remarkable, died before it was completed'. Robinson M. Yost, *Observations, Instruments and Theories: The Study of Terrestrial Magnetism in Great Britain, c. 1770s–1830s* at http://www.kirkwood.cc.ia.us/faculty/ryost/minneapolis.htm states: 'During the early nineteenth century, one of the few British measurers of magnetic phenomena was George Gilpin. Gilpin, who served as an astronomical assistant on Cook's second voyage and afterwards as an assistant at the Royal Observatory (1776–81), recognized the lack of activity and called for increased magnetic observations. In 1806, he noted as Clerk of the Royal Society that magnetic observations made for only limited periods were "not sufficient for minute purposes".'

[1] See journal entry for 23 April 1811.

[2] There is no illustration in the journal. However, the device is illustrated in *Account of the Arctic Regions*, II, Plate II, Fig. 2.

[3] In fact, of course, there is no proof of the actual temperature at the place where the water sample is taken. Scoresby assumed (justifiably in most cases) that the vertical temperature gradient indicated in a series of measurements would be consistently maintained.

[4] 262 tons, Captain John Mitchison, from Hull: Credland, *Hull Whaling Trade*, pp. 126, 138.

a temporary exchange. The Fish remained down about ¾ of an hour, then appeared but was not reached in time, made her Second appearance in 15 Minutes, received a Second Harpoon & a lance, ran down about 200 Fathoms & then appeared again. In five minutes she was killed. In the interim we had cast the Ship off from the Ice: we now again moored her to a point end received the Fish alongside & began to <u>Flinch</u>.

Friday 21ˢᵗ of May Lat. 77°35' Lon. 2°35'E
NE to E. SE & SbE

Fine weather, with fresh breeze of wind in the morning, afterwards a fresh Gale with thick snow crystallized in fine small particles. The Fish being stripped of its fat & whale-bone, we cast the ship of on account of loose Ice drifting <u>upon us</u> – At 6 am. the John made Sail, we attempted to follow, but the Ice closing in her trail [threw?] us astern whereby we had to work round a Floe in stiff Bay Ice that the Ship could scarcely crush. The opening we quitted was rapidly closing, much room appeared to the Eastwᵈ we therefore aimed that way following the leads of water amongst the Floes which were thickly scattered about, often connected by Bay Ice & interspersed with loose or drift pieces. By 2 Pm. we had traversed several Miles & came near a large opening where lay several Ships separated from us by a neck of Bay Ice – all hands were required to work the Ship the navigation being exceedingly difficult, we accomplished our object followed by the John (she having stopped by ['Barometer 29.90 Ther. 30° *in margin*] some Fish), worked to the weather side under the lee of close Ice & Floes then lay too.

Saturday 22ᵈ May Lat. 77°48' Lon. 2°35'E
SbE to SW, W & NW

Fresh or Strong Gales – thick Snow or haze. At 4 am. the Ice having considerably close [*sic*] and about 10 ships having Collected themselves together within a narrow compass so that we had some trouble in keeping clear of one another, caused us to make fast to a small Floe. At 9 am. on the Snow clearing away somewhat we discovered an extensive opening to windᵈ & apparently a passage into it to the East of us, ['operation of Boreing' *in margin*] whilst here we were partly beset, we cast off, sailed towards the passage which on the John's having gone through <u>drew the pieces of Ice together</u> whereby the way was stopped & we were obliged to <u>bore</u>, that is force the pieces out of the way by a pressure of sail, pushing in between them at every opportunity, at one time the Ship stopped & was likely to fall to lee-ward into the thickest part of the patch but by giving her a <u>sallying</u>[1] or rolling motion her sides were freed & she started through; in this operation ships must doubtless be liable to receive heavy blows whenever they fall off rapidly upon a piece or receive too much head way in any small space of water in a direction too far before the wind to be stopped by the backing of the Sails, hence it is sometimes necessary to get ropes out a Stern to ease the blow. In about an hour we got through, found plenty of room, pieces of Ice & Floes being scattered around us, began to ply to windwᵈ[.] The John & Duncomb[2] saw a Whale or Whales having Boats in pursuit.

[1] See journal entry for 3–4 May 1811.
[2] Correctly, the *Duncombe* of Hull, 276 tons, Captain Joseph Taylor: Credland, *Hull Whaling Trade*, pp. 122, 139.

At 6 Pm. the Temperature of the Atmosphere was 32° we had at that time hazy weather – At 7 the wind had veered to NW & the Therm^r was at 26° at 8, 22° & at 10 or 11 pm 18°! being a variation of temperature of 14° in about four hours! The weather now amended, the Sky cleared up & we changed our direction & worked up to the weather close Ice consisting of Floes & heavy pieces, where we lay too. About 3 miles within the Ice lay two Ships beset, the one in the act of <u>Careening</u> displaying a Signal of distress.[1] The Ice being close between us we could not come near them to afford our help. 14 Sail in sight several near us. Ice not very open.

Sunday 23^d of May Lat 77°19′ Lon. 2°½E
NW to NNW
In the morning the wind was moderate, weather charming fine & clear. We find ourselves now hemmed in by Ice in every direction, small openings appear in different quarters but none likely to lead us off into a better situation for Fishing, a more northern Latitude, we have drifted quite off the ground to which they resort. At 8 am. the John entered amongst close Ice to the Eastward, we were preparing to follow (anxious to be nearer the Sea & amongst navigable Ice) when the Signal of distress was again exhibited by the above mentioned Ship which we now discovered to be the Royal George, the Prince of Brazils lay beside her; supposing our Armourer or Carpenters might be of service to assist them in repairing their damages, & observed an opening where we could come within about half a mile of them, we tacked about and worked up that way where I quitted my ship taking with me our Mechanics, and walking across a Floe & several pieces of loose Ice, in about 20 minutes arrived alongside of the distressed Ship. I found the principle [*sic*] part of the leak already stopped, whilst they were employed a second time in heaving the Ship more down by purchased fixed by lee-anchors to the Ice, assisted by a towline under the Ship's Keel which was hove on by the Cant[2] of the Prince of Brazils laying alongside, they had started the water in the Casks foreward where the damage was sustained & had filled Casks placed under the quarter-deck, by this means they had already got sight of the only remaining leak which before they had passed considering it of no importance, as it consisted only of the removal of a small piece of the doubling but so low down that they had not before come at it. The damage was sustained on Friday Evening last during the Southerly Gale, they were passing to lee-ward of a heavy piece of Ice & approaching too near struck a <u>tongue</u> of the Ice which was probably not perceptible: the blow was tremendous: in two hours the second tier of Casks in the hold was floating both pumps were scarcely sufficient to keep the Ship from sinking. The <u>wound</u> was under the Fore Chains on the Starboard side; they [careen^d?] until the Main Chains of the larboard side were in the water: the whole bow for six feet square was deeply indented & shivered[3] both planks, timbers & fortifications – the [*sic*] filled the hollow or concavity with planks up & down & covered the whole smooth & fair

---

[1] 'Hoisted in the main top-mast rigging, or indeed in any other situation <u>union downward</u>, the ancient, or national flag, is a universal sea signal of distress.': Scoresby, *Account of the Arctic Regions*, II, p. 523.

[2] I.e. the tackle used normally by the *Prince of Brazil* to turn a whale during flensing.

[3] *OED*, s.v. 'shiver': 'To break or split into small fragments or splinters.'

with other planks in their proper direction, which were nailed & bolted to the Ship. The Master declined any assistance as they had nearly finished: I returned to the Esk. Made all Sail & proceeded about 10 miles in a NE direction in a considerable opening, we found much room at the termination, but now a more formidable barrier than ever shewed itself, to the North & round to East is a Solid firm body of Fields & Floes without an apparent vacancy of any description. The John still in Sight about 8 miles SE. of us. All the rest of the Fleet aiming at the situation we obtained here. The success of the Ships around us run thus: The John, Prince of Brazils, Dexterity, & 3 others, one Fish each; the Royal George half a Fish; the Vigilant & two others clean. Saw 3 or 4 Fish.

Monday 24th of May Lat. 77°9′+ Lon. 2°¾E
North to NNE & NEbE
At 6 am. blowing a Fresh Breeze of wind we made sail & steered away to the SSW^d or SW^d determined if possible to extricate ourselves from our present situation. A Ship which attempted to gain the Sea by Steering to the SE^d was presently stopped by Floes; I therefore judged a more southern track to be the more ['eligable?], at any rate more certain. Having sailed, winding amidst Floes & <u>drift</u> Ice about 10 miles to the SW^d we hauled up about SE the Slackest Ice appearing in that direction, at 10 am. we arrived at a close stream of exceedingly heavy Ice, evidently arisen from the breaking up of some Field or heavy Floe very recently. No passage shewed itself either round the stream or through it – boring hence was our only resource. We therefore made a tack to get a little to wind^d & made towards the narrowest part which might be about 400 yards through. The Ice being so tremendous we could not avoid ['striking' *deleted*] receiving some heavy Blows. In two hours we got through, found the Ice beyond it very <u>cross</u> or [untoward?], had to bore through another stream as [broad?] as the former but much lighter Ice; we now met smaller Ice & more open, steered about 10 miles EbS we came to a patch over which we could see an appearance of the <u>Ocean</u>. This patch was unnavigable except in an ENE direction, which course we could not steer, the wind having veered to NE, with a great deal of attention we managed to work through it & accomplished the end in view of reaching the <u>Sea</u>, or <u>Land Water</u>[1] at 6 pm. after 12 hours, difficult & sometimes dangerous sailing. No Ice now appeared without us to Sea ward except a few small streams. The 10 Sail of ships in Company with us before we started, attempted a retreat from amidst the Ice in a more windw^d direction, notwithstanding the Ice favoured them by separating in their course, yet we were out of sight before we could observe them obtain their release; though I doubt not but they will accomplish their wishes.

No Fish being now seen & an open navigation before us we ['began to' *deleted*] cleared the main hold & about MidNight commenced the operation of making off, putting the Ship under easy sail – wind a Fresh breeze – Sky Cloudy – Thermometer 23° 6 am 16°.

Tuesday 25th of May Lat 77°20′ Lon. 3°E
NE Variable
Fresh breezes, with cloudy weather, & considerable Easterly Sea. The Fore part made

[1] See Introduction, p. liv.

considerable progress plying to windward whilst under shelter of detatched Streams, but in the afternoon becoming exposed to a strong swell & having the wind variable we made small advancement in Latitude. The Ice along the edge of which we worked ['is a' *deleted*] seemed a close pack. Several of the Ships we left yesterday now appear in sight to lee-ward of us, carrying every sail they can display. Employed making off in the Main Hold, had all hands engaged about 12 hours, before & after wards the half Watch. No whale seen. An Ice bird[1] perched on the Ship.

Wednesday 26th of May Lat 77°20′ Lon3°E
N.erly, NW.erly, NE.rly variable
Very little wind, exceedingly variable all the day, with cloudy fine weather. In the morning set all the Sails, could gain little ground however: a Short way from us to the Northward appears by the Blink a deep sinuosity of the Ice where the pack besides us here seem to change into Streams & favourable fishing Ice. I regretted to remain <u>unemployed</u> in the way of Fishing in such charming weather & took great pains to obtain this bight of Ice, the wind however being adverse & so variable, we gained but small advantage by all our endeavours. 10 Ships in sight, several ['Finish making off. 57 Casks. Rules for reducing Butts of Blubber to Tons of Oil' *in margin*] of which being favoured by the wind & a fresher breeze than us came up with & even passed us. At 6 am. finished making off, having filled Casks as follows; viz, 38 of 252 Gallons or Tons; 8 of 300; 2 of 400; & 9 of 200 Gallons equal to about 115 Butts of Blubber. Several different methods of calculation or proportion are made use of for ascertaining the quantity of oil a certain number of Butts will produce: this must depend on the quality or richness of the Blubber, the following scheme I should offer for the different cases met with: – 1st Old Davis's Streight's Fish or those where Blubber is very coarse & the least rich, say 11 Butts = 4 Tons; 2d Best old free Fish of Greenland; 8 Butts to 3 Tons; 3d The finest Blubber of young Fish of Greenland, 5 Butts to 2 Tons. Now 80 Butts according to the 1st proportion would produce: 29¼ Tons; 2d 30 Tons; the 3d 32 Tons.[2]

---

[1] Scoresby did not use this term in his description of birds in *Account of the Arctic Regions*, I, pp. 527–38. This may be another reference to the ivory gull (see journal entry for 12 April 1813).

[2] In *Account of the Arctic Regions*, I, p. 461, Scoresby made the simple statement 'Four tons of blubber by measure, generally afford three tons of oil.' He also noted (p. 461, footnote) that 'The ton or tun of oil is 252 gallons wine measure.' Smyth, *Sailor's Word Book*, defined a 'butt' as 126 gallons wine measure. In a small notebook from 1810 in the Scoresby Papers (WHITM:SCO682), Scoresby created the following table:

English Measures

	Gallon Cub. Inches	Pint Cub. In.	Weight Avoirdu. pound
By the Coal Act	277.183	36.648	10.025
– – Malt Act	268.8	33.6	9.722
Wine Measure	230	28.875	8.354
Ale Measure	282	35.25	10.1995

The 'weight' in the fourth column is presumably that of one gallon.

Thursday 27th of May Lat 77°35′ Lon. 3¼E.
Variable NE.erly. NW.erly, NE.erly very var.
Light airs inclinable to Calm, the Forepart, a moderate breeze after 8 am. very variable however – used all attention to get to the NE.ward along the edge [of?] the Ice laying in about that direction – at 8 Pm. suppose we had got about 25 Miles of Latitude, when I observed the Ice to be slack as far as could be seen from the Mast Head to the W^d & N^d a Ship within laid too. We therefore reached thro' a very cross & close patch of light Ice & in about an hour got into comfortable quarters, where we saw a Fish, the 2^d only since Sunday night last. The 10 or 11 sail of ships in Company with us, remained on the outside of the Ice except the three most lee-wardly which followed us. Plying to windward the rest of the day on the inside of a stream of Ice, or between an extensive stream & the pack edge which lay about 10 miles to the westward of it.

Friday 28th of May Lat 77°45′ Lon. 3°¼E
NE.erly N.erly Variable.
Fresh breezes all this day: charming fine weather – By 8 am we had worked out into the open Sea, no longer finding shelter from a strong E.rly Sea we gained little ground until towards Evening when the wind veered to the N^d[.] A Ship near us got a Fish – we saw two in the Forenoon, had Boats in pursuit of one of them. Since we last made off the Esk proves very lee-wardly when exposed to the least swell on account of being of too light draught of water, to remedy the inconvenience as much as possible we filled about 10 Tons of Casks in the Main Hatch Way, third tier, a vacancy we had left for a Flinch Gut. Four strange Sail in Sight to wind^d the eleven ships in Co. yesterday likewise in sight 8 to lee-ward 3 to windw^d of us. At Mid Night thick Frost Rime. Ther*mome*ter about 18°.

Saturday 29th of May Lat. 78°0′ Lon. 3°15′
NbW Variable
Blowing Fresh with thick weather proceeding From a <u>Frost Rime</u>, apparently not arising from the water but from a <u>Fog inclined</u> cloud as we sometimes see in England. Showers of small snow likewise assailed us ['occasionally' *deleted*] frequently. Making all possible progress to the Northward, tacking occasionally to keep in with the Ice, which in general Shewed to be a close pack. In the Forenoon we met with much small scattered Ice, passed amidst it until noon, when the thick Sky cleared away and exhibited to our surprize upwards of 40 Sail of Ships! Not one of which was Fishing: the John was amongst them, on coming up with her I went on board & heard the following particulars of news: John <u>two</u> Fish, Aimwell, ['Greenland news; loss of the Latona!' *in margin*] Lively, Volunteer, Clean; Henrietta, Resolution: two Fish each: Sarah & Eli*zabe*th 3: Walker, Venerable, Margaret of London, 5 or 6 large Fish each: the Latona wrecked! The casualties of this Ship & her final unfortunate catastrophe are somewhat remarkable. This Ship was one of the Aberdeen fleet laid in the Roads when the Oscar was lost,[1] she likewise drove with her anchor, but providentially brought up scarcely a length from the shore: some time ago she was stove by

---

[1] See journal entry for 2 May 1813.

the Ice, it said twice, the damages were patched up, the late Southerly Gale about Friday or Saturday last in the act of wearing she struck a piece of Ice near the wales[1] in midships, the planks were indented, & shattered like a [broom?], the wound tho' not above three feet square caused the ship to fall over after filling her with water, in less than an hour: the Crew shook the reefs out of the Top-sails & attempted by laying the sails flat aback to the mast, to careen the damage out of the water, but the leak had gained so much on the pumps & brought the ship too deep to effect their purpose: at length she fell over so quickly that the Crew with difficulty saved themselves, leaving behind them all their Chests, beds, & spare clothes. The Volunteer of Whitby & James of Liverpool met with the wreck lying on her broad side; all sails standing or rather set & hanging by the masts: I suppose they plundered everything they could come at – Aberdeen sent 14 ships out for the Fishery two are already lost![2] After hearing the news we worked to wind^d some miles but seeing no Fish & the Ice becoming very close, and dangerously navigable we reached out by the wind to the WSW amongst sailing Ice about 20 Miles, where so far to wind^d that the Ice assumed the appearance of a pack we saw a few Whales, had three Boats in chase but all returned unsuccessful: the John got a Fish – at Mid N^t Thermometer 16° thick Frost rime.

Sunday 30th of May
NW.erly W.erly Var
Little wind inclinable to Calm all this day. We shifted our ground very little, and saw but two or three Fish – The Volunteer & another ship flinching to lee-ward. Many ships in sight: Aimwell in Company. Weather fine, Thermometer 16° to 22°.

Monday 31st May Lat 77°41′+ Lon 3½E
Werly SW.erly & S.erly
Soon after Mid-Night being within Sight of the Latona's wreck, & wanting old rope for the purpose of making spun yarn [nittles?][3] &c of which useful articles we have not a bit, we reached towards it & moored to it whilst the Aimwell laid it alongside & hove it nearly upright – we got one side of the Fore top Mast & lower rigging, several pieces of stays, small ropes, blocks; 3 or 4 Ice anchors, 3 Ice axes, 2 Ice Grapnels, a cask of thin treacle, 20 feet of the Foremast, an old stick; some Gumming knives, &c, &c, we likewise saved several articles of Cloathing, bedding, &c. which we gave to a man present ['Save some articles from the wreck' *in margin*] who had belonged the vessel & knew the rightful owners. The Aimwell got a hundred articles; saved several Chests which were freely delivered up to their original proprietors. When the wreck was first met with by the Volunteer & James, she might easily have

---

[1] Smyth, *Sailor's Word Book*, s.v.: 'Strong planks extending all along the outward timbers on a ship's side, a little above her water-line.'

[2] The contemporary printed list of 13 ships from Aberdeen included the *Latona* but omitted the *Oscar*, presumably because she was wrecked at the very outset of her voyage. Lubbock, *Arctic Whalers*, p. 194, erroneously recorded the *Latona* as having been wrecked 'in Davis Straits'.

[3] Presumably what Smyth, *Sailor's Word Book*, terms 'nippers': 'NIPPERS. Are formed of clean, unchafed yarns, drawn from condemned rope, unlaid … .[U]sed in various ways, viz. to bind the messenger to the cable, and to form slings for wet spars, &c.' See also journal entry for 27 July 1813.

been saved, the wound was quite dry they could have closed it in two hours, they then might have hove her up by cutting the Topmast away at any rate, if not without; the hatches might then have been secured, the Cabin windows rather lifted & the water pumped out. I have not the least doubt but two ships might have done all this in 30 or 40 hours, might have saved a ship! This 30 or 40 hours might have been no loss or detriments to the Ships so humanely engaged, although it might have been otherwise.

Mr Johnstone informed me of the particulars of the Separation of 14 of the Volunteers Crew from their Ship:[1] on the commencement of the heavy Gale May the 11th these men left the Ship to ['make' *deleted*] ['Separation of 14 Men from the Volunteer' *in margin*] set an anchor in a large piece of Ice whereby to hang the Ship, the Sails were clewed up, & the ship moored; in a few minutes however, the anchor flew out & the ship was adrift, the sails were [again?] set, the Ship reached about 2 miles to the Eastward & having attempted to wear her, she refused after running near 2 miles to lee-ward they reached out to Sea & left the men! The Thermometer was at 15 or 16° & these poor wretches left upon the Ice with a single Boat for their conveyance, which Boat on account of the high Sea could not attempt to follow the ship.

A division now took place amongst the party, death stared them in the face wherever they turned, some were for remaining by the Ice, but here the Ice could afford no shelter from the extreme Cold & would probably soon be broken to pieces by the inchoative swell, the rest were for attempting to row to the Ship, but here likewise death seemed inevitable, the Boat could not live with so many men on board, & what added to their distress the Ship was already out of sight – they at length however determined to attempt to row to the Ship, judging that by remaining where they were, death was but ['Providential escape' *in margin*] prolonged for a short time as the cold must speedily, benumb their faculties & sleep overcome the remains of animation, 'twas better to risk being drowned than to be starved, to be frozen without resource: poor souls what must have been their sensations, a premature dissolution seeming inevitable, & the sparks of life yet remaining lighting but a feeble flame – they tried to row, found the plan utterly unfeasible & attempted to return to the Ice. How great must have been their delight when at this critical juncture a Ship hove in sight – oh! How opportune, how extatic the view: they displayed their flag & were observed by the vessel & all taken safely on board the Lively, greeted by their [townsmen?], received by their companions, who were not backward in assisting towards the restoration of their benumbed limbs & congratulating them on their narrow escape, their highly Providential deliverance; oh! God thine eye thy benignant eye cannot behold the distresses of the work thine hands with['out' *deleted*] [unconcern?]; perhaps some of those very men a few hours before were calling down imprecation ['of' *deleted*] upon their own heads or Souls, and themselves impiously unthinkingly invoking their own destruction or the damnation of their fellow Beings – O God thy forbearance is wonderful, ['thy' *deleted*] mercy is thy darling attribute & judgment, severe, just, judgment thy strange work! Oh! That wretched man would consider what he owes to the Sovreign [*sic*] of the World, to that Being in whose hands are both his Body & Soul, & who could annihilate him in a Moment.

[1] See journal entry for 17 May 1813.

That several <u>Foreign</u> Ships are in Greenland this year I was likewise told, Fresh Gales in the Evening with <u>thick Fog</u>, plying to windw^d under all sails in Company with the John. The Fishery this Season proves so critical, so uncertain, & the haunts of the Whales not to be met with, it seems of little moment which way we proceed provided we shift our ground when it becomes deserted by the objects of our search: the appearance of thick Fog with a Temperature of 30° to 32°, is an object far from being grateful: Fog is the most serious obstacle to Fishing which this country presents, dangerous, & highly disagreeable = open seasons are frequently foggy Seasons & often prove [sky?] <u>Fisheries</u> = appearances just now are not by any means so favourable as we could wish – Several Ships were in sight at noon but at mid n^t we had distanced all the Fleet except the John & an other supposed to be the Capham.[1] At Mid Night we reached in with the Ice the Fog cleared away when we came close to the edge found no shelter from the Sea, nor opening that was at all feasible. The rigging covered with transparent Ice from the moisture of the Fog congealing on its application to any solid substance.

Tuesday 1st of June Lat 77°25′ Lon. 5°0′E
SbW or SSW
Strong Gales the Fore part, accompanied with thick Fog, showers of sleet or <u>pure Rain</u>! Towards mid night Calm, still thick weather. We reached to a considerable distance from the Ice to determine whether the Whales were more plentiful in the Clear Sea than at the edge of the Ice; we did not see one however. The water which near the Ice was of a deep Olive Green Colour, very opaque & highly favourable for whale Hunting, was here of a transparent Blue. Several Seals seen. Ther. 32°[-?]30.

Wednesday 2^d of June Lat 78°14′+ Lon. 4°50′E
Calm NNW Calm.
About 2 am. a Breeze of wind sprang up from the NNW to NWbN, the Fog likewise began to thin away, having seen no whales during our traversing towards the South we made all sail by the wind to the NE.ward ['excep' *deleted*] expecting to fetch in with some point of the Ice extending far into the Sea. At Noon we saw a strong blink of Ice & soon afterwards the substance, of which this was the Reflection, was visible from the Mast Head: a Fish likewise made its appearance & as we reached towards the Ice saw others; one of our Harponeers struck at a large Whale, a <u>Fall was called</u>, but it proved, unfortunately, a false alarm, the Harpoon had not penetrated deep enough to secure its hold, on account of the Fish in the act of sinking, having twisted itself in an unfavourable position. The Ice by which we lay proved to be a slender point extending from the Main Body near ten Leagues into the Sea in a SE.erly direction: its breadth as shewn by the <u>blink</u> could not exceed 15 miles: at the extremity of the point we saw different Whales, had three Boats in full chase; my Father likewise was equally active & equally unsuccessful. Calm towards Mid N^t The place where we saw the Wreck of the Latona we judge to lay about 30 miles west of us. At 12 Night Lat. Observed 78°25′N Weather fine, cloudy or Showers of Snow.

[1] *Sic.* The *Clapham* of Hull presumably intended.

Thursday 3ᵈ of June Lat 78°31′ Lon 5°10′E
S.erly SSW to West.

Little wind, variable, inclinable to Calm, thick Snow Showers about 2 Pm. We run along the edge of the Ice round the point, NE, North, & NW saw several Fish early in the morning, but found them more scarce as we proceeded. At 4 Pm. we had obtained a deep sinuosity laying farthest westerly of any within sight, here although appearances were so favourable, not a Fish was to be seen. Lay too. Upwards of 20 Sail of Ships made their appearance to lee-ward, most of them plying towards us under all Sails – we spoke the Neptune of London with one Fish, gives an account of the Margaret of London having 5; Sisters Clean, Aurora Sadler 7 or 8, Neptune of Aberdeen 5, & of ['three' *deleted*] two Hamburghers ['all' *deleted*] both Clean; who bring news of the Fall of Hamburgh under the attack of the Russians, the Death of <u>Murat</u> in its defence & some other political news which as it is not altogether to be depended on I will not take the trouble to insert here.[1]

The Neptune has lately been as far north as Lat. 80°15′ found firm Ice to [the Wᵈ?] but an open Sea to the NEwards the Ice laid very near the Land & no fish!

The Foreland in Sight to the Eastward of us about 50 Miles Distant.

Friday 4ᵗʰ of June Lat 78°45′ Lon. 5°0′E
Easterly Variable

Little wind & very variable all the day, dodging near about the same <u>bight</u> of the Ice into which we yesterday sailed, the pack begins to slack, three ships worked some distance within the edge; snow showers then commencing we were unable to trace their progress. Spoke Several Ships, amongst the rest a Hambro' Brig,[2] heard different statements relative to the situation of the northernmost Ice; Robinson[3] says much water lies to the NEᵈ and Nᵈ of the Head Land, that he sailed NW 40 miles from this part of Spitzbergen, others affirm that the Ice lies close to the land & affords no passage, that the Sea is not navigable so far as 80°. Robinson must be correct, he could not [well be deceived?] . Whales are so difficult to be met with that the ablest Commanders are at a loss how to proceed, the prospect at present is certainly bad; Some suppose Fish may be found round the Head Land. Robinson says not; and all agree that there are no Fish along the edge of the Ice to the Northward. The wind have been lately & indeed, most of the [past?] part of the Season highly unfavourable for the Fishery, having generally had a tendency to pack the Ice which prevents us from penetrating to explore the Common haunts of the Whales: I firmly believe that

---

[1] Scoresby was right to be doubtful. Hamburg, occupied by the French since 1806, had been abandoned by them without a fight on 12 March 1813 following reports of the approach of Russian troops. The town was then occupied by a detachment of Cossacks until the end of May when Marshal Davout retook the town and eventually surrendered it only after the fall of Napoleon in 1814. Leipzig did fall in the crucial Battle of the Nations, but not until October 1813. Joachim Murat, Napoleon's brother-in-law, took part in the Russian campaign, and the Leipzig battle; he was executed in Italy in 1815.

[2] *OED*, in defining the 'hamber-line', gives 'hambro' as an alternative spelling, and considers both as corruptions of 'hamburgh', i.e. Hamburg, Germany. See also Smyth, *Sailor's Word Book*, s.v. 'Hamber, or Hambro'-Line.

[3] *Sic*, but the contemporary printed lists give the *Neptune*'s master in this period as 'Robertson'.

were we 30 or 40 miles within we should have plenty of Room; as we so experienced whilst amongst the Floes a few days back to the Southward. Strong North or Westerly winds we expect would away [*sic*] the loose Ice & expose the edge of the Floes & Fields & it is highly probable would admit us to the presence of the Whales & for such an event then we anxiously wait: at present the wind seems tollerably favourable & already has the Ice been seen to slack. 30 Sail in Sight. Bar. 29.75 stationary.

Saturday 5ᵗʰ of June Lat 78°48′ 4°0′E
WSW, SW, SSW
Early in the day we had thick <u>Rimy</u> weather, a Fresh breeze & clear sky prevailed afterwards until 6 Pm. when a thick Fog Commenced. Anxious to ascertain whether the Ice was penetrable up to <u>Fishing ground</u>, under all sails we plyed to the Westward, at first amongst open Ice, but laterally[1] surrounded by hundreds of pieces laying very near each other & at the best affording but a difficult & dangerous navigation: ['the ship' *inserted above the line*] we received two or three heavy blows from the Ice, when circumstances occurred preventing all possibility of steering clear of the pieces. At 2 am. the Ice closed around us & we could proceed no farther, being in the vicinity of a small but heavy Floe we made fast to it together with 6 or 7 ships accompanying us, the John penetrated somewhat further but at length stopped about two miles from us. The <u>Rose in Bloom</u>,[2] Hamburgh Ship, having started some hours before us found the Ice slacker at that time & sailed 8 or 10 miles from us; To the South we can perceive the Seas suppose near that <u>Bay</u> where we left the <u>Wreck</u> of the Latona, on the NW hand are seen many Floes of various dimensions & quality. 9 Ships in sight in the Sea water, 4 to the westward far distant & upwards of 20 near us or attempting to come at our situation. In the Evening a thick Fog commenced: the wind southering, set the Ice about us & partly beset us. At 8 pm. Thermometer 35°. Bar. 29.80 Inches.

Sunday 6ᵗʰ of June Lat 78°41′+ Lon. 4°E
South
Fresh Gales, with thick Fog in the Morning, snow showers afterwards. About noon we could see a very large & clear space of water to windward, extending far westward but inaccessible to us. At 4 Pm. the loose Ice slacked on all sides of the Floe to which we lay moored, and a very difficult Communication appeared on the East side of the Floe, between us & the above noticed break of the Ice, we cast off, & made sail, found the Ice to set down upon us so rapidly in the small opening formed between the Floe & a close pack to the Eᵈ, that it was with the greatest attention & difficulty that we gained about a mile in four hours, frequently tacking every five minutes; at one time we had not room to give the Ship velocity enough to tack, had to strike a piece of Ice on the lee-bow to heave her about which produced the desired effect, without this maneuvere [*sic*] we should certainly have been obliged to return drifting to the place from whence we set out; five of the Ships out of 8 moored to the

---

[1] *Sic*: 'latterly' presumably intended.
[2] A contemporary printed list of whaling vessels from the Elbe and Weser in 1818 (Scoresby Papers, WHITM: SCO607) included the *Rosenboom* of Hamburg.

same Floe with us, got on the way at the same time & all steered to the westward, two got out shortly after us, but the rest were many miles to lee-ward amongst the Ice at 9 Pm. when we had gained an extensive clear opening where a few Ships lay, having their Boats in pursuit of Whales. The William & Ann, with 2 large Fish, got a third near us to day which in the act of killing upset one of the Boats without however doing the Crew any injury, and producing little inconvenience except a thorough wetting. Two other Fish were got by Ships within sight of us, although partly beset.

Monday 7th of June Lat. 78°46′ Lon. 3°45′E
South SW SbE
Moderate breezes with Snow Showers the Fore part of this day, the latter part Fresh Gales with thick Fog or Rain. Spoke the Royal George with half a Fish still, the Prince of Brazils near with four, two small. The mate of the former tells me, that the Ice to the W^d of us lying about NE & SW is the main pack, that in a Southerly direction, nothing separates us from the Sea but a heavy <u>Sea Stream</u> which keeps off the swell. At 1 am. we ran down into a deep Bight nearly before the wind where we saw several whales, had Boats in pursuit several hours; at length, 7 am, a Fish was struck & I was agreeable aroused from my Bed by the joyous Cry of "a Fall, a Fall." I remember hearing of a <u>landman</u>, who was unacquainted with the forms of the Fishery, being roused from his sound Sleep by this cry, attended with stamping and every other present means that could be used to increase the ['anecdote' *in margin*] noise, jumped out of his bed in the utmost fright, which was nothing abated by seeing every Man seize his Clothes in his hand, spring upon deck, & each seat himself in a Boat, he amongst the rest was wishful to get a place but finding all the Boats occupied & himself refused admittance; he ran too & fro, up & down the deck, crying in the most piteous manner "Will nobody take me in, must I be left here to be drownd. O Dear, O Dear, I will be drowned, I cannot swim!"[1]

The spot where the above Fish was not so favourable as might have been wished; a close patch of Ice lay to windw^d another of a mile's breadth to leew^d much Ice to the westward, & to the Eastward alone was clear water. The entangled Whale after descending about 700 Fathoms took to lee-ward & in about half an hour after being struck made her[2] appearance, near the edge of the patch of Close Ice to lee-ward, through the midst of this it passed, was seen blowing several times. It was not until 10 am. that a second Harpoon was struck after the

['Robt Dowell **M.** N° 6 = 9″5.' *in margin*]

Fish had taken 11 lines or 1320 Fath. from the fast Boat & had made its way Completely through the patch of Ice into a tollerable clear place where two Boats were laying in wait ready to receive it. After this the Fish was speedily dispatched. We made the Ship fast to a small Floe, & began to flinch. At 5 pm. finished: the loose Ice in the interim had so drifted down upon us that by this time we found ourselves beset

---

[1] Scoresby repeated this anecdote in *Account of the Arctic Regions*, II, pp. 243–4.
[2] Scoresby again initially described this whale as female, but the margin entry indicates a male.

in a close pack of heavy Ice, containing many Floes – we however lay very safely & under no apprehension save the danger of the swell breaking through upon us whilst the wind increased to a Strong Gale which was doubtless much heavier without. So long as the Sea Stream before mentioned continues entire we ['shall be in' *deleted*] apprehend little or no danger, but should this stream give way to the force of the Sea, and thereby admit the waves to approach the Ice around us our situation might become highly dangerous. Several ships are in sight beset around us in different directions. ['midnᵗ Bar. 29.80 2 pm. Ther. 44°! *in margin*]

Tuesday 8ᵗʰ of June Lat 78°50′ Lon. 3°40′E
SSE
All this day we had Strong Gales of wind accompanied with Rain, Sleet, or Fog; very disagreeable weather. Ship close beset. A Bear came near us having a very small cub with it. Saw three whales not far distant. About noon we cleared the Hold (close by the Main Mast, fore part) & began to make off. Therm. 35° to 38°. Bar. rising.

Wednesday 9ᵗʰ of June Lat. 78°49′+ Lon. 3°38′
SW.erly
W.erly Calm E.erly Calm Soon after Mid Night the weather shewed signs of amendment, the Fog cleared away, the Rain ceased, & the wind abated. About 4 am. finished the operation of Making off, having filled 21 Casks, 13 whereof were in the ground tier: this completed the lower tier from the Bows to the Main Mast & Second tier, same space except five Casks which remain full of water. Stowed the Casks of the 3ᵈ tier which were removed & filled them with water, as ballast. In the Forenoon we had delightful weather, the wind fell to Calm, the sky cleared, the Sun shone bright & hot. At 8 am. the Thermometer was at 40° & at Noon in the shade 48°! a Temperature higher than I ever recollect of before observing in this Country.[1] The Ice continues close for several miles distant all round us – in a South direction we can see the Sea & much water to the SW, a firm pack every where else. 10 Ships in sight beset – About 15 others under sail, part of them bearing SW & part ENE. Having no employment we put the Harpoon Gun into a Boat & fired it with a string by way of trial, we afterwards repeated the shot several times, by hand, for the purpose of exercising the Harponeers. About [*blank space*] oz. of Double Sealed powder forced a Harpoon of [*blank space*] lbs weight to the distance of 15½ Fathoms dragging along with it a Whale line the whole way. The Gun seemed to act very well, altho' we only put one half of the charge recommended by Wallis of Hull the Maker, having been warned by my Father & others who had made trial according to directions that the charge was far too capacious, had damaged two Boats & endangered the lives of the men who fired the Gun.

About Noon when the Thermometer stood so high, & the Sun shone bright, the reflection of light from the Snow covered Ice was so strong, that for a while it was absolutely intollerable: the eyes could not bear it without the greatest inconvenience

---

[1] The same temperature was recorded by Scoresby on 24 July 1818 at 79°8′N 9°15′E. See *Account of the Arctic Regions*, I, p. 366 and Appendix I.

['Remarkable light' *in margin*]. I never knew the glare of light so oppressive, I could almost as well look on the bright face of the Sun as on the Ice on which he shone: I found great relief from the use of a pair of spectacles with ['having' *deleted*] plain <u>Green Glasses</u>; having provided them for the express purpose of relieving the eyes when exposed to too intense a light.

At Mid Night as well as the whole Evening we had thick Foggy weather. Ice still close. Barometer 30.30 Thermo*mete*r 35°. Three Bears seen.

Thursday 10th of June Lat. 78°50' Lon. 3°40'E
WSW
At 10 am. the thick Fog cleared away & a fresh breeze of wind Commenced; at the same time the <u>Sea water</u> made its appearance scarcely three miles from us to the SE^d of us; during the thick we had set near a large Floe which lay between us & the Sea, we cast off from our piece of Ice & warped with the help of the Sails to a SE direction about half a mile & then moored to the edge of the large Floe, should have proceeded within a Mile of the Water but the Ice closed upon us & stopped our progress. Some ships to the NE^d of us Fishing! 9 Sail beset: the John & several others to the S^d & SW^d of us in the open water, apparently amongst Fish. The Prince of Brazils, & Margaret of Hull, both beset near us, appeared to be <u>careening</u>!

In the Evening the loose Ice cleared away from the edge of the Floe on which we lay, so that within two hours we could have worked to windward under sail, & in one hour more we had not room to turn the Ship! The loose Ice ['drifted' *deleted*] [set?] to the NW^d of us & a very heavy small Floe being likely to endanger us we had to heave a stern about 200 yards & even then it approached us within twenty yards & I believe would have touched the ship had it not been kept off by a piece of heavy Ice laying against the side of the Floe. Our situation was highly dangerous, should we unfortunately have lain in the point of collision & any considerable pressure accompanied the contact, the ship must inevitably have been crushed, as far as possible to Secure ourselves we lashed a piece of Ice of about a Foot in thickness alongside to ease the force of any blow, whilst we hauled a heavy piece to the bows & confined it to the Floe edge that it might take the brunt from the Ship.

[*no break in paragraph of main text in original*]

Friday 11th June Lat 78°50' Lon. 3°44'E
WSW, Calm NW.erly NE.erly
After Mid Night the Floe side was again clear: we warped out of the way of the small heavy Floe & in the morning warped round a point end about 200 Yards to the SW^d & were then stopped by the pressure of loose but very heavy Ice. The weather was at this time foggy, Snow Showers occasionally: on its clearing away about 10 am. the Main Water which yesterday was within three miles of us, was not to be seen from the mast; slack Ice lay to the SE^d of us about 1¼ miles off, between which & our Ship was heavy [Close?] Ice & some Floes. The wind now inclining from the NE or E^d and a large heavy Floe having approached within half a mile of us in an ENE direction we attempted to warp up to it & accomplished our wish after ['in' *deleted*] about four

hours hard labour and moored the Ship to the SE point end distant from slack Ice not a mile, but separated from us by a long Floe & close heavy Ice. Several Ships in sight in the Sea to the E^d, & SE^d of us several running along the edge of the Ice to the SW^d Seven or Eight Sail of ships which yesterday were only about a mile to the W^d of us, have all accomplished their emancipation, the Ice having slacked to the very Floe to which they lay moored & afforded them an['y' *deleted*] easy egress. The Margaret of Hull is now the only companion we have within sight beset. At Mid-Night Ther-m*ometer* 31° Wind a Fresh breeze.

Saturday 12th of June Lat. 78°50′ Lon. 3°40′E
ENE North & NW
About 2 Am. I was informed that the narrow slip of a Floe above noticed was setting towards us, its weathermost end setting along <u>our</u> Floe edge with a great pressure & was at this time within twenty yards of us: when I arose I was alarmed to see the pressure of the Ice break a piece from off the point end near which we lay & lift it upon the closing masses altho' apparently half the weight of our Ship, at the same time the [***] Floe as it pressed towards us was broken in two although at least 200 yards Broad & perhaps 10 or 15 feet in thickness – we hauled the Ship alongside the Ice where at [*sic*] was about 8 feet above the Surface of the Sea, took a towline out astern for the purpose of heaving the Ship clear of any <u>squeeze</u> should we be so unfortunate as to lay in the way – unshipped the Rudder & hung it across the Stern. [There are?] smooth hills of Ice upon the Floe to which we are moored at least 20 feet above the water & some rough hummocks that have been thrown up by mere pressure are elevated more than 30 feet! The wind at this time blew a moderate breeze at NEbE or ENE it afterwards gave us fresh spirits by shifting to the wished for quarter the NW. I should suppose that if any wind can open the Ice this must be the most suitable direction. A thick Fog commenced at 6 am. & on clearing away at 3 Pm. the Main water, that yesterday was navigable within a mile of us & was clear of Ice at about 5 Miles distance, was no longer visible from the Mast Head. The Ice still close around us, slacked at Noon, but afterwards came together again – seems to slack to the SE^d of us, but the openings inaccessible to us, on account of [three?] Floe having drifted from the NE to the SE of us, cutting off our passage from the nearest Water. The strange, unaccountable convolutions of Floes renders our situation highly dangerous: whilst we have room to move the Ship backward or forward a few paces, by a careful watch, under the care of Divine Providence, we may evade the most alarming pressures, but should the Ice close us immoveable we can then make no effort towards the preservation of the ship & can only have confidence in Him who is alone able & willing to save to the uttermost those who put their trust in him and serve him in so far as in them lies. May this powerful Being take us under his charge; then shall we be secure tho' the Earth be shaken to its centre & winds & waves in mad contention rage. Short sighted is Man: he knows not what is for his good – apparent evil sometimes proves a real good, & spiritually often an Eternal advantage. The Lord will deal with us as he sees meet, may we be enabled to cry [under?] very dispensation of his providence, "thy will be done", and with Pope may we be convinced,

All Discords, Harmony not understood,
All partial evil, Universal good:
And, spite of pride, in erring Reason's spite
One truth is clear, Whatever is, is right.[1]

At Mid Night a light breeze of wind accompanyed by thick Fog which fell on the rigging like Frost rime & befringed the windward side of every Rope above an Inch in thickness. Little alteration in the Ice. Shot a young seal in the water.

Sunday 13th of June Lat. 78°48′ Lon. 3°50E.
Calm WbS

The long Floe near us alternately pressed & slacked, but not sufficiently so as to encourage us to venture into the trap until 4 am. when the wind springing up a Fresh breeze at WbS which drifted the loose Ice near us against the weather Side of the Floe where we lay and a heavy Floe to windward seeming rapidly to approach us, obliged us to risque a press of the Floes or encountering certain danger whilst laid alongside of Ice deeper than the Ship's keel (13 f^t): accordingly on the Floes abating their pressure, preceeded by a piece of the Ice broader than the Ship, thereby securing our safety, we forced into the opening & in about two hours got thro' between the points where they overlapped 200 yards; here we found a small vacancy bounded in every direction by Floes, being formed by the contaction of <u>four</u>, to the ESE lay about 300 Y^{ds} of loose Ice closely set together & the mouth of the gap beyond was stopped by a heavy piece of Ice or a small Floe, between which & the Southernmost Sheet lay a few heavy piece [sic] of Ice enduring a severe pressure. Beyond this appeared slack Ice & fewer Floes apparently navigable some miles: this being the only possible outlet we warped by the edge of the South Floe into the E.ern [Corner?] waiting for an abatement of the pressure: in the interval as usual we performed Public worship agreeable to the Forms followed by the Church of England & on its conclusion, found the Floes we wished to pass had slacked: we immediately began to push the pieces of Ice from between the overlapping points some we hove towards the N. of the Ship where we had a little vacant space & the rest we forced out into the more open water. Having completely cleared the way, by removing at length a piece of Ice at least 100 Tons in weight, which we left until the last to prevent the points from closing, we followed it closely by the Ship, dragged forward by 40 Men upon the Ice, we happily got out into sailing Ice & comfortable quarters about 3 Pm. In ten minutes the points were again close! Thus we providentially had egress from a most dangerous & anxious situation; I say providentially because in every movement we made, the places closed which we left & were not observed to slack again, but became highly more dangerous quarters – the first spot we quitted was met by the heavy windward Floe above mentioned in two hours time, & with such a force, that had the ship been there, she must have been crushed to pieces:[2] the last place we quitted became so contracted & its boundaries so effectual that a possibility of emancipation until some very remarkable change was

---

[1] These lines, accurately quoted in the journal, close Epistle 1 of Alexander Pope's 'An Essay on Man' (1734).

[2] The preceding passage, commencing 'Thus we providentially ...' was reproduced, with minor alterations, in Scoresby-Jackson, *Life*, p. 89, together with a full-page 'Plan showing The Situation

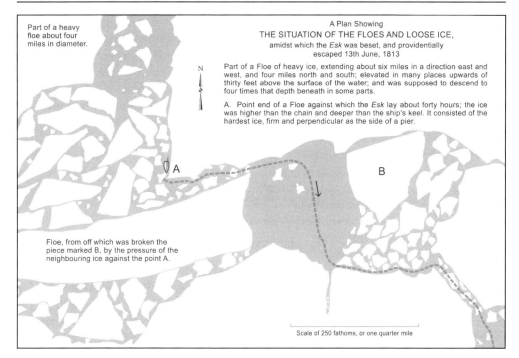

Fig. 5. Ice distribution. This has been redrawn from the illustration facing p. 88 in Scoresby-Jackson's *Life*. That illustration was itself based on the sketch in Scoresby's manuscript autobiography. The format of the linear scale has here been slightly modified. The fact that the track of the *Esk* in the southeastern corner of the map was drawn so as to appear to pass through pieces of ice may indicate that this ice was moving in the same direction as the ship.

entirely set aside. Moved on the SE. side of the ['Easternmost' *deleted*] Southernmost Floe and hung the Rudder: Saw many Narwhales & one running Whale. Several Ships on the outside of the Ice in sight, amongst the rest the John which seemed to have got a Fish at least a Jack was displayed, the signal for being Fast. The Margaret effects an escape.

About 8 Pm. seeing no Fish, the Ice rather closing around us & our sphere of action being contracted to a small space by an impervious body of Ice in every direction except SSW or SW, we cast off & made all sail to the ['East' *deleted*] S^d aiming at the clearest point: we found the Ice exceedingly untoward & so close that in three tacks we did not gain 5 yards of ground – At Mid N^t Saw a Fish: at this time the place we left bore about NE distant 5 or 6 miles. Wind a light breeze.

Monday 14th of June Lat 78°35' Lon. 4°10'E
West, to North, or NNE.
Light airs or moderate breezes. After ['some' *deleted*] much tedious sailing, & some

of the Floes and Loose Ice amidst which the Esk was beset, and providentially escaped 13th June, 1813.' A redrawn version is reproduced here as Fig. 5.

boring we at 6 am. got into slack Ice but heavy – the Sea then made its appearance to the SE^d[.] At the same time saw a great many Whales & although the Boats approached 3 or 4 within 9 yards we could not entangle one. At 10 am. the Ice had closed considerably with the Change of wind, the pieces were very numerous & some large. All the Fish having disappeared we aimed at the Sea to the Eastward & about 3 pm. we had the pleasure of finding ourselves once more in partly unbounded space. Spoke the Earl Piercy with One Fish yet – were informed thereby that the week wherin we have been beset has been the best Fishery the whole Season, several Ships having got 2 some three or more Fish. The John to lee-ward got a Fish about Noon. The edge of the loose pack which we have quitted lies North & South: about 6 miles to Windward it trends more Easterly & finally turns down to the SE thereby forming a semi-round bay, the Ice to the E^d of us is slack & only a few miles broad, the northern boundary appears to be a firm body of Ice. Here then is a likely place for Fish: judging so we made

['John Trueman **M.**   N° 7 = 9 ..5' *in margin*]

all sail & at 8 pm. had worked to the top of the bight as far as we could get. a large Floe being near us separated only by a Stream of Ice too close to be sailed through, bearing from us W. to North, I saw no Fish near it, however fortunately sent two Boats off towards it at a venture, they had scarcely got to the edge of it before one of them struck a Fish. We observed several holes in the Floe & in these the Fish found unmolested rest to breath, our men passed over the Ice & disturbed its repose by the plunge of a lance. In about 3 hours time it made its appearance at the Floe [**Tuesday 15**^th **of June** Lat 78°26' Lon. 4°E. North. to NNE.' *in margin*] edge & a second Harpoon was struck & in half an hour or less the Capture was complete. By this time the Stream of Ice which before opposed us had slacked & cleared the edge of the Floe to a considerable extent, we worked the ship through made fast to the Ice & began to Flinch. The Earl Piercy got a Fish near us, several others were seen. Having freed the whale of its covering of adipose matter, gave the remnant as Food for Sharks[1] & Bears. at 5 am. with a moderate breeze of wind a thick Fog commenced. At 8 am. of a sudden we found ourselves completely surrounded with Ice, the Fog prevented us seeing more than 100 yards: we cast off, made sail & after boring, drifting, sailing, warping, & towing about two hours amongst heavy drift Ice we were happy in procuring our extrication. Several Ships which moored to the Floe beside us gave us the following news. That the Old Manchester[2] of Hull having come out late fell in with whales very numerous on her arrival near Cherry Island, she there got four of large size in a very short time, then left the place! and came to the Northward

[1] Scoresby commented in *Account of the Arctic Regions*, I, pp. 538–40, that the Greenland shark had not previously been described. The Latin name he gave, *Squalus borealis*, has now been superseded by *Somniosus microcephalus*. Scoresby remarked that 'Though the whale-fishers frequently slip into the water where sharks abound, there has been no instance that I have heard of, of their ever having been attacked by the shark.' This is apparently due in part to its sluggish or lethargic behaviour, but more because in summer it normally lives at depths of 200 to 700m (Canadian Shark Research Laboratory, on-line).

[2] See note to journal entry 1 June 1811.

about a week ago where seeing no Fish & a bad prospect, she returned again to Cherry Island accompanied by several ships. This Manchester brings news from England up to the 3ᵈ of May I believe. On the 10ᵗʰ of June I remarked thus, "Some ships to the NEᵈ fishing["] Those ships were the James of Liverpool, Henrietta, & Resolution of Whitby & Sarah & Eliza*beth* of Hull. The James (the source of our intelligence) sent all his boats away at the time I saw him & each Boat brought a small Fish! Mʳ Clough never saw Fish more plentiful. He got 9 in that place which made his amount 14 whereof 2 only were size: calculated not more than 60 Tons. The Henrietta last Friday had 7 Resolution 3 & Sarah & Eliza*beth* 5.

At Noon the Fog cleared away & I observed the water of the bight in which we the preceeding day worked up to the Nᵈ several miles to the westward with a considerable deal of Ice between it & us, we made sail towards it & altho' the Fog recommenced we found our way out & lay too when we had reached the edge of a Floe lying on the west side of the opening & which Floe bore South of us 4 miles off when we got the last Fish. At 4 Pm. the wind increased to

['Thoˢ Wilburn F.   Nᵒ 8 = 9ᶠᵗ..11ⁱⁿ' *in margin*]

a Fresh breeze & the Fog became attenuated: saw a Fish & afterwards 3 or 4 more amongst loose Ice bordering the Main body of west Ice of which the Floe mentioned was a part: the clear water we found here yesterday was now covered, though openly, with pieces of loose Ice. At 6 Pm. we enjoyed "a Fall" and having moored the Floe at 8 pm. received a fine whale alongside of the Ship. A heavy piece of Ice set towards the Floe having a rapid motion that was likely to bring some troublesome Ice about us, we seized the drift piece & let the Floe slip: – started the 10 tons of water we filled 9ᵗʰ of June, took the Casks out & put the Blubber of the Fish in the vacancy as we flinched – At Mid Night thick weather – 20 Sail in Sight all to lee-ward except two.

Wednesday 16ᵗʰ of June Lat 78°20′ Lon. 3°50′E
NNE or Calm
Fine cloudy weather. Therm. 8 Am. 38° Bar. 30.10 Inches – Wind light breeze. At 11 am. got under way – a crooked piece of wood was sticking up from the surface of the piece of Ice we quitted, firmly frozen to the firm Ice: we cut it away. Slack Ice laying between us & the Main body in a NNW direction made sail by the wind & worked up therin, as we approached the Main Ice saw a Fish sent two Boats in pursuit whereby this or another whale was struck. She ran out [*blank space*] lines, remained beneath the surface 35['o' *deleted*] Minutes & then received a Secon*d* Harpoon[.] in less than an hour more she was killed. Our success these three days in the Fishery has been remarkable, one Fish only has been killed near us tho' 8 or 10 ships constantly lay within 2 or 3 miles of us: it is true we have each time been a single Ship, that is we have always been first to the place where the Fish were found, yet had not Providence particularly blessed our endeavours such unbounded success could not have been dreamt of – "Surely the Lord is on our side."[1] And yet why should the Almighty God

[1] A paraphrase of the repeated phrase in Psalms 124:1–3: 'If it had not been the Lord who was on our side'.

take any regard of the secular concerns of his Creation, concerns which have no relation to good or evil?

['John Dunbar **M.** ⬯⬯⬯ N° 9 = 8 ..7' *in margin*]

It seems more than we have a right to expect, nevertheless, it is beyond a doubt the case. May we alway be aware of the Mercies of God, may His Spirit teach us suitable gratitude and sancify [*sic*] every instance of the goodness of the Lord.

Calm the rest of the day: Fog showers – Several Fish seen: Made the Ship fast to a Heavy piece of Ice. 20 Sail of Ships in sight.

Thursday 17th of June Lat 78°10' Lon. 3°45'E.
Calm, NNE. NE to North.

In the Morning a Fresh Gale of wind commenced, attended with Snow Showers. Saw several Fish at 8 Am. It seems the Harpoon Gun which should have got us a Fish was the means of losing one. R. Dowell having struck a fine whale with a heave of the hand Harpoon when meeting her, the Gun Foreganger running beneath the Boat's bottom was suddenly checked when became tight from the Harpoon in the Gun & although the Gun was turned with Mussel downwards the Harpoon did not slip out so that when the line pulled it, at right angles, the Harpoon was <u>bent</u> in the Gun & the resistance offered by it drew the Harpoon out of the Fish! The John passed us at 8am. with 9 Fish 80–90 Tons of Oil. A <u>vast</u> of water appears to the westw[d] apparently [formed?] by the edge of a Field: the John sailed towards it & after about an hours boring got into it & lay too – our Ship broke adrift at 9 am. by the Anchor tearing away the Ice to which it was fast, (not being very firm): very narrowly escaped striking a heavy piece of Ice with her Rudder as she went astern, might have been productive of very serious consequences:– We now made sail, being about to cast off before the accident, after two or three tacks we reached to the Westw[d] meaning to join Co. with the John, whose <u>Jack</u> was displayed while we were yet about 4 Miles off:– <u>bored</u> through a patch [of?] Ice & reached up to the edge of the Field – By this time the John had killed two Fish & was fast to two more: we saw but one. The Neptune of Aberdeen got one & struck another before we arrived & the Earl Piercy struck one afterwards. I soon observed the extensive water which was here two hours before, to be rapidly Closing, a body of Floes was drifting down the edge of the Field, at the rate of at least three knotts p hours: I never was more astonished: we had not been an hour at rest before we made sail to the Eastern part of the vacancy wishing to get out again: we passed between a Floe & some drift Ice which actually closed as fast as the Ship sailed, in a Minute they ['it' *deleted*] were [in?] close contact: the drift Ice disturbed the water over which it passed, filling it with <u>eddies</u> like a Strong tide in shallow water.[1] In a few minutes the John was beset, & the two Ships entangled with

---

[1] In *Account of the Arctic Regions*, II, pp. 343–6, Scoresby gave a detailed account of these events, under the heading 'Dangers arising from Ice, when Boats are enclosed and beset, and their Crews thus prevented from joining their Ships.' He described the behaviour of the ice as follows: 'The sea was as smooth as the surface of a pond; but the ice, I observed, was in a strange state of disturbance. Some floes, and some large pieces, moved with a velocity of three or four miles *per* hour, while other similar

Fish, ['were' *deleted*] had above a Mile of packed Ice between them & their Boats. We likewise left a Boat behind us which I had sent after the John offering assistance if it was needed as no Fish were to be seen: the Boat was not halfway before I hoisted signals to re-call it, the Ice closed as fast as they rowed & they with difficulty extricated them selves. We now entered the same patch of Ice we had awhile before so eagerly passed through, found it much closed, were three hours hard <u>boring</u>, whereby the Ship received some severe blows, before we got through. The Ice in every direction except from SW, to NW appears open but consisting of heavy piece [*sic*] & laying very unfavourably for sailing, or as the Greenlanders term it <u>lying very cross</u>. We worked a little to windward with some trouble, saw several Fish had three Boats in pursuit, but were unsuccessful. At Mid N^t fine cloudy w*eathe*r wind a fresh breeze. Therm*omete*r 35° . 8 Sail in Sight.

Friday 18th of June Lat 78°04' Lon. 3°58'E
North NNW

['John Trueman F.   N° 10 = 6..4' *in margin*]

Fresh or moderate breezes, fine cloudy w*eathe*r Snow Showers occasionally. Having worked about four Miles to the N^d we got a Fish – <u>She</u> remained 30 Minutes down after being struck, then 10 minutes, & was afterwards speedily killed. Moored to a small Floe to flinch: A Ship to windw^d beset – The Neptune & Earl Piercy have still their <u>Jacks</u> flying but whether they have yet received their Boats on board or are making a Success-ful fishing I cannot say. At 6 pm. the wind shewed Signs of increase & afterwards blew a strong Gale, accompanied with thick Showers of Snow. Our situation amidst so much Ice lying highly unfavourable for Navigating, would be particularly dangerous in bad weather; to better ourselves therefore we made all Sail to the NE^d steering various courses accordingly as the Ice laid more open, we sailed about 20 miles without tacking, having passed through much loose Ice & Floes. At 10 Pm. we saw three Ships made fast to windw^d of us, worked up towards them & found more room as we proceeded until we came into a fine navigable space; bounded on the W. by open Ice & Floes, likewise to the SW, & South; on the SE & E by a heavy Floe, on the North & NW by an apparently firm body of Floes. At Mid N^t Therm*omete*r 32°. Barom*ete*r 29.83 In. 8 Sail in Sight.

Saturday 19th of June Lat 78°20' Lon. 4°5'E.
NNW
Strong Gales, with almost Constant Snow, or Sleet. Lay too when we came to the weather Ice. I was surprized & highly gratified by the receipt of a Letter from my affectionate wife dated May the first, brought by the Perseverance of Hull,[1] which ship having been frozen up in the Baltic could not sail before the 7th of May! has now two Fish. I was rejoiced to hear of the continued good health of my dear Mrs S. to

---

masses were at rest. Some sheets of ice, though quite detached from the main body, moved towards the south, as it were by magic, and with such a degree of rapidity, that they left traces in the water over which they passed, resembling the eddies produced by a strong current in a shallow river.'
  [1] 244 tons, Captain James Hunter: Credland, *Hull Whaling Trade*, pp. 126, 137.

peruse her varied protestations of unalterable Love & increasing tenderness: on the other hand the indisposition of our Son was a cause of sincere regret – I trust God will spare him.

Spoke the William & Ann with 6 Fish about 50 Tons; Volunteer 4 Fish; & Richard[1] 11 Fish. Plying about, two miles from the windward Ice, saw two Fish sent away two

['John Dunbar **M.**   N° 11= 9..5' *in margin*]

Boats one of which soon got fast to one of them, that was playing near some pieces of Ice. It ran out 11½ Lines after [staving?][2] the fast Boat, appeared in about 56 minutes, at least a mile to windw^d of the fast Boat, having sent a Boat in that direction, the Whale presently received a Second Harpoon, dived 300 yards & died down without a lance although 9½ feet Bone. Flinched drifting to lee-ward all sails clewed up. Fog Showers at MidN^t. 50 Sail in Sight.

Sunday 20th of June Lat. 78°4' Lon. 4°5'E.
NNE to NNW
Strong to Fresh Gales with frequent Showers of Snow. We completed the flinching operation in 2½ hours with ⅔^ds of our Crew, that is we took all the Blubber, about 35 Butts & ¾ Ton of Whalebone within this time, from the Carcase of the Whale. At 2 Am. made sail & worked up to the Boats which were engaged getting the Lines in. The Ice closing around us at 2Pm. accompanied by several Ships ran to leeward a few miles & then hauled out by the wind to the E^d amongst Floes & loose Ice. From different Ships we spoke we had the following melancholy intelligence. The Laurel of Hull last Thursday (the day the John got beset, remarkable for the amazing velocity of the Ice) which within Sight of us it seems was caught between two Floes running as fast as the Ship could sail, the sheets of Ice made no stop at the ['Disasterous Events.' *in margin*] Ship but in a moment severed her in two pieces: all the Crew were I believe saved.[3] On the same day I remarked that the Neptune of Aberdeen & Earl Piercy of Kirkaldy both entangled with Fish were separated from their Boats: I am now informed that what we took to be their Jacks displayed on Friday was their Ancients in distress: the former Ship having lost ['her' *deleted*] five Boats with the Master & all the Crew except a young Second mate & 11 or 12 Men four only of whom are sailors: the latter lost (at least for the present) two Boats & Crews: On Friday Evening, they both came away to the Eastward leaving men & Boats behind the Ships being no longer safe in that situation: the Boats were not far from the John it may

---

[1] Hull whaler, 304 tons, Captain William Hurst, loc. cit.

[2] Smyth, *Sailor's Word Book*: 'STAVE, To. To break a hole in any vessel.'

[3] 'The *Laurel* of Hull was wrecked in the ice at Greenland': Lubbock, *Arctic Whalers*, p. 194. That is consistent with Scoresby's journal. Credland (*Hull Whaling Trade*, p. 125) listed two ships of this name, *Laurel I*, 286 tons, sailing from Hull from 1809 until 'Lost at the fishery 1830' and *Laurel II*, for which the only information is '1812–14'. The contemporary printed list for 1813 indicates two vessels of that name sailing from Hull, one under Captain Harper to Davis Strait, the other under Captain Blenkinsop to the Greenland Sea. In the copy of this list in the Scoresby Papers, a manuscript note beside the latter vessel states 'wrecked'.

therefore be confidently expected they would all reach her in safety. I sincerely trust she will be secure & [firmly?] hope the Father of Mercies will take my Parent & his Crew under his immediate protection: I am exceedingly anxious about him. O God grant him thy ready help, [***] every danger, & favour his exertions that he may be enabled to make ['his' *deleted*] a speedy escape: may he feel more his dependence on thee & may every trial be sanctified to his Eternal Welfare.

['*vide 7ᵗʰ of July' *in margin*] *¹It is reported that the Royal Bounty of Leith is lost with all hands! I hope it is not true. Merciful God prevent us in all our doings from [running?] into the Snares which would swallow us – uphold us with thy Mighty Arm – & preserve us from all dangers.

Spoke the Aimwell with 6 Fish 60 Tons of Oil, informs us the Gilder,² Walker, & Elizabeth (of London) near full. Resolution (Whitby) 7 Fish, Henrietta 4 = 35 Tons, &c, &c, &c. At Mid Night we found ourselves in very open Ice, scattered patches & streams; near 30 Sail in Sight, many near us. Aimwell & Dexterity in Co.

Monday 21ˢᵗ of June Lat. 78°2′+ Lon. 4°40′E.
NNW W.erly, SSW
Light winds the Fore part, about Noon thick Fog, afterwards a Fresh Gale with Fog Showers. Steered to the NE until we came to the extremity of a deep <u>bight</u> of the Ice, Saw no Fish; the Ice slack but lying cross to the Westwᵈ – not navigable to the Nᵈ & scarcely so to the Eᵈ we had to ply to windwᵈ two hours, then continued our reach to the SEᵈ by the wind in much water, wherin ware [*sic*] disseminated streams, & drift Ice with some small Floes. After sailing about 30 miles, at mid nᵗ we came to the Sea edge. Lay too within the Sea Stream. About 20 Ships in Sight, some plying to windwᵈ others laying too. Barometer 30.00 Inches. Several Seals Seen resting themselves on the Sea Stream.

Tuesday 22ᵈ of June Lat 78°12′+ Lon. 6°E
SWbS. to SSW
Fresh Gales all the day, Fog Showers occasionally. Killed Six Seals, a great many were seen but were difficult to take. At 10·am. being out at Sea, made sail to the NEᵈ along the edge of the Ice. At 2 Pm, saw a Fish, hauled under a jutting point, discovered much water within side the Ice, sailed in by the wind amidst a quantity of loose Ice & streams, made a few tacks & then reached near 10 miles to the Wᵈ: fell in with Floes & ample water: saw only One Fish which was pursued by two Boats near two hours. The Aimwell, Dexterity & another ship following us. 7 Sail lay too on the outside. About Mid Night reached to the westwᵈ under the lee of a flat Floe where we saw several Fish, had three Boats [**Wednesday 23ᵈ of June** Lat 78°30′N Lon. 6¼°E SSW to SbE *in margin*] in chase & had several good chances, ['although' *deleted*] but they proved unsuccessful. The Floes exhibited rapid movements, the loose Ice drifted or rather sailed with full two knotts velocity in an East direction, apparently impelled by a strong upper Current. In some places a strong Rippling of the water was seen; & the

---

¹ It seems that the asterisk and marginal note, together with the corresponding asterisk in the main text, were inserted after the transcript had been made.
² Hull whaler, 360 tons: Credland, *Hull Whaling Trade*, p. 123. The name is spelled correctly here, but as 'Guilder' later in the journal.

surface passed over by the drift Ice was marked by strong eddies similar in appearance to those formed by rapid tides over rocky ground in shallow water. A space of clear water containing at least 40 square miles, was within four hours time reduced to one third the surface. Considering the situation dangerous, and observing much Room to the W^d of us, we plyed a little to wind^d then reached a few miles west amongst a quantity of loose Ice, during a thick Fog, found our progress stopped by a close stream, where a loud [dashing?] noise heard indicated the proximity of the open Sea. Remained here during the Morning – at Noon we had less wind; on the Fog clearing away we discovered the Sea close by us: bored thro' the Stream in a narrow spot, reached a little to the westw^d then lay too. A deep sinuosity to lee-ward of us, wherin lay three Ships, one of them in the act of Flinching. Saw two or three Fish. Several Ships in sight, some of them making off. In the Evening we had again thick ['The Aimwell being short of Bread lent them [our?]'180 Gallon Casks filled with that indispensible Blessing of God' in margin] Fog, attended with little wind. Began to clear the after Hold for making, observing the Blubber begins to waste, shewn by the Oily water drawn up by the Pumps.

Thursday 24th of June Lat. 78°26' Lon. 5°55'E.
SbE to SW.
The disasterous effects occasioned by the rapid motion of the Ice, or the winds & Ice combined, have not of late Years been equalled. Of Ships known to be stove most, of them severely, we have the following list, Royal George, Prince of Brazils, Venerable,[2] Sarah & Elizabeth, Margaret of Hull – wrecked, the Latona, Laurel, & the Thornton ['Losses & accidents' in margin] people affirm, that in one day they saw four wrecks!*[3] The Margaret of Hull ['*a mistake: vide 26th June.' in margin] about the time the John got beset, saw a Ship far in amongst the Ice to the westw^d with only lower Masts & Bowsprit standing! A Brig said to be the Perseverance[4] was seen many miles NW of the John & a Ship suppose the Sisters of Hull[5] we saw closely beset bearing North from us Sunday last. The damages sustained during the passage by ships contending for the Davis's Streights, are not calculable. The Dexterity lost Foremast, Bowsprit & Main yard, the London lost Main Yard, James of Whitby: rudder & other damages, with many more Casualties too numerous to insert here, indeed I cannot recollect the half of the disasters which have been related by different persons. The news current of a more favourable character, represents the Guilder, & Walker of Hull & Elizabeth of London as nearly full. The Augusta, Margaret (London) & several others as being far forward. We are likewise told that the Neptunes 5 Boats &

---

[1] Perhaps a transcription error for 'four', but that reading is not possible in the transcript.
[2] Hull whaling bark, 328 tons, Captain John Bennett: Credland, *Hull Whaling Trade*, pp. 128, 135.
[3] Another asterisk and marginal note evidently added later, when accurate information became available. The rumour about the loss of the Thornton was also incorrect; Credland (ibid. p. 126) listed her as continuing whaling until she was lost in 1821.
[4] According to the contemporary printed list there were two vessels of that name in the Greenland Sea in 1813: from Hull (Captain Hunter) and Peterhead (Captain Penny). Credland (ibid., p. 126) listed the Hull whaler as a bark, so this probably refers to the Peterhead whaler.
[5] 303 tons, Captain Richard Marshall: Credland, *Hull Whaling Trade*, pp. 126, 138.

Crews, left the John (where they had taken refuge) when no Ship could be seen from the Mast Head; they fell in with the Thornton & were by her conducted to their own vessel. Happy function!

We had light winds all day, mostly thick Fog, lying near the same spot a Short distance from Ice in every direction except from SSW to SSE. Saw three or four Fish: the Hercules captured one of them. Employed making off: completed two tiers fore & aft by Mid Night, wherin are contained [*blank space*] Casks. Several Ships in sight. Barometer 30.03. Therm. 35°-39°[.] Aimwell in Co.

Friday 25th of June Lat 78°20′ Lon. 5°46′E
SW to West
Light or Moderate Breezes; the latter part constant thick Fog, the Fore part Cloudy with Fog showers. At 4 Am. finished making off, filled Casks, as viz, 5 of 300 Gallons 27 of 252; 15 of 200; 11 of 180; 8 of 160; & 17 of 126 Gallons, containing 132 Butts of Blubber = about 48 Tons of Oil.

Plying all day to Windward to get out of a bight at least 30 miles deep, from 10 to 1¼ miles wide & lying in a direction SW & NE.[1] Expect the Sea on the outside of the bight to the SW^d Entered some scattered Ice on the Sides as we worked up, in search of Fish, but saw not one. The Aimwell got one early in the Morning. In the afternoon Rigged Fore & Mizen Royal Masts & the Flying Jib-boom. At Noon 20 Ships in Sight. Saw many narwhales. At Mid Night the Fog was so thick that we could not see a hundred yards.

Saturday 26th of June Lat 78°16′ Lon. 5°40′E.
WNW NW to NbE NE Calm
Wind a moderate Breeze, constant thick Fog until 8 am: afterwards Snow Showers. On the Fog clearing away we found the Ice still trending in the form of a bight as far as could be seen to the SSE, the place where the angle was formed between the SW & SSE direction we yesterday took to be the Main Sea. The wind having veered to the NE^d we reached to the NW^d amongst loose Ice ['until' *deleted*] about

['Robt Dowell **M.** N° 12 = 9..6.' *in margin*]

two miles & then came to an impervious body consisting of Floes & loose Ice: we here saw a Fish <u>playing</u> amidst a few pieces of Ice; on its Second appearance we were fortunate enough to entangle it. It did not remain under water above a Minute before it again appeared, dashing the water with its Fins & Tail expressive of its suffering & exhibiting amazing strength – in a few minutes a Second Harpoon was struck & soon afterwards another. Whilst lancing it tore down the Gunwale of a boat & otherwise stove her. In 45 Minutes after the Fall the Fish was killed. In 5½ hours it was flinched (from the fall): the Flinching was performed in 2½ hours. We saw two More Fish, one of which we were very near. Reached in a SSE direction towards the Sea, met a brisk

---

[1] Originally written 'WSW & ENE', but the two initial letters then deleted.

swell, a proof of the water seen being the Sea. All the Ships near us about 13 Sail, followed us out. I was to day informed that when the Neptune's Boats left the John, she had 18 Fish! was perfectly safe lying in the <u>midst</u> of a Bay Floe. The intelligence was gratifying. On Thursday last I noticed an account given by the Margaret of having seen a partial wreck in the Ice seems to be a mistake. The Neptune's Boats leaving the John with Jacks placed on oars occasioned the deception. At Mid Night 26 Sail in Sight. Weather Calm: fine Cloudy sky – no Fish; Narwhales numerous.

Sunday 27th of June. Lat. 78°10′ Lon. 5°50′E
Calm. S to SE & E to NE. NNE
Calm fine weather, the Fore part of this day, the latter part a fresh Breeze accompanied by Fog Showers. Reached about 15 Miles to the Eᵈ fell in with a point of Ice, tacked: meaning to ply up a deep sinuosity bearing from us about North or NNW; clear water separated from us by a narrow stream of Ice seemed to extend many miles in that direction: 10 Ships all plying to the Northward appeared within the Stream. 38 Sail in Sight. Two Fish killed within sight of us.

Monday 28th of June Lat 77°54′ Lon. 6°20′
NE
Wind a fresh breeze – Fog or Snow showers. Having come to the stream of Ice above mentioned, we could find no passage through it: Seeing no Fish, neither the Ships to windwᵈ we ran a few miles to the SEᵈ & then steered SSE in the open Sea. At 8 Am. no Ice was to be seen & only two Ships – at this time we fell in with two fish or more, pursued one, (remarkable for a White Scar near

['John Dunbar **M.** Nº 13 = 10ᶠᵗ 2ⁱⁿˢ' *in margin]*

the Blowholes) above six hours & on lowering a third Boat down we were favoured to get Fast. Like the last Fish it scarcely ever disappeared: three Harpoons were struck within 15 minutes & the Fish was killed in about 45 minutes from the Striking. Clewed the Sails up at the Mast Heads & at 3½ Pm. began to Flinch. The Aimwell near us; an <u>appearance</u> of Land to the Eastward. In 2ʰ 50′ finished, set the Sails & plyed about, shifting our situation but a little: saw Several Fish, had three Boats in pursuit; were not successful.

Tuesday 29th of June Lat. 77°50′ Lon. 6°E.
NE.erly. Variable
Fresh to light Breezes, Snow Showers all day; fine cloudy weather. In the Morning reached near the Ice, saw several Fish; most of the day had two to four Boats in pursuit. The Augusta & Vigilant got a Fish each near us. Upwards of 20 Sail in sight. The Masters of the Aimwell, Clapham, & Enterprize visited me. The Clapham has 9 Fish, 100 Tons, Enterprize 14, 140 Tons, Aimwell 7 as before mentioned. I had the following news – Guilder, 18, 210–220 Tons! Augusta 13, 130 Tons, has now 14 –; Resolution, 9; Henrietta 9; James 9; & Lively of Whitby 3; Margaret of London 11; Eweretta, 9; Ipswitch 11; Neptune 4; Catherine, 2; Hope 3; Vigilant, 8; – Zephyr, 5;

Mary Francis, 5; Perseverance, 2; Trafalgar, 4; North Britain, 1;[1] Ellen, 2; Perseverance (Peterhead), 3; &c. &c. &c.

At Mid Night reached out into the Sea. Cooper employed setting up <u>Shakes</u>.

Wednesday 30th of June Lat. 77°50' Lon. 6°E

NE.erly Variable E.erly.

Moderate breezes all day, snow Showers frequent: fine weather. Sailing about in various directions, pursuing Fish with 2 or 3 Boats & followed by the Ship when the wind would allow us. All the whales however which we saw escaped us by running too swiftly for our Boats. Our Boats had some hard races. At least 10 Fish were killed, or flinched within Sight of us, during this day. At Noon 36 Ships were in Sight. Spoke the *William* & Ann of Whitby with 6 Fish = 55 Tons of oil. In the Evening reached about 20 Miles to the Eastw^d. Saw three Ships flinching but no loose Fish. Returned by the wind. At Mid Night still fine cloudy weather. No Ice or Fish to See. Thermometer 33° Barom. 30.30 Inches.

I was surprized at the distance which the whales [saw?] one another underwater. Several instances occurred within these two days where two Fish have been seen about a miles distant from each other, which on their next appearance were seen in Company.[2] Water Green.

July 1 Thursday at noon Lat 77°25' Lon. 3°30'E

E, SE S, SW.erly Variable[.][3]

Moderate or light Breezes, Snow or Fog Showers in the Morning, about Noon charming fine weather: Thermometer obliquely exposed to the Sun shewed a Temperature of 54° & in the shade 38° the Tar oozed out of the Rigging & the pitch on the Ship's sides was melted! The Neptune of Aberdeen passing us I sent a Boat on Board to enquire the particulars of the John's situation, &c: I was delighted to hear the following good tidings. Neptune saw the John last Sunday near the Ice edge, had 26 Fish, 180–190 Tons of oil, had come out to make off & returned the same ['Sun' *deleted*]

---

[1] The preceding 5 ships, together with the *Gilder,* 360 tons, Captain Joseph Sadler, and *Augusta,* 386 tons, Captain William Beadling were all from the Hull fleet: *Zephyr,* 342 tons, Captain Edward Bell; *Mary Frances,* 386 tons, Captain Martin Morris; *Perseverance,* 244 tons, Captain James Hunter; *Trafalgar,* 330 tons, Captain Wake; *North Briton,* 262 tons, Captain Peter Jameson. The *Resolution, Henrietta, James* and *Lively* were Whitby ships; the *Margaret, Eweretta, Ipswich, Neptune, Catherine* (or *Catharine*), *Hope* and *Vigilant* were from London, and the *Ellen* was from Kirkwall. (Compiled from Credland, *Hull Whaling Trade,* Appendices 1 & 3, and the contemporary printed list.)

[2] Scoresby, *Account of the Arctic Regions,* I, p. 465: 'Its sense of seeing is acute. Whales are observed to discover one another, in clear water, when under the surface, at an amazing distance. When at the surface, however, they do not see far.' What Scoresby believed was due to vision was almost certainly a result of acoustic communication. 'Although communication by sound is difficult to prove for whales, it is likely that the vocal displays described are used by bowheads to stay in touch with each other, and perhaps to gauge activities such as traveling, feeding, or socializing. Underwater sounds allow whales to remain in touch over distances of at least 5–10 k. …': Würsig and Clark, 'Behavior', p. 192.

[3] Much of the margin for this day's entry is occupied by drawings of the two knots described in the text.

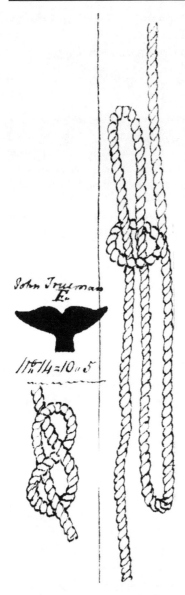

Plate 9. Knots. Drawing by
Scoresby. Whitby Museum
(Transcripts SCO1253, 1 July
1813, margin)

day as seen by ['the' *deleted*] our informer. The
Neptune's men were 4 days on board the John; she
lay in perfect safety: after they left her [a run?] of
small Fish enabled my Father to take 8 at a Fall: he
only wanted 6 or 7 more of the same kind or 2 or 3
large Fish to <u>fill</u> the Ship.

At 2 am. having reached near the Ice lying NE we
tacked & stood 10 hours to the S^d first & afterwards
westward as the wind shifted. Coming

['John Trueman F.   N°14 = 10..5'

in margin]

near the Ice (an open pack) saw a few whales, sent
three Boats in pursuit & at 1 Pm. one was struck, in
15 minutes it re-appeared & in 10 minutes more
three Harpoons were struck. It just reached the
borders of the Ice as it yielded up its life under our
Lances. Took it alongside & made sail off the Ice,
flinching as we reached.

I have hitherto neglected to mentioned [*sic*] a curious circumstance or rather phenomenon which
appeared, on hauling in the first fast Boat's lines of
our 6th Fish June the 7th Two perfect knotts were
formed on the line; the one like a figure of 8 the other
a hitch over [the' *deleted*] a bight of the same continuation of lines. The former was within about 80
yards of the Harpoon the latter farther distant, & the
bight contained within the hitch, comprised near 100
yards of line. The speed of the Fish must have been
amazingly rapid & its evolutions very peculiar to
form two separate, distinct knotts, of a description
difficult to conceive the mode of formation. The
figures in the margin represent these knotts. – At 7
Pm we made sail & began to ply to windward. 12
Sail in Sight, whereof 3 & ourselves have been flinching.

Friday July 2^d Lat. 77°20' Lon. 3°10'E
SW.erly
Fresh to light Breezes with Showers of Snow, all the
day. Plying to windward the fore part, off the face of
the Ice, saw 3 or 4 Fish. Spoke the Resolution's Boat,
has 10 Fish, could not learn what Oil. About noon,
<u>Fish scarce</u>, cleared the after hold & began to make

off with half watch, whilst another Crew manned a Boat on watch for Fish. In the Evening saw several, had two Boats in pursuit: I fancy it was owing to the transparency ['"Making off' *in margin*] of the water that they did not get fast. About Mid Night Completed the four tiers of the after hold, stowed the greatest part of the Gummed Whale Bone upon the Casks between the Beams. 15 Sail in sight, two Flinching. The Eliza Swan's Boat came on board of us to enquire if we had seen the Monarch: the Eliza Swan was driven by a Gale of wind into a Pack, in the Month of May, were obliged to cut up several Ropes for fenders to preserve the Ship, narrowly escaped, got out: the Monarch, Aurora of Hull, & Royal Bounty, were left in a similar situation to that the Eliza Swan providentially quitted; those three Ships have not been seen or heard of since!!![1]

Saturday July 3ᵈ Lat. 77°18′ Lon. 3°20′
Variable ENE, NE. NNE
We had light winds with charming fine weather all the morning & forenoon. Fell in with a number of large Fish, although making off had Boats on watch. At 8 am. "a fall", was called' [*sic*] : the fish was entangled by a heave, it is probable the Harpoon was not very well fast, that by the fish rolling over the Foreganger had been cut by it, as it was hauled in & found to be severed: three lines were run out when the

['J. Wellburn.   Foreganger broke' *in margin*]

Fish escaped, carrying away the Harpoon in its back. It is remarkable that this Harpoon is the first Fishing Instrument of any description that we have lost this voyage. Harpoons, lines, lances, &c. we lost not one or any part before today. We have been highly favoured in the Fishery: this being but the Second Fish which has escaped us after being struck, since the Commencement of our labours. In the hope of better luck we kept all the Boats on watch 3 or 4 hours, they came near Several whales but were not successful. After the Fall ceased making off, the Blubber of the two first captured Fish being all put away in Casks: chiefly in the After hold, but 9 Casks about the Main Mast & in the Main Hold. The Wind increased after Meridian & in the Evening blew a Strong Gale accompanied by Snow or Sleet. I have observed the Augusta of Hull flinch 2 or 3 large Fish within these 30 hours past, of 20 sail in sight 2 or 3 others shewed successful by the cleuing up of their Sails. Many Fish were seen in the Evening, but the Sea making rapidly, obliged us to relinquish the pursuit. At Mid Night reduced our sails to double reefed Top Sails & Fore Top Mast Stay Sail.

Sunday 4ᵗʰ of July Lat. 77°29′+ Lon. 2°40′E.
NNE to SSW or SW
The wind ceased towards Morning, veered to the SWᵈ & again blew a Strong Gale

---

[1] The *Eliza Swan*, *Monarch* and *London* were the three Montrose whalers in the Greenland Sea. The *Royal Bounty* was a Leith vessel. The *Eliza Swan*'s misfortunes were not yet over. On 24 July 1813 she was captured by the American 44-gun frigate *President* in latitude 67°40′N, 4°E and was released on payment of a ransom of £5000: Lubbock, *Arctic Whalers*, p. 193.

attended with Snow Showers & considerable Sea. Reaching near the Ice about noon, saw the <u>John</u>, approaching us, in the act of running before the wind, lay too to speak her. Proved to have 28 Fish (16 size) about 180 Tons of Oil. Had been mostly amongst the Ice since we before parted with her. Saw but few Fish lately, got two last week. Seems very deep: wants 2 or 3 Fish more!

Plying under easy sail in Co. with the John. Several Ships in Sight.

Monday 5th of July Lat. 77°24′ Lon. 2° E
SW.erly
Strong to Fresh Gales, much Snow in the Morning, after Meridian cloudy weather. At 1 am. re-commenced making off & at 8 Pm made a finish: Completed the hold, about 3 feet before the Foremast Beam of the Main HatchWay, together with every winger & one Cask besides. Since our commencement on Friday last have filled Casks as follows: Tons or 252 Gallons 29; 200's, 4; 180's, 23; 160's, 9; & 126's, 3; in all 68 Casks containing 110 Butts of Blubber.

At 4 Pm made more sail; reached near the Ice in a deep Bay: saw no Fish steered out again. At Mid Night just within the Sea stream, lay too.

Tuesday 6th of July Lat. 77°26′+ Lon 2°20′E.
Calm, NE. to NbW
Calm weather until noon, a fresh Breeze then sprang up at NE. made all Sail & reached 10 or 12 Miles into the Sea, saw 3 Fish, were partly fast to one by a heave, the Harpoon however did not fix itself. Took on board some Fresh water Ice. 10 or 12 Sail in Sight. Plying to windward the rest of the day, out of sight of the Ice. It seems the late Gales of wind have dispersed the Fish & caused them to quit their ground: in the clear water where they were so numerous on Friday & Saturday scarcely one is now to be seen. The John in sight to windward.

Wednesday 7th of July Lat. 77°46′ Lon. 3°10′E.
NNW. NW. West. WSW
Light to Fresh Gales, fine cloudy weather. Sailing or plying to the westward all the day expecting the Fish must have taken to the Ice as none are now to be seen in the clear water. Fell in with the Jane, Captⁿ. Newton of Aberdeen, who gives us the following interesting intelligence. I may premise that on the 20th of June, I mentioned a Report of the loss of the Royal Bounty; at the same time 10 or 12 other ships were in missing, that is they had not been seen by any ship since the fore part or middle of May: a rumour prevailed that 7 Ships had been severely stove & had left the Country, these were supposed to be the missing Ships – the whole tale however seems without foundation except that such Ships were actually in missing – they were the, Dundee, ['Elizabeth' *deleted*] & Aurora of London; the Cove, Leviathan, & British Queen, of Shields; the Aurora, & Gardiner & Joseph[1] of Hull; the Monarch of Montrose & Jane of Aberdeen, & the Royal Bounty of Leith: the Elizabeth of London, was said to

---

[1] The *Gardiner and Joseph* was one vessel, not two.

have 18[1] Fish in May & was believed to have gone home. It appears from Capt[n] Newton's account that himself in the Jane, with the Elizabeth, & the rest of the Ships just mentioned took the Ice, finding Shelter within a Sea Stream, during the heavy gale of the 15th of May which continued with some abatement however, for several days – they were then in Lat. 77° or 77½°N. perhaps 30 Miles to the S[d] & considerably to the Westward of us: that finding the Ice slack they worked in to the NW[d] fell in with large Floes & several Fish; the Ice began to close around them in a day or two, & very shortly altho' the wind with them continued from the Northward they were closely beset: the Jane sawed a Dock in a Floe for their ['Where & how beset' *in margin*] preservation. They continued amidst this ice until about the 14th of June, having at that time drifted down into Latitude 75° & amazingly to the westward, so that they expected to have seen the Western Land.[2] The Jane, Royal Bounty & Monarch, were beset Eastward of the rest of the Ships, which except the Gardiner & Joseph that seemed to escape about the 25th of May, were all turned or <u>slewed</u> round to the NW side of a Floe. The Jane, Royal Bounty, & Monarch came away in Company; Mr Newton declares he has made good 190 Miles of distance in a direct NE line ([freed?] from the Variation) from the place which he left until he reached the edge of the Ice where abouts he got beset!! He says they frequently saw Fish & that some of the Ships made captures. The success of the Ships he left he states as follows: June the 14th Dundee, Elizabeth, Leviathan, & British Queen, all clean[;] the two Aurora's two Fish each; & the Cove 3. The Jane has now 3 having got two since he left the Ice; states Royal Bounty 2; & Monarch 4 Fish on the 4th Inst[t].

We spoke the William & Ann with 7 Fish; Resolution 10; 100 Tons, & heard of the James of Whitby having 14 Fish 170 Tons.

Until the above account has reached us, we were scarcely sensible of the danger we escaped on the 24th of May: our critical situation on the 13th of June was glaringly evident at the time; yet our extrication now seems a more providential interference than at that time although so deemed, could possibly be duly appreciated. May we live in remembrance of God's mercies.

Thursday 8th of July Lat. 77°35′ Lon. 2°0′E.
WSW SW Calm
With a Fresh Gale of wind we continued or[3] reach to the NW[d][.] at 6 am. came to the edge of a large Floe lying close by the Sea, some Fish were seen at it. Sent all the Boats away, or in the technical phrase, we <u>"made a loose Fall"</u>.[4] The John, William & Ann, & Resolution in Co. The William & Ann got two fish in a very short time equal to near 20 Tons of Oil whilst no other ship got any. We had several good opportunities but adventitious circumstances always foiled every endeavour & obliged the Boats to return without success. Moored to the Floe: large pools of Fresh Water stood on the surface near where we lay sent Casks to the Ice & filled 8 Butts very readily. After Meridian the wind fell to near Calm; Fog Showers enveloped us in the Evening. At 9

[1] Possibly '15'.
[2] I.e. the east coast of Greenland.
[3] *Sic.* 'our' intended?
[4] See journal entry for 25 June 1811.

Pm. we were obliged to cast off from the Ice on account of several small Floe pieces setting up where we lay, removed about half a Mile to the South. Sent two Boats to the Floe to keep watch;[1] one of them observing a Fish blowing in a hole of the Ice, dragged the Harpoon & the line over the Ice to a distance of 350 yards & struck the Fish as she was in the act of quitting the Spot. She ran out 10 lines, was supposed to be seen blowing in different holes of the Ice, at length however (Mid Nt.) she came out to the edge ['**Friday 9th of July** Lat 77°46' Lon. 2°0E Calm. S.erly, SW, SbW.' *in margin*] & the Resolution's Boat which had come to our assistance struck a second Harpoon. The Fish immediately took under the Ice again & after running out 50 Fathoms of line broke the Ice where it was near a foot in thickness whereby to <u>Breathe</u>; lances now flew over the Ice & wounded her wherever she[2] appeared. Irritated by repeated

['John Dunbar **M.** N° 15 = 9..5' *in margin*]

assaults it moved onwards several yards breaking the Ice with its <u>Crown</u> all the way. Some time before the dissolution the Second ['fast' *deleted*] Harpoon was observed to be very slightly fast, an active Sailor leapt upon the living Whale's Back, actually cut the Harpoon out with his <u>pocket knife</u> & with the help of a messmate re-struck it, up to the Socket! This was an act Clever & highly opportune, since on this Harpoon depended the Capture of the Fish & had it drawn out, it would have been in vain to kill the Fish as no means would then have offered of ['drawing' *deleted*] getting it out without the most laborious exertions of sawing the Ice & the practicability of this method would have depended on the winds, weather, & favourable disposition of the ambient Ice. After being killed, the Fish was fortunately readily drawn out and at 4 AM, received alongside of the Ship, that had been re-moored to the Ice. A Breeze of wind springing up & the Ice again setting towards us, we were obliged again to cast off, flinching drifting to lee-ward. 5 Ships in Co. Several within Sight.

A fresh gale of wind in the afternoon attended with hazy weather. Plying to windward along the Floe edge. Fearing least the Ice should close us in, or the wind shift to the Eastward, on the Fog clearing away for a short time in the Evening we reached out & Starboard tacked, by the wind, for near 15 Miles found ample room, loose Ice & scattered Floes, all laid very open. Began to ply to windward.

Saturday 10th of July Lat. 77°30' Lon. 2°10'E.
South to SWbW or WSW
Strong Gales the fore part; towards night moderate breezes, thick Fog, haze, or small Rain occasionally throughout the day: plying to the Southward amongst much Ice, streams, patches & Floes, scattered variously abroad. At 8 Pm. we found more room & had apparently a view of the Sea – 16 Sail in Sight, most of them to lee-ward. Not

---

[1] The events described in the following passage were recounted by Scoresby, *Account of the Arctic Regions*, II, pp. 263–5, introduced by the comment 'I cannot pass over a circumstance which occurred within my own observation, and which excited my highest admiration.'

[2] Again the whale is identified in the marginal note as a male.

a Single Fish seen all the day. Spoke the Clapham with 12 large Fish 140–150 Tons of Oil. Water transparent Blue.

Sunday 11th of July Lat. 77°20' Lon. 1°50'E
WSW to West
We had light or moderate Breezes of wind all this day – foggy with but short intervals of partly clear except during heavy rains when the Fog was in a measure dissipated. Continued plying to windward all the night amongst Floes & drift Ice most of the pieces detatched from each other, saw no signs of a Fish: several Ships at 10 am. being observed running to the NEd & having come from far in a windward direction it appeared of no avail working up any further: lay too a few hours, & at 2 Pm. made Sail wishing to get out to Sea on a['n' *deleted*] SE course, passed much Ice in the thick, soon met a swell, a favourable sign, & at 8 Pm. we found ourselves in ample room, supposed it to be the Sea, hauled by the wind to the Sd & kept our reach the rest of the day. 4 sail in sight.

Monday 12th of July Lat 77°0' Lon. 2°50'E.
WbS, SW SSW South. Var.
Weather commonly foggy, Rain Showers, with a moderate or Fresh Breeze of wind. Continued our reach lying SbW or SSW with making only one short tack until Noon, frequently passing much heavy Ice & large Floes: owing to the thick Fog we were not able to discern the clearest road & I fancy occasionally we passed through the thickest Ice, when rather clear we constantly observed very close Ice to the Eastwd of us. At 10 am. the wind veered SSW & at Noon was at South – and at this time Fog very thick we fell in with very close Ice, tacked several times always however reaching, most to the ESE when the Ice would allow us. The Royal Bounty joined Company in the Evening, confirmed the account delivered by the Jane & before stated herein, those two Ships having escaped with the Monarch after being beset seven weeks. The Royal Bounty has now 2 Fish the same which she got before she was beset. Captn Kelly visited me – despaired of getting more Fish this Season.[1]

We began to make off in the Morning finished in 8 hours having filled filled [*sic*] 4 Ton Casks, 19 of 180 Gallons & 4 of 80 Gallons which together with one Ton Cask of Crang not before enumerated completed the lower hold (not well stowed however owing to the want of suitable Casks) together with 5 Casks of 180 Gallons remaining in the Twin decks. At 10 Pm. we reached out to Sea. 9 Ships seen.

Tuesday 13th of July Lat. 76°50' Lon. 5°E
South to SWbS..
Wind a Fresh Gale attended with constant thick Fog & occasionally much Rain throughout this day. Having in the beginning of the month, seen so many Fish in the

---

[1] Lubbock, *Arctic Whalers*, p. 194: 'The *Aurora* and *Eagle* of Hull, and the *Royal Bounty* of Leith, were beset in the ice from the middle of April to early in July, the first to get clear being the *Royal Bounty* on July 4, when Captain Kelly wrote home saying that, after being seven weeks beset, he intended to stay as long as there was any chance of doing good.'

clear water, with a view to prove whether any yet remained we reached to the ESE about 60 miles, saw no living creature save our constant attendants the Fulmars, at noon therefore tacked, made all sail, wind a Beam to the WNW & at 10 Pm. fell in with Ice, straggling pieces the noise of much Ice was heard from to windw^d the drift pieces however becoming numerous we tacked ran out clear of all Ice & lay too. I was much astonished & not a little pleased with an amazing concentration of sound of the Ice around us, from the concavity of wet mizen stay Sail, the focus of which I passed through as I walked too & froe [*sic*] on the Quarter Deck, such aloud [*sic*], harsh, splashing noise at first much astonished me, I did not perceive what was the cause, & whenever I turned to where the sound seemed to arise it was no longer heard & nothing which could cause it was to be observed – the focus was confined to a small space & varied with the motions of the Canvass as well as the Ship; the noise resembled that of a rope rapidly drawn over the surface of a wet sail, but more intense. I was amused by the effect this concentration had on the sailors as they occasionally heard the noise – they stared about in all directions, but were ever disappointed in discovering from whence it proceeded. ['**Wednesday 14**^th **of July** Lat. 77°10′ Lon. 2½°E SSW.' *in margin*] Perhaps some benefit might arise from the knowledge of this curious property of a wet sail swelled by the wind; probably the Crew of Boat separated from the Ship in a Fog might be heard shouting, more readily ['here than' *deleted*] in such a situation of a sail than in any other part of a Ship, any noise would doubtless be concentrated which should reach the surface of the Sail. I have frequently observed that sounds are more readily distinguished & heard at a Ship's Masthead than on the Deck, the reason I do not pretend to surmise – yet it is well known that the Blowing of a Whale is distinct, nay loud, whilst on the Deck no sound is heard. In a Calm a Fish may be heard blowing at more than a mile's distance, at the Mast Head. Whether the sound may be reflected by the Hull of the Ship & any way concentrated by the sails or urged more directly to the Ear, thereby, I cannot pretend to determine.

Fresh Gales, with almost constant Fog throughout. Showers of Rain frequent, the Fog always of a very wetting nature. Having lain too most of the night & morning near streams of Ice as we supposed from scattered pieces seen; at Noon we bore up & steered 5 hours NEbE afterwards altered our Course to north seeing no Ice & having seen no Whale since the 9th Inst^t except two of the species of Razor Back (finned Whale) vulgarly so called. Passed the Thornton. Having steered north 5 hours hauled up by the wind to the westward & at Mid Night falling in with a stream of Ice tacked. Fog very thick & wet.

Thursday 15th **of July**
SSW or SW
Fresh Gales all the day; Fog occasionally ['less in' *deleted*] more pervious than usual. Having passed through a large extent of open water & seen no symptoms of a Whale, it seems needless labour or lost time to traverse the <u>Sea</u> any longer with the same view: our only remaining hope must depend on a change of situation amongst the Ice & yet this attempt is rendered critical & dangerous from the prevalence of thick Fogs. A change of wind to the N. or W. might very probably afford likewise a change of

weather whereby we may be enabled to prove for the last time this Season whether any Fish are to be found amongst the Ice. In the Latitude in which we now lay we amply explored the recesses of the Ice a few days ago, to the Southw^d we have like-wise been, a higher Latitude therefore seems the only probable change of situation likely or possible to be advantageous. During the intervals between the thickest Fog showers we reached several miles amongst streams & patches of Ice. Saw several Ships. The Ipswitch gives account of having spoken the John this morning, still with 28 Fish, thinking of going home. They described the John as having run to the NE^d otherwise we must have fallen in with her. Was informed the Resolution of Whitby had been at a Field very recently & he nor any ship I could hear of has seen a Fish since the day we got our last. From the face of <u>the times</u> it seems very unlikely that we shall get any more success this year & very probable that we may not be able to find, to see, a Single Fish. At 10 Pm. the atmosphere was cleared of its Fog the first time for this 4 or 5 days past: altho' every ship in sight (12 in N°] were beating to windw^d under a press of sail, we steered before the wind to the North 3 ['**Friday 16th of July** Lat 78°2' N Lon. 1°10'E SW, WSW. or W.' *in margin*] hours about 12 miles, lay too during a Fog shower & then reached 5 hours or 25 Miles to the NW amongst very open Ice, streams, patches, & some Floes. At 9 am. the Fog re-commencing obliged us to lay too. Wind a Strong Gale. The rest of the day, constantly thick Fog, of a drier nature than hitherto, so much so that although the rigging sometimes dripped its moisture, yet the Sails [&c?], the decks were to all appearance dry. The density of the Fog prevented us seeing a piece of Ice, at a greater distance than 100 yards. Lay too in consequence, plying occasionally a little to windw^d to keep to nearly the same situation. Saw a <u>Razor Backed</u> Whale, several Seals in the water & some Fulmars as usual following us invariably for the grease which is left in the Ship's track &c.

Saturday 17th of July Lat 78°15' Lon. 1°15'E
SW to S.

The weather continued without any amendment until the afternoon when the Fog was displaced by a heavy continued Rain: we had been engaged several hours scraping the Ships sides, gunwales, Rails, scrubbing the Decks, &c; having finished as the weather became clearer, we made sail, reached about 12 miles to the WNW amongst streams & patches of Ice with some small Floes, & fell in with a firm body of Floes – here we hoped to see Fish, a few Narwhales however were the only Cetacea to be met with. Towards Mid Night the Fog re-commenced & the wind abated lay too. The Ice to the W^d of us seems to be the Main body, consists of ragged Floes intimately approximated, containing some small Holes: the Surface is bare: the Snow all dissolved & standing in large pools of water in various places – such spots are of a fine Green colour, the rest still retains in a great measure its whiteness.

Sunday 18th of July Lat 78° 20' Lon. 1° E
S. West WNW to NW & N.
Calm weather for several hours attended with thick Fog: afterwards a Brisk Gale sprang up from the W^d the Fog disappeared & Snow Showers commenced. Worked up to the edge Body of Ice, seeing no Fish we prepared to change our ground by

making all sail. To the NW^d not a particle of Ice is to be seen, suppose Fields might there be met with but to work to wind^d to any distance would spend too much time especially as there is so little chance of benefit; to the S^d lies much Ice aggregated into patches & streams offering considerable obstacles to the Navigation that way; steered therefore to the ESE, the way we had penetrated until having cleared the thickest of the Ice, we then hauled up South. Having changed our Latitude about 30 miles we steered to the W^d with a few[1] of examining the Main Body of Ice in this parallel. Snow Showers commencing & much loose Ice opposing us we tacked & endeavoured to find our way out to Sea in an ESE direction.

Monday 19th of July Lat. 77°40′ Lat 1°10′E
NNE. Calm. W.erly SW
Soon after Mid Night the wind abated & thick Fog showers took the place of Snow; having steered too much to the Southward whilst I was in Bed, at 6 am. we found ourselves entangled amidst many Floes, & thick patches of heavy drift Ice. The weather was calm, therefore lowered three Boats to tow the Ship; we persevered in the <u>thick</u> in an Easterly Direction & in about 6 hours found more room. Whilst the Boats were towing a Fish sprang up near us (the first we have seen since the 9th Inst^t) sent the three Boats to the spot; saw the whale no more. About 2 Pm. a breeze of wind commenced from the W^d by means of which we were enabled to make better progress, so that by 8 Pm. we found ourselves extricated from all difficulties & no Ice to be seen on the Fog clearing away except disseminated patches. A phenomenon similar to what has been observed from the top of high mountains was pleasingly exhibited by the Sun ['Natural Phenomenon' *in margin*] shining in through the Fog this morning. To an observer at the <u>Mast Head</u> a complete coloured circle was exhibited – the upper segment similar to the rain Bow, the lower part of the same description also but occupying a situation descending nearly down to the <u>Nadir</u>. Its plane seemed to lay at right angles to a line drawn from the observer to the centre of the circle, I regret I did not measure the diameter, it might be about 30°. At the centre of the circle I observed my own figure represented on the water, whilst a lucid appearance surrounded it, particularly the head which was adorned with a <u>glory</u>. The lucid character was impressed on the Fog, whilst the figure appeared a Shadow on the water; I have reason to believe however from similar appearances observed by naturalists that had there been no material object in the way, the Fog would have represented the Same Shadow.[2]

As the atmosphere was cleared of its density seven Ships were seen a stern, discovering some <u>Friends</u> amongst them we lay too & afterwards ran to lee-ward & joined

---

[1] *Sic.* 'view' presumably intended.
[2] Scoresby described this event again in *Account of the Arctic Regions*, I, pp. 394–5, commenting that 'I remained a long time contemplating the beautiful phenomenon before me.' Scoresby's description may be compared with the definition of a glory in the *International Cloud Atlas*, p. 59: 'One or more sequences of coloured rings, seen by an observer around his own shadow on a cloud, consisting mainly of numerous small water droplets, on fog or, very rarely, on dew.' The *Atlas* noted that 'When the shadow seems to be very large, because the clouds or fog are near the observer, it is called a "Brocken spectre", whether a coloured glory is seen or not.'

them, they proved to be the Henrietta, Aimwell, Volunteer, William & Ann of Whitby the Dexterity, Earl Piercy, & Berwick Lively:[1] as the Masters of the four former Ships were collected on board the Volunteer I joined them. I had the following interesting particulars communicated to me. The Volunteer got a Fish in the midst of the Blubber of ['Interesting Fact.' *in margin*] which, whilst making it off, they found the mouth of a lance formed of Blue sclate, about three Inches long & two Broad & evidently from the form & quality had been the manufacture of the Esquemaux's of Davis's streights – such lances are alone used by them, hence it is evident this Fish must have been attacked by the Natives of Davis's streights & has removed from thence hither; this is a further proof that it is not uncommon for the Whales to shift from one Country to the Other; it has been remarked that a good fishery in one Country has been attended with the reverse in the other, hence it is probable that the whales occasionally remove from one place to the other, not merely in wounded individuals (which alone can be proved) but the great Bulk of the species, collected together in high Latitudes.[2] The other proof that I refer to was the Circumstance of a fish having been Captured in Greenland last year by the Aurora of Hull in the Blubber of which was found a Harpoon of the native Greenlanders which doubtless had been struck in Davis Streights. The fish got by the Volunteer shewed no wound, the place where the lance had entered was completely healed up, marked only by a small white scar. – Another relation likewise interesting was the following:– the Henrietta has lately taken a Fish; in the Back of which was found sticking a Harpoon, two thirds concealed within the Blubber, the stock of the Harpoon still remained attached. remarkably swelled with the water, ['Interesting Fact.' *again in margin*] the shank of the Harpoon that was acted upon by the salt water was deeply corroded with rust – the wound was healed up, its extent marked by an indentation of a portion of white, gristly skin. The Harpoon from the engraving was found to have belonged to the Inverness[3] & a leathern mark in the socket proved it to have been struck last year! and from the circumstance of the Inverness losing but one fish last Season & doubtless this was the Individual, it must have carried ['it' *deleted*] the Harpoon in its Back ever since June 25th 1812, the time the Fish was proved to have been struck. The Fat on this wounded animal was very inconsiderable in proportion to its Bulk, its vigour & health must have been impaired by the wound & doubtless the cause was sufficient to reduce the poor whale's Blubber.

The following is the alledged success of the Whitby Ships in Co. The Henrietta 11

---

[1] Not to be confused with the *Lively* of Whitby.

[2] Scoresby used this evidence from the *Volunteer* in *Account of the Arctic Regions*, I, p. 11, to support his belief that there must exist 'a sea communication between the Atlantic and Pacific Oceans by the North'. In that recounting, Scoresby made clear that it was not based on hearsay: 'The master of the Volunteer whaler of Whitby … shewed me part of a lance which had been taken out of the fat of a whale killed by his crew a few weeks before. It was formed of hard grey stone, of a flinty appearance, about three inches long, two broad, and two-tenths thick. Two holes were pierced in one end of it, by which, it appeared the stock or handle had been secured.' In the modern survey, *The Bowhead Whale*, both Moore and Reeves ('Distribution and Movement', p. 356) and Woodby and Botkin ('Stock Sizes Prior to Commercial Whaling', p. 387) noted a lack of evidence about interchange among the different bowhead stocks.

[3] Of London.

['Success of Whitby Fleet.' *in margin*] 95–100 Tons of Oil; Aimwell as before 7 = 65 Tons; William & Ann as before 9 = 80–85 Tons; Volunteer 7 = 70 Tons – The Dexterity 7 = 70 Tons; Earl Piercy 7; – &c. &c. The Fleet thus collected are all for <u>home</u> – home how pleasant the thought? Under any circumstances the idea must have agreeable feelings, but especially under prosperous circumstances. <u>We</u> have particular cause to be grateful, we have been favoured above our fellows – Providence has Blessed our endeavours & though the ship is far from being full, yet thanks be to God, we have a <u>good</u> ['<u>voyage &</u>' *deleted*] <u>Cargo</u>. We trust this same good Providence will not desert us, but continue to protect & uphold us, grant us a safe & speedy passage, favour us with a happy meeting with those Friends our hearts <u>hold most Dear</u> – Add to which the Better Blessings of Divine Grace whereby through the Merits of the Redeemer we may obtain Everlasting Life.

Tuesday 20th of July Lat 77°10′ Lon. 7°E.
SW to South, SW & W.
Fresh Gales, Strongest in the Night, always accompanied by Rain or Fog, whenever the Rain ceased, thick Fog always commenced & continued in showers throughout the day – Steered by the wind making p Compass a Course ESE until noon, when we tacked in Company with the 7 before mentioned Ships – furled the Main Sail Top Gallant Sails & Stay Sails, & reefed the Topsails, on account of wind & our outsailing ['Left the Ice' *in margin*] the rest of the fleet. The wind veering to the W^d at 7 Pm. we again tacked, lay too near two hours & then made sail by the wind lying South or SSW against a heavy head Sea. The <u>watch</u> employed cleaning the Ship. <u>No Ice to see.</u>

Wednesday 21st July Lat. 76° 42′ Lon. 7°30E
WSW West
Fresh or Brisk Gales with Fog Showers or Rain. Sticking all the day by the wind to the S^d under a [Smart?] Sail, in Company as above. Sent down the Crow's nest, placed the Main Royal Mast – &c. Shortened Sail in the Evening for the Fleet, all astern but the Henrietta & two Scotch Ships. No Ice to see.

Thursday 22nd of July Lat. 75°9′ Lon 7°¾E
WNW, NW, NNW
Immediately after Mid Night the wind veered to NW^d the weather presently began to amend & fine Cloudy weather followed: under a Brisk sail all the day, steering as we supposed SW or SWbW at the rate of 4 to 5½ knotts p hour.[1] I cannot be certified of

---

[1] The lengthy discussion of compass variation that follows was to become a major preoccupation of Scoresby, resulting in several scientific reports, notably the paper 'On the Anomaly in the Variation of the Magnetic Needle, as Observed on Ship-Board', *Philosophical Transactions of the Royal Society*, 1819 and reprinted in *Account of the Arctic Regions*, II, Appendix IX. In that paper, Scoresby noted that 'ever since the year 1805, I have been in the habit of allowing only 2 to 2½ points variation on the passage outward to Greenland, with a northerly or north-easterly course, but generally three points variation on the homeward passage when the course steered was S.W. or S.W.b.W. Without this difference of allowance, a Greenland ship outward bound will be generally found to be several leagues to the eastward of the reckoning, and homeward bound will be as much as 4 or 5 degrees to the eastward of it.' See Introduction, pp. lvii.

the Course steered on account of the different Indications of our Compasses; those 3
in actual service constantly differed a point from each other, whilst the Starboard
Binnacle shewed SW, the larboard was at SWbW & the Cabin Hanging Compass
shewed a WSW course; I take the Mean as being most likely to be nearest the truth:
this great difference in the Compasses renders our acts[1] of navigation very uncertain
– the case is not very ['Dissimilar Indications of three Compasses' *in margin*] uncommon: the Cause seems to be the attraction of the different bulky Metallic or rather
Iron Bodies which occupy a variety of situations in the Ship, thus the Guns are spread
in equal spaces along the Deck, some of them must be near the Compasses; whether
this be the sole cause, or whether the whole mass of Iron in the Ship may not form a
Pole or centre for attraction, or whether some concealed Iron very near the Binnacle
may have some effect I cannot determine. That some foreign attraction is the cause
may seem to be proved[2] from the Circumstance of every compass agreeing in the self-
same situation: that is suppose the Starboard Binnacle Card indicate a SW Course the
Ship being kept perfectly steady, the other Compass which pointed SWbW is put into
the same place & the former removed it is now found to point likewise to SW & each
when alternatively Shifted pointed to the same direction which its partner shewed in
the same spot:– I removed one Compass, no change took place in the one remaining,
which proved that their mutual attraction was not the cause – the removed compass
I placed near the helm it indicated 1½ points ['Supposition concerning the cause.' *in
margin*] more westerly than the Starboard Binnacle; I then placed it [close by?] the
Companion on the Starboard Side – one point was the difference, as likewise when
shifted to the Main Mast, Stern Boat, & other places about the deck freest from Iron.
From the whole I judge the Mean to be true as it agreed well with itself in various
positions throughout the Ship. I found no fault in any Compass, each ever agreeing in
the same exact spot. In cases like this I have generally found that the errors decrease
as the ship decreases her Latitude so that by the time we reach England, they will
probably all agree. This I think may be accounted for; the direction of the magnetic
attraction Shewn by the dipping needle ['The oblique action of the Magnetic Fluid, or
the Oblique Position of the Magnetic Poles, renders its power inefficient.' *in margin*]
in Greenland forms an angle of about 80°–82° with the horizon, or approaches the
perpendicular within ten degrees – hence the power is very oblique, the force by
which an horizontal needle is directed to the Pole becomes almost insufficient for
overcoming the friction on the point of the Centre, at least though the friction may be
overcome when the needle is far from the line of N&S. yet when its vibrations
become reduced to a small angle the friction on the point stops it at the extremity of
an oscillation and according to the size of such oscillation the Compass directs
wrong, in many cases stands altogether in [any?] position when undisturbed by any
motion of the vessel. Now when the power of attraction is in the best circumstances
insufficient to fix the needle accurately parallel with the magnetic poles, the least
foreign attraction applied must act with powerful influence, hence it is that any object
in the ship or any part of the ['Calculation of the proportional effective influence of

---

[1] Or 'arts'.
[2] Possibly 'found'; there is an ink stain partly obscuring the word.

the Magnetic Fluid under different angles of the <u>Dipping Needle</u>' *in margin*] ship which has the power of attracting the needle causes it to diverge from the line in which it ought to point. Supposing the magnetic influence to be equal throughout the Globe, the proportional power which is applied in directing the needle to the North may be easily calculated for any Latitude where the *dip* is known; the <u>natural versed Sine</u>[1] of the angle formed by the dipping needle & a perpendicular to the Horizon will give this proportional force of attraction in every elevation from the horizontal. Thus calling the power of attraction acting on the magnetic needle whereby it is conformed to the pole, at a maximum, or when the dipping needle lies horizontal 1,000 – The proportional power under other elevations follows the course of the versed sines: thus, as in the following Table,[2] the <u>Co-versed sines</u> under every angle formed by the

0°	5°	10	15	20	25	30	35	40	45	50	55	60	65	70	75	80	85	90
1000	913	826	741	658	577	500	426	357	293	234	181	134	94	60	34	15	4	0

<u>dipping needle</u> & the <u>Horizon</u> (the way in which the scales of Dipping needles are commonly graduated) ['Comparative magnetical influence' *in margin*] marks the force of attraction whereby the magnet is conformed to the pole. Now we see this attractive force is in Greenland only 15/1000 parts of what it is where the needle lies horizontal (that is supposing the whole or perpendicular force or impulse to be the same in all Latitudes & situations[)]. In England where the Dip is about 73½° the attractive force is 41/1000 or near treble that of Greenland, whence the magnetic needle must be supposed to be much more certain in its indications.[3] In Greenland Heavy Compass Cards do not answer, the water being commonly smooth, no agitation on the point of the Centre to ease the friction, the card is liable to stand in any position, whilst a very light card presses with less force on the Centre, which is also less liable to be [blunted?] & at any rate produces less friction.

Supposing ourselves now out of the reach of further Success this voyage from the [Mate's?] account of the Casks filled with Blubber, I frame the following Manifest.

[1] *OED*: '*Versed sine* ... the quantity obtained by subtracting the cosine from unity.'

[2] Thus, sine 5° = .0872; 1000 – 87 = 913; sin 40° = .6428; 1000 – 643 = 357, etc..

[3] I am grateful to Dr Larry Newitt, Geomagnetic Laboratory of the Geological Survey of Canada, for the following comments on this passage: 'Scoresby is talking about the decrease in the horizontal component (H) of the magnetic field as one approaches the latitude of the north magnetic pole. The pole's position about 1820 is believed to have been approximately 71°N 100°W. At some point, varying according to the quality of manufacture, the frictional force in the pivot of the compass becomes larger than the horizontal force, causing the compass to become erratic. Scoresby seems to have believed that the horizontal force is proportional to the naturally versed sine of the magnetic inclination or dip.

His result (that the horizontal force in the Greenland Sea is about one-third that of England) is correct, but that may be coincidence. In actual fact, the formula for calculating horizontal force is
$$H = F*\cos(I)$$
where F is the total field strength and I is inclination.

It was not possible to measure the true field strength in Scoresby's era, so he could only calculate a ratio. F is also not uniform over the globe, and cosines are not the same as "naturally versed sines". For example, his table gives 15 (actually .015) for 80 degrees of dip, whereas the cosine is .174. However, if you go through the math, the horizontal strength in the Greenland Sea is indeed about one-third that of England.'

Manifest of the Cargo of the Ship Esk, British Built, Burthen 354 73/94 Tons; William Scoresby Junr Master from Greenland of & for Whitby. To say,

2 Casks of 400 Gall*ons*

16 "	——	300	
134 "	——	252	
38 "	——	200	
59 "	——	180	
20 "	——	160	
24 "	——	126	
3 "	——	80	

296 Casks of Blubber, & 1 of Crang
Containing 508 Butts of half a Ton
each, Eight Tons of Whale Finn; &
7 Seal's Skins.
The Produce of 15 Whales: 7 Seals.

Thomas Brodrick Esq.

Greenland Seas 20th day of July 1813

William Scoresby Junr.

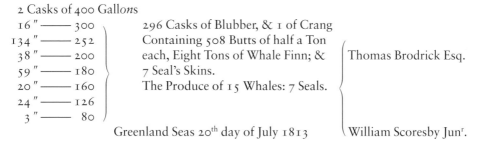
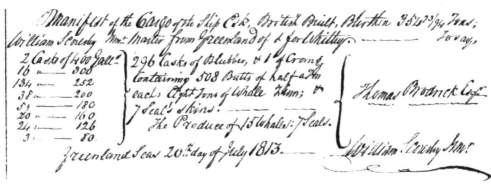

All hands were employed a few hours, suspending three pairs of [Jaw?] Bones in the Fore Rigging, making off the Blubber of two Tails, clearing the Twin Decks for receiving the Boats, placing the Guns, & other needful work. In the afternoon all the Fleet parted Company by steering more to the westward than us, except the Henrietta which continued to follow, under three [Stearing?] Sails & Royals besides all other Sails. At 8 Pm. steered SWbW½W. Wind a moderate Breeze.

Friday 23^d of July Lat. 74°18′ 7°17′E
Variable SWbW
At 1 am. the wind shifted to SWbW & continued throughout the day, a light or moderate Breeze, Steered SSE[1] generally – always close by the wind. In the Morning dismantled 4 Boats, washed their lines & put them in two Coyls on the Quarter Deck. The Boats we stowed between the Decks. Some of the Ships which parted Co. yesterday appeared astern at 8 pm.

Saturday 24th July Lat. 73°16′+ Lon. 10°56′E
SW.erly Var. West
Wind variable a light or moderate Breeze, weather Clear charmingly fine in consequence of which we suspended the washed whale lines on spars between the Main & Mizen Rigging before night they were tollerably dry. Coyled them roughly in the

---

[1] Possibly 'SBE' (but not 'SbE').

Gun-room. 13 Sail in Sight. Suppose the Fleet parted with & others. At 9 am. finding ourselves far to the Eastw^d & the wind rather southering tacked, lay WbN; to NWbW under all sails, made little progress. Tacked again at 8 pm. lay SSW to SWbS. Showers of Rain in the Night.

Sunday 25th of July Lat. 72°47′ Lon. 10°¼′E
WSWerly Werly WNW.
Light Breezes, variable squally, with Showers of Rain. Strong SE swell. We persevered by the wind to the S^d & SW^d expecting a wind from the same quarter as the swell prevailed in, were however disappointed. Made but small progress. Nearly Calm in the Evening. 15 Sail in sight. The Volunteer & *William* & Ann, joined Co. with us & the Henrietta, the Aimwell to the SE, 3 miles distant.

Monday 26th of July Lat. 71°42′ Lon. 7°51′E.
['WNW', *deleted*] NW, Variable NEbE SEbE
Light airs Inclinable to Calm, until 4 Am. the wind then veering to the SE^d the Breeze increased to a Brisk Gale: had fine cloudy weather. Rigged Royal yards & set the Royals. 15 Sail of Ships in sight, the Henrietta, *William* & Ann in Company. Steering about SWbW the fore part of the day, towards Evening SW½S at the rate of 5 or 6½ Knotts. At Mid Night the Centre of the Sun appeared 49 minutes above the Horizon. Weather Warm. Saw several of the Cetacea vulgarly called Bottle Noses. Steering Sails Set.

Tuesday 27th of July Lat. 69°45′23″ Lon. 5°5′E.
SE.erly SEbS. Calm
Some Rain in the Night, Fog Showers towards Morning, delightful fine weather at Noon with a Moderate Breeze of wind. Therm. 8 am. 56° noon 59°! Sailing by the wind to the SWbS at the rate of 6 to 3 Knotts p hour. All hands employing making Points, [Gaskets?] , Nittles, &c sundry needful & useful works.

At Meridian Alt. of Sun's lower limb – – –		39°	21′	50″
Index error or Error of Sextant		- _	1	15
		39	20	35
☉'s Semidiameter	+		15	47
		39	36	22
Dip for [14?] feet … .. 3′ 36″				
Mean Refraction 1′ 9″				
Correction Therm^r ≈58° − 1				
Barom^r 29.63 − 0	1″ 8 = -	4		44
['Variation Compass True Alt. ☉'s Centre	39	31	38
30°W' *in margin*]	90	0	0
Zenith Distance =	50	28	22
Sun's Declination 19° 16′ 50″			
Corr^n for 5° E. Long + 11 =	19	17	1 ^{N}
Latitude of the Ship	69	45	23 North

In the Evening Fog Showers commenced & at 10 Pm. the wind fell to a Calm. The report of two Guns were [*sic*] heard, supposing they proceeded from the *Willia*m & Ann & Henrietta, with a view to learn our situation, the better to keep Company, we answered them, by the discharge of an 18 Pounder. 10 Pm. Therm. 57°!

Wednesday 28ᵗʰ of July Lat. 69°24′ Lon 4°57′E.
Calm. Variable NW.
Calm all the Night, & during the Morning, with thick Fog or Fog Showers. At Noon called all hands to Quarters: Classed & distributed the Crew, as Captain, Second Captⁿ 4 Men & a Boy to each Gun on one Side, of these, one in each Gun's Crew was nominated "Sail trimmer" to be withdrawn when needed, & another Small arm man likewise at a Call; delivered to each small arm man & sail trimmer a Musquet for to keep in order. The three First Officers to superintend the Braces, one at each mast, & to keep order & every man at his duty, in their different districts. Thus arranged all the Guns were loaded & everything prepared for an attack.

At 3 Pm. a Breeze sprang up at NW, set studding Sails & every other Sail, steering SW from 4 to 5½ Knotts p hour. Henrietta & *Willia*m & Ann near us, some other Ships occasionally in Sight.

Thursday 29ᵗʰ of July Lat. 68°8′ Long. 4°15′E.
NW, NNW Var. Calm. SSW, S.
Variable winds & changeable warm Weather, mostly cloudy or Foggy, [but?] at 2 Pm. a fine Clear sky, sometimes a fresh Breeze of Wind at others Calm. The forepart we made good progress on a SW course, towards night closehauled by the wind larboard tacked. Saw Several large Mollusca in the water; those animals are seldom seen above 100 or 150 miles from land, and as they increase in abundance mark the gradual proximity to terra firma – on near approach they are seen attended with Sea weed & commonly land Birds, or Birds frequenting the shores: in [these?] Latitudes, Ducks, Loons ['&' *deleted*] Teistas,[1] Sea Parrots,[2] [Solon?] Geese,[3] a large Brown Gull, &c, &c. are the Birds most commonly seen on approaching ['Remarks on the appearance of molusca [*sic*] & SeaWeed.' *in margin*] the Shores of Shetland, Ferroe, or Norway. Mackrill abound particularly on the Norway Coast. According to my Reckoning we are about 150 miles distant from the nearest Islands on the Norway Coast, from the appearance of the Mollusca, it would seem we are not more at any rate, although the variation as ascertained on tuesday indicated a situation at least 5 degrees of Longitude more westerly, from the variableness of our Compasses however it is probable ['Appearance of a Current setting to the Eastward' *in margin*] the azimuth (magnetic) might not be correct. Thirty degrees of west variation in the Greenland & North Seas, is what is commonly met with near the meridian of London or a little westward of it. Owing I suppose to the prevalence of westerly winds at this Season of the Year, which probably occasions an Easterly Current, it is a most difficult matter keeping a correct Reckoning on a Greenland passage home, with westerly winds great allowances must

---

[1] The Shetland name for the Black Guillemot, *Cepphus grylle*, is 'Tystie': Butler, *Isle of Noss*, p. 45.
[2] An alternative name (*OED*) for the puffin, *Fratercula arctica*.
[3] The gannet, *Sula bassana*. The Shetland name for the gannet is 'Solan': Butler, *Isle of Noss*, p. 45.

be made, if a point of the Compass is not allowed to the Eastward of the apparent Course, the Ship will assuredly be found to the Eastward of her Reckoning.[1] Thus it is that most of strangers & junior Captains get upon the Norway Coast at the time they expect they are perhaps 200 miles distant. Even the most experienced are unable to account for the Easting made in some cases. In consideration of this liability to error it is always best in returning from Greenland to keep <u>well</u> to the <u>westward</u>; a mistake in this respect is seldom material as westerly winds may be expected & seldom fail in offering the means of a speedy rectification.

Mr Kearsly & Stephens dined with me, departed to their respective ships at 6 [pm?]. The commonly received theory of the <u>waves</u>, but imperfectly accounts for all their phenomena – that waves should be impelled an hundred miles beyond the acting principle & always nearly in the direction of the wind by which raised, that should thus proceed in defiance of opposite winds & opposite waves, is what I cannot ['Remarkable swells some thoughts on this subject' *in margin*] account for or apply, on the principles of gravity & that oscillatory motion by it produced. To day we had a remarkable instance of different waves passing each other without any apparent effect being produced on either: in the morning a swell prevailed from the ENE & in the evening a <u>heavy western ocean swell</u> made its appearance from a WSW direction. They both continued remarkably apparent for several hours although the wind was from the same quarter as neither of them. 10 Sail in sight. In Company as before. Several Bottlenoses seen. Thermometer all the day 58 to 60. Barometer about 30 Inches.

Friday the 30th of July Lat 67°30′ Long. 3°45′E.
SSW WbN to WSW SW SSW.
Wind a light or Fresh Breeze accompanied with heavy Rain in the morning & Fog Showers or ['thick' *deleted*] [dark?] Cloudy weather the rest of the day. At 2 am. tacked, lay SbW to SbE & at 6 Pm. the wind having veered to SbW tacked again in Company as before. Three London Ships in sight. Heavy Swell from the WSW. Under all sails except Royals.

I dined today off a chine of Beef, killed in March & never salted except [with?] scarcely an ounce of Salt to preserve the external parts, consequently it was perfect fresh & although we have little no Frost for these two months past, the Mean Temp. in June being … . & in July … . & tho' the Temperature of the air for the last four days has never been below 55° yet it was almost perfectly Sweet. It is true that some portion of the outside was slightly tainted with the peculiar effect of beginning putre-faction, yet only in such wise as to improve the flavour, according to the taste of an Epicure. This chine had not ['Fresh Beef kept 4½ months' *in margin*] parted with its moisture, on being cut gravy sprang out in sufficient store, the flesh was particularly tender fine grained & delicately flavour. A practical, indulgent, experienced, <u>gour-mand</u> would have had an invaluable treat; at his Table I should not have been surprized to have seen venison, nay Turtle removed untouched whilst any of the choice of such a Roast remained. This chine finished our stock of Fresh Beef, we had

[1] See Introduction, p. lvii.

sufficient to use freely the whole voyage: no means are necessary except covering with Canvass & suspending in the Air – a few grains of salt may be rubbed in the moist parts, & should very Rainy weather take place soon after the first suspensing it may be necessary to dip the Beef in salt water or pour Sea water over it. In Greenland it is generally frozen & of course not liable or even capable of putrefaction, when thawed a leg, or other large piece must be and very speedily[1] when once cut on, when the air is allowed to come in contact of a fresh part it is then incapable of resisting its influence when no frost prevails.

Saturday 31st of July Lat. 66°57′54″ Long. 2°35′E.
South to SW.
Moderate Breezes to Fresh Gales of wind – Cloudy in the Morning: charming fine Clear weather at Noon, in the Evening Rain. Heavy Swell from the WSW. Suspended the last two Boats lines upon spars between the Main & Mizen Masts. Took them down before the Rain Commenced, coyled them roughly down beside the lines of the other Boats in the Gun-Room. Steering all day by the Wind, making near two Points lee-way, 23 hours WSW to W, tacked to the SSE^d at 11 Pm. Sailed with the Mizen TopSail aback & Top Gall^t Sails furled most of the day, the Ships in Co. being far to leeward & astern.

Sunday 1st August Lat. 66°25′59″+ Lon. 1°11′E Long. by Ob^n 0 51 45.
SW, S, SW & WbS
Fresh Gales all day with high SW.erly Swell. Weather on the whole fine, at Noon clear & pleasant, heavy clouds in the Evening. Under a Brisk Sail steering by the wind to the SSE^d, WSW, W, WNW &c. on the most favourable tacks. At 4 am. tacked, & at 4 Pm. tacked to Starboard, afterwards lay SbE, or. S. the rest of the Night. At 3^h 31′ 37″ Pm. apparent time the angular distance betwixt the Sun & Moon was (reduced & corrected) 61°53′38″ the Mean of five sights from which obtained the Longitude of the Ship 51′ 45″ East. Barometer at noon 29.75 Thermometer 8 am. 64° noon 62° 8 Pm. 57. Clouds ∩ \∩ & / & \∩_.[2] The Aimwell Henrietta, William & Ann, in Co. 3 other ships in sight.

Monday 2^d of August noon Lat. 65°46′41″ 3½ Pm. Lon. 57′ 9″ E.
WSW SWbW Calm. SSE SE
Delightful fine weather the whole day. Thermometer 8 am. 59° Noon 64° 8 pm 60°. Barometer 29.90 at Noon. Under all Sails by the wind Starboard tacked lying SbW to SSE during the SWerly wind's continuance. In the afternoon we had 6 hours Calm. Mr Johnstone visited me. A light Breeze towards Mid night. Ship larboard tacked.
  Suspended again all the Six Boats Whale Lines on spars between the Masts, at 4

---

[1] Apparently a word omitted in transcription: 'eaten'?
[2] In his 1804 paper 'On the Modifications of Clouds', Luke Howard had proposed (p. 345) seven symbolic abbreviations for clouds: '\ Cirrus. ∩ Cumulus. _ Stratus. \∩ Cirro-cumulus. _ Cirro-stratus. ∩_ Cumulo-stratus. \∩_ Cirro-cumulo-stratus, or Nimbus.' If the entry '/' is a transcription error for '\', the symbols in Scoresby's record therefore indicate 'cumulus, cirro-cumulus and cirrus, and nimbus.'

Pm. they were charmingly dry, coyled them finally in single lines & stowed them in the Line Room. The quantity & variety of business we carried on during this day was somewhat singular, the following is a list of our engagements. Making <u>Rope</u>, Royal Stay Sail, Pails, [Gratings?],[1] Top Rails, Top Nettings & fringes, [Spunyarn?],[2] nittles, Points, Roebands,[3] Gaskets; various Iron work; dried & coyled 36 whale lines; Painted my <u>Cutter</u> with her [***] masts, yards & oars. Worked & dried a quantity of whale's hair, & determined the time by the Mean of 10 observations & likewise by a single set two hours afterwards which shewed the error of the Watch, differing only 4 Seconds! Likewise by the Mean of eleven sets of observations determined the Ship's Longitude at 3^h 24′ 17″ Pm. Apparent time 57′ 9″ East from Greenwich.

Tuesday 3^d of August Lat 65°6′ Lon. 0°45′E.
SEbE to SE Calm
Fine weather: wind a light or Fresh Breeze about Noon – Steering about SSW under a Brisk Sail, took the Royals in, & sailed with the Mizen TopSail about 8 hours for to allow the Henrietta & Aimwell to come up. Washed all the Ice ropes, but did not complete the drying, coyled one cable in the Tier. In the Evening Calm weather: at the earnest solicitation of our two Shetlandmen engaged March the 23^d we put them on Board the William & Ann, that Ship being under the necessity of calling to muster her Crew; sent with them 40 lb of Beef & about 20 of Bread, directed the agent, Mr Spence, to pay them monthly wages until the day of the *Willia*m & Ann's arrival at Lerwick. The errors in our Compasses continue irreconcilable: by an amplitude of the Sun at setting, the variation seems to be 33°35′W. whilst in the Longitude I am confident it can be no more than 2¼ pts or 28°7½W. When the Sun was in the Meridian, one Compass shewed <u>One Point</u>, another, 2, & a third 2¼ Pts. variation. Stars now make their appearance, & become at first an object of as much consideration as the Sun at Mid-N^t on our entry into Greenland. At Mid Night heavy clouds seen travelling in a NE. direction, an adverse wind may be expected to follow. ['Therm*ome*ter 8 Am 62° Noon 64° 10 Pm 61° Bar. Noon. 29.87' *in margin*]

Wednesday 4th of August Lat 64°22′49″ Lon. 50′E
SW SSW SE.
Charmingly fine weather: wind a light Breeze, Calm sometimes[.] Steering to the SE^d or SSW by the wind, made small progress. Coyled the Ice ropes in the Cable Stage when dried, scraped the three lower masts & Bowsprit & painted them, set up a Troysail mast for the Mizen to traverse upon, the sail being too small for the size of the Ship the alteration proved an amazing improvement, set Royal stay sail; – whilst we waited for the Aimwell, the Henrietta went far ahead: the *Willia*m & Ann & Aimwell in Company. A strong SW.erly swell. Saw a Number of large Mollusca, 4 to

---

[1] Smyth, *Sailor's Word Book*, s.v.: 'An open wood-work of cross battens and ledges forming cover for the hatchways, serving to give light and air to the lower decks.'

[2] Ibid.: 'SPUN-YARN. A small line, formed of two, three or more old rope-yarns not laid, but twisted together by hand or winch. Spun-yarn is used for various purposes as seizing and serving ropes, weaving mats, &c.'

[3] Smyth, *Sailor's Word Book*, s.vv. 'Robands, or Robbens' and 'Rope-bands'. Rope-bands, the lines that secure the head of a sail to the yard.

8 In diam*et*er Brownish [moss?] like on the underside & giving out a variety of large fibres from every part of the circumference: they are a sign of land. ['Ther. 8 Am. 62° Noon 65° 8 Pm 63° Bar. noon 29.87 *in margin*]

Thursday 5th of August Lat. 63°40′42″+ Lon. 43′E.
SSE Calm. ESE EbS. Variable.
Fine weather; wind a light or moderate Breeze, fair, all the day after 4 am. Steering p Compass SSW at the rate of 2 to 6 knotts p hour. Left the Aimwell out of sight astern the Henrietta 10 miles to the NWd Will*ia*m & Ann in Company. The same description of <u>Mollusca</u> as we yesterday saw were seen more numerous during this day, some seemed near 12 Inches in diameter & most of them gave out gelatinous spines. Some flocks of Teistas Seen; Gulls, Fulmars, & Sea Parrots. A whale I supposed of the description which occasionally are stranded on the Coasts of Shetland exhibited itself in performing repeated leaps out of the water: its shape was nearly Pointed at the nose & tail swelling from thence to about the middle where it was thickest, it might seem to be about 15 feet in length & ¼th or ⅕ the diameter. Therm*ometer* 65 to 62°. Bar. 29.83. Strong west swell.

Friday 6th of August Lat. 61°56′ Long. 1°3′E
ESE East to NEbE
Steering all day SSW wind fair, 3 to 5 knott Breezes. Water of a Green Colour. Employed scraping decks, stuffing[1] the Sides, &c. At 8Pm in Latitude 61°20′ sounded with 120 Fathoms of line in a Boat; no Bottom: at the same time caught a Mackrell. Mollusca plentiful. Soundings are the chief criterion of an Easterly or Westerly situation with regard to Shetland. In Lat. 60½° to 61°N no soundings are to be obtained on the west side with 200 Fathoms when 40 or 50 Miles from Land; on the East side on the Contrary, unless very near the Norway Coast ground is generally struck with 120 to 65 or 70 Fathoms.[2] A strange sail in sight. Weather Cloudy; wind a light or moderate Breeze. Therm. 62° to 60° Bar. 29.70.

Saturday 7th of August at 60°14′56″ Long. 1°4′E.
NEbE to North & NNW
At 4 am. lowered a Boat & struck Soundings in 70 fathoms water, fine white sand with small stones & some shells. This determines the correctness of our lunar observation & subsequent reckoning, at least it shews we are between Shetland & Norway, nearer the former than the Latter. Afterwards steered SW. The Will*ia*m & Ann at 4 am. hauled away about WbS to make Shetland. At Noon Observed in Latitude 60°14′56″ Lerwick by account bearing p Compass wnw Distant 61 Miles. The Strange Sail near us apparently a Greenlandman. A Strong Breeze towards night under all sails made good progress 4 to 7 knotts p hour. At 9 Pm. a Strange Sail steering by the wind made its appearance, shewed to be a Merchant Ship, should have spoke her, but for the departure of day light. Fine weather. Barometer 29.89 Therm. 60° to 63°.

---

[1] Smyth, *Sailor's Word Book*: 'STUFF. A *'coat of stuff*, a term used for any composition laid on to ships' spars, bottom, &c.'
[2] See journal entry for 9 August 1812 and Introduction, p. lviii.

Sunday 8ᵗʰ of August Lat 58°8′13″ Long. a/c 11′W.
NNW, NW, W. SW, & Southerly.
Strong to light Breezes, delightful fine weather. Until noon steering under every sail to the SW, afterwards by the wind lying SSW, SSE, & SE tacked at 4 Pm. at Mid Night Calm. Sounded at noon in 83 Fathoms soft mud. The Signs of Land seen were Gulls, & Sea Weed. At noon Bucchaness p. account bore due SW¾W Distance 64 Miles.[1] In the Evening a Strange Sail seen far SW of us. Barometer at 12 noon 29.93 Thermometer. 8 am. 63 Noon 66. 8 Pm. 64° . Clouds \∩ & ∩ modification.[2]

Monday 9ᵗʰ of August Lat. 57°19′27″ Long a/c 15′W.
Calm, SE, E, NE, North, NW, WNW. Var.
At 2 am. a Small Breeze sprang up, made Sail Steering first SSW afterwards SW. At 4 am. in Lat. 57°41 & Long. by a/c 15′ W Sounded in 80 Fathoms water soft mud; & at 9 am. in Lat 57°24 in 50 Fathoms fine white sand with a few Brown specks & at Noon in 45 Fathoms similar ground. A Brig in sight. The Ship seen these two days past left out of sight astern. A westerly Swell, shews we are a considerable distance from Land. Caught two Mackrell & a Ling. At Noon p account Aberdeen bore due W¾S Distant 63 Miles & Whitby p. Compass SSW¾W Distance 172 miles. At 8 pm. nearly calm Lat 57° Long. a/c 27′W. Sounded in 45 Fathoms fine sand as before: about this time caught a Cod Fish, two Dog Fish & several Mackrell. Thermometer 60° to 66° Bar. noon 30.00.

Tuesday 10ᵗʰ of August Lat. 56°20′54″+ Long. 18′W.
WNW, W, SW, WbS, West.
A light or moderate Breeze all the Morning, fine weather all day: Thermometer 61° to 66° Barometer at noon 30.15. Close hauled by the wind starboard tacked[.] At Noon by Account Whitby bears due S4°E Distance 114 Miles p Compass SEbS nearly. Hauled the small Bower Cable up, out of the Cable Stage, coyled it in the Tier & bent it the anchor. In the Afternoon & Evening a Fresh Breeze which towards Mid Night became a light Air: Saw three Fishing vessels, made a Short tack & boarded one which lay at anchor fishing, they furnished us with some fish, & a newspaper a month old containing some interesting intelligence, stating the defeat ['Good National News' *in margin*] of the French army by Lord Wellington at Vittoria[3] & the Capture of the American Frigate Chesapeake 49 or 60 Guns & 440 Men by the Shannon British Frigate of 330 Men & 44 Guns[.][4] after fighting within half pistol shot 13

[1] Buchan Ness is a promontory a few miles south of Peterhead, Grampian, 57°28′N, 1°47′W.
[2] I.e., following Luke Howard, 'On the Modifications of Clouds', cirro-cumulus and cumulus. Modern terminology now distinguishes between cirrocumulus clouds, composed of ice crystals, and the more common altocumulus, formed by water droplets. What Scoresby described as cirrocumulus was probably altocumulus.
[3] The battle of Vittoria took place on 21 June 1813.
[4] HMS *Shannon* was in fact a 38-gun frigate. She may have been known to Scoresby because in 1807 she had protected the Greenland whaling fleet, reaching a latitude of 80°6′N. The engagement took place on 1 June 1813 20 miles east of Boston lighthouse between Cape Ann and Cape Cod: Phillips, *Ships of the Old Navy*.

minutes the Enemy was carried in 3 Minutes by Boarding. The account likewise states that so confident were the Yankees of success that a Sumptuous dinner was prepared for the Captain & Officers when they should return with their prize into Boston from which port the Chesapeake had just emerged in consequence of a challenge from Captain Broke ['Barom. at noon. 30.15' *in margin*] of the Shannon: some thousands of persons in [sloops?] Boats, & other Craft accompanied their Frigate off & were spectators of the Conflict.

The Fishing Vessel from whom we received this pleasing intelligence, belongs Yarmouth, had not seen the land for <u>6 weeks</u>, suppose themselves 60 miles from St Abbs' Head by their soundings & which agrees within 4 miles of my calculations. At this time 8 Pm. had 40 Fathoms water. Caught several Mackerell.

Wednesday 11th August Lat 55°19'35"+ Long. 17'W.
W, NW[?] , WNW, W, WSW, SW, South & West
We had a fair wind two Hours in the Morning steered WSW, SWbW, SW, & after 5 am. close hauled by the wind lying SWbS or SSW. Saw several fishing vessels, from Yarmouth & Shetland. Some Brigs seen about Noon, apparently Coasters. At Meridian [***] in Latitude 55° 19'35" Whitby by account bearing p Compass SWbS¼W Distant 52 Miles & Tinmouth W½N 35 miles Barom^r 30.18. Therm. 62° to 66°.

The three Compass [*sic*] which on the 22^d of July & many following days, differed 2½ Points (the extremes) all now agree uniformly within one Quarter Point! this must be owing the more powerful effective attraction on the needle owing to the Magnetic Pole assuming a position father removed from the Perpendicular or Zenith:– Since writing this last sentence I find the compasses merely agree when the Ship is on a Southerly course, for some hours afterwards when steering west a difference of a point was again observed.

At 3 Pm. tacked & lay WNW to WbS making of a progress of 4 to 6½ knots p hour close by the wind until 10 pm. when on the wind shifting we again tacked: we imagined we could perceive the grateful effluvia arising from Hay & other [vegative?] production of the Land, a sign of our proximity to terra firma.

Thursday 12th August Lat 54°56' Long. 0°45'W
West Var SSW WSW or SW
Strong or Moderate Breezes Continuing with fine cloudy weather[.] on the wind shifting at Mid Night we again tacked & steered by the wind, WbS WbN, WNW, NWbW, &c – 4 to 6½ knots until 11 am. At 6 am. descried land & presently distinguished [Hemtcliff foot?] bearing SW Distant 8 Leagues. At 11 tacked Sunderland bearing due West about 6 Miles distant: from my Reckoning the situation of Sunderland appears too far westerly by 44 Miles of Longitude hence the error of our accounts equal 25 Geographical Miles westerly & therefore in the [few?] recent days where soundings in certain Longitudes have been given it will be necessary to apply the miles of Longitude equal to 25 miles of Departure in an Easterly direction: thus the Longitude yesterday instead of 7 miles west should be ['Barom*eter* 30.02 Therm. 67° to [66°?] *in margin*] corrected 38'E. Longitude. At noon made all possible sail lying SSE to SbE with a Brisk breeze of wind, expecting almost to fetch Whitby before the

turn of tide. At 3 Pm saw Whitby Abbey – bearing SbE , the wind withal scanting,[1] & at the same time failing so it was not until near 6 pm. that [were?] off the Town with the harbour open, about 3 miles distant. At 6 being nearly Calm & seeing the dilatory Pilots scarcely half the way towards us I left the Ship under the charge of the mate with orders to make every exertion towards obtaining a Road Stead, towed with?] all the Boats if necessary. At 6¾ hours Pm. I landed from my own Cutter at the Pier steps & was received by an immense crowd of spectators, chiefly the wives & relatives of the Crew & the different Fishing Ships belonging the Port, together with the interested Gentry & many nay some Hundreds of [spectators?] concerned from friendly feelings or curiosity. It was a Pleasure to me that the former class I had nothing but good news to communicate,[2] to the owners &c my communications were perhaps not so agreeable as the success of the ship's [sic] was not equal to the expectations of many. I cannot perhaps better express myself, than in the Greenland idiom, for shewing my situation on landing, I was in fact completely beset amongst women, men, & children, the former however were most solicitous & altho I assured every one we were all well through [Mercy?] on board the Esk yet every individual must be like wise assured of the particular welfare & health of their[3] connexions. The numerous congratulatory expressions, on my success & safe arrival were beyond any thing I ever before experienced & were doubtless grateful to the feelings.

It was not long before I was assured of the health & wellfare of all my Relatives. I was received on emerging from the Crowd by my Dear mother & sisters, my worthy owner & friend Major Brodrick accompanied them. In a few minutes more I had the delight of embracing my Beloved partner my adored wife in full health & our Dear Child likewise Blessed. The former as might be expected had been long anxious for my arrival & hailed this auspicious day as the most delightful of her life, she had not been apprised of her approaching happiness more than two hours – the latter I found strengthened, improved, exceeding my most sanguine hopes: exhibiting a pleasing form, an amazing [expression of] countenance, a liveliness, quickness and sagacity much beyond his Age & far surpassing even what I conceived would have determined the summit of my ambition. Our gratitude for our happiness in meeting under such flattering, delightful circumstances was withal augmented by the representation of dangers which we escaped unknown, & of course undreaded: had we known that Commodore Rodgers in the Frigate President of American interest was during the time of our passage committing depredations on the Archangel trade, & Greenland Fishery ship [sic], that two had been captured by him, whilst we essayed homewards; had we been apprised of this Fray, we should have had an anxious passage, well grounded fears, & might perhaps by using schemes to avoid the Enemy have rushed more directly into his way. The Benignant Being in whom I trust, from whom I have derived timely comforts, & assistance together with an incalculable number of other & varied mercies, has once

---

[1] Smyth, *Sailor's Word Book*: 'SCANT. A term applied to the wind when it heads a ship off ....'
[2] An unexpected remark, in view of the death of John Dodds on 24 April.
[3] 'her' inserted above the line, apparently as a grammatical correction.

again consummated my Bliss and that of my Valued, Dear, Relatives by bringing me healthful & prosperous to their anxious, open arms. "Oh that men would praise the Lord for his goodness, & for his wonderful works to the Children of Men / For he hath been mindful of us & hath blessed us' – In my distress I cried unto the Lord & he heard me, therefore Praise the Lord O my Soul, all that is within me Bless & praise the Lord."[1]

Light variable winds the Evening a heavy Northerly squall accompanied with Rain towards Midnight. At 10 Pm. the Esk came to an anchor in Whitby Roads, 7 Fathoms water, half a mile from the west Pier head. At Mid Night on the first appearance of Flood tide I returned on board.

Friday 13th August
NWerly Var

Charming weather wind a light to a fresh Gale. At 3½ Am. "all hands up anchor" aroused our sleeping Crew, who joyous to the windlass bend their rapid steps – soon was the anchor withdrawn from its hold the sails unfurled & set & the Ship under way, the wind being light, ['tide' *deleted*] somewhat scant, the tide rapid & channel narrow we tacked about ['Moored in Whitby Harbour !" *in margin*] until near 5 am. which we judged the full high water, then made all sail for the Harbour, withdrew the canvass as we passed the Scotch Head but never stopped the Ship until she was secure, above the Bridge. Loosed all Sails to dry. The James is the only Fishing ship in the Harbour, she brought a Cargo of 14 whales about 170 Tons of Oil, arrived in the roads the … .th & in the Harbour yesterday morning. No account has been received of the arrival of the John at Clyde.[2] The West winds may have retarded her progress or they may have contended longer in the Country. Unbent the sails in the Afternoon, [attended?] tide but got very little higher up the Harbour. At 3 Pm. the Aimwell & Henrietta made their appearance in the roads & just [saved?] the tide. They both moored safe above Bridge.

Saturday 14th August
NW.erly

Fresh Gales of wind, fine weather. Arrived the Volunteer. The Resolution appeared in Sight. Sent Sails to the loft & Gunpowder to the Fort Magazine.

Monday [*sic*] 15th August[3]
NW.erly

By this time all the Whitby Fleet were safe in port except the Lively & she in the offing. Paid the Esk's Crew their whole Sea wages, Fish Money, &c and oil money up to 140 Tons agreeable to Contract p Articles.

[1] Scoresby appears to have been quoting from four psalms: the 107th, verse 8; the 115th, verse12; the 120th, verse 1; and the 103rd, verse 1.
[2] I.e. at Greenock on the Firth of Clyde.
[3] It seems reasonable to assume that Sunday was taken as a day of rest, and therefore it is the dates, not the days of the week, that are inaccurate in these last two entries. Monday was the 16th of August, not the 15th.

Tuesday 16ᵗʰ Augᵗ
Landed a few Blubber Casks at the Boiling House Quay, Boiled a Copper of Oil in the Evening & afterwards continued the operation with all speed.

		Ton-nage	Length of Voy.	Whales	Seals	Narwh	Bears	Butts	Tons of Oil	Whale-bone	Value Cargo	Divi-dends
Esk	Scoresby	354		15	7			508	176	17½	9968	?
James	Smith			14					171			?
Henrietta	Kearsley			11								?
Resolution	W. Kearsley	291		10								
Willᵐ & Ann	Stephens			9								
Aimwell	Johnstone	262		7								
Volunteer	Dawson			7								
Lively	Wilson			4								

The above Cargos Sold at the following Rates: Viz. Fine Train Oil from 49 to 52 £ p Ton delivered in Whitby or 53 to £55 delivered in London & Whalebone 140 to 160 £ p Ton of 6 feet length & upwards, the undersized laminæ being sold at half price. The above cargoes are calculated according to their values in Whitby which is less by £3 p Ton than their intrinsic value in the market.[1]

[1] Lubbock (*Arctic Whalers*, pp. 194–5) noted that , for the British whaling fleet as a whole, 'The return shows a great falling off in the amount of oil, which was under 3600 lbs. [*sic*; throughout this sentence 'lbs' should presumably be 'tons'] as compared with 6561 lbs. in 1812; 5300 in 1811; and 4928 lbs. in 1810. The ships, however, that were well fished made handsome profits, as, during the autumn, oil was selling up to £60 per ton, a higher price than had ever been known before.'
'Old Captain Scoresby in the *John* of Greenock returned with a full ship (17 fish), making £11,000, and his son, in command of the *Esk* of Whitby, with 15 whales, filling 508 butts, making over £10,000' (ibid., pp. 195–6).

Works Cited

Abbass, D. K., '*Endeavour* and *Resolution* Revisited: Newport and Captain James Cook's Vessels', *Newport History*, 70, 1, 1999, pp. 1–20.

Barrow, Tony, *The Whaling Trade of North-East England*, Sunderland, University of Sunderland Press, 2001.

Birse, Ronald M., *Science at the University of Edinburgh, 1583–1993*, Edinburgh, Faculty of Science and Engineering, University of Edinburgh, 1994.

Brewer's Dictionary of Phrase and Fable (centenary edn, revised), London, Cassell, 1981.

Burder, George, *Village Sermons; or … plain and short discourses on the principal doctrines of the Gospel; intended for the use of families, Sunday schools, or companies assembled for religious instruction in country villages*, 7 vols, London, Mathews, 1798–1816.

Burns, John J.; Montague, J. Jerome; Cowles, Cleveland J., eds, *The Bowhead Whale*, Lawrence KS, Society for Marine Mammalogy, 1993.

Butler, David, *Isle of Noss*, [Lerwick ?], Garth Estate, 1982.

Canadian Shark Research Laboratory, 'Greenland Shark', on-line at http://www.mar.dfo-mpo.gc.ca/science/shark/english/greenland.htm

Columbia Encyclopedia, The, 6th edn, New York, Columbia University Press, 2000.

Cotter, Charles H., *A History of Nautical Astronomy*, London, Hollis & Carter, 1968.

Credland, Arthur G., *The Hull Whaling Trade, An Arctic Enterprise*, Beverley, Hutton Press, 1995.

Crowl, Philip A., *The Intelligent Traveller's Guide to Historic Scotland*, London, Sidgwick and Jackson, 1986.

De Jong, C., 'The Hunt of the Greenland Whale: A Short History and Statistical Sources', in Michael F. Tillman and Gregory P. Donovan, eds, *International Whaling Commission, Historical Whaling Records, including the proceedings of the International Workshop on Historical Whaling Records, Sharon, Massachusetts, September 12–16 1977*, Cambridge, International Whaling Commission, 1983, pp. 83–106.

Dellenbaugh, Frederick S., ed. *Seven Log-books concerning the Arctic Voyages of Captain William Scoresby, Senior of Whitby, England*, 8 vols, New York, The Explorers Club, 1917.

Emsley, Clive, ed., *North Riding Naval Recruits: The Quota Acts and the Quota Men 1795–1797*, North Yorkshire County Record Office Publications No. 18, Northallerton, North Yorkshire County Council, 1978.

English Pilot, The, Describing the Sea-Coasts, Capes, Headlands, Soundings, Sands, Shoals, Rocks and Dangers. The Bays, Roads, Harbours, Rivers and Ports in the Whole Northern Navigation …, London, Mount and Page, 1770.

Gad, Finn, *The History of Greenland*, 2 vols, Montreal, McGill-Queen's University Press, 1971–3.

Garitee, Jerome R., *The Republic's Private Navy: The American Privateering Business as Practiced by Baltimore During the War of 1812*, Middletown, Conn., Wesleyan University Press, 1977.

Girouard, Mark, *Town and Country*, London, Yale University Press, 1992.

Greenland & Davis's Streights Whale-Fisheries, 1811, 1812, 1813. (Annual lists of ships, masters and home ports, preserved in the Scoresby Papers, Whitby Museum. They were apparently printed in Whitby, as the 1812 list includes the statement '[Rodgers, Printer, Whitby.]'. Cited in the present volume as 'contemporary printed lists'.)

Haldiman, Jerrold J. and Tarpley, Raymond J., 'Anatomy and Physiology', in John J. Burns *et al.*, *The Bowhead Whale* (q.v.), pp. 71–156.

Hall, Marie Boas, *All Scientists Now: The Royal Society in the Nineteenth Century*, Cambridge, Cambridge University Press, 1984.

Hamblyn, Richard, *The Invention of Clouds: How An Amateur Meteorologist Forged the Language of the Skies*, London, Picador, 2001.

Houston, R. A., *Scottish Literacy and the Scottish Identity, Illiteracy and Society in Scotland and Northern England 1600–1800*, Cambridge, Cambridge University Press, 1985.

Howard, Luke, 'On the Modifications of Clouds,and on the Principles of their Production, Suspension, and Destruction; being the Substance of an Essay read before the Askesian Society in the Session 1802–3', *Philosophical Magazine*, 16, 1803, pp. 97–107, 344–57; 1804, 17, pp. 5–11.

Hutchinson, J. R., *The Press-Gang, Afloat and Ashore*. London, Bell, 1913.

Jackson, Gordon, *The British Whaling Trade*, London, A. & C. Black, 1978

Jones, Stephanie Karen, 'A Maritime History of the Port of Whitby, 1700–1914', University of London (UCL) PhD thesis, 1982.

Koski, William R. *et al.*, 'Reproduction', in John J. Burns *et al.*, *The Bowhead Whale* (q.v.), pp. 239–74.

Layton, Cyril W., *Dictionary of Nautical Words and Terms*, 4th revised edn, Glasgow, Brown, Son & Ferguson, 1994.

Ley, Willy *et al.*, *The Poles*, New York, Time Inc., 1962.

Lloyd, Charles C., *Mr. Barrow of the Admiralty. A Life of Sir John Barrow, 1764–1848*, London, Collins, 1970.

Lowry, Lloyd F., 'Foods and Feeding Ecology', in John J. Burns *et al.*, *The Bowhead Whale* (q.v.), pp. 201–38.

Lubbock, Basil, *The Arctic Whalers*, Glasgow, Brown, Son & Ferguson, 1937.

Melville, Herman, *Moby-Dick; or, The Whale*, London, Bentley, 1851.

Montague, J. Jerome, 'Introduction', in John J. Burns *et al.*, *The Bowhead Whale* (q.v.), pp. 1–21.

Moore, Sue E. and Reeves, Randall R., 'Distribution and Movement', in John J. Burns *et al.*, *The Bowhead Whale* (q.v.), pp. 313–86.

Norie, J. W., *Formulae for Finding the Longitude, in which a Method Invented by Mendoza Rios is Used for Clearing the Observed Distances from the Effects of*

Refraction and Parallax, with Rules for Working the Observations, London, Norie, 1816.

North Sea Pilot, Part III, East Coast of England, From Berwick to the North Foreland, Including the Rivers Thames and Medway, London, Admiralty Hydrographic Office, 8th Edition, 1914.

Partridge, Eric, *A Dictionary of Slang and Unconventional English. Colloquialisms and Catch Phrases, Fossilised Jokes and Puns, General Nicknames, Vulgarisms and such Americanisms as have been Naturalised*, 8th edn, London, Routledge & Kegan Paul, 1984.

Philbrick, Nathaniel, *In the Heart of the Sea: the Tragedy of the Whaleship* Essex, New York, Penguin, 2001.

Phillips, Michael, *Ships of the Old Navy*, on-line at http://www.cronab.demon.co.uk/intro.htm

Philo, L. Michael *et al.*, 'Morbidity and Mortality', in John J. Burns *et al.*, *The Bowhead Whale* (q.v.), pp. 275–312.

Robinson, Francis K., *A Glossary of Yorkshire Words and Phrase, Collected in Whitby and the Neighbourhood: With Examples of their Colloquial Use, and Allusions to Local Customs and Traditions*, London, Smith, 1855.

Ross, W. Gillies, 'Commercial Whaling in the North Atlantic Sector', in John J. Burns *et al.*, *The Bowhead Whale* (q.v.), pp. 511–77.

Salisbury, W., 'Early Tonnage Measurement in England. Part V. Colliers, Deadweight, and Displacement Tonnage', *The Mariner's Mirror*, 54, 1, 1968, pp. 69–76.

Scammon, Charles M., *The Marine Mammals of the North-Western Coast of North America, Described and Illustrated: together with an Account of the American Whale-Fishery*, San Francisco, Carmany, 1874.

(Scoresby, William), *The 1806 Log Book, Concerning the Arctic Voyage of Captain William Scoresby [Senior]*, Whitby, Caedmon, 1981.

Scoresby, William, *An Account of the Arctic Regions, with a History and Description of the Northern Whale-Fishery*, 2 vols, Edinburgh, Constable, 1820. (Facsimile reprint, with an introduction by Alister Hardy, published by David & Charles Reprints, Newton Abbot, 1969.)

Scoresby, William, *Journal of a Voyage to the Northern Whale-Fishery; Including Researches and Discoveries on the Eastern Coast of West Greenland, Made in the Summer of 1822, in the Ship Baffin of Liverpool*, Edinburgh, Constable, 1823. (Facsimile reprint published by Caedmon, Whitby, 1980.)

Scoresby, William, *My Father, being Records of the Adventurous Life of the Late William Scoresby, Esq., of Whitby*, London, Longman, Brown, Green and Longmans, 1851. (Facsimile reprint published by Caedmon, Whitby, 1978.)

Scoresby, William, *Sabbaths in the Arctic Regions*, London, Longman, Brown, Green & Longmans, 2nd edn, 1850.

Scoresby-Jackson, R. E., *The Life of William Scoresby, M.A., D.D., F.R.S.S.L. & E.*, London, Nelson, 1861.

Smithsonian Meteorological Tables, 6th revised edn, Washington, D.C., Smithsonian Institution, 1951.

Smyth, William H., *The Sailor's Word Book of 1867; an Alphabetical Digest of*

Nautical Terms, London, Blackie, 1867. (Facsimile reprint published by Conway Classics, London, 1991.)

Stamp, Cordelia, *The Scoresby Family*, [Whitby?], n.p. [1989?]

Stamp, Tom and Cordelia, *Greenland Voyager*, Whitby, Caedmon, 1983.

Stamp, Tom and Cordelia, *William Scoresby, Arctic Scientist*, Whitby, Caedmon, [1975?]

Tactical Pilotage Chart TPC B-1A, Scale 1:500,000, St Louis, Missouri, Defense Mapping Agency Aerospace Center, 1986.

Taylor, Eva G. R., *Navigation in the Days of Captain Cook*, Maritime Monographs and Reports No. 18, [London], National Maritime Museum, 1975.

Times Atlas of the World, The, 7th comprehensive edition, London, Times Books, 1985.

Trethewey, Ken and Forand, Michael, eds, *The Lighthouse Encyclopaedia*, 2003 edn, published in compact disc (CD) format by the Lighthouse Society of Great Britain, Torpoint, Cornwall, 2003.

Twigger, Robert, *Inflation: the Value of the Pound 1750–1998*, Research Paper 99/20, London, House of Commons Library, 1999.

United Kingdom, Hydrographic Office, *Harbours and Anchorages on the East Coast of England and Scotland*, Admiralty Chart 1612, Taunton, 2002.

United Kingdom, Meteorological Office, *Observer's Handbook*, London, HMSO, 1952.

Ventress, Monica, *Admiral Sir Robert Moorsom, 1760–1835*, Whitby, Whitby Literary and Philosophical Society, 1998.

Weatherill, Richard, *The Ancient Port of Whitby and its Shipping*, Whitby, Horne & Son, 1908.

Wilson, Leonard G., 'Uniformitarianism and Catastrophism', in *Dictionary of the History of Ideas: Studies of Selected Pivotal Ideas*, ed. Philip P. Wiener, 5 vols, New York, Scribner's, 1973, IV, pp. 417–23.

Woodby, Douglas A. and Botkin, Daniel B., 'Stock Sizes Prior to Commercial Whaling', in John J. Burns *et al.*, *The Bowhead Whale* (q.v.), pp. 387–407.

World Meteorological Organization, *International Cloud Atlas, Abridged Atlas*, Geneva, WMO, 1956.

Wright, Joseph, ed., *The English Dialect Dictionary, being the Complete Vocabulary of all Dialect Words Still in Use, or known to have been in use during the last two hundred years. founded on the publications of the English Dialect Society and on a large amount of material never before printed*, 6 vols, London, Frowde, 1896–1905. (Reprinted by Oxford University Press, 1981.)

Würsig, Bernd and Clark, Christopher, 'Behavior', in John J. Burns *et al.*, *The Bowhead Whale* (q.v.), pp. 157–99.

Yost, Robinson M., *Observations, Instruments and Theories: The Study of Terrestrial Magnetism in Great Britain, c. 1770s–1830s* on website http://www.kirkwood.cc.ia.us/faculty/ryost/minneapolis.htm

Young, George, *A History of Whitby and Streoneshalh Abbey: with a Statistical Survey of the Vicinity to the Distance of Twenty-five Miles*, 2 vols, Whitby, Clark and Medd, 1817. (Reprinted in facsimile by Caedmon of Whitby in 1976.)

Index

Note: Because they are continual themes throughout much of the journals, no attempt has been made to index the details of navigation, sail-setting, ice distribution or whaling activities; there are similarly no entries for William Scoresby Junior or his crews. Scoresby's frequent references to other ships in the whaling fleet are indexed separately.

Index of Whaling Vessels

Note: This is not a complete listing of whaling vessels active in 1811–13, but only those mentioned in Scoresby's journals. It includes a few vessels of the Davis Strait fleet, especially in 1813. Home ports and masters are shown in parentheses, based on the contemporary printed lists: *Greenland & Davis's Streights Whale Fisheries, 1811, 1812, 1813*. As mentioned in the footnotes to the journal, in some cases other sources indicate different masters or spellings from these lists. Where vessels of the same name sailed from different ports, there is uncertainty in some cases as to which vessel Scoresby's journals refer. Neither the *Resolution* nor the *Esk* is indexed for the journals when captained by Scoresby, but references to both vessels in the Introduction are indexed, and the *Resolution* is indexed for 1813. Whaling vessels not mentioned in the 1811–13 journals (e.g. *Baffin*) are listed in the main index.

[1] There is no *Britannia* in the contemporary list for 1812, when Scoresby mentioned the vessel; in 1813 her master was Captain Mills.

[2] Master's name inserted on printed list by hand.

[3] In the 1811 contemporary list, the *Ewretta* (*sic*) was listed as a Newcastle vessel, Captain Boswell. In 1812, the *Eweretta* was included among the London whalers, but without the name of her master. In 1813, the list in the Scoresby Papers shows the *Eweretta* as a handwritten addition to the London vessels, again without a master's name. See also Barrow, *Whaling Trade of North-East England*, pp. 56–8, who gives the correct spelling as *Euretta*.

[1] In 1812 and 1813 another *Laurel* (Captain Harper) also sailed from Hull, but in both years to Davis Strait, not the Greenland Sea.

[2] 'Lyon' sometimes in Scoresby's journals.

[3] 'Stevens' in the 1812 list; probably an error.